A TREASURE TROVE OF
SCRIPTURAL TRANSMISSION

THE SEVEN TREASURIES SERIES

This series consists of the volumes written by Longchen Rabjam that, as a group, have come to be known as *The Seven Treasuries*. Although Longchenpa did not intend them to be a series, scholars traditionally treat them as such because of their interrelated themes.

Published Volumes

The Precious Treasury of the Way of Abiding

The Precious Treasury of the Basic Space of Phenomena

The Precious Treasury of Pith Instructions

The Precious Treasury of Philosophical Systems

A Treasure Trove of Scriptural Transmission

A Commentary on *The Precious Treasury of the Basic Space of Phenomena*

Longchen Rabjam

Translated under the direction of
His Eminence Chagdud Tulku Rinpoche
by Richard Barron (Lama Chökyi Nyima)

Edited by members of
the Padma Translation Committee:
Susanne Fairclough, Jeff Miller,
Mary Racine, and Robert Racine

PADMA PUBLISHING

2001

Published by Padma Publishing
P.O. Box 279
Junction City, California 96048-0279

Printed in the United States of America

Second Printing 2003
Third Printing 2011

Jacket design by Daniel Tesser

Library of Congress Cataloging in Publication Data
Kloṅ-chen-pa Dri-med-'od-zer, 1308–1363
[Chos dbyings rin po che'i mdzod ces bya ba'i 'grel pa. English]
A treasure trove of scriptural transmission : a commentary on "The precious
treasury of the basic space of phenomena" / Longchen Rabjam;
translated under the direction of
His Eminence Chagdud Tulku Rinpoche by Richard Barron (Chökyi Nyima);
edited by members of the Padma Translation Committee,
Susanne Fairclough . . . [et al.]
p. cm.
Includes bibliographical references.
ISBN 1-881847-30-6
1. Rdzogs-chen (Rñiṅ-ma-pa). 2. Rñiṅ-ma-pa (Sect)—Doctrines—
Early works to 1800. I. Title: A treasure trove of scriptural transmission.
II. Barron, Richard. III. Fairclough, Susanne. IV. Title.
BQ7662.4.K535 2001
294.3′420423—dc21   00-059853
                                                              CIP

ISBN 1-881847-30-6 (hardback)

Contents

Foreword

His Eminence Chagdud Tulku Rinpoche

The publication of Longchen Rabjam's *Seven Treasuries* should be a cause for rejoicing among deeply committed English-speaking Buddhists who aspire to realize the *dzogchen,* or great perfection, teachings of vajrayana Buddhism. Though there are many spiritual traditions in this world, Buddhism offers the deepest examination of what constitutes the root of samsara, and of how to deal with all levels of obscuration and attain liberation. Among Buddhist teachings, none are more profound, more capable of freeing the mind from its most subtle obscurations, than those of the great perfection.

Yet, because great perfection transmission leads to wisdom beyond words and concepts, the translation of dzogchen texts presents tremendous difficulties. Some lamas have said that it is not even worth the attempt, that too much distortion results. I respect their opinion, but feel that those of us with the supreme fortune to have received authentic transmission from great dzogchen masters have a responsibility to maintain the oral lineage, including the translation of texts, as well as the mind-to-mind lineage of realization. If we eschew this work, the precious great perfection teachings will remain inaccessible to some excellent Western practitioners who have potential as meditators but who do not know Tibetan. An avenue for the flourishing of the transmission will be cut off.

I am also gravely concerned about the translations of great perfection texts produced by Westerners who know Tibetan but who rely solely on scholarly knowledge, without recourse to teachers. Intellectual understanding alone, without the ripening process that takes place under the direction of qualified dzogchen teachers, will certainly result in misguided translations, perpetuated in misguided meditation by those who base their spiritual practice on such translations. But again, if qualified dzogchen masters refrain from working on translations because they fear imperfect results, can they lament when even more erroneous translations are published?

The translator of these texts, Richard Barron (Lama Chökyi Nyima), has truly mastered both literary and spoken Tibetan, but his deeper understanding is based on an extended retreat under the guidance of His Eminence Kalu Rinpoche, on a number of six-week dzogchen retreats, and on listening to and translating the teachings of many eminent lamas. He has translated other great perfection texts and sadhanas, notably Dudjom Lingpa's *Buddhahood Without Meditation,* under my direction. He thus brings more capability to his work than mere theoretical and intellectual competence. The other members of the translation committee have a grounding in the study of dzogchen terminology and have likewise participated in annual dzogchen retreats. The learned scholar Khenpo Chödzö has been consulted on many details of this translation of *A Treasure Trove of Scriptural Transmission.* I myself have brought to the process whatever understanding of great perfection I have attained in the course of a lifetime of study and meditation.

This means that while we have not necessarily produced flawless translations, we have confidence in this groundbreaking attempt. It should be understood that works of this kind are not casually read and easily comprehended. In fact, for most people, the texts are quite difficult to fathom; their meaning unfolds according to the depth of the reader's spiritual preparation. However, simply having these books in one's home is more valuable than having statues or stupas, for they are truly relics of the dharmakaya. Such holy works carry powerful blessings and are worthy objects of faith and devotion.

The project of translating Longchen Rabjam's *Seven Treasuries* is ongoing. We encourage anyone with knowledge and experience of the great perfection to contact us with suggestions, clarifications, or corrections, which we will consider for incorporation into future editions. May these precious texts illuminate the minds of all who read and venerate them.

Introduction

Venerable Tulku Thondup Rinpoche

Chöying Dzöd is the meaning of the innate nature of mind,
dharmakaya.
It elucidates naked primordial wisdom without affirming
or negating anything.
It is the heart essence of the visions of the Omniscient Lama
[Longchen Rabjam].
It is the most profound of all profound teachings.

It is the vivid arising of pure dharmakaya as the teaching.
This excellent teaching is a living buddha.
It fulfills the Buddha's activities in this world.
It manifests the absolute vision of the Buddha.
Even if you were to see the Buddha in person, there would not be
[any] greater [teaching] than this.[1]

Paltrul Rinpoche[2]

    Chöying Dzöd enshrines the essence of Dzogpa Chenpo teachings
written by Longchen Rabjam, the Omniscient Master.[3] It consists of a set
of source verses—*The Precious Treasury of the Basic Space of Phenomena* (or *The Precious Treasure on the Ultimate Sphere*)—and Longchen
Rabjam's commentary on these, which constitutes the present volume.

---

[1] *mDzod bdun la lta bar bskul ba,* by Abu Hralbo (Paltrul Rinpoche), *Paltul Sung
bum,* Vol. Ka, folio 2a/6 (Sikhron Mirig Petrun khnag).
[2] For the life of Paltrul Rinpoche, see *Masters of Meditation and Miracles* (hereafter
MMM), by Tulku Thondup (Shambhala, 1996), p. 201.
[3] For the life of Longchen Rabjam, see *The Nyingma School of Tibetan Buddhism,*
by Dudjom Rinpoche (Wisdom, 1991), Vol. I, p. 575, and MMM, p. 109.

Chöying Dzöd is not a composition contrived by a conceptual mind, but a manifestation of dharmakaya in the form of naturally arisen words. For centuries, it has remained one of the most sacred meditation manuals and has inspired thousands to attain the ultimate realization of Dzogpa Chenpo.

Dzogpa Chenpo and Prasangika-Madhyamaka

The general view of Dzogpa Chenpo is similar to that of Prasangika. Dzogpa Chenpo, however, stands alone not only in its approach to meditation, but also in its view. Longchen Rabjam writes:

> Dzogpa Chenpo's view of freedom from extremes is similar to Prasangika-Madhyamaka's for the most part. [The main difference is that] the important basic view of Madhyamaka is of a spacelike empty aspect, while the principal basic view [of Dzogpa Chenpo] is of primordially pure and naked intrinsic awareness, which is ineffable and unceasing. According to Dzogpa Chenpo, intrinsic awareness and everything that arises within it are free from all extremes, like the [nonexistence of] limits to space.[4]

The Third Dodrupchen (1865–1926)[5] writes:

> *Chöying Dzöd* and other [Dzogpa Chenpo] sources praise the view of Prasangika-Madhyamaka. So [Dzogpa Chenpo] is in accord with Prasangika regarding the definition of the limits to the object-of-negation (*dgag bya'i mtshams 'dzin*).
>
> However, in Prasangika—having separated the aspects (*ldog ch'a*) of appearances and emptiness by distinguishing the particularities (*spu ris*) of each or by separating the emptiness aspect [from the apparent aspect]—one apprehends the aspect of emptiness that is a nonaffirming negation (*med dgag*). This is a method of maintaining [the view] using concepts. It also asserts that after conceptually distinguishing between them and gaining experiences [of it] in meditation, one attains what is called "the fruition of the blissful, clear, and nonconceptual intellect."

---

[4] *Ch'os dbyings mdzod kyi 'grel ba Lung gi gter mdzod,* by Longchen Rabjam, folio 76b/1 (Adzom ed., reproduced by Dodrupchen Rinpoche).
[5] For the life of the Third Dodrupchen Rinpoche, see MMM, p. 237.

Dzogpa Chenpo, on the other hand, solely maintains intrinsic awareness (*rig pa*) [the true nature of mind], and uses it as the path. It does not employ concepts (*rtog pa*), since concepts [are the province of] mind (*sems*), and Dzogpa Chenpo involves meditation [on intrinsic awareness after] distinguishing mind from intrinsic awareness.[6]

Dzogpa Chenpo teachings are classified into three divisions. The Mind Division (*sems sde*) teaches that the nature of mind is enlightenment. It is primordial wisdom, just as it is. All phenomena of samsara and nirvana arise as the manifestative power (*rol pa'i rtsal*) of the mind, like the arising of reflections in a mirror.

The Space (or Vast Expanse) Division (*klong sde*) teaches that primordial wisdom (*ye shes*) and its manifestative power, phenomenal existents (*chos*), are attributes (*rgyan*) of primordially liberated space, the ultimate sphere (*chos dbyings*).

The Instruction Division (*man ngag sde*) teaches that direct realization of primordial purity is beyond concepts, designations, and dimensions. The profundity, or radiance (*gdangs*), of primordial purity arises naturally as the avenue of spontaneously accomplished appearances (*lhun grub kyi snang ba'i sgo*).

The view of the Mind Division falls into the extreme of apprehending everything as the power (*rtsal*) of the mind, while the Space Division apprehends everything as the ultimate sphere. But in the Instruction Division, where one has awakened the self-arisen ultimate nature as it is, everything arises as the natural radiance of primordial purity itself.

Chöying Dzöd and the Three Divisions

Many scholars consider *Chöying Dzöd* to be a teaching on the ultimate sphere according to the Space Division of Dzogpa Chenpo. Others see it as embodying the teachings of all three divisions. The Second Zhechen Rabjam (1713–1769) writes:

> Many early scholars [of Nyingma] assert that *Chöying Rinpoche'i Dzöd* is a teaching on the crucial meaning of the instructions of the Space Division. But, in fact, it is a profound and detailed

---

[6] *rDzogs ch'en*, by Jigmed Tenpe Nyima, *Dodrupchen Sungbum*, Vol. Cha, folio 7b/2 (Dodrupchen Rinpoche).

instruction that establishes the basis, path, and result of all three divisions of Dzogpa Chenpo.[7]

In concluding the *Chöying Dzöd*, Longchen Rabjam writes:

> I composed *Chöying Dzöd* according to the twenty-one scriptures of the Mind Division,
> three classes of the Space Division, and four cycles of the Instruction Division.[8]

In *Chöying Dzöd*, Longchen Rabjam cites many Instruction Division tantras, such as *The Reverberation of Sound*, and many great masters agree that the heart essence of *Chöying Dzöd* is the Instruction Division. Khenpo Ngakchung (1879–1941)[9] studied *Chöying Dzöd* with his root teacher, Nyoshul Lungtok (1829–1901),[10] who was a student of the great Paltrul Rinpoche (1808–1887). In his autobiography, Khenpo recalls some of his dialogues with his teacher about *Chöying Dzöd* and how it was transmitted to him:

> He [Nyoshul Lungtok] told me, "*Chöying Dzöd* is the mind profile of the omniscient Longchen Rabjam. The first nine chapters teach the view [of Dzogpa Chenpo]. The tenth teaches meditation; the eleventh, conduct; the twelfth, the immediate results of the path; and the thirteenth, the final results. You must study it and treasure the understanding of its meaning in your mind."
>
> I prayed strongly to the Great Omniscient One and studied the text, but didn't have much understanding. One day [Nyoshul Lungtok] asked me, "Did you understand any of it?" I responded, "It has many quotations from [the tantras of] the Mind Division, the Space Division, and the Instruction Division, but more from the Mind Division. Because of my preconceptions about the differences between the crucial points of the Mind Division and the secret class of the Instruction Division, only confusion has developed in my mind."

---

[7] *mDzod bdun ngal gso gsang tik (dkar ch'ag) skal bzang rna ba'i dga' ston*, by Gyurmed Kunzang Namgyal, p. 123/6 (Dodrup Sangyay Lama, 1979).

[8] *Ch'os dbyings rin po ch'e'i mdzod*, by Longchen Rabjam, folio 26a/1 (Adzom ed., reproduced by Dodrupchen Rinpoche).

[9] For the life of Khenpo Ngakchung, see MMM, p. 266.

[10] For the life of Nyoshul Lungtok, see MMM, p. 222.

He said, "[Generally,] it is easy to stretch the meaning of quotations in whatever way you want. Nevertheless, [teachings] do not use citations of higher teachings to [affirm] lower views. Rather, they quote lower teachings to [affirm] higher views." Then he added, "Now I will try to teach you *Chöying Dzöd.*" And he proceeded to give me the teachings.

[One day] he said, "You are so lucky that you can study sitting down. I received these teachings [alone] from Abu Rinpoche [Paltrul Rinpoche] at Dzogchen Kangtrod, at the expense of his sleep [or rest]. If he sat down, Abu tended to fall asleep [because of his advanced age], so I would walk backward holding the text in my hand for him, and he would teach me walking after me. The teachings continued in this way for many days and nights."

He continued, "Since it is said that *Chöying Dzöd* is the essence of [all teachings], it was Abu's main meditation [manual] and it is supposed to be mine, too. Now, you must treasure this teaching in your heart. If you develop a good understanding of *Chöying Dzöd* based on my instructions, you will never confuse it with the teachings of the Mind Division.

"*Chöying Dzöd* contains the teachings of [the Instruction Division, including] the *Unexcelled Ultimate Secret Tantra Without Text,*[11] *The Testaments of the Buddhas and Knowledge Holders with Their Instructions,*[12] and *Two Kinds of Introduction: One Based on and the Other Not Based on Khyungchen Khading,*[13] by Shri Singha."

After that I studied *Chöying Dzöd* again and again and arrived at an awareness that wasn't the same as what I had earlier. I presented this discovery to him and he said, "That is right! Progress is made gradually."[14]

---

[11] *rNying ma rgyud 'bum,* Vol. Ta, folios 182b/1–218b/5 (Adzom ed., reproduced by Dilgo Khyentse Rinpoche).

[12] *Bima sNying thig: gSer yig chan,* by Vimalamitra, Vol. E, folios 8a/4–36b/1 (Adzom ed., reproduced by Lama Jigtrak and Tulku Pema Wangyal).

[13] *Bima sNying thig,* by Vimalamitra, Vol. Ma, folios 21b/2–27a/3 (Adzom ed., reproduced by Lama Jigtrak and Tulku Pema Wangyal).

[14] *Padma las 'brel rtsal gyi rtogs bjod Ngo mtshar sgyu ma'i rol gar* (Autobiography of Khenpo Ngakchung), p. 138/2 (Sonam T. Kazi).

Chöying Dzöd as a Liturgy

Chöying Dzöd has also been used as a liturgy (Skt. *sadhana*)—that is, a daily prayer or meditation guide. My teacher Kyala Khenpo (1893–1957)[15] used to read a chapter of *Chöying Dzöd* and meditate on it every day. I remember his telling Tulku Dorje Dradul (1891–1959), the youngest son of Terton Dudjom Lingpa (1835–1904), "I have vowed to read a chapter of *Chöying Dzöd* every day until death comes to me." Tulku responded, "It is the best practice. It is the sadhana of dharmakaya, the ultimate body of the buddha." Even on the very morning that Khenpo drew his last breath, he recited a chapter of *Chöying Dzöd* and meditated on it. It was Chapter Three, which ends with

Always remain in the unchanging state.
There is no straying, even in the slightest, from awakened mind.[16]

Chöying Dzöd for Dying Meditators

Chöying Dzöd has also been used as a sacred introduction (*ngo sprod*) for dying meditators. By reciting it, a practitioner introduces the person passing away to his or her true nature and reminds him or her to remain in the right mental state. Generally, the process of dying is the most crucial experience in life, the time when we need the greatest support. It is also a time when our mental attitudes can make a significant difference in our future, because at the time of death we are suddenly free of the bonds of our gross body and all its limitations.

In my teens, when Kyala Khenpo and I performed death services for a great master called Pushul Lama, Khenpo advised me, "First, chant the *Chöying Dzöd* very slowly next to the lama's body. Chant the verses clearly and think about their meaning as you do so." Lama had died two days earlier, but his mind remained in a meditative state.

Khenpo added, "*Chöying Dzöd* was recited at the time of death of many highly accomplished Dzogpa Chenpo masters. For such masters, there is no method of introduction greater than this."

---

[15] For the life of Kyala Khenpo, see MMM, p. 283.
[16] *Ch'os dbyings rin po ch'e'i mdzod*, by Longchen Rabjam (Adzom ed., reproduced by Dodrupchen Rinpoche).

Under the guidance of the Dzogpa Chenpo master Chagdud Tulku Rinpoche,[17] *lotsawa* Chökyi Nyima and a team of editors have brought this precious teaching to English through years of devotion and dedication. On behalf of omniscient Longchen Rabjam's lineage of blessings, I offer my gratitude to all who have dedicated their lives and support to bringing this precious teaching to English readers. I entreat readers to enshrine this volume with the greatest respect. I also request that they study it with an open mind and a devoted heart in order to awaken the sublime wisdom light within themselves and let it shine for all beings. I humbly invoke the power of the blessings of the compassionate buddhas, lineage masters, and powerful protectors. I ask their forgiveness for all the mistakes that have crept into our efforts to bring this sacred teaching to the public, as well as their blessings, so that the absolute meaning of Dzogpa Chenpo may awaken in the minds of all who read it.

[17] For the life of Chagdud Rinpoche, see his autobiography, *Lord of the Dance* (Padma Publishing, 1992).

Translation Committee's Preface

Among the works in Longchen Rabjam's famous collection, *The Seven Treasuries,* is that commonly known as the *Chöying Dzöd,* which consists of two texts: a set of source verses entitled *The Precious Treasury of the Basic Space of Phenomena* and Longchenpa's own commentary on those verses, which constitutes the present volume. Although we have published these texts individually, they are considered companion volumes. Buddhist works are often structured in this way: the source verses provide a poetic summary of the subject matter examined at length in the prose commentary. The advantage of this in the past, when studying such texts included committing them to memory, was that it was much easier to memorize the source verses than the larger commentary. The advantage to contemporary practitioners is that, once they have studied the commentary in depth, reading the source verses will enable them to recall the detailed explanations presented in the commentary. As well, the source verses stand as a profoundly inspiring poetic work in their own right.

To some extent, each volume of *The Seven Treasuries* addresses the spiritual approach of the great perfection, or *dzogchen,* the pinnacle of Buddhist thought and practice according to the Nyingma school. The *Chöying Dzöd* focuses on the great perfection approach of *trekchö,* or "cutting through solidity," within the framework of view, meditation, conduct, and fruition. In the present volume, Longchen Rabjam writes that trekchö is "the ultimate meaning of the ground of being, which brings the most excellent individuals, those of the very highest acumen, to freedom effortlessly."

This work has been held in the highest esteem by masters of the great perfection tradition. In the later part of his life, Paltrul Rinpoche, a major figure of the tradition in the eighteenth century, carried a copy of the work with him constantly. In his history of the great perfection lineage, the late Nyöshul Khenpo Jamyang Dorjé, one of the foremost modern masters of this lineage, notes that Paltrul Rinpoche had a vision in which Longchenpa conferred on him the transmission of the ultimate lineage—the awakening of enlightened intent. Thereafter, Paltrul Rinpoche made the *Chöying Dzöd* the very heart of his personal spiritual practice. He gave extraordinary explanations of the text to his close students and helped to preserve the great perfection tradition by emphasizing the study of *The Seven Treasuries* and other works by Longchenpa.

The great perfection approach is said to "speak its own language," employing terminology and styles of presentation that are often unique. As such, it must be understood in its own right, and too literal an interpretation can lead to misunderstandings. In the tantric sources from which Longchen Rabjam quotes so liberally—especially *The All-Creating Monarch* (traditionally considered the primary source tantra of the Category of Mind) and many of the seventeen source tantras of the Category of Direct Transmission—the language employed is sometimes quasi-theistic. However, these are not the words of a divine creator speaking to others, but rather the direct expression of awakened mind. As well, the exegesis found in the present text is geared to students of the highest acumen and so does not employ the argumentation and lines of reasoning of lower spiritual approaches. Longchenpa assumes that the reader will grasp the implications without requiring more elaborate conceptual proof.

It is common for terms used in the great perfection approach to differ in meaning from the same terms used in other contexts. In translating key terms, we have attempted to convey their meanings within the expansive view of this approach. But as translators and editors, we have not taken it upon ourselves to try to supplant the role of a personal teacher, without whose guidance a student cannot realize the deeper significance of this text.

To aid the reader, we have composed chapter titles and, where the material is especially complex, have inserted subheadings. The text is further divided into sections, which consist of an introductory sentence, one stanza of the source verses (printed in boldface type), and Longchen

Rabjam's detailed explanation of those verses, including his citation of supporting material from the tantras and other scriptural sources. Our interpolations, which are confined to the English translation of Sanskrit and Tibetan terms, are enclosed in square brackets. Terms or phrases in parentheses consist of either Longchenpa's own explanatory material or Tibetan terms from the original that we have retained to help the reader follow the various etymological analyses. We have not translated certain Sanskrit terms. Some of them are well on their way to becoming familiar in colloquial English or are already in Western dictionaries (for example, "samsara"). Others (for example, "vajra" and "dharmakaya") carry a wealth or breadth of meaning that is not easily conveyed in English. For the most part, Sanskrit proper names in the text do not have diacritical marks.

In preparing this translation, we consulted three different editions of the *Chöying Dzöd*. Our primary source, and perhaps the most readily available of these editions, is the one printed from wood blocks carved at the Adzom Chögar printery in eastern Tibet, presumably in the early part of this century. These prints were brought out of Tibet and published by H.H. Dodrupchen Rinpoche in Gangtok, Sikkim, as a photo offset edition. Folio references to this edition of the commentary appear in brackets in the present text. We were also fortunate to have access to a recently corrected and reissued edition of the same blocks (which we refer to in the endnotes as the "revised Adzom Chögar edition") acquired by H.E. Chagdud Tulku Rinpoche on a visit to eastern Tibet in 1987. The third edition is a photo offset of prints made from blocks carved at the printery in Dergé (the cultural and political center of eastern Tibet before 1959), published in 1983 by Sherab Gyaltsen and Khentse Labrang in Gangtok, Sikkim. Our handling of variant readings within and among these editions is documented in the endnotes.

Throughout this project, we have had the invaluable guidance of Chagdud Tulku Rinpoche, who patiently answered the many questions that inevitably arose in the course of our work. We wish to express our deepest gratitude to him for envisioning the task of bringing this seminal collection by Longchen Rabjam to English-reading practitioners and for his continuous blessings, inspiration, and guidance.

In addition, we wish to acknowledge the contributions of Khenpo Chödzö (Orgyen Trinlay), who studied at Khenchen Jigmé Puntsok's monastery in Serta, in the eastern Tibetan region of Golok, and of

Khenpo Chöga of Dzogchen Monastery, also in eastern Tibet. Khenpo Chödzö, whom we consulted on numerous occasions, repeatedly emphasized the necessity of training under a qualified teacher in order to understand the *Chöying Dzöd* on a profound level. Khenpo noted that even those whose native language is Tibetan cannot fathom such a text without a long and systematic course of study and training. Khenpo Chöwang Dorjé Rinpoche of the Institute of Higher Nyingma Studies, Sikkim, very kindly helped Susanne Fairclough in the translation of Paltrul Rinpoche's "Exhortation to Read *The Seven Treasuries*." Finally, our thanks go to Linda Baer for typesetting the book.

A Treasure Trove of
Scriptural Transmission

A Commentary on *The Precious Treasury of the Basic Space of Phenomena*

༄༄།།ཆོས་དབྱིངས་རིན་པོ་ཆེའི་མཛོད་ཀྱི་འགྲེལ་པ་ལུང་གི་གཏེར་
མཛོད་ཅེས་བྱ་བ་བཞུགས་སོ།།

In Sanskrit: *Dharmadhātu ratna koṣa nāma vṛtti*

།རྒྱ་གར་སྐད་དུ། རྨ་རྨ་རྟུ་རཏྣ་ཀོ་ཥ་ནཱ་མ་བྲྀཏྟི།

In Tibetan: *Chos dbyings rin po che'i mdzod
ces bya ba'i 'grel pa*

བོད་སྐད་དུ། ཆོས་དབྱིངས་རིན་པོ་ཆེའི་མཛོད་ཅེས་བྱ་བའི་འགྲེལ་པ།

Longchen Rabjam

Introduction

In the language of India, the short title of this treatise would be *Dharmadhātu ratna koṣa nāma vṛtti;* in the language of Tibet, it is *Chos dbyings rin po che'i mdzod ces bya ba'i 'grel pa (A Commentary on "The Precious Treasury of the Basic Space of Phenomena").*

Homage to all the vast hosts[1] of victorious ones!

I pay homage to the original protector, Samantabhadra—
flawless and totally pure like space,
the deity of the kayas and timeless awareness, which do not come
    together or separate,
the glory of both conditioned existence and the peace of nirvana.

For all beings in samsara, which is like an illusion—
    clearly apparent without truly existing—
bound by their reifying perceptions as though in a dream,
the ultimate meaning of great perfection is that they are by
    nature totally free.
I will give a detailed explanation of this supremely spacious state
    of spontaneous equalness. [2a]

When enlightenment—the kayas and timeless awareness, which do not come together or separate—is discovered within primordial basic space, it dwells as the very adornment of the spontaneous realm Ghana-vyuha [Dense Array]. Like rays of light shining from the unobscured orb of the sun, emanations occur due to the nature of the continuum of inexhaustible adornment—enlightened form, speech, mind, qualities, and activity. Throughout infinite realms in the ten directions, as vast as

3

the boundless reaches of both ordinary space and the basic space of phenomena, appears an array of those who enlighten—transcendent and accomplished conquerors capable of guiding beings under any circumstances. The causal factors involved are the quality of innate responsiveness that is spontaneously present in these guides and the fact that those to be guided augment what is positive in themselves. The fruition of all turnings of the wheel of dharma—the consummate perfection of what has ultimate meaning— [2b] is natural great perfection, the spiritual approach of the unsurpassable secret. *Secret Conduct: The Tantra of the Potential* states:

> This is unique, genuine being.
> It is spoken of, is revealed, is explained
> that in the seeds of what has ultimate meaning
> lies the definitive heart essence itself.
> The enlightened speech that reveals this is a vast ocean;
> in some cases the purpose is of a more immediate nature,
> in other cases it is something that becomes relevant in the future,
> while in others it is specifically to guide beings.
> The very heart of the heart essence
> cannot be established for everyone with just a few words.

Let me define the topic of this text. Of the two means of practice, [3a] this work concerns the ultimate meaning of *trekchö* [cutting through solidity]—the ground that brings the most excellent individuals, those of the very highest acumen, to freedom effortlessly. A great many developmental treatments of this approach can be found in the tantras and the instructions of direct transmission. In this work I give a very clear explanation, summarizing the definitive vajra topics from the perspective of their single nature.

Here I explain in detail my composition *The Precious Treasury of the Basic Space of Phenomena*. Those who wish their work to be very thorough meticulously establish the underlying reasons for writing it. At this juncture, let me comment on the title in detail. This is so that people of keen acumen can comprehend the ultimate point of the text merely on hearing[2] the title and so understand it to be an "overview of the vajra body of the text." In fact, a title is composed in one of three ways: through the use of a metaphor, the meaning underlying that metaphor, or a combination of the two. Any of these will ensure that the title is relevant to the work.

In this case, I have carefully chosen the title by the method of combining a metaphor and its underlying meaning. The metaphor is "The Precious Treasury," while its underlying meaning is "the Basic Space of Phenomena." The basic space of phenomena—naturally occurring timeless awareness, totally pure by nature—is mind itself, ultimate truth. The metaphor and underlying meaning are thus connected, because all phenomena of nirvana and samsara without exception occur due to awareness or a lack of recognition of that awareness. This is analogous to all that is desired coming from a treasury of jewels that grant whatever one imagines. [3b]

Original basic space is described as buddha nature—buddhahood that is spontaneously present by nature. Given that neither nirvana nor samsara exists—only realization of this nature or the lack of such realization—the conventional designations "buddha" and "ordinary being" do not refer to anything whatsoever that has ever existed, because without awareness nothing could be ascertained to be nirvana or samsara and there would be no basis for distinguishing freedom from confusion. The explanatory tantra *Naturally Arising Awareness* addresses this in the following passage:

> Previously, before me,
> there were neither buddhas nor ordinary beings.
> How, then, could there be a path or accomplishment?
> There is not a single thing[3] that does not come from me.
> I am supreme emptiness.
> The five elements develop from me;
> I am the great master of the elements.
> I am the ancestor of all buddhas.
> Previously, before me,
> there was not even the name "buddha."
> I am the perfection of skillful means.
> Since I have no characteristics,
> my mind does not vacillate.
> I am the tomb of all buddhas;
> they are buried in me,[4] the unchanging burial ground.
> I am the dwelling place of all ordinary beings;
> their habitual patterns manifest as bodies.
> I am inalienable sublime knowing.
> Outer, inner, and secret are perfect in me.
> I am the embodiment of the vajra heart essence.

Buddhas are born from me.[5]
I am the ultimate meaning of unborn awareness.
I am free of being a phenomenon with substance.
Since I have no characteristics,
I raise beings from the grave.
Since innate responsiveness arises from me,[6]
I am beyond any talk of emptiness. [4a]
Since what is to be illuminated[7] comes from me,
I illuminate the darkness.

Thus, awareness—naturally occurring timeless awareness—is the basic space of phenomena. The term "treasury" describes this very aptly, for from that basic space come the phenomena of samsara and nirvana without exception. Although there are limitless explanatory methods using terms that are more or less synonymous, I shall explain the title according to three vajra themes.

The naturally pure ground is your fundamental nature—buddha nature, mind itself, inherently and utterly lucid. It is the basic space of phenomena in the sense that it abides as a precious treasury of the spontaneously present qualities with which this fundamental nature is timelessly endowed.

The ripening process of the path constitutes the stages of empowerment, including empowerment into the dynamic energy of awareness as spontaneous presence. It is the basic space of phenomena in the sense that all excellent qualities come from it. The aspects of the liberating process—that is, a guru's advice and the superb qualities that derive from one's view, meditation, and conduct in applying this advice—are said to be like precious jewels. The unlimited arising of dynamic energy as meditative experiences and insights—realization, meditative absorption, and so forth—is understood to be a treasury of all enlightened qualities.

The fruition, self-knowing awareness free of distortion, is sacred dharmakaya endowed with twofold purity; it is the basic space of phenomena in the sense that it abides as the flawless ground for the arising of enlightened qualities. It is sambhogakaya, the perfection of spontaneously present mastery and power, similar to a precious jewel. It is nirmanakaya, [4b] which entails enlightened activity and is shown to be like a fine treasury, for it completely fulfills the hopes of those to be guided.

With this, I have completed my explanation of the meaning underlying the title of this work.

Now, the salutation has two parts; the concise version is as follows:

Homage to glorious Samantabhadra!

Here "glorious" carries the meaning of bringing to full expression the qualities that derive from renunciation and realization. From the point of view of one's own welfare, this is the discovery of sacred dharmakaya, and from the point of view of others' welfare, it is the benefit that the sacred rupakaya—while not straying from basic space—ensures for beings for as long as samsara endures. You may ask, "Who or what has such glory?" It is attributed to "Samantabhadra" [that which is wholly positive]. This primordial guide manifests as the guru for all samsara and nirvana, ensuring the spontaneous accomplishment of noble enlightened activities. It is to this most perfect teacher—the timeless perfection of mastery and power as the sacred guide who demonstrates the path—that the author pays "homage" with fervent faith and great devotion of body, speech, and mind.

You may wonder, "Is homage paid solely to Samantabhadra?" No, for homage is also paid to all that aids beings in fathoming the subject matter of this work and that abides as the five aspects of Samantabhadra—that is, to all buddhas, who have awakened to buddhahood within the essence of Samantabhadra, as well as to all aspects of ground, path, and fruition.

Samantabhadra as teacher is the fact that all buddhas, while abiding as sambhogakaya and dharmakaya in Akanishtha, the pinnacle pure realm, [5a] ensure benefit by sending forth emanations to all realms of those to be guided. *The Detailed Commentary* states:

> Homage to the total effulgence
> of wholly positive rays of light—
> the complete loosening of the net of concepts
> and mastery of the profound and vast kayas.

Samantabhadra as ground is the true nature of all phenomena, suchness itself. This is called "Samantabhadra as nature."

Samantabhadra as adornment is the manifestation of all phenomena—that is, the natural arising of the display of objects in the phenomenal world. This constitutes all that is completely pure in that its nature is illusory.

Samantabhadra as awareness is naturally occurring timeless awareness—buddha nature. *The Highest Continuum* speaks of this in the following passage:

> Because the kaya of perfect buddhahood is pervasive,
> because of the undifferentiated state of suchness,
> and because of the birthright of all beings,
> they are forever endowed with buddha nature.

Samantabhadra as realization is the fundamentally unconditioned way of abiding. This constitutes the discovery of the vision of liberation that comes through complete realization. It is called "Samantabhadra as path."

Furthermore, concerning these aspects, *Samantabhadra: Mirror of Enlightened Mind* states:

> You should understand that the nature of all phenomena is that of the five aspects of Samantabhadra. What are these? you ask. They are Samantabhadra as nature, Samantabhadra as adornment, Samantabhadra as teacher, Samantabhadra as awareness, and Samantabhadra as realization.

As for the extensive explanation of the salutation, [5b] this is a eulogy to awakened mind, which is equal to space:

> **Naturally occurring timeless awareness—utterly lucid**
>   **awakened mind—**
> **is something marvelous and superb, primordially and**
>   **spontaneously present.**
> **It is the treasury from which comes the universe of appearances**
>   **and possibilities, whether of samsara or nirvana.**
> **Homage to that unwavering state, free of elaboration.**

The preceding verse demonstrates the general subject matter of this treatise. In effect, what it says is as follows: Mind itself, totally pure by nature, is spontaneously present as the ground aspect of buddhahood—dharmakaya, suchness itself, without any transition or change—for it occurs naturally and primordially without being created by some agent. Mind itself abides as something marvelous and superb, for the qualities of basic space abide timelessly as the kayas and timeless awareness, which do not come together or separate. Mind itself abides as awakened mind, naturally occurring and utterly lucid—timeless awareness that never changes. Although nirvana or samsara comes about under conditions of realization or its lack, this essence—mind itself—is the true nature of phenomena, which undergoes no transition or change whatsoever, abiding as natural great perfection. To this sacred embodiment I pay homage as an expression of my understanding of the way in which it abides. *Naturally Arising Awareness* states:

> Within the essence of ultimate truth,
> there is no buddha or ordinary being.
> Since awareness cannot be reified, it is empty.
> Given that it does not dwell in emptiness,
> it abides in its own state of supreme bliss.
> The majestic ruler of all buddhas is understood to be one's
>   own awareness.
> This monarch, naturally manifest awareness, is present
>   in everyone, but no one realizes it. [6a]

Following this, I state my commitment to compose this work:

> **The very pinnacle of spiritual approaches, the expanse in**
>   **which the sun and moon orbit the most majestic mountain,**
> **is the expanse of the vajra heart essence—spontaneously**
>   **present and utterly lucid—**
> **the expanse of the naturally settled state that entails no effort**
>   **or achievement.**
> **Listen as I explain this superb, timelessly infinite expanse.**

Although mind itself is identical to naturally occurring timeless awareness, there is a developmental process by which one reaches a definitive conclusion about this, and so numerous spiritual approaches are explained, taking into account individuals' differing degrees of acumen. These can be subsumed concisely under nine headings, as *The Supreme System of Ati* states:

> The lesser stages are threefold,
> their teachings in accord with the intellects involved.
> The shravaka approach is for those consumed by concepts,
> the pratyekabuddha approach for those whose thinking
>   is methodical,

and the bodhisattva approach for those who apply concepts
  with discrimination.

The intermediate approaches are shown to be threefold.
For the most inferior, there is kriya,
for the inferior, charya,
and for those with discursive minds, there is yoga.

As for the three greater stages,
there is the development stage for those with expansive minds,
the completion stage for those whose minds are more focused,
and the sublime secret, the great perfection approach, for the
  most excellent.

Of these nine approaches, atiyoga, the vajra heart essence, is the pinnacle. Furthermore, the very pinnacle of its three categories is the unsurpassable sphere of the Category of Direct Transmission, which is
therefore called "the expanse in which the sun and moon orbit the most
majestic mountain." The same source states:

There is the Category of Mind for those with conceptual minds,
the Category of Expanse for those with minds like space, [6b]
and that of Direct Transmission for those who need not strive
  step by step.

Ati is the expanse of the utterly lucid vajra heart essence by virtue of
being naturally pure and beyond anything to be established or removed.
It is the expanse of the naturally settled state by virtue of being beyond
effort or achievement. It is the superb, timelessly infinite expanse by virtue of being timelessly pure in its very essence. My commitment is to
compose this work in order to explain, for the sake of future generations, the ultimate meaning of awareness—awakened mind—the spacelike vajra heart essence of ati. A eulogy of this basic space as the very
pinnacle of all views is found in *Naturally Arising Awareness:*

It is explained that the very pinnacle of all views is ati,
  great perfection.
Since it is spacious,[8] it should be understood that the significance
of its unlimited potential is that it is like space.
The significance of its being vast and profound, and therefore
  difficult to fathom,
is analogous to the depths of the great ocean.

The significance of the light rays of lucidity gathering
is understood to be analogous to the orb of the sun itself.
Because it is free of conceptual limits,
the secret mantra approach is said to be the most majestic
    of skillful means.

With the foregoing, I have finished demonstrating the reasons for composing this treatise. Now, in order to explain in detail the subject matter of the main body of the treatise, I will discuss the topics of this most majestic secret in thirteen chapters.

1

The Adornment of Basic Space

First it can be demonstrated that since samsara and nirvana do not
stray from basic space, all phenomena are without transition or change
within the context of supreme perfection, which is equal to space. [7a]
To this end, it can be shown that although what arises as samsara and
nirvana does so naturally within the scope of awareness—the supreme
spontaneous presence of the three kayas—it does not stray from spontaneously present basic space:

> Within the expanse of spontaneous presence is the ground
>   for all that arises.
> Empty in essence, continuous[1] by nature,
>   it has never existed as anything whatsoever, yet arises as
>   anything at all.
> Within the expanse of the three kayas, although samsara
>   and nirvana arise naturally,
> they do not stray from basic space—such is the blissful realm
>   that is the true nature of phenomena.

Thus, given that awareness is pure by nature, its essence as emptiness
is dharmakaya, its nature as lucidity is sambhogakaya, and the way in
which its innate responsiveness arises is nirmanakaya. These three are
timelessly and spontaneously present without having to be sought. This
great, undiminishing treasure is the utterly lucid mandala that abides
as the ground of being. Even as anything at all arises within that context—be it awareness's own manifestations as perceived purely by buddhas or as perceived impurely by ordinary beings—it is only the display
of basic space as the true nature of phenomena. Nothing else arises, just

as nothing you dream about, be it good or bad, goes beyond the context of sleep. *Naturally Arising Awareness* states:

> Due to the sun of awareness rising within the realm of emptiness,[2]
> the five unchanging kayas arise directly from the mandala of
>   the great, undiminishing treasure.
> They present a nondual display[3] within a nonconceptual state.
> On the level of truth, the five mind-body aggregates, without
>   being deliberately structured,
> are revealed as a magical display of appearances, however they
>   manifest. [7b]

And *The All-Creating Monarch* states:

> The three kayas are subsumed within me, the all-creating one.
> All phenomena, however they manifest,
> have three uncontrived aspects—nature, essence, and
>   responsiveness.
> I reveal these three kayas to be my suchness.

Therefore, it can be shown that the universe of appearances and possibilities, which manifests as samsara and nirvana, is the magical expression of basic space:

> **Mind itself is a vast expanse, the realm of unchanging space.**
> **Its indeterminate display is the expanse of the magical**
>   **expression of its responsiveness.**
> **Everything is the adornment of basic space and nothing else.**
> **Outwardly and inwardly, things proliferating and resolving are**
>   **the dynamic energy of awakened mind.**
> **Because this is nothing whatsoever yet arises[4] as anything at all,**
> **it is a marvelous and magical expression, amazing and superb.**

In the spacelike context of one's self-knowing awareness, this display of myriad phenomena—this animate and inanimate universe that seems to endure—is revealed to be amazing and superb, since it arises timelessly as a continuous magical expression within an unborn state. *Naturally Arising Awareness* states:

> Awareness,[5] difficult for anyone to realize,
> is subtle, hard to comprehend, and seen by no one.
> It cannot be reified, but is equally present everywhere

as the expanse of naturally occurring well-being.
It arises as the display of samsara and nirvana within
    a continuous context.[6]

And *The All-Creating Monarch* states:

All phenomena are awakened mind, and to use a metaphor—
the universal metaphor—their nature is like space,
which is also the ultimate meaning of awakened mind.
Space, air, water, earth, and fire—these five
are the superb manifest aspect of buddhahood within
    awakened mind. [8a]
The manifestations of the three planes of conditioned existence,
    the five paths, and the six classes of beings
are also the manifest aspect of buddhahood, which is not
    affected by the consequences of karma.
The three realms are timelessly the form, speech, and mind
    of enlightenment.
And so, just as there is nothing in the entire universe—
    the universe of all appearances and possibilities—
that does not abide within the realm of space,
so too the enormous scope of the vast expanse of awakened mind
is such that buddhas, ordinary beings, and the entire universe are
    present therein.[7]

The way in which the display arises within the expanse of awakened
mind can be explained in detail:

**Throughout the entire universe, all beings and all that
    manifests as form
are adornments of basic space, arising as the ongoing principle
    of enlightened form.
What is audible, all sounds and voices without exception,
    as many as there may be,
are adornments of basic space, arising as the ongoing principle[8]
    of enlightened speech.
All consciousness and all stirring and proliferation of thoughts,
    as well as the inconceivable range of nonconceptual states,
are adornments of basic space, arising as the ongoing principle
    of enlightened mind.**

Within this scope of awareness, all the sensory appearances that manifest as the universe of appearances and possibilities, whether of samsara or nirvana, arise naturally as awareness's own manifestations, their very essence being nothing other than that of a dream, their nature that of the moon's reflection in water. All manifest forms are the mandala, or display, of enlightened form as an aspect of naturally occurring timeless awareness. All sounds and voices are the mandala of enlightened speech. Ordinary consciousness and the vast range of nonconceptual timeless awareness arise naturally as nothing more than the display of the supreme mandala of enlightened mind. Not even afflictive emotional patterns, which manifest due to the six sense faculties and their attendant objects being invested with identity, stray from the context of this single mandala of naturally occurring timeless awareness. [8b] *The Tantra Without Letters* states:

> Everything that occurs—perceptions based on confusion—
>   is my mind.
> Everything that abides—perceptions based on confusion—
>   is my enlightened mind.
> Everything that manifests—perceptions based on confusion—
>   is my enlightened form.
> Everything that is audible—perceptions based on confusion—
>   is my enlightened speech.

And *The All-Creating Monarch* states:

> Ah! The all-creating monarch, teacher of teachers,
> arrays the heart essence as the mandala of enlightened form.
> However phenomena appear and remain,
> they are all arrayed within the realm of the unborn basic space
>   of phenomena.
> Moreover, because there is no acceptance or rejection with regard
>   to the ultimate meaning of this heart essence,
> I, the all-creating one, have also arrayed them.

> Ah! The all-creating monarch, teacher of teachers,
> arrays the heart essence as the mandala of enlightened speech.
> However phenomena are audible and endure,
> they are all arrayed through words as enlightened speech[9]
>   within the realm of unborn basic space.

This essence is subsumed within indescribable
    enlightened speech.
The all-creating monarch has also arrayed this.

Ah! The all-creating monarch, teacher of teachers,
arrays the heart essence as the mandala of awareness.
All consciousness, all thoughts, whatever their content[10]—
one is aware of them as the ultimate meaning of the unborn
    all-creating one.
The enlightened form, speech, and mind of me,
    the all-creating one,
are the threefold mandala of resting without contrivance
    in genuine being,
not deliberately arranged, but perfect all at once.
With this realization, one enters into the ultimate meaning of the
    spontaneously present heart essence.

Now, everything can be summarized as the single miraculous display of
basic space, and the way in which this is realized can also be discussed:

Beings born in the six classes through the four avenues of
    rebirth, moreover, [9a]
do not stray in the slightest from the basic space of phenomena.
The universe of appearances and possibilities—
the six kinds of sense objects manifesting in dualistic
    perception—
appears within the realm of the basic space of phenomena
    just as illusions do, manifest yet nonexistent.
Without underlying support, vividly apparent yet timelessly
    empty, supremely spacious, and naturally clear, just as it is,
the universe arises as the adornment of the basic space of
    phenomena.

Thus, within the scope of awareness, all phenomena of the universe
of appearances and possibilities—the three realms and the six classes
of beings—are awareness's own manifestations arising and are nothing more than a magical display, clearly apparent without truly existing. This is similar to an illusory city or some other enormous illusory
manifestation appearing in the sky. Even as phenomena manifest they
do not know existence, arising naturally as nothing more than inherent

expressions of emptiness. Appearances that manifest as objects of the six avenues of consciousness arise naturally within this scope of awareness as a display of dream images or magical illusions. *The Tantra Without Letters* states:

> Seeing is continuous—things manifest in a manner consistent
>   with my form.
> Hearing is continuous—things are heard in a manner consistent
>   with my sound.
> Smelling is continuous—things are smelled in a manner
>   consistent with my scent.
> Tasting is continuous—things are tasted in a manner consistent
>   with my flavor.
> Sensation is continuous—it is readily perceived in a manner
>   consistent with my conceptual mind.
> On the secret level, afflictive emotions are my miraculous display.
> Buddhas and ordinary beings are my tomb.
> I, the all-creating one, am the supreme natural clarity of sensory
>   appearances.
> Originally, before there were sensory appearances,
> the six open avenues of the conceptual mind that readily
>   investigate [11] things
> ensured that the process of consciousness would remain
>   continuous, with these six avenues arising in a relaxed way.

And *The Source Verses on Sublime Knowing* states:

> Like dream images, like magical illusions, like mirages of castles
>   in the air— [9b]
> thus, it is said, do things originate, thus do they endure, and thus
>   are they destroyed.

Now, all phenomena are subsumed within naturally occurring timeless awareness. So even as they arise naturally as awareness's own manifestations, appearing and imputed to exist outwardly and inwardly, there is infinite evenness in their supreme equality, in which nothing need be done:

> **However things appear or sound, within the vast realm**
>   **of basic space**

they do not stray from their spontaneous equalness as
    dharmakaya, awakened mind.
Since the timeless state of utter relaxation is naturally empty
    and without transition or change,
whatever manifests constitutes the scope of naturally occurring
    timeless awareness, the true nature of phenomena,
merging in a single blissful expanse, without any effort,
    without anything needing to be done.

Even as anything at all manifests, this is nothing other than the
scope of awareness, just as when any dream image appears, this is nothing other than the realm of sleep. Given that such awareness is like space,
timelessly empty and without transition or change, the manifestation of
sensory appearances within its scope is a display of empty appearances
that do not exist. Therefore, since nothing whatsoever has ever existed
in its own right, things have always arisen within the crucial context
of their needing to be neither accepted nor renounced, requiring neither
hope nor fear. Now, without becoming involved anew in effort or in
hope and fear, you are instructed solely to rest in the uncontrived state
of genuine being, which extends infinitely throughout that realm within
which things fade equally in and of themselves. *The Perfect Dynamic
Energy of the Lion* states:

> The all-encompassing state of infinite pervasiveness is
>   the sublime, ultimate meaning of the heart essence.
> Sense objects are perceived within the state of equalness
>   and dissolve into the naturally occurring state.
> The meaning of boundlessness is experienced as that state
>   of self-knowing and supremely blissful awareness.[12]
> The manifestation of the essence of being is subsumed within
>   the expanse of the kayas.
> The all-pervasive nature of being is a boundless manifestation
>   within basic space.
> Inexhaustible, it occurs naturally, free of the limitations
>   of elaboration.[13] [10a]
> It is the infinitely pervasive nature of lucidity—the unity
>   of basic space and awareness.
> It is beyond being an object[14]—neither a creator nor something
>   created.

> It displays itself in everything—the consummate natural
>   manifestation of spontaneous presence.

And *The All-Creating Monarch* states:

> Ah! The all-creating monarch, teacher of teachers,
> has uttered a prophecy to the authentic retinue.
> The way sensory appearances manifest leads one
>   to a definitive conclusion
> concerning the uncontrived heart essence, the root of
>   all phenomena.
> If one fathoms the ultimate meaning of the single nature[15]
>   of this heart essence,
> one realizes that the nature of everything is subsumed
>   within that all-creating one.

Thus, the essence that is beyond concerted effort—dharmakaya, which involves neither acceptance nor rejection—is awareness, naturally occurring timeless awareness. Given that this is so, its pure and inherently lucid nature can be shown to be sambhogakaya, uncontrived and unadulterated:

> **Sambhogakaya is unwavering natural lucidity.**
> **Even as anything at all manifests, it is by nature**
> **   spontaneously present,**
> **uncontrived and unadulterated—a pervasive state**
> **   of spontaneous equalness.**

Abiding as natural lucidity, the very essence of awareness arises naturally as the spontaneous presence of sambhogakaya, so there is a supreme, uncontrived state of equalness. This constitutes the nature of being, the unchanging unity of emptiness and lucidity.

In the same vein, the continuous way in which awareness expresses itself is the timeless arising of nirmanakaya:

> **Due to the way in which the distinct, myriad display arises,**
> **emanations occur naturally—the amazing magic of what has**
> **   ultimate meaning.**
> **They never stray from the wholly positive state in which**
> **   nothing need be done.**

By virtue of its essence, images arise vividly and continuously in a highly polished mirror, yet the mirror itself is unaffected. [10b] Similarly, regardless of the way in which awareness arises, its essence is unaffected and its dynamic energy arises continuously; this is nirmanakaya.

The perfection of the three kayas within the scope of awareness is stated in *The All-Creating Monarch*:

> Due to the nature of me, all-creating enlightenment,
> the three kayas—the heart essence of all victorious ones—
> are naturally and spontaneously present without having
>   to be sought.
> My uncontrived nature is ensured as dharmakaya,
> my uncontrived essence as sambhogakaya,
> and my fully evident responsiveness as nirmanakaya.
> I do not reveal these three to be results ensured by being
>   sought.
> The three kayas are subsumed within me, the all-creating one.
> All phenomena, however they manifest,
> have three uncontrived aspects—nature, essence, and
>   responsiveness.
> I reveal these three kayas to be my suchness.

And *The Tantra Without Letters* states:

> Since the five kayas manifest naturally in me,
> I am the pure realm—the completely perfect nature
>   of phenomena.[16]

Thus, when I explain that the kayas and timeless awareness, which constitute basic space, are perfect in their spontaneous presence, certain deluded people who have not studied and contemplated sufficiently disparage this vehemently, saying, "Wouldn't it indeed be wonderful if even now the kayas and timeless awareness of buddhahood were present and perfect in ordinary beings? But that is impossible!" They are similar to those who hold that the sun is not present when it is obscured by dense clouds, so I would not stoop to debating with such fools. Nevertheless, I would assure them that it is hardly fitting for them to be upset about this. It is said that enlightened qualities are spontaneously present in one's fundamental nature. If they were not, where would they come from as something new when one awakened to buddhahood? [11a] As

Maitreya explains, they are "uncompounded and spontaneously present." And *The Two Chapters* states:

> Ordinary beings are truly buddhas,
> but this fact is obscured by adventitious distortions.
> Once these are removed, truly there is buddhahood.

You can gain some understanding from such scriptural citations. I am certainly not suggesting that these qualities are present in their total purity under current circumstances. But it makes perfect sense, even for those with limited intelligence, to respect as authentic spiritual teaching the fact that these enlightened qualities are totally pure by nature. Thus, I would speak to them as the Blessed One did in Vaishali when he persuaded some irreligious monks to respect the dharma.

Now, it can be shown that within awareness—awakened mind—the kayas and timeless awareness do not come together or separate:

> Within awakened mind itself, which is without pitfalls,
> the spontaneous perfection of the three kayas, entailing
>   no effort,
> is such that, without straying from basic space, they are
>   spontaneously present and uncompounded.
> The spontaneous perfection of the kayas, timeless awareness,
>   and enlightened activity, moreover,
> is a great amassing—the supreme expanse that is timelessly
>   perfect, timelessly arising.

Because the kayas and timeless awareness are forever and always spontaneously perfect within the essence of awareness, they—like the radiance of the sun—are not subject to transition or change. This is the state of naturally occurring timeless awareness, and as such it is perfect in that its nature is the continuum of the inexhaustible adornment of enlightened form, speech, and mind. *The Perfect Dynamic Energy of the Lion* states:

> The ultimate meaning is expressed within a single awareness.
> The three kayas manifest as the essence of victorious ones. [11b]
> From the kayas occurs the miraculous expression of timeless
>   awareness.

This is neither manifest nor nonmanifest.
It is free of the extremes of realization and a lack of it.
Illuminating timeless awareness abides as the essence of being.
The elements are the embodiment of what is unsullied
    by conditions.[17]
Illuminating timeless awareness [18] displays itself in everything,
totally free of spiritual paths, innumerable though they may be.
Within the vast range of worlds in the three-thousand-fold
    universe,
however many mandalas of enlightened form there are,
they are all, without exception, clearly apparent as sensory
    appearances.
Within the vast range of worlds in the three-thousand-fold
    universe,
however many mandalas of enlightened speech there are,
they are all, without exception, revealed in what is audible.[19]
Within the vast range of worlds in the three-thousand-fold
    universe,
however many mandalas of enlightened mind there are,
they are all, without exception, pristine in light of realization.[20]
Enlightened form, speech, and vajra mind—
from what is not manifest, everything manifests.
Buddhahood is the kayas and the radiance of timeless awareness.
Sensory appearances are present as awareness's own
    manifestations.
Samantabhadra is self-knowing awareness.[21]

Given that the kayas and timeless awareness are perfect within the
scope of awareness, it can further be shown that all that is experienced
as the expanse of awareness—the pure realms of vast hosts of victorious
ones and the range of enlightened wisdom—is the miraculous expression of that awareness:

Timelessly and spontaneously present, this pure realm is
    without transition or change.
With the perception of the true nature of phenomena within
    basic space,
wisdom arises continuously as the adornment of that space.
Not created or achieved, it abides timelessly.
Like the sun in the sky, it is amazing and superb.

When enlightenment, endowed with twofold purity, is discovered, at that point [12a] all that constitutes the timeless awareness and perspective of dharmakaya, sambhogakaya, and nirmanakaya is simply the natural manifestation of awareness—buddhahood itself—expressing itself fully. Nothing has ever existed as anything other than that, because there is nothing other than that—only the perspective of the kayas and timeless awareness that are present within you and become fully evident at that point.

You might object, "Doesn't this enlightenment derive from the accumulations of merit and timeless awareness?" My reply is that the two accumulations are termed "spontaneously present" in the sense that their qualities of manifestation and emptiness are already perfect. The purely nominal label "the two accumulations as causal factors" refers to the incidental reinforcing of these factors as merely conditional circumstances that dispel distortions. This is like describing the cleaning rag and cleanser used to polish a gem covered with dirt as the "causes" of seeing the gem.

Therefore, given that the three kayas are subsumed within the perspective of naturally occurring timeless awareness, this awareness abides as the guiding principle, the ground from which factors such as the three kayas arise. *The All-Creating Monarch* states:

> Naturally occurring timeless awareness is unique as the guiding
>   principle of everything.
> From the manifestation of my threefold nature
> comes the threefold enumeration of guiding principles.

Given that, in manifesting and arising naturally, all phenomena are thus subsumed within awareness—awakened mind—they can be shown to be like a spectacular illusion since, however they manifest, at the same time they have never existed:

> Within this ultimate womb of basic space, timelessly
>   and spontaneously present,
> samsara is wholly positive, nirvana is positive. [12b]
> Within the wholly positive expanse, samsara and nirvana
>   have never existed.
> Sensory appearances are wholly positive, emptiness
>   is positive.

Within the wholly positive expanse, appearances and
emptiness have never existed.
Birth and death are wholly positive, happiness and suffering
are positive.
Within the wholly positive expanse, birth, death, happiness,
and suffering have never existed.
Self and other are wholly positive, affirmation and negation
are positive.
Within the wholly positive expanse, self, other, affirmation,
and negation have never existed.

Within the essence of awareness—of awakened mind, which is like
space—nothing whatsoever has ever existed. So while anything at all
can manifest—samsara and nirvana, sensory appearances and emptiness, birth and death, happiness and suffering, self and other—none of
it has ever existed. These are awareness's own manifestations that appear continuously and are simply the scope, or dynamic energy, or display, of that awareness. Because they manifest yet have no independent
nature (like magical illusions, dream images, the reflection of the moon
in water, hallucinations, castles in the air, or phantom emanations), all
possible phenomena of samsara and nirvana are such that, though apparent, they have never known existence. Having no such basis, they do
not stray from the enlightened intent of the union of Samantabhadra
and Samantabhadrā, the masculine and feminine aspects of the wholly
positive state. *Samantabhadra: Mirror of Enlightened Mind* states:

There is not a single thing that does not come from me;
I am Samantabhadra, all that occurs.
I am Samantabhadra, the guiding principle;[22]
there is not a single thing that I do not reveal.
Different natures come from me;
I am Samantabhadra, the nature of being.
I am free of conventional designations;
I am Samantabhadra, the state of oneness.
The five aspects of supreme illumination are perfect in me;
I am Samantabhadra, the supreme ruler.[23]
I bring about liberation into pure realms; [13a]
I am Samantabhadra, the liberator.
Whatever manifests is perfect within my mind;
I am Samantabhadra, realization.[24]

. . . .

Samantabhadra is vast, displaying itself everywhere.
Samantabhadra and Samantabhadrā comprise a single
  nondual state;
the nonduality of masculine and feminine completely permeates
  all beings.
Samantabhadra, awakened mind, does not entail reification
  or progress.
Samantabhadra's face gazes in all ten directions.
The embodiment of all-seeing Samantabhadra has no front
  or back.
Everything merges in the bhaga of the feminine aspect, the single
  blissful expanse.
It does not abide in any finite way[25] and cannot be characterized
  with words.
The miraculous expression of Samantabhadra takes place within
  the realm of ultimate truth.
It is a treasure of Samantabhadra that ensures the fulfillment
  of all wishes.
The expanse of Samantabhadrā is an inexhaustible wealth
  of enjoyment.
It is imbued with the sublime signs of timeless awareness that
  accord with what is meaningful.[26]
The mandala that cannot be drawn is the blissful expanse[27]
  of utter lucidity.
This mandala of Samantabhadra completely permeates
  all beings.[28]

And *The Perfect Dynamic Energy of the Lion* states:[29]

Samantabhadrā—the basic space of phenomena—manifests as
  sense objects.
Samantabhadra—complete purity—appreciates those objects.
Samantabhadrā—timeless awareness—enjoys space.
Samantabhadra—awareness—enters into that basic space.
The complete purity[30] of the masculine and feminine aspects
  in union is not subject to affirmation or negation.
Samantabhadrā—awareness's own manifestation—is not subject
  to restrictions.

Samantabhadra—realization—unites everything.

Samantabhadra—the elements manifest as identical with her.

Samantabhadra—sublime knowing—reveals what manifests
naturally.

Samantabhadra—spacious sky—is unmoving, [13b]

and Samantabhadra—equalness—is nonconceptual.

In Samantabhadra—the coming together of things—everything
merges in oneness.

Samantabhadra—awareness[31]—engages what has ultimate
meaning.

Samantabhadra—sublime knowing—forms all variety of things.

Samantabhadra—sublime skillful means—manifests as
awareness.

Samantabhadra—brilliant lucidity—cannot be reified.

Samantabhadra—transcendent and accomplished conqueror—
arises instantaneously.

Samantabhadra—involving no reification—abides in her
own ground.

Samantabhadra—the sphere of being—is in essence empty.

Samantabhadra—the source of phenomena—is not created.

Samantabhadra—the nonconceptual state—is undistracted.

Samantabhadra—relative reality—is the actual seed.

Samantabhadra—ultimate reality—reveals her miraculous
expression.[32]

Samantabhadra—lovely adornment—manifests in
sense objects.

Samantabhadra—the unity of basic space and awareness—
is actual dharmakaya.

Samantabhadra—the nature of being—is continuous.

Samantabhadra—the essence of being—is unchanging.

Samantabhadra—the responsiveness of being—manifests as
anything whatsoever.

Samantabhadra—the guiding principle—tames afflictive
emotions.

Samantabhadra—emptiness—is free of conventional
designations.

Samantabhadra—lucidity—is free of being anything identifiable.

The masculine and feminine aspects together are the wholly
positive expanse of awareness.

Manifesting like dream images within such a context, sensory appearances perceived in confusion can be shown to arise in and of themselves for all beings as awareness's own manifestations:

> Labeling takes place in confusion, for what is nonexistent is
>   taken to exist.
> Given that the nature of things is similar to that of dream
>   images, which have no basis,
> how exceedingly strange it is to fixate on samsara and nirvana
>   as though they existed in their own right!

That is to say, one's self-knowing awareness—the essence of spontaneously present dharmakaya, empty yet lucid, like space—has no characteristics or substance. [14a] However, there are two aspects of the non-recognition of awareness that occur simultaneously—an aspect that is coemergent with being itself and is the failure to recognize the very essence of awareness, and an ascriptive aspect that reifies things so that they seem to be what they are not. This leads to confusion based on dualistic perception, so that what is perceived in that confusion and constitutes samsara arises in a variety of ways. Just as by reifying the environments and images in a dream one gives them identity, beings in their confusion are obsessed about the universe of appearances and possibilities. Since they thus invest clearly apparent yet nonexistent phenomena with ultimate meaning, it is as though they were fixating on the images in a magical illusion as somehow truly existing. You should understand this, thinking, "How very strange!" *The Pearl Garland* states:

> Thus, sensory appearances in all their variety
> are like a rope being perceived as a snake.
> From reification, so that things seem to be what they are not,
> both the inanimate universe and the life it contains are formed.

And *The Heart Essence of Secrets* states:

> How marvelous! Given that there is buddha nature,
> one's thoughts flow because of karma.

And *The Compendium* states:

> However many beings there are, whether inferior, middling,
>   or superior,
> the Sugata has stated that they all come from the nonrecognition
>   of awareness.

It can be shown that, even as sensory appearances perceived in confusion thus manifest as samsara, their nature is that of dream images, for
in actuality confusion has never known existence:

> Everything is wholly positive, a supreme state of spontaneous
> presence.
> Since there never has been confusion, is no confusion, and
> never will be confusion,
> conditioned existence is merely a label.
> It is beyond the extremes of existence and nonexistence.
> Since no one has ever been confused at all in the past,
> no one is confused at present and no one will be confused
> later on.
> This is the enlightened intent of the original purity of the three
> planes of conditioned existence. [14b]

As soon as you fall asleep and in your dreams see any and all beings and environments of the three realms arising simultaneously, in
that very moment, these manifest to your mind,[33] are reified by your
mind, and are fixated on by your mind. But in actuality they have
never known existence, because there is no denying the fact that you
have only fallen asleep in your own bed. Similarly, in the case of sensory appearances that are perceived in confusion as samsara, regardless
of what manifests, what arises, and what is perceived, in that very moment, these appearances do not stray from the scope of awareness. So
they are simply manifest sensory appearances and have never existed as
anything whatsoever. Because they are clearly apparent without truly
existing, they have never known existence in the first place, and since
confusion is impossible when nothing exists, they have never been subject to confusion in the first place. If there was no confusion initially, it
is impossible for there to be confusion at present or confusion later on.
By analogy, because a barren woman can never give birth to a child, no
child could be born from that woman in the first place, and so it would
be impossible for the child now to be approaching the prime of life and
middle age, and absolutely impossible for the child to eventually grow
old and die.

Thus, it is impossible for what simply manifests as samsara and nirvana to exist. To give an example, when you confuse a rope for a snake,
the rope that causes your terror is of such a nature that it deceives you
on the relative level, for in the face of your confusion you perceive it as

though it truly were a snake. Some people will argue that when it is shown to be a rope, the perception of the snake is undermined and it seems to truly exist as a rope. But upon further examination, the rope is found to be empty, since it can be reduced to its individual strands and these in turn to subatomic particles until there is nothing left to divide. Similarly, ordinary consciousness reifies its confusion on the basis of sensory appearances perceived in that confusion. [15a] But when holy ones demonstrate that these are empty and you realize that by nature they are not what they seem, their apparent truth is undermined, just as the perception of the snake is undermined. Moreover, upon examination, the factors in this situation—the so-called negating factor, the object of negation, and the phenomenon in question—are found never to have existed as anything, just as the rope itself does not exist as such.

Coming to the decisive experience of all phenomena finally resolving into a supreme state beyond labels is the enlightened intent of the original purity of the three planes of conditioned existence. *The Pearl Garland* states:

> . . . like a rope being perceived as a snake.
> From reification, so that things seem to be what they are not,
> both the inanimate universe and the life it contains are formed.
> But upon examination, there is just a rope.
> Timelessly, the universe is emptiness.
> The ultimate is expressed in the relative.
> The perception of the snake is convincing enough as a perception,
> but the perception of the rope is the valid one.
> For example, like a bird perched on high,
> the nature of the two levels of truth
> is such that the ordinary world is merely relative.
> It has no connection with what is authentic.
> Everything is free within the essence
> of the basic space of emptiness.

And *The Heaped Jewels* states:

> The root of the nonrecognition of awareness, without having
>   to be examined,
> is determined never to involve confusion.
> But none of this is perceived in any way by anyone.
> Moreover, with all the coarse elements
> naturally cleared away from the very beginning,

there are no longer any realms of ordinary beings, for these are
   naturally cleared away.
In the timeless nonexistence of one's body
lies the awareness that it has never existed and never will. [15b]

Generally speaking, there are distinct ways of perceiving and approaches to evaluating outer and inner phenomena according to the
level of one's acumen. The Vaibhashika [Analytical] school of the shravaka approach holds that the material forms of the universe, for example, are relatively real in their coarse manifestation and ultimately real
on the indivisible subatomic level.

Followers of the Chittamatra [Mind Only] school, who accept sense
data as true but distorted, hold phenomena to be specific forms presented to one's consciousness.

The division of the Madhyamaka [Middle Way] school of philosophy
called Svatantrika ["allowing provisionally for autonomous existence"]
holds that, on the relative level, phenomena are like reflections, simply
appearing outwardly due to the interdependent connection between
causes and effects. The division called Prasangika ["using syllogistic
reasoning"] holds that they are clearly apparent without truly existing,
like the reflection of the moon in water or an optical illusion.

Proponents of the Category of Mind in the great perfection approach
hold that phenomena are simply the arising of dynamic energy as the
display of awareness, awakened mind.

Proponents of the Category of Expanse hold that phenomena are
simply awareness's own manifestations, for they do not hold that awareness itself arises, but that these phenomena are arrayed as its naturally
manifest adornment.

Proponents of the Category of Direct Transmission hold that awareness's own manifestations are factors that obscure naturally occurring
timeless awareness, but that they nonetheless arise naturally through
the avenue of spontaneous presence. In this approach, then, awareness's
own manifestations—which do not exist anywhere at all, whether outwardly, inwardly, or in between—are held to be simply manifestations
that arise timelessly. And so these proponents consider the universe of
appearances and possibilities to be an illusion—simply the arising of
empty forms—in that it is a naturally clear manifestation of what does
not truly exist, appearing within the scope of awareness. They consider
sensory appearances to be simply awareness's own manifestations that

are based on confusion and have never existed as anything whatsoever—
not as mind or anything other than mind. The three realms have never
known existence. Their nature is timelessly pure, like that of reflections,
and they abide in their own place, timelessly free. Having initially realized their nature and having become familiar with it, you gain freedom
in what is actually the case in all its immediacy. Confusion vanishes,
with there being no sense of where it has gone, [16a] and the unique
state of awareness—naturally occurring timeless awareness—abides in
its natural place of rest as originally pure dharmakaya. It is held that
benefit is ensured by the rupakaya arising as a spontaneous presence
while never straying from basic space.

Since not even the label "confusion" exists, it can be shown that nothing
has ever existed as some unconfused state, for it would be dependent on
the former:

> Since there is no[34] confusion, nothing exists as some[35]
>   unconfused state.
> Supreme, naturally occurring awareness is timelessly and
>   spontaneously present.
> Since there never has been freedom, is no freedom, and never
>   will be freedom,
> nirvana is just a label and there is no one who has ever
>   known freedom.
> There never will be freedom, for there never has been bondage.
> Complete purity, like space, is free of being restricted or
>   localized.
> This is the enlightened intent of the original purity of total
>   freedom.

In this regard, once the basis on which something depends has been
eliminated, the dependent phenomenon is eliminated; and with the
elimination of the relationship of mutual dependence, the phenomena
that depend on that relationship are eliminated. In the present case, because confusion—the phenomenon on which the absence of confusion
depends—has been eliminated, nothing has ever existed even as some
unconfused state, and so nirvana is merely a label. *The All-Creating
Monarch* shows that samsara and nirvana, bondage and freedom, are
transcended:

Nor do I explain that there is some "ultimately true phenomenon"
   or "higher plane."
There is no confusion, nor is enlightenment attained by gaining
   realization on the path.
Moreover, naturally occurring timeless awareness itself is free of
   the limitations of words.

And *The Great Garuda* states:

There is no buddha, and who creates the fetters that bind?
There is no name for, let alone the possibility of, confusion
   or nonrecognition for any being. [16b]
Therefore, since nothing has ever been freed, freeing later on
   is a fallacy.
For anyone who posits a goal when it is said that "the path has
   no basis,"
liberation remains obscured precisely because of this supposition.
Emptiness and lucidity, existence and nonexistence,
affirmation and negation, cause and effect—there are no
   such extremes
as these four pairs of eight factors.
This is analogous to the realm of space.

And *The Heart Essence of Secrets* states:

Nothing binds, for there is no bondage,
nor is there anything to be bound.
With no bondage, there can be no total freedom.
 In order to teach the timelessly and spontaneously
   perfect dharma,
myriad emanations occur.

Now, the topic of this chapter can be summarized. With samsara and
nirvana never having known existence, basic space is a supremely spacious state of spontaneous equalness:

In brief, within the ultimate womb of basic space, spacious
   and spontaneously present,
whatever arises as the dynamic energy of its display—
   as samsara or nirvana—
in the very moment of simply arising has never known
   existence as samsara or nirvana.

> Whatever arises in a dream due to the dynamic energy of sleep
>   does not actually exist.
> There is only self-knowing awareness, the blissful place of rest,
> extending infinitely as the supremely spacious state of
>   spontaneous equalness.

The theme of this chapter is the determination that basic space and what arises within its scope—whether as samsara or nirvana, since both are like dreams—constitute a supreme state of equalness that has no underlying basis. Here the meaning of the foregoing sections is summarized by a single point.

Regardless of what phenomena arise within the scope of awareness—the universe of appearances and possibilities, whether of samsara or nirvana—they simply constitute the natural and continuous way the display arises through the avenue of spontaneous presence. It can be shown that in actuality this display has never existed as anything whatsoever. [17a] This is similar to the fact that regardless of what kind of dream you have, whether good or bad, your awareness as you lie asleep in bed does not go anywhere else. Awareness's own manifestations, which are not subject to restrictions or extremes, arise naturally such that they have no true existence. *The Great Garuda* states:

> Mind is never subject to extremes.
> To whom can samsara and lower states of rebirth appear ever
>   to have existed?
> Without true existence—like dreams, magical illusions, and
>   castles in the air—
> they are false appearances.
> It is impossible for them to have the impact of truth.

And *The All-Creating Monarch* states:

> Since buddhahood does not exist, not even the name
>   "buddha" exists.
> Conditioned existence is just a label, for phenomena thus
>   imputed have been transcended.[36]

This is the commentary on the first section of *The Precious Treasury of the Basic Space of Phenomena,* demonstrating that samsara and nirvana by nature do not stray from basic space.

2

Awakened Mind as a Pure Realm

With the definitive conclusion having thus been reached that basic space is by nature the ground for all that arises, it can be shown in detail that the following has great import: basic space and appearances manifesting within that space arise timelessly and naturally as a pure realm. To begin with, this infinitely extensive expanse can be described as being like space:

> Given that basic space is by nature primordially and
>   spontaneously present,
> it is infinitely pervasive, with no division into outer and inner.
> Without any limiting boundaries, it is beyond division into
>   above and below or any other direction.
> Beyond the duality of spacious versus narrow, awareness—
>   pure like space—
> is this very expanse,[1] free of the elaborations of a conceptual
>   framework.

Within awakened mind, in essence timelessly and totally pure and equal to space, nothing has ever existed as something external or internal, as any component, [17b] as anything either spacious or narrow, as some finite essence, or even as anything in the slightest that could be identified. To elicit the underlying meaning of this, one can speak metaphorically of the nature of space. *The All-Creating Monarch* states:

> Mind is the essence of what simply is.
> What simply is, is nondual and supremely blissful,
>   and while allowing for all manifestation, it is itself
>   completely nonmanifest.

35

Given that it abides timelessly, like space, free of elaboration,
it is not[2] some objective construct and cannot be reckoned
   even as a unity.

Thus, it can be shown that samsara and nirvana arise as natural expressions of emptiness within the basic space of empty awareness:

**The magical expressions that originate within unborn
   basic space
are completely indeterminate and not subject to any
   restrictions whatsoever.
They cannot be characterized as "things," for they have
   no substance or characteristics.[3]
In that their nature is like the panoramic vista of space,
they are unborn, spontaneously present, and free of any
   time frame, any beginning or end.**

Regardless of what manifests within the scope of primordially unborn awareness—whatever comes into being and so forth—it is the display of what is unborn. It is beyond restrictions or extremes. *The Perfect Dynamic Energy of the Lion* states:

Great perfection is my awakened mind.[4]
This essence of awareness, being nonconceptual,
is nothing in itself, yet occurs as anything at all.

And *The All-Creating Monarch* states:

The spacelike nature of phenomena
can be characterized by the metaphor of space.
The true nature of phenomena cannot be conceptualized;
it is revealed in being characterized as inconceivable.
Given that it cannot be described with words,
it is spoken of as "indescribable." [18a]
It is revealed to be the ultimate, inconceivable essence.

It can be shown that such spontaneous presence is enlightened intent, beyond coming or going:

**The essence of all samsara and nirvana is awakened mind.
Spontaneously present—not occurring, not originating,
   and not finite—**

it has not come from anywhere, nor does it go anywhere at all.
The expanse of awakened mind, with no linear time frame,
does not come or go, for it is infinitely pervasive.

It can be shown that the essence of awareness, spontaneously present
and beyond any basis for description, is the basic space of samsara and
nirvana. *The All-Creating Monarch* states:

Fundamentally, all phenomena are identical in awakened mind.
In enlightenment—the heart essence of all that occurs—
buddhas, ordinary beings, and the entire universe of appearances
    and possibilities
are not one thing, yet defy enumeration.
The forms and speech of buddhas, and the bodies and speech
    of ordinary beings, moreover,
are awakened mind, timelessly free of dualistic perception.

It can be shown that this is pivotal—the supreme expanse that is equal
to space:

The true nature of phenomena—suchness—has no beginning,
    middle, or end.
This state of infinite evenness, equal to space and pure by
    nature, has no beginning or end.
It is beyond any time frame.
It is unborn, unceasing, and has no substance or
    characteristics.[5]
It neither comes nor goes and cannot be characterized
    as some "thing."
It involves no effort or achievement or anything needing
    to be done.
The ground of suchness itself has no periphery or center.
Since it is[6] nonreferential and uninterrupted, it is the expanse
    of equalness.

Thus, since awareness has never existed as anything whatsoever,
[18b] it is beyond any independent nature or any metaphors that could
characterize it as "this" or "that." It is therefore described as "having
no beginning or end," "not originating or ceasing," "neither coming nor
going," "involving no effort or achievement," and "having no limit or
center." *The Six Expanses* states:

It is beyond the numerous attempts to characterize it.
Not created through mantra, it is timeless perfection itself.
It is completely free of causes and conditions
and free of[7] all distortions of view and meditation.
It is without limit and cannot be conceived of as a center.
It has no specific form and no sensory qualities.[8]
There is no deity, or even a mantra.
It is not some phenomenon, for it is beyond all labeling.
There is no enemy, or even an ally.
There is no body; there are no sense faculties or sensory
    appearances.
Phenomena do not manifest through thought.
Nothing exists, for there is nothing to reify.
I do not exist, nor does my retinue.
There is no basic space or any embodiment of awareness.
There is no virtue, nor are there any inevitable consequences
    of harmful actions.
There is no life force, so no idea of it being cut off.
There are no accumulations or objects to be amassed.
There are no buddhas, no ordinary beings.
There is no location, or even emptiness.[9]
There are no skillful means and no retinue to listen.
There are no sense objects.
Not even the three times exist,
nor does a continuum of the three times.

It can be shown that such a nature is in fact "the enlightened intent of basic space as a state of supreme equalness and purity":

> Since the true nature of all phenomena is equalness,
> there is not a single thing that does not abide within
>   the expanse of that equalness. [19a]
> The scope of awakened mind is a single state of evenness
>   in which everything is equal.
> Since it is unborn—an infinite evenness so vast that it is equal
>   to space—
> the scope of equalness is without interruption.

Within the scope of awareness—awakened mind—everything is equal in being unborn, unceasing, and not abiding in any finite way. So nothing strays in the slightest from the enlightened intent that involves no coming or going. *The All-Creating Monarch* states:

> Within suchness—the nonconceptual state of equalness—
> there is nothing in the least for this state of being to teach itself.

And *The Six Expanses* states:

> I manifest as undivided and indivisible.
> Since my objects, actions, and conduct
> cannot be differentiated from me,[10]
> in the equalness of the three times
> I am not an object and am free of any concept
>   or underlying basis.

This very mode, the spontaneous presence[11] of supreme equalness, constitutes a single context—the true nature of phenomena, which undergoes no transition or change—within the pure realm of vajra basic space. So it can be shown that awareness is timelessly fashioned as the "fortress" of the vajra heart essence:

> Therefore, the fortress of infinite pervasiveness is
>   spontaneously present and beyond extremes.
> The fortress of the spacious and timeless expanse has no
>   division into higher and lower or in between.
> The fortress of unborn dharmakaya encompasses everything
>   impartially.
> The fortress of the precious secret is unchanging and
>   spontaneously present.
> The universe of appearances and possibilities, whether of
>   samsara or nirvana,
> is perfect as the timeless fortress of a single state of equalness.

Since everything abides timelessly in totally pure awareness—naturally occurring timeless awareness—there is nothing whatsoever other than this. [19b] It is beyond the threat of confusion—of all-consuming emotional affliction (the nature of pleasure and pain) or any other state of confusion—as well as of karma and its inevitable consequences. Since there is no context for negative influences or potential error, the way in which all phenomena timelessly constitute buddhahood "fashions the fortress" within vajra basic space, the state of supreme equalness. *The Perfect Dynamic Energy of the Lion* states:

Supremely spacious awakened mind
is unchanging, inconceivable, and inexpressible,
and so erects a vajra stronghold as a fortress.
It cannot be destroyed by any means and is free of any flaw.[12]

. . . .

The vajra of self-knowing awareness blazes everywhere.
The vajra beyond characterization blazes as awareness's
   own manifestation.
The radiantly fearless vajra is supreme emptiness.
The vajra unsullied by what is subtle or coarse blazes intensely.
The great vajra crown is all-pervasive emptiness.
The limitless vajra is not conferred, but naturally perfect.[13]

And *The All-Creating Monarch* states:

The vajra nature of causality serves as a condition.
Having no origin, it cannot be destroyed.
In the primordial heart essence of enlightenment,
basic space is not disturbed by thoughts of seeking it.

Given that such awareness can be compared to the domain of a prosperous ruler, the "palace" of the naturally occurring heart essence is built on the "foundation" of the true nature of phenomena as basic space:

**On this infinite foundation, extending everywhere impartially,
the stronghold of awakened mind does not distinguish between
   samsara and nirvana.
Its imposing and lofty summit is the spacious expanse that is
   the true nature of phenomena.
At the very center of the panorama of this uncreated nature, [20a]
the entranceway that frees one from developmental effort
   is wide open.**

The essence of naturally pure basic space is uncontrived and unadulterated, such that nothing need be added or removed, yet insofar as everything relies on it, it is comparable to a foundation. It is also analogous to a naturally occurring palace, without limiting boundaries, for it is not at all subject to any restrictions or extremes, whether of samsara or nirvana. The true nature of phenomena, a spacious vault that cannot be measured or identified, is described simply as imposing and lofty, while the fact that it is timelessly beyond the four alternatives—which involve such factors as effort and affirmation or denial—corresponds to the panorama of the four directions. The avenue through which those of the very highest intelligence enter into that nature lies across the threshold leading beyond the causality of developmental effort—a doorway that is timelessly and naturally in place. All this constitutes "the palace of awakened mind, the true nature of phenomena." This nature is discussed in *The Six Expanses:*[14]

> Timeless awareness is uncontrived and totally pure.
> Its colors are uncontrived, yet distinct and clear.
> Nonduality is uncontrived—the scope of emptiness.
> What occurs naturally is uncontrived—the expanse
>   of awareness.

And *The All-Creating Monarch* states:

> The doorway through which one enters is the doorway that
>   cannot be sought.

As for the adornment and array of that palace:

> **Within that palace, adorned by the spontaneously present**
>   **array of wealth,**
> **the king, naturally occurring timeless awareness, sits on**
>   **his throne.**
> **All aspects of the dynamic energy of that awareness,**
>   **manifesting as thoughts that proliferate and subside,**
> **serve as ministers, exercising control over the domain.**
> **The holy queen, naturally abiding meditative stability, [20b]**
> **is accompanied by the royal heirs and servants, naturally**
>   **arising enlightened intent.**
> **This encompassing**[15] **expanse of supreme bliss is naturally lucid**
>   **and nonconceptual.**

So naturally arising and spontaneously present awareness is the array of the palace. This is the perfection of all phenomena—the kayas and timeless awareness, which do not come together or separate. As *The Tantra Without Letters* states:

> Since I am not divided into outer and inner,
> the quality of lucidity is completely perfect.
> Since I am neither void nor substance,
> manifest phenomena are completely perfect.

Thus, this spontaneously present heart essence is such that, essentially, it is naturally occurring timeless awareness, like a king who never leaves his throne. To abide naturally within that essence is natural meditative stability, which is like the queen in that it has never been separate from awareness. When the ultimate meaning of this has been realized, the warmth of enlightened intent is present as a natural quality; this is likened to the royal heirs and servants. Within the scope of awareness, its natural dynamic energy is consciousness that functions in the immediacy of sense objects; this is likened to the ministers who accomplish the king's wishes, exercising control over the domain. If I did not make these distinctions, I would be no different than a raving lunatic.

Therefore, there is naturally occurring timeless awareness that, under all circumstances, is in essence naturally abiding and spontaneously present, and that does not take sense objects as its reference point. And there is timeless awareness that is dynamic energy functioning as cognition, which arises in the immediacy of sense objects and takes those objects as its reference point. But there is an enormous and crucial difference between this and ordinary thinking, which is what occurs when you do not know how to truly relax. So once you have identified the inner, naturally occurring aspect, its dynamic energy is freed in the immediacy of the ground of being, and within the scope of the original purity in which phenomena resolve you come to a decisive experience. If you have not identified it, [21a] this naturally occurring aspect is of neutral value, and its dynamic energy constitutes thoughts that engage sense objects. Therefore, it is crucial that you recognize the very essence of awareness to be enlightened intent without interruption, entailing natural meditative stability. *The All-Creating Monarch* refers to the essence and specifics of this:

> Ah! Listen, great and courageous being!
> What is called "timeless awareness," "timeless awareness"—
> timeless awareness is awareness that is always the case.
> "Naturally occurring timeless awareness" is awareness that
>   is always so.
> As for "timeless awareness that cognizes sense objects,"
> it is not naturally occurring, in the sense that it depends on
>   those objects.
> In the mere absence of objects, it is not evident.
> Therefore, naturally occurring timeless awareness

is timeless awareness in the sense that it is awareness that is
   always the case.
That is what is called "timeless awareness."
As for timeless awareness as "the teacher of the retinue,"
that timeless awareness which cognizes sense objects
is cognizant of each and every sense object;
it is "timeless awareness functioning as cognition."
Sense objects that are cognized come from awakened mind,
and so they are awakened mind, which takes no object.
Since timeless awareness occurs naturally,
it is not cultivated in meditative absorption.
Since it is not cultivated,
meditative absorption does not reinforce some habitual pattern.
The true nature of phenomena, entailing no habitual patterns,
is explained to be the enlightened intent of the buddhas
   of the three times.
The enlightened intent of all buddhas of the three times
does not entail conceiving of sense objects.
It abides timelessly in a state of equalness.

Within naturally occurring timeless awareness, which does not conceive of sense objects, naturally abiding meditative stability is present
spontaneously, without deliberately being made to happen. This is the
meditative stability of a yogin. [21b] But any integration of calm abiding and profound insight that involves concentrating one-pointedly on
an object is the mundane meditative stability of one who is spiritually
undeveloped. The difference lies in whether or not habitual patterns
continue to be reinforced. The essence of naturally abiding awareness,
being awakened mind, is called "the enlightened intent of the true nature of phenomena." Consciousness that arises with respect to sense
objects, called "the mind of samsara," takes the form of object–subject
perception. Once you have identified this and understand how to truly
relax within that context, naturally occurring dynamic energy subsides
into the ground of being, so that enlightened intent arises as the true nature of phenomena.

The difference between these two kinds of meditative stability is so
crucial that it bears repeating. The same source states:

   Ah! Listen, great and courageous being!
   Because there are no concepts

in naturally occurring timeless awareness—
the enlightened mind of all buddhas of the three times—
the enlightened intent of buddhas is not deliberate.
It is free of all objects of thought.
If any yogins of ati, whoever they may be,
abide in a nonconceptual state,
they ensure the enlightened intent of buddhahood.
Since naturally occurring timeless awareness does not conceive
    of sense objects,
it is not sullied by habitual thought patterns.

Thus, the enlightened intent of basic space that undergoes no transition
or change is ascertained to be the ongoing domain of awareness:

**Within that very context, unwavering and beyond imagination
    or description,
mastery is gained over the entire universe of appearances and
    possibilities.
This is the vast dominion of the basic space of phenomena.**

These lines provide a summation. Since the innately abiding scope of
naturally occurring timeless awareness [22a] and the consciousnesses of
the five sense faculties that arise within that scope are naturally pristine
and naturally free, they do not stray from the true nature of phenomena.
So the universe of appearances and possibilities arises as the pure realm
of dharmakaya. *The Testament* states:

This awareness, which has never existed as anything,
has a naturally manifest way of arising that is perfectly
    continuous,
so the entire universe of appearances and possibilities arises
    as the pure realm of dharmakaya.
That very arising is free in its own immediacy.

And *The All-Creating Monarch* states:

The five expressions of nonconceptual, naturally occurring
    timeless awareness
are explained to be[16] the nature of mind as the five senses.
This naturally occurring timeless awareness is unceasing.
With the essence of awakened mind actually manifest,

naturally occurring timeless awareness is unceasing and evident
in distinct ways.

In general, awareness in its very essence is such that it has never existed as anything whatsoever, is not conceptual in any way whatsoever,
and does not abide in any finite way whatsoever. Many labels are applied to it—"awakened mind," "ultimate truth," "naturally occurring
timeless awareness," "dharmakaya," and so forth—but this labeling
amounts to nothing more than distinguishing individual facets such as
its lucidity, emptiness, and so forth. In actuality, awareness is such that
there is nothing to prove or refute. The same tantra states:

> The oneness that is the nature of me, the all-creating one,
> is labeled according to the wishes of my retinue.
> Some label it "awakened mind,"
> some label it "the element of space,"
> some label it "naturally occurring timeless awareness," [22b]
> some label it "dharmakaya,"
> some label it "sambhogakaya,"
> still others label it "nirmanakaya,"
> some label it "omniscience,"
> some label it "totality,"
> some label it "the four (or three) expressions of timeless
>   awareness,"[17]
> some label it "the five expressions of timeless awareness,"
> while others label it "basic space and timeless awareness."
> These apply to just one thing, naturally occurring
>   awakened mind.
> All that can be perceived is said to be me, the naturally
>   occurring one.

It can be shown that the ultimate meaning of all this is that everything is
encompassed within the single blissful expanse of awakened mind, the
true nature of phenomena:

> If one abides in that domain, everything is dharmakaya.
> With no wavering from this single, naturally occurring
>   timeless awareness,
> there is an unfabricated, timelessly ensured transcendence
>   of effort and achievement.

> Given that the sphere of being, without any "hard edges,"
>   is inclusive,
> everything, just as it is, is encompassed within the expanse
>   in which there is no differentiation or exclusion.

The essence of undistorted awareness abides timelessly as the unique sphere of being, dharmakaya. It can be shown that the true nature of phenomena, beyond concerted effort and the realm of imagination, is naturally occurring timeless awareness. *The Pearl Garland* states:

> Since the ground of all ordinary experience arises naturally
>   as dharmakaya,
> the root of its continuity[18] is severed.
> Since the fulfillment of all wishes abides timelessly
>   as enlightened intent,
> factors that stir the mind settle in and of themselves.
> Since the flow of the breath is cut through timelessly,
> primordially there is no birth or death. [23a]
> Since sensory stimuli are timelessly perfect,
> the extremes of fixation are meditation itself.
> Since one has already arrived without taking a step,
> the very path to follow has already been traversed.
> Since there is nothing to describe with the spoken word,
> the realm of expression and imagination is forever transcended.
> Since the proliferation and resolution of thoughts[19] are
>   timelessly empty,
> there is timeless abiding in supreme meditative stability.
> Since distortions are naturally pure,
> there is abiding in a supremely unobstructed, undistorted state.
> Since nothing has ever been created,
> there has been freedom from plans and actions from the very
>   beginning.
> Since there is only the ground of being—no phenomenon that
>   exists as something else—
> this is the unique, naturally occurring primordial state.
> Since attempts to evaluate things as a unity or as dualities have
>   fallen away,
> the sphere of being is unparalleled.
> Since the darkness of ignorance is primordially and totally pure,
> manifestations of awareness are pervaded by utter lucidity.
> Since samsara has already ceased without changing,[20]

there has always been spontaneous, perfect buddhahood.[21]
Since things that can be characterized are pristinely empty,
the mind that reifies their identity falls away timelessly.

It can be shown that all phenomena are of one taste in the essence of awareness—awakened mind:

> Neither the realms of the six classes of beings nor even the pure
> realms of buddhas exist elsewhere.
> They are the realm of space, the true nature of phenomena.
> Given that they are of one taste in naturally lucid awakened
> mind,
> samsara and nirvana are fully encompassed within the scope
> of awareness.

Just as dreams share an identical context in sleep, all possible phenomena are of one taste within the scope of awareness, and so it can be shown that they are subsumed within awakened mind as their source. [23b] *The All-Creating Monarch* states:

> The source of all phenomena is all-creating awakened mind.
> Whatever manifests is my essence;
> whatever occurs is my magical expression.
> All sounds and words—whatever is audible[22]—
> are expressions of my very meaning in words and sounds.
> The kayas, timeless awareness, and enlightened qualities
> of buddhas
> and the bodies, habitual patterns, and so forth of ordinary
> beings—
> all that is subsumed within the entire universe of appearances
> and possibilities
> is timelessly the essence of awakened mind.

Because all phenomena are perfect in such a context, even the phenomena of nirvana abide as a supreme spontaneous presence, without having to be sought:

> In[23] this treasury of the basic space of phenomena, the source
> of everything,
> nirvana is timelessly and spontaneously present, without
> having to be sought.

> So within dharmakaya—unchanging, nonreferential,
>   and infinitely extensive—
> the manifestation of the outer and inner universe is
>   sambhogakaya,
> and the natural arising of things like reflections is nirmanakaya.
> Since there is no phenomenon that is not perfect as an
>   adornment of the three kayas,
> everything arises as the display of enlightened form, speech,
>   and mind.
> Moreover, without exception, the countless pure realms
>   of the sugatas
> arise from the very same source—mind itself, the expanse
>   of the three kayas.

Thus, all phenomena are dharmakaya (in that, timelessly, they are supreme emptiness), sambhogakaya (in that they manifest naturally), and nirmanakaya (in that they arise continuously in all their variety). As for those who manifest from pure realms as holy masters to guide ordinary beings, [24a] their nature is also that of the three kayas. Because these masters are naturally perfect within awareness—that is, awakened mind—they abide in the essence that is spontaneously present without having to be sought. *The All-Creating Monarch* states:

> Ah! Listen, great being of courageous resolve!
> Due to the nature of me, all-creating enlightenment,
> the three kayas—the heart essence of all victorious ones—
> are naturally and spontaneously present without having
>   to be sought.
> My uncontrived nature is ensured as dharmakaya,
> my uncontrived essence as sambhogakaya,
> and my fully evident responsiveness as nirmanakaya.
> I do not reveal these three to be results ensured by being sought.
> The three kayas are subsumed within me, the all-creating one.
> All phenomena, however they manifest,
> have three uncontrived aspects—nature, essence, and
>   responsiveness.
> I reveal these three kayas to be my suchness.
> There is only me and my suchness itself—
> nothing positive called "buddha" to glorify,
> nothing negative called "ordinary being" to disparage.

Thus, there is abiding in a nonconceptual state of equalness.
Given that there is nothing other than this,
buddhas do not receive any transmission greater than this
from me, the all-creating one.

Thus, the manifest realms of the six classes of beings arise within the basic space of awakened mind, encompassed within the single sphere of being, free of elaboration:

As well, the "cities" of the six classes of beings, whose nature is
that of samsara,
are simply reflections arising within the scope of the basic space
of phenomena. [24b]
Moreover, the various manifestations of birth and death,
pleasure and pain,
are like phantasmagoria within this expanse—mind itself.
Although they do not exist, they appear to, and in manifesting
they have no basis,
and so they are like clouds in the sky, simply occurring
adventitiously due to circumstances.
Neither existent nor nonexistent, they are by nature beyond
extremes,
fully encompassed within the sphere of being, free of elaboration.

All phenomena—all that appears or is possible—particularly appearances based on confusion that are endemic to the six classes of beings, are expressions of emptiness that have no independent nature. For people who lack realization, appearances manifest as layer upon layer of confusion, as though such people were caught up in a phantasmagoria; yogins experience them as mere illusions. They are clearly apparent without truly existing, are by nature adventitious, and, although arising due to the incidental circumstance of a lack of realization, have no finite essence or independent nature. They are like images that manifest in optical illusions caused by hypnotic spells. If you do not examine them, they are convincing enough as seemingly individual things, but if you do, they prove to be devoid of any finite essence. *The Great Garuda* states:

Without cause and free of conditions, awareness's own
manifestations are unobscured.
Free of effort, unique, and not created by anyone or anything,

> the timelessly perfect heart essence expresses itself in
>   the spontaneous presence of sense objects.
> Things are like water in an illusion;
> the hundreds of qualities exhibited by forms
> and conceptual speculation about them have come
>   to an end.

And *The All-Creating Monarch* states:

> What are called "the six classes of beings" are empty,
>   merely labels that are applied.[24]

Karma and afflictive emotions are what define an ordinary being. If you reflect further, you see that these have no basis [25a] and so are free of the extremes of being one thing and being many and are devoid of any finite essence. *The Great Garuda* states:

> In this mind, about which it is fundamentally impossible
>   to posit anything,[25]
> habitual patterns and the consequences of actions have no basis,
>   so what could support them?
> Just as a flower has no place to grow in the sky, having
>   no support,[26]
> the mind is not localized in the body, so there is no possible
>   support for habitual patterns.

And *The Pearl Garland* states:

> The five afflictive emotions of ordinary beings
> do not exist in actuality.
> Like clouds in the sky,
> they are adventitious and depend on circumstances.
> If one understands that clouds come from the sky itself
> and likewise dissolve[27] into the sky,
> one understands the expression "a single indivisible state."
> Likewise, afflictive emotions are simply distortions.[28]
> If it is understood that they occur naturally and
>   subside naturally,[29]
> how can an ordinary being be bound by them?

And *The Detailed Commentary* states:

> The nature of mind is utter lucidity.
> Distortions are adventitious.

Now, the meaning of the preceding points—the mode of supreme equalness—can be summarized as vajra basic space:

> Mind itself—that is, the nature of awakened mind—
> is pure like space, and so is without birth or death, pleasure
>   or pain.
> It has no substance to delimit it and is free of the phenomena
>   of samsara and nirvana.
> It cannot be characterized as some "thing," and being an
>   infinitely spacious expanse,
> it is unchanging, without transition, spontaneously present,
>   and uncompounded.
> Given that buddhahood lies within the vajra heart essence
>   of utter lucidity,
> everything is a naturally occurring realm of bliss—
> the very context of sublime enlightenment, a state of
>   spontaneous equalness. [25b]

The essence of awareness—by nature like space, without transition or change—is the essence of what simply is. Given that samsara and nirvana are already and forever free within its scope, buddhahood lies within the vajra heart essence. This can be shown to be sublime awakened mind, by nature a state of spontaneous equalness. *The All-Creating Monarch* states:

> However things appear, they are identical in suchness.
> Let no one meddle with this!
> The nonconceptual intent of dharmakaya is
>   spontaneously present[30]
> in the majestic state of uncontrived equalness.
>
> . . . .
>
> Mind is the essence of what simply is.
> All phenomena are ensured in suchness.
> Given what simply is, do not meddle with anything.
> Given this very essence, do not look elsewhere and try
>   to achieve something.
> Even if they sought it, victorious ones would not find anything
>   but basic space.
> Since it is already created, there is no need to create it anew.
> Since it is already ensured, there is no need to try to achieve
>   it anew.

> Settle in a state of equalness, without thinking and without
> intending anything at all!

Elsewhere in the tantra just cited, the term "awakened mind" refers to mind itself—that is, to naturally occurring timeless awareness, free of any extremes of elaboration. Where required by the demands of meter, this term is contracted to "mind," as in the following passage:

> I, the all-creating one, have never revealed
> buddhahood to be anything other than mind.

Mind that goes out to sense objects is termed "dynamic energy functioning as cognition" or "mind as display." Given that this is not awakened mind in the actual sense of the term, it is very important to understand the distinction between these two.

This is the commentary on the second section of *The Precious Treasury of the Basic Space of Phenomena,* [26a] concerning the universe of appearances and possibilities arising as a pure realm.

3

Metaphors for Awakened Mind

The nature of awakened mind having thus been revealed, it can now be explained that all phenomena are subsumed within its scope as great perfection:

> Everything is subsumed within all-inclusive awakened mind.
> Since there is no phenomenon that is not included in
> awakened mind,
> the true nature of all phenomena is that of[1] awakened mind.

All phenomena occur within the scope of awakened mind, arising within it. So it can be shown that, just as the entire universe is subsumed within the realm of space and the taste of all sugar is contained within the taste of a single piece of sugar, both the essence of samsara and nirvana and the enlightened intent of all buddhas are subsumed within this scope. *The All-Creating Monarch* states:

> I am the all-creating monarch,
> and the ultimate meaning of the enlightened intent of all buddhas
> throughout the three times
> is subsumed within[2] me.
> Within my nature, their embodiment is subsumed,
> their speech is subsumed, and their intent is subsumed.
>
> . . . .
>
> Given the nature of the all-creating monarch,
> it can be shown that all things are unborn,
> just as, given that all buddhas are unborn,
> it can be shown that they are subsumed within their
> unborn nature.

> Given the nature of the all-creating monarch,
> the true nature of phenomena is unceasing.
> Similarly, as I explained before,
> the true nature of all buddhas is unceasing.
> Therefore, I have revealed that they are subsumed within
>   the true nature of phenomena.

Such a state of awakened mind is to be understood in three ways—by a metaphor, its underlying meaning, and the evidence. [26b] First, there is the metaphor:

> **Space is a metaphor for awakened mind.**
> **Since that mind has no cause and is not an object that comes**
>   **into being,**
> **it does not abide in any finite way, is inexpressible, and**
>   **transcends the realm of the imagination.**
> **The phrase "the realm of space" is simply a way of illustrating**
>   **it metaphorically.**
> **If even the metaphor itself cannot be described as some "thing,"**
> **how could the underlying meaning that it illustrates be**
>   **imagined or described?**
> **It should be understood as a metaphor for what is**
>   **naturally pure.**

Mind itself—naturally occurring timeless awareness—has no substance or characteristics. Since it is empty yet lucid and free of elaboration, it cannot be conceived of as "this" or "that." Although it can be illustrated by a metaphor—"It is like space"—if one reflects on space as the metaphor, it proves to have no color, or shape, or anything about it that is identifiable. Therefore, if the metaphor being used does not refer to some "thing," then the underlying meaning that it illustrates—mind itself, pure by nature—is not something that has ever existed in the slightest. At a certain point, this comes down to understanding space to be a convenient metaphor for what simply cannot be illustrated within a conceptual framework. *The Perfect Dynamic Energy of the Lion* states:

> The enlightened intent of buddhahood is a state of equalness
>   free of substance.
> Naturally manifest timeless awareness is dharmakaya,
>   pure like space.[3]
> Awareness free of elaboration is equal to space.

With no reification of sense objects, which are empty, conduct
    is free in its own place.
The natural abiding of enlightened intent is meditative
    absorption as a state of resting imperturbably.
Awareness's own manifestations have no actual substance
    but are the actuality of all mandalas.
The unchanging, inherently pristine nature of phenomena
    is the universal environment.

And *The All-Creating Monarch* states:

Ah, great and courageous being! [27a]
All phenomena are of the nature of space.
There is no nature of space.
There is not even a metaphor for space.
There is not even a measure of space.
The ultimate meaning of all phenomena without exception
should be understood in this way.

To illustrate the meaning thoroughly with this metaphor:

The underlying meaning is that awakened mind is self-knowing
    awareness equal to space.
It is not within the realm of the imagination, for it defies
    illustration or description.
Naturally lucid and unwavering, the spacious expanse
    of utter lucidity
is not created but is spontaneously present, with no fixed reach
    or range.
Dharmakaya is the spacious domain that is the heart essence
    of enlightenment.

Naturally arising timeless awareness, being spontaneously present
as the heart essence of dharmakaya, is free of conceptual or descriptive
elaboration. *Naturally Arising Awareness* states:

Dharmakaya is unimaginable[4] and free of elaboration.
In the true nature of phenomena[5]—timeless awareness that
    is buddhahood—
the nonconceptual essence of buddhahood is evident.
In the supreme state of natural purity that cannot be reified,
awareness that is Vajrasattva is evident.

In timeless awareness, lucid, pure, and empty,[6]
the true nature of phenomena, which has no characteristics,
    is evident.

And *The Root Tantra of the Reverberation of Sound* states:

Free of anything needing to be done, it is completely perfect.
Free of limiting boundaries, it does not abide in some center.
Since it is completely perfect, it is free of the need to dedicate
    anything.[7]
Since nothing is extraneous to it, it is not incomplete.
It is not one thing, and dualistic extremes have fallen away.
It does not manifest as a multiplicity, yet transcends being a unity.
Indescribable, it is nevertheless the basis for words. [27b]
The real significance of the heart essence of emptiness is that it is
    free of being some "thing."
The real significance of view is that it does not fall into extremes.

And *The All-Creating Monarch* states:

The view and conduct of great perfection
are not like effects, which are achieved as a result of causes.
The nature of the view and conduct of awakened mind
is like that of space.
Space is beyond thinking and analysis.
Enlightenment, which is like space, will not come about
for those who indulge in thinking and analysis.

Given that the nature of view and conduct is that of space,
enlightenment, which is like space, will not come about
for those who indulge in dualistic perception.
The onset of dualistic perception constitutes error
    and obscuration.

Just as space is nondual,
there is no duality in enlightenment.
Enlightenment, which is like space, will not come about
for those who indulge in dualities.
The onset of a dichotomy between view and conduct constitutes
    error and obscuration.

The nature of enlightenment is that of space.
There is no acceptance or rejection[8] in space.
Enlightenment, which is like space, will not come about

for those who indulge in acceptance and rejection.[9]
Acceptance and rejection[10] constitute error and obscuration.

The nature of enlightenment is that of space.
There is no effort or achievement in space.
Enlightenment, which is like space, will not come about
for those who indulge in effort and achievement.
Engaging in effort and achievement constitutes error
    and obscuration.

The nature of enlightenment is that of space.
There is no cause or effect in space.
Enlightenment, which is like space, will not come about
for those who perceive in terms of the duality of cause and effect.
Perception in terms of cause and effect constitutes error
    and obscuration. [28a]

Thus, one can be certain about the line of reasoning which shows that the nature of awareness, awakened mind, is totally pure like space and not restricted or localized:

The evidence is that anything can and does arise due to
    the dynamic energy of awareness.
Even as it arises, there is no place of arising or anything arising.
"Arising" is simply a label, for if examined, it is found to be like
    space.
Everything being encompassed within a supreme state of
    equalness without bias
constitutes the expanse of infinite evenness, which entails no
    dualistic perception.

The continuous way in which things arise within the scope of awareness is like the reflection of the sky in a limpid ocean. Although things seem to arise in all their variety, in actuality there is no place for them to arise or anything arising. So you come to the decisive experience of their resolving into emptiness within the indivisible state of dharmakaya.

Using the line of reasoning that it is a supreme state of indivisible equalness, it is possible to prove that mind itself is like space. The subject under discussion is the essence of awareness. To describe it as being like unborn space is a valid conventional way of saying that it transcends imagination or description. It is valid because ordinary mind, arising as dynamic energy, is identical in essence to awareness, but that essence cannot be identified as anything whatsoever, being like space— timelessly empty and free of elaboration. *Naturally Arising Awareness* states:

> The true nature of phenomena, which cannot be reified,
>   is the expanse of naturally lucid bliss.[11]
> Not entailing concepts and permeating space, the true nature
>   of phenomena displays itself as everything.
> The true nature of phenomena, which cannot be reified,
>   is pure in its own place.
> Natural freedom, which does not entail concepts, is the force
>   of bliss.
> The natural manifestation of an undistracted state is
>   all-pervasive.
> One has reached the authentic nature of phenomena,
>   the level of supreme bliss. [28b]

And *The All-Creating Monarch* states:

> The evidence is awakened mind, which labels everything.[12]

The preceding discussion shows that awareness is pristine in the immediacy of sense objects, without any interruption between thoughts arising and being freed, and is fully encompassed within the vast realm of the "sky" or "ocean" that is the true nature of phenomena. *The Perfect Dynamic Energy of the Lion* states:[13]

> In the sky that is the true nature of phenomena, free of labels,
> soars the garuda of awareness's own manifestations, with none
>   of what characterizes sense objects.
> It is uncontrived   self knowing awareness that is experienced
>   as blissful.
>
> In the ocean that is the true nature of phenomena, naturally
>   occurring and free of elaboration,
> swim the golden fish of what cannot be characterized
>   as anything.
> They are fully encompassed within the single taste of naturally
>   manifest dharmakaya.
>
> In the sky of total purity, free of elaboration,
> soars the golden garuda of dharmakaya, free of elaboration.

Not the ordinary mind of effort, it is fully encompassed within
    the realm of the "lamps."

In the naturally occurring ocean that is the boundless nature
    of phenomena
swim the golden fish of self-knowing awareness, free of concepts.
They are fully encompassed within the empty yet lucid realm free
    of samsara and nirvana.

In the sky that is lucid yet free of reifying attachment
soars the golden garuda of naturally abiding enlightened intent.
It is fully encompassed within the scope of the true nature of
    phenomena, spacious and all-pervasive.

In the sky in which elaborations disperse in their own place
soars the garuda of awareness's own manifestations, free of plans
    and actions.
It is fully encompassed within the scope of the true nature of
    phenomena, free of effort and achievement.

In the ocean of timeless awareness, uncorrupted and
    spontaneously perfect,
swim the golden fish of lucid, pure awareness.
They are fully encompassed within the naturally occurring realm
    free of any conditional basis.

The ultimate meaning of these points can be summarized in the context
of the true nature of phenomena, [29a] which has no limit or center:

> Given that naturally occurring timeless awareness—the true
>   nature of phenomena—is boundless,
> analogies are used so that it can be ascertained through
>   metaphor, underlying meaning, and evidence.
> Equal to space, that nature, which subsumes everything and
>   is without differentiation or exclusion,
> is exemplified by these three linking factors.
> In the womb of basic space, a supremely spacious state
>   of equalness,
> everything is timelessly equal, with no time frame of earlier
>   or later, no better or worse.[14]
> This is the enlightened intent of Samantabhadra,
>   of Vajrasattva.

Awareness is free of limitation and transcends imagination and description. Through the three linking factors by which it is ascertained—metaphor, underlying meaning, and evidence—it can be shown never to deviate from the scope of the true nature of phenomena. *The All-Creating Monarch* states:

> If you wish to gain definitive realization of this ultimate meaning,
> consider space as a metaphor for it.
> The underlying meaning is the unborn nature of phenomena.
> The evidence lies in mind itself, which is unceasing.
>
> The spacelike nature of phenomena
> can be characterized by the metaphor of space.
> The true nature of phenomena cannot be conceptualized;
> it is revealed in being characterized as inconceivable.
> Given that it cannot be described with words,
> it is spoken of as "indescribable."
> It is revealed to be the ultimate, inconceivable essence.
>
> The meaning of what has been revealed in this concise way
> is a commentary on that ultimate essence.
> With this, realize me, the ultimate meaning.
> If you do not realize me, the ultimate meaning, with this,
> regardless of the terms and words used to demonstrate
>   that meaning
> you will never encounter me.
> You will stray from me.
> I will be obscured, and so you will never see[15] the heart essence of
>   phenomena. [29b]

Awareness that is thus illustrated by the metaphor of space is free of elaboration and is beyond imagination or description. Its essence is the enlightened intent of Samantabhadra, Vajrasattva, and so forth. The same tantra states:

> The embrace of Samantabhadra's enlightened intent
> is that of the all-creating one making evident[16]
> all appearances, however they manifest,
> without their being accepted as good or rejected as bad.
> The embrace of Vajrasattva's enlightened intent
> is that of unborn, unceasing enlightened intent.
> The seven successive buddhas ending with Shakyamuni,

the one thousand and two buddhas, and others as numerous
    as atoms,
as well as the benefit ensured through their enlightened forms,
    speech, and minds—
in occurring, all of this occurs due to enlightened form, speech,
    and mind.
The way in which benefit is ensured through enlightened form,
    speech, and mind
lies in the very nature of enlightened form, speech, and mind.
And that, furthermore, is subsumed within the all-creating one.
In the palace of the basic space of phenomena,
there is not a single thing that is not subsumed within me.
In the immeasurable mansion of the realm of space,
there is not a single thing that is not subsumed within me.

Such awareness can be shown to be comparable to the orb of the sun:

Awakened mind can be compared to the sun.
It is utterly lucid by nature and forever uncompounded.
With nothing to obscure it, it is unobstructed and
    spontaneously present.
Without elaboration,[17] it is the scope of the true nature
    of phenomena, which does not entail concepts.

This is a brief treatment. Spontaneously present dharmakaya—
utterly lucid by its very nature, yet uncompounded—is supreme, unobstructed awareness. *Naturally Arising Awareness* states:[18]

Supreme dharmakaya, free of the four extremes,
is without distortion and utterly lucid, like a pure crystal. [30a]
Dharmakaya, free of extremes, is the kaya that dispels darkness.
Flawless and dispelling darkness, it is like the sphere of the sun.
Dispelling the darkness of the four extremes, it is timelessly
    and spontaneously present.

As for a more extensive explanation:

In being empty it is dharmakaya, in being lucid it is
    sambhogakaya, and in being radiant it is nirmanakaya.
The three kayas do not come together or separate.
Since these enlightened qualities are already and forever
    spontaneously present,

they are not obscured by the darkness of flaws and faults.
They are identical in being without transition or change
   throughout the three times,
identical in permeating all buddhas and ordinary beings alike.
This is called "naturally occurring awakened mind."

From the point of view of its emptiness, mind itself is called "dharmakaya"; from the point of view of its lucidity, it is called "sambhogakaya"; and from the point of view of its arising, it is called "nirmanakaya." Although it can be described in such terms, in essence it has never existed in the slightest as anything that can be identified. It is the very enlightened intent that is spontaneously present, without any transition or change throughout the three times, because it is the heart essence that permeates all samsara and nirvana. As is said:

Buddha nature, sugatagarbha, permeates all beings completely.

It can be shown that all of these descriptions refer to naturally occurring timeless awareness, empty yet lucid. *The All-Creating Monarch* states:

For me, all-creating awakened mind,
the three uncontrived aspects of my nature
reveal the way in which the three kayas, which are
   just labels, arise.
By nature, the three kayas[19]
definitely do not stray from suchness itself.

For me, all-creating awakened mind, [30b]
unborn and free of dualistic perception,
"unborn dharmakaya" is just a label.
Dharmakaya is definitely just a label.
There is no straying from suchness itself.

For me, all-creating awakened mind,
my essence is plainly just a label—
the mode of sambhogakaya, again just a label.
Sambhogakaya definitely
does not stray from suchness itself.

For me, all-creating awakened mind,
my responsiveness is nirmanakaya becoming evident.
The mode of nirmanakaya, which occurs

due to the uncontrived nature of responsiveness,
is just a label.
Nirmanakaya also definitely
does not stray from suchness itself.

It can be shown that the universe of appearances and possibilities arises
within such a context:

> **Its dynamic energy arises as anything at all—**
> **whether there is realization or not,[20] there is the universe**
> **   of appearances and possibilities**
> **and beings' perceptions in all their variety.**

Within the mirrorlike nature of awareness, its natural dynamic
energy abides as the ground for all that arises, like reflections. So, although experiences of the universe of appearances and possibilities arise
in all their variety, there is no sullying of, no transition or change in, the
essence of awareness. This is similar to a mirror being unsullied by, and
undergoing no transition or change due to, the reflections in it. *Naturally Arising Awareness* states:

> The supreme, naturally occurring state manifests outside of time.
> Like the magical display of the sun and moon in the vault
>   of the sky,
> a continuous magical display occurs within the realm of what
>   is unborn.
> Thus, this supreme magical display poses no difficulty.

And *The All-Creating Monarch* states:

> I am enlightenment, the authentic essence of everything. [31a]
> Since I am the essence of unelaborate basic space,
> I am the supreme secret[21] of all buddhas,
> and so the display of the three realms and the six classes of beings
>   arises from me.

It can be shown that, in the very moment of arising, things have no independent nature:

> **Though things arise, none of them has any independent nature**
> **   whatsoever.[22]**

> Like water in a mirage, a dream, an echo,
> a phantom emanation, a reflection, a castle in the air,
> or a hallucination, all things are clearly apparent yet do not
>   truly exist—
> they merely manifest adventitiously, without basis or support.
> You should realize that all these manifestations are temporary,
>   adventitious phenomena.[23]

Dream images that manifest do not exist either before one has gone to sleep or after one wakes up, but they manifest in the interval when one is asleep. Similarly, perceptions based on confusion (which constitute samsara) do not exist in the context of either the ground (the true nature of phenomena) or the fruition (nirvana), but they manifest to confused ordinary consciousness in the present interval. However, even as they manifest they have never existed as anything whatsoever, being simply appearances, expressions of emptiness that are in essence clearly apparent yet nonexistent. This is because all phenomena, having no independent nature, have never existed in any of the three phases of their origination, duration, or cessation. *The Source Verses on Sublime Knowing* states:

> Like dream images, like magical illusions, like mirages of castles
>   in the air,
> thus, it is said, are things born, thus do they endure, and thus are
>   they destroyed.

And *The Discourse on the Most Majestic State of Meditative Absorption* states:

> It is as though beings in conditioned existence were in a dream.
> Therein, no one is born and no one dies. [31b]
> No beings, human or otherwise, not even life force itself,
>   can be found.
> The accumulation of karma—of actions committed—
>   does not exist, nor will it ever.

It can be shown that these appearances do not stray from their true nature:

> Due to the nature of spontaneously present awakened mind,
> there is a continuous display, the magical illusion of samsara
>   and nirvana.

> Since this entire magical display is fully encompassed within
>   basic space,
> you should know that it does not stray from the scope of
>   primordial being.

As much as samsara and nirvana manifest, even as they manifest they do not stray from the realm of awakened mind in its essence. *The All-Creating Monarch* states:

> The source of all phenomena is all-creating awakened mind.
> Whatever manifests is my essence;
> whatever occurs is my magical expression.

Since everything is perfect in basic space, it can be shown to be great perfection:

> Within this, everything is the scope of awakened mind.
> With that single perfection, all is perfect—without being
>   made so, everything is perfect.
> Naturally occurring timeless awareness is by nature
>   spontaneously perfect.

All phenomena of the universe of appearances and possibilities, whether of samsara or nirvana, are spontaneously perfect within the essence of awareness. *The Tantra Without Letters* states:

> Since I do not undergo birth or death,
> phenomena subject to cessation are[24] completely perfect.
> Since I am not divided into outer and inner,
> the quality of lucidity is completely perfect.
> Since I am neither void nor substance,
> manifest phenomena are completely perfect.
> Since I have no conceptual framework,
> perceived phenomena are completely perfect.
> Since I have no body or mind, [32a]
> naturally manifest phenomena are completely perfect.
> Since I am neither self nor other,
> expressions of awareness[25] are completely perfect.
> Since there is no causal factor that creates me,
> supreme meditative stability is completely perfect.
> Since I have no destination,

naturally manifest objects are completely perfect.
Since I am not subject to bias or division,
secret timeless awareness is completely perfect.
Since sensory appearances are continuous in me,
the three aspects of basic space are completely perfect.
Since I am neither a unity nor a duality,
phenomena within the sphere of being are completely perfect.
Since in me there is neither darkness nor illumination,
manifest phenomena are completely perfect.
Since I have neither of the concepts of identity,
empty phenomena are completely perfect.
Since I have neither of the two distortions,
the five aspects of lucidity are completely perfect.
Since I involve no proliferation or resolution,
the meanings of all letters are completely perfect.

In this regard, let me show the way in which all that manifests continuously is subsumed within awakened mind while simply seeming to exist in relation to it. *The Six Expanses* states:

Within mind itself, there is origination:
the manifestations of the six classes of beings arise naturally,
and so[26] in the perception of distinct forms,
the ripening of sensory appearances as forms is perfect.

Within mind itself, there is cessation:
impermanence arises naturally as the cause of this cessation,
and so the manifestation of what has no independent nature
is perfect, as though, for example, in a dream. [32b]

Within mind itself, there is elaboration:
myriad appearances arise naturally,
and so, in being perceived through the five distinct senses,
they are perfect from the point of view of holding their own place.

Within mind itself, there is what can be revealed:
terms, words, and names arise naturally,
and so, within the natural purity of minds caught up in
    conventional designations,
the secret pith instructions of the guru are perfect.

Within mind itself, there is perception:
numerous conditions influencing events arise naturally,

evident in the objects of perception,
which are perfect in their distinctness and natural clarity.

Within mind itself, there is what is always present:
the aggregates of one's perceptions arise individually,
and so, given that they are naturally connected within a supreme
    state of primordial unity,
they are perfect in being endowed with the power of total recall.

Within mind itself, sense objects are present:
sensory appearances arise naturally,
and so, given that the two ways of reifying identity are
    naturally pure,
the objects of the six senses are perfect in their individuality.

Within mind itself, there is what can be described:
calm abiding and profound insight arise naturally,
and so, in formal meditation and periods thereafter,
they are perfect as unwavering meditative stability itself.[27]

Within mind itself, there is what can be seen:
the universe of appearances and possibilities arises naturally
    as oneness,
and so the natural freedom of the three realms in their own place
is perfect as ati, the supreme state of natural rest.

Within mind itself, there is what can be attained:
hope itself is pure in its own place,[28]
and so, being free of effort and achievement,
the three kayas are completely perfect in themselves.

Within mind itself, there is what can be quantified:
individual spiritual approaches arise naturally, [33a]
and so, without conceited intellectual speculation,
the heart essence is perfect as the supreme and innermost secret.

Within mind itself, there are conceptual frameworks:
myriad appearances arise naturally,
and so, with their individual names and colors,
they are perfect in the dualistic way they manifest as forms.[29]

Within mind itself, there is what can be fathomed:
the objects of one's perceptions are experienced as true,[30]
and so, given that they arise[31] naturally as reference points,
they are perfect in entailing conceptual frameworks.

Within mind itself, there is what is audible:
all words are marvelous, arising naturally,
and so all things that can be described,
as well as the words that point them out, are perfect in their
    own place.

Within mind itself, there is what can be brought to rest:
the natural state of rest with regard to sensory appearances
    arises within the ground of being,
and so, from the standpoint of the supreme state of resting
    imperturbably,
they are perfect in that they need not be sought.

Within mind itself, there is what can be transformed:
afflictive emotions arise naturally,
and so, like poison being transformed into medicine,
they are perfect as the epitome of the kayas and
    timeless awareness.

Within mind itself, there is what can be purified:
objects of the five senses are naturally pure,
and so, like unsullied water that is naturally limpid,
sensory appearances are perfect in their own place.

Within mind itself, there is what can be freed:
sense objects manifest as they do,
and so, being like a knot in a snake that releases itself,
they are free and perfect in their own place.

Within mind, there is what can be evaluated:
the full measure of awareness's own pure manifestations
    is perfect,[32]
and so, like a scale being in complete balance, [33b]
experiences are perfect on higher and higher levels.

That is to say, far from awareness being simply nonexistent, like
some kind of void, it is called "great perfection," because both the true
nature of phenomena and phenomena themselves are perfect as the essence of both the two levels of truth and the three aspects of purity. *The
Web of Magic: The Heart Essence of Secrets* states:

Through the four aspects of sublime realization—
the single cause, the mode of letters and syllables,

consecration, and direct perception—
everything is the great king of manifest perfection.

Given that the essence of being has never existed as anything whatsoever
yet gives rise to anything at all, it can be shown that what arises does so
continuously within a context that is unborn:

> Given that awakened mind is neither apparent nor not
>   apparent,
> the outer and inner worlds of samsara and nirvana do not
>   exist as phenomena
> yet arise nonetheless as a myriad display—
> the universe of appearances and possibilities, whether of
>   samsara or nirvana—
> because they are, by nature, the stirring of mind's dynamic
>   energy.

Although a single crystal ball is nothing other than transparent and
flawless in essence, upon contact with a beam of sunlight it refracts an
effulgence of five-colored light. Similarly, although the essence of awareness, which has never existed as anything whatsoever, abides as pure
dharmakaya, empty yet lucid, nevertheless, due to the dynamic energy
of awareness, the display of the universe of appearances and possibilities arises in all its variety as either nirvana or samsara, depending on
whether or not there is realization. Within mind itself, just as it is, supremely and completely pure—whose nature is that of space, without
specific form—all sensory appearances in their myriad forms are perfect
in being spontaneously present. This is what is meant by the expression
"supreme emptiness endowed with the sublime capacity for everything
to manifest." [34a] The ordinary mind, which invests the six kinds of
sense objects that manifest from this emptiness with identity, creates
the range of karma (pleasurable, painful, and so forth), habitual patterns, and the universe. These are perfect in their very essence. *The All-
Creating Monarch* states:

> Ah, great and courageous being!
> Mind is the essence of what simply is.
> What simply is, is nondual and supremely blissful,
> and while allowing for all manifestation, it is itself
>   completely nonmanifest.

> Given that it abides timelessly, like space, free of elaboration,
> it is beyond any objective construct and cannot be reckoned
>   even as a unity.
> Though awakened mind cannot be quantified or illustrated,[33]
> the phenomena created by mind can be quantified.
> If you wonder about the things created by mind—
> the universe of appearances and possibilities, buddhas and
>   ordinary beings—
> they are created from what is essentially the nature of mind.
> They are revealed in that they are created and become evident.
> The five major elements, the manifestations of the six classes
>   of beings,
> and the two aspects of the rupakaya that ensure benefit—
> these can be quantified, being evident as[34] the pure nature
>   of mind.

Since in its very essence awareness has never existed as anything what-soever, it is beyond being either manifest or empty. Due to the key point that it is not an object that can be characterized or described, it can be shown that what arise within its scope are false appearances that have never known existence:

> In simply arising, forms are by nature empty.
> From what is unborn there manifests what seems to be born,
> but even as it manifests, nothing whatsoever has been born.
> From what is unceasing there manifests what seems to cease,
>   but there is no cessation. [34b]
> These are illusory expressions of emptiness.
> Even with abiding there is nothing that abides.
> There is no basis on which anything could abide.
> Within the context in which there is no coming or going,
> regardless of what manifests, it never exists as what it
>   seems to be,
> and so one is reduced to merely labeling it as "having no
>   independent nature."

You can reach a definitive conclusion concerning the true nature of phenomena through logical reasoning. It is because sensory appear-ances manifest that they have no independent nature, being like magi-cal illusions. Thus, you should understand that their nature is such that even as they appear to originate they do not, that even as they appear to endure they do not, that even as they appear to cease they do not, that even as they appear to come and go they do not. *The Discourse Unifying the Enlightened Intent of All Buddhas* states:

How marvelous! This is truly marvelous and superb!
The secret of all perfect buddhas
is that all things are born within what is unborn,
yet in the very act of their being born, there is no birth!

How marvelous! This is truly marvelous and superb!
The secret of all perfect buddhas
is that all things cease within what does not cease,
yet in the very act of their ceasing, there is no cessation!

How marvelous! This is truly marvelous and superb!
The secret of all perfect buddhas
is that all things endure within what has no duration,
yet in the very act of their enduring, there is no duration!

How marvelous! This is truly marvelous and superb!
The secret of all perfect buddhas
is that things come and go within what does not come or go,
yet in the very act of their coming or going, there is no coming
    or going!

And *Naturally Arising Awareness* states:

All phenomena occur in the space of an instant. [35a]
How marvelous—precious awakened mind!
Present in everyone, it is perceived by no one.
This drop of nectar, naturally occurring timeless awareness,[35]
arises naturally and occurs naturally,
without there being anything to strive for or any effort to make.[36]
The enlightened intent of buddhahood arises naturally,
    without origin.
It is the supreme, naturally arising state that has no duration
    or onset.[37]
Supreme natural freedom,[38] which involves no reifying
    attachment,
should be understood within the scope of awareness,[39]
    not within ordinary mind.

The significance of this can be summarized by the essential fact that, regardless of what manifests, even as it does so it has no independent nature:

> Sensory appearances, moreover, arise naturally due to
>   the dynamic energy of awareness,
> and so their nature is described in a purely symbolic way as
>   one of "interdependent connection."
> Even in the very moment that things seem to arise due to
>   that dynamic energy,
> they do so without being subject to extremes or divisions—
> with no question of whether or not something arises—
> and even "dynamic energy" is just a symbolic term, with no
>   finite essence whatsoever.
> So within the context that is never subject to transition
>   or change,
> nothing strays in the slightest from awakened mind.

Even the statement that things arise as samsara and nirvana due to the dynamic energy of awareness is merely conventional, for in essence nothing has ever existed as anything in the slightest—nothing being distinct in itself as the process of samsara or nirvana arising or as some "thing" that arises. And so there is no straying from the state of equalness that is the true nature of phenomena.

Reflections of planets and stars appear to arise in the limpid water of the ocean, but in actuality there is no arising. The context in which their arising seems to occur is the expanse of the ocean itself—simply limpid water. What arise are the planets and stars themselves, which do not stray from the vault of the sky. Given that all this coming together does not exist as some phenomenon, [35b] these are simply reflections that arc apparent yct empty. Analogously, all phenomena are such that they manifest yet do not cease, do not originate, do not come, do not go, cannot be categorically denied, cannot be naively affirmed, and have never existed as ultimately distinct or ultimately identical. Rather, it should be understood that they are simply illusions based on interdependent connection. *The Source Verses on Sublime Knowing* states:

> I pay homage to that most sacred
> exposition of the perfect Buddha—
> revealing that things occur in interdependent connection,

without cessation, without origin,
without being denied, without being affirmed,
without coming, without going,
without ultimate distinctness, and without ultimate identity,
and revealing that the thorough subsiding of elaboration is peace.

And *The Reverberation of Sound* states:

All phenomena are without basis, without foundation.[40]
Without desire and free of conditioned existence,
mind is by nature uncontrived and beyond description.
Concepts based on the confusion of plans and actions fall away.
There are no phenomena, no buddhas, no ordinary beings,
no "I," no identity, and no dualistic perceptions.

This is the commentary on the third section of *The Precious Treasury of the Basic Space of Phenomena,* presenting the metaphors for awakened mind.

4

The Essence and Display
of Awareness

On the basis of the preceding decisive demonstration using a metaphor, the nature of awakened mind—that is, awareness—is now ascertained so that you can thoroughly understand the underlying meaning:

> It is the nature of all-inclusive awakened mind that it is
>   not apparent,
> for it transcends that which is apparent.
> It is not empty, for it transcends that which is empty.
> It is not existent, for it has no substance or characteristics. [36a]
> Nor is it nonexistent, for it permeates all samsara and nirvana.
> Neither existent nor nonexistent, it is primordial basic space,
>   spontaneous and uniform,
> not subject to extremes or division, and without substance,
>   foundation, or underlying basis.

Given that the essence of awareness is free of the limitations of conceptual or verbal elaboration, it has never existed or not existed, yet it timelessly permeates all samsara and nirvana. *Naturally Arising Awareness* states:

> Without origin, it is without cessation.
> Without reification, it is free in its own place.
> Having no conceptual framework, it entails no elaboration.
> Not having come about by being made,[1] it is present everywhere.
> Being uncompounded, it is the basic space of total purity.
> It is free of the conventional designations that reify.[2]
> Without any independent nature, it is free of description.

75

The authentic nature of phenomena is the expanse of awareness.
Permeating everything, it is the realm of the masculine principle.
Giving rise to everything, it is the basic space of the feminine
     principle.
The supreme transmission that cannot be demonstrated
abides[3] in inexpressible sublime knowing.
Meditative absorption without a conceptual framework
is clearly evident in dharmakaya,
in which there is nothing to discard or adopt.
Within the vast, uncompounded expanse,
timeless awareness, the most majestic state of awareness, radiates.
Within the vast expanse, unborn and unceasing,
what is clearly perceived by the eye of naturally occurring
     sublime knowing[4]
is the unique state that permeates everything.

In being pure and infinitely extensive by nature, the very essence of
being is perfect as the true nature of phenomena:

Uninterrupted, awareness is the expanse of awakened mind.
Without transition or change, the "sky" of basic space is
     timelessly and infinitely extensive.
Naturally occurring timeless awareness,
which has ultimate meaning in that nothing compares to it,[5]
is subsumed within the single sphere of being, unborn and
     unceasing. [36b]
Indeterminate and all-pervasive, it is absolutely without
     limiting extremes.

Basic space—naturally occurring timeless awareness—is a supreme
state of spontaneous presence, infinitely extensive and pervasive. In
essence it is all-inclusive and without interruption. It abides timelessly
as the source of the mandala of a wish-fulfilling treasure. *The Array of
Inlaid Gems* states:

A single kaya manifests to all beings.
A single kaya is the consummation of benefit for beings.
A single kaya reveals its manifestation everywhere.
This single kaya does not abide in any extreme.
The kaya of timeless awareness, the vajra heart essence,

lies at the very heart of meditative stability, beyond words,
evident as the very embodiment of manifest enlightenment.
Timeless awareness is the sole decisive state, free of dualistic
   perception.
The kaya of the vajra holder has never existed in actuality.[6]
It is supreme natural lucidity,[7] not abiding in either of
   two extremes.
The vajra that seals reality is unchanging.
The true foundation—this utterly stable kaya—
occurs within the immutable mandala.
The myriad spheres constitute the wealth[8] of this kaya.
The colored[9] mandala is the perfection of the three kayas.
Entailing no plan or action, it is imbued with basic space.
Dharmakaya does not stray from this oneness.
There is no duality; sense objects are awareness's
   own manifestations.
The duality of ultimate versus relative is transcended.
The dualistic extremes that reify are completely eliminated.
The mandala is the vajra wish-fulfilling treasure.
The scope of equalness does not stray into any extreme.
Thoughts, which constitute both straying and obscuration,
   are cleared away.
Dharmakaya is not made to occur;
unapproachable through reification, it is like the moon's
   reflection in water.
Responsiveness manifests naturally as skillful means;
like the sun's rays, [37a]
it is totally present due to the dynamic energy of sublime knowing,
so the ultimate mandala is one of boundless manifestation.
Mind itself, which constitutes this kaya, is empty and
   without identity.
The amassing of timeless awareness is free of origination
   or disintegration.
The true nature of phenomena, a state of peace, is beyond
   imagination[10]—
freedom within the pure realm of boundless manifestation.
This naturally occurring kaya itself is[11] totally pure;
due to the samaya of emptiness,
it manifests fully as the scope of awareness.[12]

Although such basic space is present everywhere, it can be shown to be the province of only a fortunate few:

> The legacy of the vajra heart essence is one of unwavering
>   spontaneity and equalness.
> The immensity of sublime basic space, which is not made
>   or unmade,
> is not some finite range that can be characterized with words.
> It is the welling forth of an expanse of sublime knowing,
>   the scope of one's self-knowing awareness.
> A yogin who is free of conceptual and descriptive elaborations
> comes to a decision that whether it can be characterized or not
>   is irrelevant.
> Since neither meditation nor anything to meditate on can be
>   discovered,
> there is no need to "slay the enemies" of dullness, agitation,
>   and thought.

The very essence of awareness, beyond view and meditation, effort and achievement, is the legacy of the vajra heart essence—that is, the nature of basic space, which is not made or unmade and is beyond characterization and description. This is not the scope of conceptual or descriptive elaboration, but rather the domain of an individual's self-knowing awareness. *The Superb Ruler* states:

> The inconceivable nature of phenomena is awakened mind.
> One cannot reach a definitive conclusion about this through
>   speculation or description.[13]

And *The Vajra Cutter* states:

> The true nature of phenomena is not an object of ordinary
>   consciousness.
> It cannot be "known."

It is, however, the domain of each individual's awareness, [37b] for as is said:

> Indescribable, inconceivable, and inexpressible, the perfection
>   of sublime knowing
> is unborn and unceasing—the very essence of space.
> It is the domain of each individual's self-knowing timeless awareness.
> I pay homage to the mother of victorious ones of the three times.

Some masters say, "The true nature of phenomena cannot be known through analytical investigation, because it is beyond speculation and description; but it can be known when discerned thoroughly, because it can serve as the domain of those who perceive truth directly."[14] I do not find this acceptable, but merely an arbitrary theoretical distinction, the words of those who have not experienced what has ultimate meaning in all its immediacy. There is elaboration whenever ordinary consciousness is engaged in thinking, but what I am discussing is not within the scope of such ordinary thinking, for it stands in direct contradiction to thought. When you rest without ordinary consciousness engaging in speculation or description, you arrive at what has ultimate meaning in all its immediacy, and so it is within the scope of self-knowing awareness. This is because the essence of awareness, which abides as the ultimate reality that is the true nature of everything, becomes evident within that context.

An individual who realizes the ultimate meaning to be the naturally settled state, supreme and spontaneously present, is one who upholds the legacy of the vajra heart essence. In keeping with the true nature of phenomena, such an individual has, moreover, the appearance of one who has nothing more to do and has put an end to effort and achievement. *The Great Garuda* states:

> Able to penetrate ordinary mind—the nature of which is difficult
>   to prove existent or not—
> timeless awareness itself involves no speculation and has put
>   an end to[15] confusion.
> Uncomplicated people with spacious minds should be easygoing,
> carefree, and as forthright as an innocent.

And *The Reverberation of Sound* states:

> In addition, they are patient and relaxed[16] [38a]
> and have the easygoing manner of an innocent.
> They have few concepts and are serene by nature.
> They are free of physical and verbal busyness,
> possess sublime knowing, and so can uphold the teachings.

Once you have understood the essence of awareness, then regardless of what happens—whether awareness is at rest or arises as thoughts, or whether dullness, agitation, and the like occur—there is nothing but the essence and display of naturally occurring timeless awareness itself. There are no errors or obscurations that must be eliminated. Errors and obscurations themselves are not something "other" that is not included in awareness; awareness abides timelessly as dharmakaya, the supreme state of spontaneous presence, in which nothing need be done. Thus, the situation is similar to reaching the fabled Isle of Gold, where one cannot find anything but gold—no ordinary earth or stone—even if one searches for it. *The All-Creating Monarch* states:

> Listen, O great and courageous one!
> Buddhas of previous generations, moreover,
> had nothing to contrive or to seek, only their own minds.
> They did not contrive what simply is.
> They did not cultivate conceptual meditative absorption.
> Accomplishment came about through natural mind, which does
>   not entail concepts.
> For those who abide now or have yet to appear,
> accomplishment also ensues from a nonconceptual state
>   of equalness.
> . . . .
> Within the vast expanse that is the true nature of phenomena,
>   the infinite extent[17] of supreme bliss,
> abides what by nature is supreme, nonconceptual evenness.
> As for the very nature of phenomena, which is nonmanifest,
> do not think about it, however intelligently!
> Do not indulge in meditative absorption!
> Abiding in the fundamental nature spontaneously ensures
>   the absence of straying. [38b]
> With natural abiding, there is nothing for anyone to contrive.
> To abide in what simply is, without its being sought,[18]
> means that nothing need be done—this is revealed[19] to be
>   the most sublime activity.

Mental dullness and agitation are impossible in naturally abiding meditative stability. *The Heaped Jewels* states:

> In natural, uninterrupted meditative stability,
> there is no dullness or agitation—how amazing!

Spontaneously present meditative stability, settled in its own place, is understood to be ongoing, like the flow of a river, without having to be deliberately cultivated. Within that context, everything arises as the true nature of phenomena, and so there is no error or obscuration, no dullness or agitation, no distraction or even the lack of it, because any object of distraction arises as the display of that nature.

Meditative adepts in approaches other than this may cultivate a state of meditation in which their consciousness is focused one-pointedly without distraction, but this does not bring them the slightest bit closer to awakening to buddhahood; rather, it is a stake that tethers them to rebirth in the formless realm of meditative stability. This is similar to the current situation of certain followers of the Zhijé [Pacification] school. *The All-Creating Monarch* states:

> To ignore what is inherent and seek afar for something else,
> eagerly trying to arouse the bliss that requires no effort—
> there is no greater debility than this.
> Undistracted meditative absorption is a stake that tethers one
> to reification.
> With respect to what is and always has been, there is no
> distraction, nothing to be lost.
> Undistracted meditative absorption seduces one with hope.
> Such are the mahayana approaches based on either causes or results,
> which reveal what is provisional.
> With respect to what is and always has been, there is no
> distraction, no loss.
> The state in which nothing need be done transcends all effort
> and achievement.[20]

Now, given that the universe of appearances and possibilities abides as a pure realm, [39a] it can be shown that it entails no acceptance or rejection, nothing being better or worse:

> **Within the timelessly abiding, omnipresent state—**
> **the true nature of phenomena—**
> **there are no concepts of self or other,**
> **and so the three realms themselves constitute a pure realm**
> **of natural equalness.**

Even though the pure realm that is permeated by awareness—the supreme, spontaneously present state of purity and equalness—manifests as the three realms and the six classes of beings, it arises timelessly and naturally as the pure realm of naturally occurring timeless awareness. So it can be shown that this mode of great perfection as the true nature of phenomena is timelessly awakened in vajra basic space. *The Reverberation of Sound* states:

> Moreover, owing to their circumstances, among ordinary beings
> there is not a single one who has not awakened to buddhahood.
> Because their nature is in harmony with naturally manifest
>   timeless awareness,
> samsara has never existed.
> Therefore, each being is naturally a buddha.
> Once one realizes what the process of birth really is,
> abiding in the womb is the basic space of phenomena,
> the coming together of body and mind is the connection between
>   basic space and awareness,
> and abiding in the body is the three kayas.
> Aging is the falling away of phenomena and the end of
>   confused perception,
> illness is the experience of the true nature of phenomena,
> and death is emptiness, impossible to identify.
> Therefore, ordinary beings are actually[21] buddhas.

And *The Pearl Garland* states:

> With the uniting of skillful means and sublime knowing,
> the causal factors—one's father and mother—are pure.
> The impetus from the subtle energy of momentum
> is enlightened awareness, self-knowing and supremely blissful.
> With the five elements as their causal factors,
> the ovum and sperm are sensory appearances[22] arising within
>   the domain of emptiness. [39b]
> The blissful union of a couple
> is sublime knowing aroused by skillful means.
> With entrance into the matrix of the womb,
> self-knowing awareness arises from the ground of being
>   as sensory appearances.
> The first seven weeks are the period in which realization
>   develops;
> by ten months, the levels of realization are traversed.

Birth is the arising of enlightened form.
The growth of the body is the ground of being manifesting
    as sensory appearances,
while abiding in the body is that ground.
Aging is the clearing away of confusion.
Illness is the indwelling confidence of realization.
With death there is freedom in the empty nature of phenomena.
Thus, all beings, manifest in form,
are effortlessly and timelessly perfect buddhas.[23]

Since in this way all ordinary beings have qualities in common with those of buddhahood, they are called "buddhas." Reaching too hasty a conclusion without understanding how to apply the significance of this similarity and saying that "everyone has always been a buddha" and "everything is awareness's own manifestations" is a case of raving stupidity. There is no difference between this and the same words mumbled by people in their sleep. Rather, by applying the significance of this similarity and the purity underlying everything, you should realize that what manifests as the realms of ordinary beings and the universe constitutes the mandala of buddhahood. *The Heart Essence of Secrets* states:

The components that are the vajra aggregates
are renowned as the five perfect buddhas.
All the many factors of the sense fields and components
    of ordinary experience
are the very epitome of bodhisattvas.
Earth and water are Lochana and Mamaki,
fire and air are Pandaravasini and Tara,
and space is Dhatveshvari—the feminine aspects.
All possible phenomena of the entire three worlds [40a]
are without exception a pure realm of buddhahood.
Even a buddha could not find
anything other than that awakened state itself.

And *The Reverberation of Sound* states:

The nature of perceptions based on confusion
has not been perceived to be timeless awareness.
Since conceptual confusion has no basis,
the ground of all ordinary experience is realized to be
    supreme dharmakaya.

The flow of thoughts inherent in confusion is interrupted.
Thus, unconfused perception
derives from the key factor of timeless freedom.
No one is aware of the fact that the aggregates of beings
are and always have been the kaya of buddhahood.

And *The Heaped Jewels* states:

As for self-identity and the objects of its reifying perceptions,[24]
from the very beginning, the true nature of all of them
has been such that they are awareness's own manifestations
    in and of themselves,
but that timeless manifestation has not been understood.
The five afflictive emotions, bound up with a sense of identity,
arise timelessly and naturally within awareness
and abide coemergent with being itself, but this goes
    unrecognized.

Just as samsara, a timeless state of buddhahood, arises as awareness's own manifestation, it can be shown that even nirvana is simply the pure manifestation of this same buddhahood and nothing else:

**For victorious ones of the three times, awareness's own
    manifestations are pure.
Since everything constitutes a single state of equalness,
    with nothing to renounce or accept,
there is nothing in the slightest to attain elsewhere.
All phenomena are clearly evident within the vast expanse
    of mind itself,
yet they do not stray in the least from the ultimate meaning
    of equalness.**

There is only awareness, pure in being free of adventitious distortions; there is no essence of buddhahood other than this—mind itself—nothing to seek through causes or conditions, effort or achievement, [40b] because the term "buddhahood" is being used merely to describe pure awareness. Given that even the perceptions of buddhas are nothing other than the way awareness manifests, even awakening to buddhahood within the basic space of awakened mind is not a matter of discovering some "state" elsewhere. *The Heart Essence of Secrets* states:

Perfect buddhahood will not be found
anywhere in the ten directions or the four times.
Since mind itself is perfectly awakened,
do not seek buddhahood elsewhere!
Even if they sought it, victorious ones would not find it.

And *The All-Creating Monarch* states:

All phenomena that manifest or are possible and awakened mind,
    which does not manifest,
come from the suchness of mind and are suchness.
Not realized to be suchness, they are perceived as separate.
To seek suchness within basic space—
even if victorious ones of the three times were to do so,
    they would not find it.

. . . .

Moreover,[25] successions of buddhas in the past
perceived and realized uncontrived natural mind.

If one realizes the very essence of such awareness, error and obscuration are cut through as a matter of course:

There is no division into outer and inner, and no disturbance
    due to thoughts arising and subsiding.
The foundation, awakened mind, dispels the darkness
    of extremes.
With nothing having to be renounced, the potential for error
    is cut through as a matter of course.

Because there is nowhere else to journey or look, given that the essence of awareness is beyond any concerted effort to reject or accept anything, there is no potential for either error or obscuration. So once you rest in the very essence of awareness, to then make an effort or engage in view and meditation is beside the point and will lead to error and obscuration. [41a] *The All-Creating Monarch* states:

The very nature of awakened mind
is the heart essence of all phenomena without exception.
Unborn and totally pure, it is unobscured.
Free of any path to traverse, it has no potential for error.

> Timelessly and spontaneously present, it is not something to seek.
> Though the oneness of awakened mind lies at the very heart of
>   all phenomena,
> error and obscuration ensue when one tries to enumerate where
>   in fact there is oneness.
> The potential for error ensues when one tries to traverse what
>   cannot be traversed.
> Obscuration ensues when one tries to look at what does not entail
>   any conceptual framework and fails to perceive it.

It can be shown that nothing that manifests within the scope of awareness strays from basic space:

> The world of myriad ways in which beings perceive—
> and even the kayas and timeless awareness of pure
>   buddhahood—
> all that[26] permeates the realm of basic space as a continuous
>   display
> arises due to dynamic energy, either in light of realization
>   or in its absence.
> There is simply realization or its lack within the realm of
>   the basic space of phenomena.
> For those with realization, who have reached a state of bliss,
>   there is pure perception.
> For those without it, there is nonrecognition of awareness
>   and the habitual patterns of dualistic perception,
> from which sensory appearances manifest in all their variety,
>   though none of this strays from basic space.

Due to recognition of the very essence of basic space—naturally occurring timeless awareness—buddhas appear to manifest, and due to nonrecognition, ordinary beings appear to manifest. But both are of one taste within the scope of awareness, and so are not subject to restrictions or extremes. *The All-Creating Monarch* states:

> Because everything subsumed within the universe of appearances
>   and possibilities
> and all who are subsumed as buddhas or ordinary beings
> have been created by me, all-creating enlightenment, [41b]

nothing has ever existed as something "other"
that is not included within awakened mind.
Therefore, everything is shown to be awakened mind.

It can be shown that such awareness is a supreme, unceasing state, empty yet lucid:

Awakened mind is the actual state of everything.
It exhibits an unceasing quality.
Whatever arises in all its variety is naturally and clearly
    apparent,
evident within[27] pure basic space, the true nature of
    phenomena.
There is no division or exclusion—the mode of awareness
    is without restriction.

Within the unborn state that is the essence of being, empty yet lucid and never existent as anything whatsoever—comparable to a flawless crystal globe—a continuous display arises as anything at all. *Naturally Arising Awareness* states:

Neither entailing extremes nor subject to restrictions,
without division into outer and inner, there is
    supreme spaciousness.
It is pure and flawless, like a crystal globe.
It is said that things manifest yet have no independent nature.

The nature of this awareness can be explained in detail:

Unobstructed timeless awareness, a naturally occurring
    spacious expanse,
is utterly lucid—unobscured, with no division into outer
    and inner—
and so self-knowing awareness is the great radiant mirror
    of mind.
The precious gem that provides for all wants is the basic space
    of phenomena.
Since everything occurs naturally without having to be sought,
naturally occurring timeless awareness is the splendid source
    of all one could wish for.

Basic space, naturally occurring and spontaneously present timeless awareness—the most precious gem—is inherently a state of utter lucidity, the flawless light rays of which shine forth, permeating the whole of samsara and nirvana, and so it is called "the great radiant mirror of awakened mind." The essence of this spaciousness, the true nature of phenomena, [42a] is such that it is beyond being an object of thought. *The Perfect Dynamic Energy of the Lion* states:

> Great perfection is my awakened mind.[28]
> This essence of awareness, being nonconceptual,
> is nothing in itself, yet occurs as anything at all.

And *Naturally Arising Awareness* states:

> Given its true nature as a continuous display,
> it is the wholly positive vastness of basic space itself that arises.
> Enlightened intent is the basic space of supreme, sublime
>   knowing.
> The true nature that underlies the reification of phenomena
>   entails no attachment.
> Not involving concepts, it is beyond the scope of[29] description
>   or imagination.
> It can be compared metaphorically to a miraculous display
>   in the sky.

It can be shown that awareness is the spacious expanse of enlightenment:

> **However many great qualities can be enumerated,**
> **they come from basic space and are of basic space, arising**
> **   continuously as sublime skillful means.**
> **Since everything is spontaneously perfect in unborn basic space,**
> **the substance of things is outshone by their emptiness**
> **   as the expanse of enlightenment,**
> **while their emptiness is outshone by self-knowing awareness**
> **   as the expanse of enlightenment.[30]**

Awareness—the realm of space—which is completely free of the four extremes, and all phenomena that arise within it, like a magical illusion or a reflection of the moon in water, are beyond existence and nonexistence. Therefore, it can be shown that their true nature is that of a pure, vast expanse. *Naturally Arising Awareness* states:

> Like a magical illusion, the moon's reflection in water,
>   or a mirage,
> things are not simply nonexistent, nor are they existent.
> Because they are beyond both existence and nonexistence,
> the essence of awareness is without origin,
> sensory appearances are by nature continuous,
> and awareness has the quality of being insubstantial. [42b]
> The fruition of that awareness is uncontrived.
> Awareness—the three kayas—is said to be the essence of being.[31]

Now, the ultimate meaning of the foregoing discussions can be summarized as a supremely spacious expanse:

> **In awakened mind, appearances and emptiness have**
> **   never existed.**
> **But do not fixate on nonduality, for the inconceivable**
> **   miraculous display still occurs.**
> **With no time frame, the unborn basic space of phenomena**
> **is an unchanging, undivided, and uncompounded expanse.**
> **Throughout the three times, buddhahood is awareness,**
> **   the basic space of timeless awareness,**
> **the expanse of enlightenment, of self-knowing awareness that**
> **   outshines dualistic perceptions.**
> **With no division into outer and inner, the true nature of**
> **   phenomena is spontaneous and spacious.**

Within the essence of awareness, neither sensory appearances, emptiness, nor anything else has ever existed, and the basic space of the equalness of the three times is uncompounded. Given that awareness arises timelessly as buddhahood throughout the three times, it is dharmakaya, which entails no dualistic perception. *Naturally Arising Awareness* states:

> Furthermore, I exhibit the quality of being unchanging.
> I am undivided—a oneness.
> I came before even buddhahood.
> I am untainted by dualistic perception.

And *The Perfect Dynamic Energy of the Lion* states:

> Nondual awareness's own manifestations[32] arise as anything
> at all.
> Dharmakaya, free of substance, is the very secret of timeless
> awareness.[33]
> The natural mode of sensory appearances is one of abiding
> in enlightened mind, timelessly infinite.
> The manifestations of inexhaustible awareness appear
> as anything at all.
> Awareness as a continuous display[34] arises in any way at all.
> The intent of nonconceptual enlightened mind is a state
> of equalness.[35]
> Throughout the three times, buddhahood is awareness free of
> dualistic perception. [43a]

This is the commentary on the fourth section of *The Precious Treasury of the Basic Space of Phenomena,* demonstrating the nature of awakened mind.

5

Transcending Effort and Causality

It can be shown that such a nature is beyond concerted effort and causality:

> Within mind itself—the essence of awakened mind—
> there is no view to cultivate in meditation, no conduct
>   to undertake,
> no fruition to achieve, no levels of realization or paths
>   to traverse,
> no mandala to visualize, no recitation, repetition, or stage
>   of completion,
> no empowerment to be bestowed, and no samaya to uphold.
> In the pure state that is the true nature of phenomena,
>   timelessly and spontaneously present,
> such adventitious factors of developmental effort and causality
>   are transcended.

In the present case, because ultimate truth has never existed as anything whatsoever from the perspective of spacelike awareness, neither has there ever existed any view, meditation, conduct, or fruition, any mandalas or stages of development and completion, or any samaya or vows, and so forth. This is because awareness—empty and without identity—is in its very essence beyond all characterization or description. *The All-Creating Monarch* states:

> Awakened mind is like space.
> In mind itself—the true nature of phenomena—which is like space,
> there is no view to cultivate in meditation, no samaya to uphold,

no effort in enlightened activity, nothing to obscure timeless
    awareness,
no levels of realization on which to train, no paths to traverse,
no subtle factors, no duality, and no interdependence.
There is no definitive or conclusive statement concerning mind.
Since it is beyond value judgments, there are no pith instructions
    for coming to some decisive experience.
This is the view of awakened mind, great perfection.

And *Naturally Arising Awareness* states:

The ultimate meaning is unborn awakened mind,[1] [43b]
wherein there is nothing to destroy with an antidote,
no extremes or biases,
no reification of "I" or of identity,
no concepts of good or bad.
It transcends the extremes of being something and being nothing,
is beyond any question of being conceptual or not,
is free of[2] the two alternatives of affirmation and denial,
is beyond any factor[3] of error or obscuration,
and entails no duality of whether there is realization or not.
It transcends the extremes of purity and impurity,
surpasses ordinary mind and consciousness,
    as well as phenomena,
and entails no duality of whether there is understanding or not.
It is beyond nonrecognition of awareness and the ordinary
    confused mind,
is free of terms, conventional designations, and words,
has none of the distortions of ordinary dualistic mind,
and dispels concepts, distortions of the spiritual path.
It transcends the plans and actions of[4] myriad speculations
and is free of being a phenomenon reified as having substance.
There are no paths or levels of realization on which to train.
Making offerings to deities is unnecessary.
The ten kinds of virtuous actions provide no protection,
and it is not sullied by harmful actions.
Where, then, are the lower realms of rebirth in samsara?
No such thing as nirvana exists,
nor does any view of self and other.
How could there be any question of deviation or not?

It is beyond the extremes of existence and nonexistence
and has no color or shape.

And *The Heaped Jewels* states:

There are no mantras or mudras in this.
There is no specific need at all in this,
even for mandalas, deities, or offerings.
There is no need to prepare ritual articles or perform
formal ceremonies.
There is nothing to be entered
and no expression of timeless awareness to be brought
down. [44a]

And *The Perfect Dynamic Energy of the Lion* states:

Great perfection is the natural language of awareness,
beyond the domain of either sensory appearances or emptiness,
beyond ordinary mind and consciousness, as well as phenomena,
and beyond the alternatives of being something and being nothing.
There is no view of good or bad,
and whether or not one is meditating is irrelevant.

. . . .

There is neither samaya nor kaya of awareness,[5]
neither observance nor anything to observe—
no samaya, whether apparent or not.
No samaya is proclaimed in self-knowing awareness,
the essence of great perfection.
The domain of supreme, sublime knowing
is that of ineffability experienced in ineffability itself,
of oneness in oneness itself,
of openness in openness itself,
and of spontaneous presence bestowed[6] in spontaneous
presence itself.

A definitive metaphor can be given for such a state in which there is no
concerted effort, no renunciation or acceptance whatsoever:

The essence of these factors is awakened mind.
Unobscured by clouds or darkness, the sun shines in the sky
by its very nature,
not as something adventitious.

The essence of the sun is its natural luminosity within the realm of space; even clouds cannot obscure that essence. Furthermore, its luminosity is not created adventitiously through a process of causality. Similarly, the very essence of awareness cannot possibly entail causality or obscuration. Throughout the world, when people look at the sun, sometimes it is obscured. While it seems that the sun is not shining, it is their own vision that has been obscured by clouds. [44b] Yet they still think, "The sun is not shining." This is called confusion. Similarly, while awareness entails no error or obscuration due to factors such as adventitious afflictive emotions, in the face of confused thinking it seems to be eclipsed. You think, "Awareness is obscured, so I should purify that. I will develop enlightened qualities!" This is what is meant by confusion, pure and simple. As *The Supreme "Mother"* states, moreover:

> No "mind" exists in mind, for the nature of mind is, in fact,
>   utter lucidity.

And as *The Ornament of Manifest Realization* states:

> There is nothing whatsoever to remove from this,
> nor anything in the slightest to add.

And as *Naturally Arising Awareness* states:

> The perspective of awareness itself
> transcends the extremes of affirmation and denial.
> The inexpressible state of total purity
> is beyond the extremes of being something and being nothing.
> The state that entails no repression or indulgence[7]
> transcends the limitations of reification and attachment.
> Flawless utter lucidity is spontaneous presence itself.[8]

Even though the essence of awareness is so, the ten attributes are taught to those with inferior acumen, but a yogin of ati understands that this is error and obscuration:

> **Any teaching concerning the ten attributes that involve effort**
> **   and achievement**
> **is given in response to the confusion that occurs adventitiously**
> **   due to the dynamic energy of awareness.**

It is a skillful means for engaging those whose acumen requires
   development through effort.
It is not given to yogins who genuinely experience
the ultimate meaning of the vajra heart essence, atiyoga.

As is stated in *Awakened Mind: The All-Creating Monarch*:

Three stages, up to and including anuyoga, [45a]
do not involve supreme, naturally occurring timeless awareness,
and so one traverses paths and trains on levels of realization.
These include ways of upholding samaya and cultivating view
   in meditation,
but in fact view and conduct do not develop slowly, by stages.
Because the view and conduct of atiyoga
are timelessly created by the all-creating one,
one does not traverse paths, train on levels of realization,
uphold samaya, or cultivate view in meditation.
Because everything occurs as the path of supreme enlightenment,
enlightenment itself need not traverse itself.
Because there is nothing but enlightenment itself to traverse,
enlightenment itself need not train in itself.
Given that the nature of samaya is enlightenment itself,
enlightenment itself need not uphold itself.
Given that the nature of meditation is enlightenment itself,
enlightenment itself need not cultivate itself in meditation.
Given that the nature[9] of view is enlightenment itself,
enlightenment itself need not view itself.
Atiyoga entails no cultivation of view or conduct,
but, rather, gradual familiarization with naturally occurring
   timeless awareness.
This is familiarization with me, the all-creating monarch,
and is not the domain of those involved in spiritual approaches
   entailing causes or results.

The four levels of yoga are "the yoga of courageous mind" (corresponding to the three outer levels of tantra), "great yoga" (the maha
yoga approach of development), "thorough yoga" (the anuyoga approach
based on explanatory commentaries), and "utmost yoga" (the atiyoga
approach of pith instruction). The same tantra speaks of the distinctions
among these:

Atiyoga, anuyoga, mahayoga, and the yoga of the lower tantras—
     [45b]
these are the four.
When one looks at the ultimate yoga of the heart essence,
     in which nothing need be done,
what one "sees" are these four outlooks.

The yoga of the lower tantras involves the perception of objects
     by the senses.
Consecration takes place through the five factors of
     enlightenment and the four miraculous displays,
and the deities are viewed as having two aspects.
But the genuine state of the ultimate heart essence cannot be seen,
so rest your courageous mind in uncontrived suchness!

Practitioners of mahayoga experience the genuine state—
the ultimate heart essence, in which nothing need be done—
perceiving the causal and resultant mandalas of deities
within the mandala of their own timelessly pure mindstreams.
Having completed the four branches of approach and
     accomplishment,
they view the shining forth and reconverging of light as
     spontaneously present.
But the genuine state of the ultimate heart essence cannot be seen,
so rest to that great degree in uncontrived suchness!

Practitioners of anuyoga experience the genuine state—
the ultimate heart essence, in which nothing need be done—
perceiving the heart essence of basic space as the cause of
     genuine being,
while seeing supreme timeless awareness as the result of that
     genuine state.
Since they see both cause and result in this single heart essence,
they do not perceive the yoga that transcends causality.
Rest completely in the yoga of uncontrived suchness!

Practitioners of atiyoga experience the genuine state—
the ultimate heart essence, in which nothing need be done—
perceiving the view of great perfection
and seeing awakened mind as the heart essence of everything.
They perceive the ultimate state of genuine being, uncontrived
     suchness.

Rest in the view that is timelessly such that it cannot be cultivated
   in meditation! [46a]

One rests in samaya that has never to be upheld.
One rests in enlightened activity in which nothing need ever
   be sought.[10]
By resting, one experiences the yoga of suchness.

Now, the classification of the nine spiritual approaches can be shown,
as can the enlightened perspective underlying them. The first six are as
follows:

> So that individuals who exert themselves in order to progress
>   developmentally
> may be led to primordial basic space—the true nature of
>   phenomena—
> there are the spiritual approaches of the shravaka,
>   the pratyekabuddha, and the bodhisattva.
> These are the stages demonstrated on the three lesser levels.
> The three divisions of kriya, upa, and yoga
> are by their very nature the three intermediate levels.

Spiritual approaches for those of differing acumen are presented as
stages, which are the skillful means, or contributing factors, that enable one to engage in the unsurpassable approach. From the standpoint
of whether or not these are direct paths that bring about awakening to
buddhahood in this lifetime, the outer approaches based on dialectics—
those of the shravaka, the pratyekabuddha, and the bodhisattva—are
classified as the three lesser levels, while the tantric approach is explained to be the greater level. In the tantric approach, furthermore, the
three outer levels are classified as lesser based on the length of time they
require.

From the higher perspective of the great perfection, all views and
meditations of these other approaches are considered to be for the spiritually undeveloped, for whatever is done misses the point, in that the
essence of awareness is not perceived. It is explained that they are erroneous and obscuring. *The All-Creating Monarch* states:

> Given that the true nature of phenomena is, in essence,
>   the oneness of awakened mind,

if one invokes the four truths concerning suffering and its origins
in order to assert that suffering and its origins are the causes of
    lower states of rebirth,
one rejects that nature, awakened mind.
In this way, one becomes lost, having failed to perceive that
    nature.[11] [46b]

Given that the true nature of phenomena is, in essence,
    awakened mind,
if one uses a twofold division of truth into ultimate and relative
to train on and traverse the path of the ten levels of realization
through generosity, discipline, and the rest of the ten perfections,
one does not perceive the true nature of phenomena, remaining
    instead on that level of training.[12]

Given that the true nature of phenomena is, in essence,
    awakened mind,
if one relies on auspicious conjunctions of the planets and
    constellations
and invokes the five factors of enlightenment and the four great
    miraculous displays
in order to consecrate all phenomena, which appear as they do,
and to meditate on these as forms of the deity,
one does not perceive natural mind, which cannot be cultivated
    in meditation.

The stages of the three inner levels of tantra are as follows:

The three divisions of maha, anu, and ati
manifest primordially as the three higher levels.
By opening the doorway that leads beyond other approaches
based on causes or results,
they guide fortunate beings to three levels of enlightenment.

Of these, moreover, the maha and anu approaches, unlike the unique
approach of ati, are not totally complete and so are not consummate approaches. This is because they are merely ways of educating the minds
of beings developmentally. *The All-Creating Monarch* states:

Given the essence of awakened mind, oneness,
if one uses the three stages of meditative absorption and the five rites

while meditating—through the four stages of approach
and accomplishment—
on the pure vajra aggregates of one's own mindstream as
the deity,
treating them as apparent yet without independent nature,
one contrives the deity from one's natural mind by trying to seek
and achieve something.
But one does not perceive this natural mind, in which nothing
need be done.

Given that awakened mind is one's own true nature, [47a]
the all-creating monarch, teacher of teachers,
does not proclaim meditation to the three kinds of teachers,
but simply proclaims that the true nature of one's natural mind
has always been free.
If you try to achieve something through meditation, that is
ordinary mind—the abandonment of natural mind.[13]

O great and courageous one, if you want to experience
natural mind,
you can do it only by not wanting to,
so do not try to dwell in a nonconceptual state of equalness.
Abide naturally in a mode that has nothing to do with acceptance
or rejection.
Abide as a matter of course in a state that does not waver.
Mind is the essence of what simply is.
All phenomena are ensured in suchness.
Given what simply is, do not meddle with anything.
Given this very essence, do not look elsewhere and try to
achieve something.
Even if they sought it, victorious ones would not find anything
but basic space.
Since it is already created, there is no need to create it anew.
Since it is already ensured, there is no need to try to achieve
it anew.

It can be shown that all of these are avenues that lead toward the vajra
heart essence:

**The culmination of all these, moreover, is found in the ultimate
meaning of the vajra heart essence.**

> They must lead toward this superb, supreme secret,
> and so utter lucidity, sublimely unchanging, is the pinnacle
>   of them all.
> This is renowned as the spiritual approach of the heart essence
>   of manifest enlightenment.

All of these spiritual approaches, moreover, must culminate in the approach of the vajra heart essence, because it is impossible to attain buddhahood without perceiving this doorway. *Secret Conduct: The Tantra of the Potential* states:

> This itself has manifested for whoever
> attains the resultant state of buddhahood.
> There never has been, nor will there ever be, [47b]
> a single buddha who has not perceived it.
> . . . .
> Innumerable Vajradharas share a single enlightened intent,
> the unique welling forth of enlightened mind.

That is to say, while these eight stages are taught as aids to those of lesser intellect, ati manifests to those with the most excellent fortune. In this regard, although in its very essence awareness involves no spiritual approach whatsoever, specific approaches do arise simply as avenues to bring about its realization. But there is nothing other than the supreme spaciousness of ati that reveals awareness in so straightforward a way. *The Perfect Dynamic Energy of the Lion* states:

> Spacious! Supreme! The supreme teaching![14]
> This is the antidote to lesser levels.
> In no way do lesser and greater stages
> exist on the level of truth.
> Such duality occurs in the minds of ordinary beings.

Of these two alternatives, the stages involving effort and achievement are as follows:

> Furthermore, of the two alternatives within spiritual teaching,
> one involves a concerted effort to accept or reject.
> It is taught in order to refine away the habitual patterns of
>   ordinary mind and mental events,

> whose nature it is to arise as a display due to dynamic energy.
> This approach holds that timeless awareness is purer than
> ordinary mind.

Since in these eight stages the spiritual path is forged using ordinary mind, the path that is forged involves making a concerted effort to accept or reject, on the assumption that there is timeless awareness if ordinary mind is free of distortion. Accordingly, those who have not realized the innermost heart essence of ati—the "heart drop"—can by association be included in that category. They insist that ordinary mind alone is the support for the ground, path, and result as aspects of enlightenment. You can gain an understanding of this distinction from my treatises: [48a] *The Precious Treasury of Philosophical Systems, The Precious Treasury of the Sublime Vehicle,* and *The Precious Treasury of Utter Lucidity.* As well, *The Perfect Dynamic Energy of the Lion* states:

> Actually, neither ordinary mind nor timeless awareness
>   constitutes habitual patterns,
> for timeless awareness is free of all habitual patterns
> and ordinary mind consolidates a plethora of such patterns.
> If the distinction between these two—ordinary mind and
>   timeless awareness—is not made,
> the root of apparent sense objects is not cut through,
> and so the true nature of phenomena, free of conditions,
>   is difficult to realize, even though it is pure.[15]

Let me summarize this briefly. "Timeless awareness" refers to enlightened intent free of any object—the very essence of awareness that is ever-present. It is free of all conceptual or verbal elaboration. "Ordinary mind" refers to consciousness that involves the reification of sense objects. The root of ordinary mind is found in timeless awareness, and what amounts to the inner glow, or dynamic energy, of timeless awareness is present in the gaps between thoughts. So one must identify the very essence, timeless awareness, by relying on this context. The lack of such identification is called "distortion." Given that there is this distinction between the essence of awareness and its dynamic energy, one can distinguish between timeless awareness and ordinary mind.

In this regard, six approaches are shown to have potential for error with respect to the great perfection. These are the three dialectical approaches based on causes (taken together as one), plus the three approaches of kriya, upa, and yoga (to make four), plus the two approaches of maha and anu (to make six). *The All-Creating Monarch* states:

> The six spiritual approaches for attaining a degree of certainty
> are shown to have potential for error with respect to the
>   great perfection.
> How is this so? you ask.
>
> The classes of sutras of the bodhisattva approach
> posit the level of realization that is total illumination.
> Assuming two levels of truth, they speculate about the empty
>   nature of phenomena [48b]
> and hold it to be space.
> Awakened mind, beyond conceptualization and analysis,
> is the supreme bliss of atiyoga.
> The classes of sutras are in the dark about this transcendence
>   of conceptualization and analysis.
> The great perfection explains that conceptualization and analysis
> are the error in the classes of sutras.
>
> The kriya teachings posit the state of a vajra holder.
> Passing through the doorway of threefold purification,
> one abides in the domain of purified dualistic perception.
> Awakened mind, beyond dualistic perception,
> is the supreme bliss of atiyoga.
> The kriya approach is in the dark about this transcendence
>   of dualistic perception.
> The great perfection explains that engaging in dualistic
>   perception
> is the error in the kriya systems.
>
> View and conduct in the upa approach
> are such that one engages in the conduct of the kriya approach
>   while accomplishing the yoga approach.
> Since there is nothing meaningful that connects view[16] and conduct,
> one does not realize the ultimate meaning of nonduality.
> Nondual awakened mind
> is the supreme bliss of atiyoga.
> The upa approach is in the dark about nonduality.
> The great perfection explains that engaging in dualism
> is the error in the upa approach.

Given that the yoga approach posits the realm of Ghanavyuha,
one emphasizes the four mudras—the "seals of practice"—
by using techniques that may or may not be structured.
But one cannot enter the state that does not entail acceptance
    or rejection.
Awakened mind, which does not entail acceptance
    or rejection,
is the supreme bliss of atiyoga.
The yoga approach is in the dark about this state without
    acceptance or rejection.
The great perfection explains that engaging in acceptance
    or rejection
is the error in the yoga systems.

The maha approach posits the state of Vajradhara.
By passing through the doorway of skillful means and
    sublime knowing,
one gains accomplishment through the four phases of
    approach and accomplishment
within the mandala of one's own pure mindstream. [49a]
Awakened mind, beyond effort and achievement,
is the supreme bliss of atiyoga.
The maha approach is in the dark about this transcendence
    of effort and achievement.
The great perfection explains that engaging in effort
    and achievement
is the error in mahayoga.

The anu approach posits the state of inseparability.
By passing through the doorway of basic space and
    timeless awareness,
one views phenomena however they appear,
viewing pure basic space as the cause
and the mandala of timeless awareness as the result.
Awakened mind, beyond cause and result,
is the supreme bliss of atiyoga.
The anu approach is in the dark about this transcendence
    of cause and result.
The great perfection explains that viewing cause and result
    as a duality
is the error in anuyoga.

The enlightened intent of ati, the very essence, is as follows:

> The supreme teaching involves no concerted effort to accept
>   or reject.
> Naturally occurring timeless awareness, the essence of
>   awakened mind itself,
> is made fully evident in that one does not waver from
>   the direct experience of it.
> So there is no need to strive for it elsewhere.
> It rests in and of itself, so do not seek it elsewhere.

The tradition specific to this spontaneously present vajra heart essence holds that awareness—uncontrived and unadulterated, not wavering from the scope of the true nature of phenomena—is dharmakaya, the ground aspect of buddhahood. Given that buddhahood would not be found even if it were sought elsewhere, it is held that "buddhahood" is just a label for what, in actuality, is simply the essence of awareness, without transition or change, expressing itself fully within the expanse of being. *The Great Garuda* states:

> Without cause and free of conditions, awareness's own
>   manifestations are unobscured.
> Free of effort, unique, and not created by anyone or anything,
> the timelessly perfect heart essence expresses itself in the
>   spontaneous presence of sense objects. [49b]

And *The Pearl Garland* states:

> Perfect buddhahood is self-knowing awareness itself.[17]

And *The All-Creating Monarch* states:

> Do not look for buddhahood: realize natural mind, in which
>   nothing need be done.
> If examined, it is found to be ineffable—timelessly lucid
>   self-knowing awareness.[18]
> In mahayana approaches based on either causes or results,
>   in which "equalness" is something other than this,
> by various means—renouncing, progressing, training, and
>   consecrating—
> one strays from natural mind, the true nature of phenomena,
>   in which nothing need be done.

To ignore what is inherent and seek afar for something else,
eagerly trying to arouse the bliss that requires no effort—
there is no greater debility than this.

The difference between these two kinds of spiritual approach is demonstrated:

> This—the ultimate meaning of suchness itself—is like
>   the essence of the sun.
> I hold that it abides as a natural state of rest, unwavering
>   utter lucidity.
> It can be shown that other approaches are like attempts
>   to create the already-present sun
> by dispelling clouds and darkness through a process of effort
>   and achievement.
> Therefore, these two kinds of approach are as different as
>   heaven and earth.

The spontaneously present vajra heart essence is the essence of awareness, which itself is already timelessly present as buddhahood, analogous to the sun actually being present. Those who follow other approaches hold that buddhahood is finally accomplished through a process of effort and achievement involving causes and conditions; this is like holding that the sun, which is always present, shines only due to causes and conditions that dispel clouds and darkness. This position is at odds with spontaneous presence, and so there are contradictions inherent in the sources used by these specific approaches. Therefore, a distinction can be made on the basis of whether or not awareness—that is, self-occurring timeless awareness—is experienced as buddhahood, already and naturally present. [50a]

The Dynamic Energy of the Lion demonstrates that the lower approaches fail to realize what has genuine meaning:[19]

> The ultimate meaning is expressed within a single mandala.
> There is a single secret mantra approach, but nine ways
>   of proceeding,
> which, furthermore, manifest simply as its specific aspects.
> The ultimate meaning of naturally occurring[20] timeless
>   awareness, the essence of being,
> is not realized through these nine stages.

It is the nature of sensory appearances that their manifestation
has two aspects—ultimate and relative.
These are not separate, but a single state.
Within the complete essence of timeless realization,[21]
all thoughts that occur concerning the characteristics of things
are simply the display of timeless awareness.
The ultimate meaning is expressed within a single awareness.
The three kayas manifest as the essence of victorious ones.
From the kayas come miraculous expressions of timeless
    awareness,
which is neither manifest nor nonmanifest.
It is free of the extremes of realization and a lack of it.
Illuminating timeless awareness abides as the essence of being.
The elements are the very embodiment of vajra conditions.

Now, the deluded position that fails to distinguish between timeless
awareness (naturally occurring in and of itself) and thought patterns
(occurring due to other factors) can be refuted:

Nowadays, those "elephants" who pride themselves on
    being ati practitioners,
allege that thought patterns, stirring and proliferating,
    are awakened mind.
All of these fools are submerged in darkness,
far from the meaning of natural great perfection.
They do not understand even dynamic energy or what
    arises from that energy,
to say nothing of the essence of awakened mind.

Although one might have a simple interest in this spiritual approach,
the chances of having the good fortune to perceive it thoroughly are not
even that of a one-hundredth portion split from a single hair. There are
those who swagger in their undiscriminating ignorance, [50b] whose
brows are adorned with golden chains of jealousy and wrongheaded
concepts, and who flatter themselves with the assumption that they understand and so have the haughty gait of an elephant. They indulge in
afflictive emotions, ignorance, and erroneous spiritual paths. This is
not all, however, for some individuals are inclined toward liberation but
have little merit and so are in danger of encountering such people, who
give the following kind of instruction to all who meet them: "Whatever

arises is the nature of dharmakaya. Concepts are in themselves naturally occurring timeless awareness"; or "Even while there is meditative absorption, there can be conceptual mind that fails to recognize awareness." In such ways they specifically teach fabrications that deceive beings, yet they are seen as people who expound profound spiritual teachings not found anywhere else. They are indeed nothing more than thieves who nowadays pervert the teachings of the ati approach.

In fact, what stirs from naturally occurring timeless awareness is the dynamic energy of responsiveness. Consciousness experiencing sense objects is explained to be the display arising due to that dynamic energy, but it is not naturally occurring timeless awareness, because the two are distinguished on the basis of whether or not sense objects are involved; because if skillful means are not applied, consciousness creates the karma and afflictive emotions that ensnare one in conditioned existence; and because the nature of conceptualization and analysis does not transcend what is inherent in samsara. As *The All-Creating Monarch* states:

> "Naturally occurring timeless awareness" is awareness that is
>   always so.
> As for "timeless awareness that cognizes sense objects,"
> it is not naturally occurring, in the sense that it depends on
>   those objects.

This is stated even in more ordinary spiritual approaches. *The Two Truths* explains:

> Ordinary mind and mental events are thought processes
> whose expression is the projection of the three realms. [51a]

And Dignaga explains:

> Conceptualization is the ultimate nonrecognition of awareness.
> It causes one to fall into the ocean of samsara.

Those wrongheaded people are extremely arrogant, for they plainly contradict these explanations. One should not even listen to opinions like theirs, let alone actively follow them.

If, at this point, you wonder what naturally occurring timeless awareness is, it can be explained precisely:

> In this discussion of mine, primordially pure awakened mind
> is ultimate truth—the true nature of phenomena as basic space.
> Beyond description or imagination, it is the perfection of
>   sublime knowing.
> Inherently unwavering, it is utterly lucid by nature
> and timelessly free of elaboration—of concepts stirring and
>   proliferating—
> and so is called "the essence of being," analogous to the orb
>   of the sun.
> Its dynamic energy is unobstructed awareness as a continuous
>   mode for what arises
> and is free of both conceptualization and analysis.
> Though vividly lucid, it does not entail dualistic perception.

Naturally occurring timeless awareness is awareness that is empty yet lucid and free of elaboration, comparable to a pure crystal globe, occurring such that in essence it does not investigate sense objects. Given that this is so, it abides in its aspect as the ground for the arising of things. However, in its very essence, whether anything arises or not is irrelevant; it is obvious in that it is naturally lucid, unobstructed in that it is empty, and immaculate in that it is originally pure.

The aspect of myriad things arising within awareness's scope is the elaboration of dualistic perception. The very essence of what arises, in all its pristine nakedness, is the aspect of awareness that abides as timeless awareness; since there is no thinking about sense objects, there is said to be "naturally occurring timeless awareness." In this regard, all those for whom direct introduction has not taken effect instead identify the view as just going along with whatever arises in all its immediacy. [51b] They do not understand the key point that "conceptualization is compounded confusion."

Even as things arise, pristinely naked awareness—in which there is no context either for the arising or for what arises—is identified as that which abides as timeless awareness, the continuous mode by which responsiveness arises. It is also identified by implication as the fundamental state that abides, in all its nakedness, in its own place as naturally occurring timeless awareness. And since there is no dichotomy between awareness's essence and its natural dynamic energy, it is nondual, naturally occurring timeless awareness, free of elaboration, referred to as "the unique sphere of being." *Naturally Arising Awareness* states:

Within awareness free of elaboration,[22]
how could there be confusion or nonrecognition of awareness?
Within timeless awareness free of ordinary mind,
how could there be habitual patterns or distortions?

And *The Reverberation of Sound* states:

It is characterized as empty yet lucid awareness,
its nature unadulterated by anything whatsoever.
The extremes of dualistic perception are resolved,
and the true nature of phenomena is pure in its very essence.

And *The Perfect Dynamic Energy of the Lion* states:

In essence, timeless awareness's own manifestations
do not entail the ordinary mind's conceptual process.
Sense objects in the past and sense objects in the future—
sensory appearances are directly cut through.

And *The Six Expanses* states:

Within mind itself, a state of supreme equalness,[23]
emanations of this supreme pervasive state manifest,[24]
and so I, Samantabhadra, have revealed
its "timeless connection to sensory appearances in nonduality."

Within mind itself, which is beyond characterization,
phenomena manifest in great number.
I, Samantabhadra, have revealed this to be
"nondual natural freedom."

Within mind itself, which is inexpressible,
words manifest yet have no basis. [52a]
I, Samantabhadra, have revealed this to be
"beyond the scope of expression or imagination."

Within mind itself, which cannot be sought,
the supreme, naturally occurring state is awareness's
        own manifestation.
I, Samantabhadra, have revealed this to be
"supreme, naturally occurring timeless awareness."

Within mind itself, which is undistorted,
sensory appearances are free of being conditioned sense objects.
I, Samantabhadra, have revealed this to be
"the enlightened intent of supreme natural purity."

Within mind itself, which is nonconceptual,
since what manifests[25] naturally and continuously does so
    without being reified,
I, Samantabhadra, have revealed this to be
"the essence of sense objects as[26] lucid, self-knowing awareness."

Within mind itself, which entails no deliberation,
the spontaneous vastness of natural abiding manifests.
I, Samantabhadra, have revealed this to be
"the enlightened intent of the natural resolution
    of the four sounds."[27]

Within[28] mind itself, which entails no focusing of attention,
what would ordinarily cause mind to stir manifests instead
    as naturally pure.
I, Samantabhadra, have revealed this to be
"meditative stability as the natural freedom underlying reification."

Within mind itself, free of ordinary mental processes,
this manifestation of profound insight entails no deliberation.
I, Samantabhadra, have revealed this to be
"the enlightened intent of the resolution of coming and going."

Within mind itself, which does not involve the reification
    of objects,
pure perceptions manifest continuously.[29]
I, Samantabhadra, have revealed this to be
"meditative absorption as the supreme display."

Within mind itself, which cannot be reified as a subjective agent,
a supreme state of natural arising manifests.
I, Samantabhadra, have revealed this to be
"unceasing, nonconceptual enlightened intent."

Within mind itself, which is without affliction,[30]
sensory appearances manifest free of any concept of their
    having identity. [52b]
I, Samantabhadra, have revealed this to be
"the enlightened intent of the supreme state of resting naturally."

Within mind itself, which cannot be affirmed or denied,
sensory appearances manifest, free of[31] being good or bad.
I, Samantabhadra, have revealed this to be
"enlightened intent free of reactions."

Within mind itself, which entails no acceptance or rejection,
natural freedom manifests without bias.
I, Samantabhadra, have revealed this to be
"supremely pervasive enlightened intent."

Within mind itself, which is without dullness or agitation,
awareness[32] is a supreme state of equanimity.
I, Samantabhadra, have revealed this to be
"the enlightened intent of the repose of the six avenues
     of consciousness."

Within mind itself, which is free of anxiety,
the state beyond hope and fear manifests.
I, Samantabhadra, have revealed this to be
"the enlightened intent of the timeless state of rest imbued
     with indwelling confidence."

Within mind itself, which has no manifest aspect,
an extremely subtle, unique state manifests.
I, Samantabhadra, have revealed this to be
"the enlightened intent of the supreme state free of elaboration."

As these quotations indicate, with respect to the very essence of timeless awareness, free of elaboration, as things arise due to its dynamic
energy it is possible to identify awareness in all its pristine nakedness,
without the reifying effect of concepts—without investigating anything
outwardly, examining anything inwardly, or deliberately settling in between these alternatives. This awareness is realized to be nothing other
than that very essence, free of elaboration, experienced in all its nakedness. Thus, it is nondual, naturally occurring timeless awareness.

To feel, because of references like the foregoing to "the essence" and
"its dynamic energy," that there are two states—consciousness as it
abides and as it arises—and so to say, "One rests in the essence without
concepts and holds to the experience of dynamic energy being free upon
arising," is to have one's practice go off in two directions. [53a] This is
an indication that the key point has not been grasped and that direct introduction has not taken effect. And so, in the present case, even though
the very essence and its dynamic energy are described separately, the
manifestation of sense objects in light of that very essence is analogous
to the arising of reflections in a mirror. Because there is nothing other
than naked awareness itself, which is identical in essence with its mani-

festations, while one continues to experience the arising one abides naturally in the ground of that very essence in all its nakedness. Although one continues to experience what is, in effect, a state of abiding, the radiance of awareness, which is a continuous mode of arising, is naturally evident.

These two aspects—naked awareness as whatever arises (analogous to a reflection) and the naturally occurring timeless awareness that is consciousness in its natural place of rest (analogous to the surface of a mirror)—are not separate or distinct from one another, but constitute the essence in which phenomena resolve (that is, the very essence of being, originally pure, pristinely naked, and free of elaboration). This can be described by the term "naturally occurring timeless awareness." No matter what term is applied—"utterly lucid timeless awareness," "ultimate truth," "timelessly free dharmakaya," "awareness as awakened mind," and so forth—you should recognize this essence as the state of natural lucidity, naked and originally pure.

Given that the real crux of what is discussed in the great perfection approach is that way of abiding, it is variously termed "trekchö," "nakedness," "unobstructedness," "timeless freedom," "original purity," or "spontaneous presence." But the ultimate meaning of all these various terms is this very state in all its nakedness—nothing but the unique sphere of being—and so I have explained this key point very clearly. The consummate enlightened intent of the "heart drop" approach being the sole point, [53b] this intent is termed "the spiritual teaching that awakens those of the very highest acumen to buddhahood without meditation," for when this key point is realized, it involves no striving or effort. There is nothing whatsoever, such as something to meditate on or some process of meditation, something to maintain or some process of maintaining. This is the ultimate point—naturally occurring timeless awareness itself, free of elaboration—because it is superior to all viewpoints and meditations that are not free of dualistic perception but rather cause the mind to dwell inwardly and one-pointedly, and deliberately refine the dynamic energy of mind as it proliferates outwardly. *The Great Garuda* states:

> Since all phenomena are unsullied and free of elaboration,
>   this key point—that they are not created and are free in their
>   natural state—is utterly supreme.

And similarly *The Single Time* states:

> Given that the nature of myriad things is not dualistic,
> even with their diversity things are free of elaboration.
> Given that there is no concept of "what simply is,"
> there is total illumination that is wholly positive.
> Since this is already so, the disease of effort has been abandoned.
> Since it abides spontaneously, there is rest.

And *The All-Creating Monarch* states:

> However things appear, they are identical in suchness.
> Let no one meddle with this!
> The nonconceptual intent of dharmakaya abides
> in the majestic state of uncontrived equalness.

In addition, a specific distinction can be made between the dynamic energy of responsiveness and dualistic concepts:

> Awareness expresses itself through its dynamic energy as
>   consciousness that involves conceptual elaboration,
> marked by the myriad dualistic habitual patterns that such
>   consciousness generates.
> Since what are not objects are misconstrued as objects,
>   there are the five kinds of sense objects,
> and since what has no identity is invested with identity,
>   there are the five afflictive emotions.
> These constitute all possible confused perception—
>   of the universe and the beings within it.
> Even what manifests as samsara arises due to that
>   dynamic energy, [54a]
> but when this is not realized, the manifestation itself is
>   one of erroneous perception.

Awareness, the unobstructed essence of responsiveness, is naturally lucid in all its nakedness, analogous to a polished mirror. From this, the ground for all that arises, emerges the bare dynamic energy of responsiveness. But because of a failure to realize this, thoughts arise, have arisen, and will continue to arise in response to sense objects, due to that dynamic energy. Given that these two states both exhibit very subtle qualities of lucidity and continuity, they are mistaken as one and the same, leading some to claim that, as awareness arises, there is timeless awareness if one does not reify what arises, but ordinary thinking if one does. They either just go along with or look at what arises. These are the "haughty elephants" preoccupied with emptiness without truly glimpsing it even partially.

At this point I shall distinguish between these two states. When sense objects manifest in light of awareness, like reflections in a mirror, the knowing quality in all its pristine nakedness, which does not proliferate as ordinary thinking, is called "dynamic energy as the ground for the arising of responsiveness." When that knowing quality is not recognized, its outward proliferation in response to sense objects is called "ordinary thinking based on dualistic perception." Due to the habit of reifying things as objects, the confused perception of outer sense objects grows stronger and things arise in all their variety. Due to the inner reification of mind, dynamic energy arises as the five emotional poisons. Due to karma and afflictive emotions, samsara—the state of confused perception—comes about for each individual.

Thus, while there is a difference between awareness that is naturally lucid and does not waver from its place of rest and awareness that becomes "lost" in response to sense objects, a major point of potential error lies in their basic similarity. *The Perfect Dynamic Energy of the Lion* states:

> Awareness's own manifestations are the most majestic
>   skillful means,
> and due to the powerful unceasing awareness that
>   underlies them,
> they are intimately bound up with one's own sublime
>   knowing. [54b]
> Meditative absorption that entails no frame of reference
> is intimately bound up with the state free of concerted effort.
> Beginningless mind, which is evident in its sense objects,
> is intimately bound up with totally pure basic space.
> This is revealed to be the ultimate meaning of enlightened intent.
> Because of their basic similarity, there is a great potential for
>   error
> in not distinguishing between the ground of all ordinary
>   experience (the source of ordinary mind)
> and self-knowing awareness (the source of sense objects).

Because of their basic similarity, there is a great potential for
    error
in not distinguishing between the nonrecognition of awareness
    (which manifests as ordinary mind)
and awareness (which manifests nonconceptually).

And *The Six Expanses* states:

Self-knowing awareness free of deliberation
and the myriad display of sensations arising in the ordinary mind—
they are similar, they resemble one another, but it would be
    a mistake to take one for the other.

Sublime knowing as the perfection of natural dynamic energy
and the attention of the conceptual mind lost outwardly—
they are similar, they resemble one another, but it would be
    a mistake to take one for the other.

This key point is extremely important! To discern this difference is
the province of only a few who are endowed with the eye of intelligence.
If you rely on those who do not understand it or who incline to a mistaken interpretation, even though I have already delineated it clearly,
what the glorious Saraha said is certainly relevant:

What is to be done about animals, who do not understand the world?

Now, the key point concerning yogins with realization is that they
are not affected by what manifests as the stirring and proliferation of
thoughts or by the manifesting of sense objects in their perceptions, for
these are merely the play of illusion:

Through realization, within the vast expanse of being,
    of the true nature of phenomena—
coming from nowhere, going nowhere, and abiding nowhere
    at all—
there is "the enlightened intent of the total freedom of
    the three realms."
This is the transmission of ati—spontaneous presence,
    the vajra heart essence,
arising from the wholly positive expanse of supreme
    spaciousness. [55a]

Yogins who have realized the ultimate meaning of this great perfection in all its nakedness experience awareness, pure and simple, in all its nakedness. And so, while sense objects manifest in light of awareness, that awareness is not lost outwardly in response to those objects. Thus, dualistic perception, the root of samsara, is rendered null and void. As an indication that awareness, pure and simple, pristine in all its nakedness, is not lost in response to sense objects, there are no attachments to or fixations on sensory appearances, or attempts to suppress or indulge in them. Since samsara is free as nirvana, we refer to "dharmakaya arising unobstructedly." *The Heaped Jewels* states:

> In emptiness, the resultant state of dharmakaya,
> substantiality is resolved—how very marvelous!
> In unobstructed timeless awareness that entails no substance,
> there is no reification—how very marvelous!

At this point, since the universe of appearances and possibilities is free of restriction, whatever manifests is free within the realization of this. This is called "the enlightened intent of the total freedom of the three realms." The realization that samsara has never known existence is called "the enlightened intent of the original purity of the three planes of conditioned existence." And the realization that all sensory appearances and imputations are insubstantial in that they lack true existence is called "the view that cuts through the momentum of the wheel of life." The same tantra contains the following passage, which you can examine closely and so come to understand:

> As for the tangible universe,
> on examination it is found to have no independent nature.
> What is ever-present as the view that cuts through
> the momentum of the wheel of life is not perceived.
> Are the avenues of the senses blocked?

It can be shown that the essence of awareness is like space, beyond being some object:

> **Within the essence of totally pure awakened mind, [55b]**
> **there is no object to view or anything that constitutes a view—**
> **not the slightest sense of anything to look at or anyone looking.**
> **There is no ordinary consciousness meditating or anything**
> **   to meditate on.**

**Due to spontaneous presence, without any duality of goal
and conduct,
there is not the slightest sense of any fruition to achieve.**

If you try to impose the schema of view, meditation, conduct, and fruition on awareness, that very awareness has no finite essence even as you make the attempt, and so nothing need be done about any of these; they are in direct contradiction to awareness. Thus, there is nothing to plan or to do, even for an instant. As well, given that self-knowing awareness—that is, dharmakaya—is already the case, view, meditation, conduct, and fruition have no ultimate meaning. Through a threefold line of reasoning to that effect, awareness can be shown to transcend view, meditation, conduct, and fruition. *The Perfect Dynamic Energy of the Lion* states:

> Given that awareness is spontaneously present and not cultivated
>   in meditation,[33]
> one will not find me by engaging in meditation.
> Given that it occurs naturally and is timelessly uncontrived,
> one will not perceive[34] me by engaging in conduct.
> Given that dharmakaya is timelessly free of limitation,[35]
> one will not see me by looking with some view.

And *The Six Expanses* states:

> I, Samantabhadra, have no view.
> Since I have no view, ordinary perception has come to an end.
> Likewise, I have no meditation.
> Since I have no meditation, deliberate attention has ceased.
> There is nothing that can be described as "conduct."
> Since there is no conduct, the body's elements resolve.

And *Naturally Arising Awareness* states:

> In atiyoga, great perfection,
> there is no view, meditation, or conduct.
> I have revealed this thoroughly, so keep it in mind.[36]
> With nothing needing to be done—nothing to achieve,
>   no concerted effort or speculation—
> the ultimate meaning of suchness itself has always been
>   spontaneous perfection.
> How could there be anything to do or any doing? [56a]

The true nature of phenomena, naturally occurring and entailing
    no conduct,
does not fall into any extreme whatsoever—it is[37] like space.
Not existent, it is the oneness of emptiness.
Not nonexistent, it is the kaya of authentic bliss.
Not created, it is a naturally occurring, nonconceptual state.

In atiyoga, great perfection,
how could the true nature of phenomena be cultivated
    in meditation?
That which cannot be discarded or adopted
is free of the extremes of meditation and a lack thereof.
Without reification, how could there be the distortions
    of ordinary mind?[38]
Authentic awareness is undistorted.
In undistorted, pure dharmakaya,
there is neither meditation nor anything to meditate on.
What is authentic cannot be found by meditating.
If it were to be found, self-knowing awareness would be negated.
Why is this so? Because, within self-knowing awareness—
    timeless awareness—
it is irrelevant whether there is distraction or not.
Reification, wherever it occurs,
is not naturally occurring timeless awareness.
Suppose that naturally occurring timeless awareness
were subject to meditation.
This would contradict what is posited to be timeless
    awareness.[39]
Therefore, in ati, great perfection,
it is explained that the ultimate meaning is not perceived
    through meditation.

In atiyoga, great perfection,
the view itself is such that there is nothing to be seen.
To hold any point of view is a distortion of ordinary mind.
The true nature of phenomena, undistorted and pure,[40]
is free of the duality of anything to be seen and holding any point
    of view.
The view itself is such that there is nothing to be seen.
Why is this? To hold to a point of view
would then negate the lamp of awareness.

Therefore, in ati, great perfection,
the true nature of phenomena is not reified through view.

In atiyoga, great perfection,
it is said that there is no fruition to achieve.
The fruition is not created,[41] but occurs naturally. [56b]
One arrives at suchness in the nonconceptual state.[42]
Within the supremely pure perspective of timeless awareness,
the natural radiance[43] of awareness entails no reification
    and is lucid.
Therefore, the existence of a fruition
would be a negation of buddhahood.
Because the fruition occurs naturally and without effort,
for its true nature to be that of something created—
in whatever way it was created—
would mean that its nature was subject to destruction.
Therefore, there is no fruition to achieve.

Similarly, you should understand that there are no levels of realization
on which to train or other such factors:

> Regarding what is nonexistent, there are no levels of realization
>   to traverse,
> and so there are never any paths to journey along.
> Since utter lucidity is already ensured as the supreme sphere
>   of being,
> there are no mandalas to visualize through the proliferation
>   and resolution of thoughts
> and no mantras, recitations, empowerments, or samaya.
> There is no nonreferential stage of completion, such as
>   a gradual process of dissolution.
> In the kayas and timeless awareness, which are already
>   ensured timelessly,
> there is no causality based on compounded adventitious
>   circumstances.
> If any of these were the case, timeless awareness would not
>   occur naturally.
> Being compounded, such awareness would be subject
>   to destruction,
> and then how could it be characterized as "spontaneously
>   present and uncompounded"?

Because awareness has no finite essence, and because suchness and deliberate activity are mutually exclusive, and because awareness is already timelessly and spontaneously present, nothing need be done concerning levels of realization on which to train, spiritual paths to traverse, mandalas to visualize, empowerments to be bestowed, paths to cultivate in meditation, samaya to uphold, enlightened activities to accomplish, and so forth. This is because there is no need to accomplish anew [57a] what is already timelessly and spontaneously accomplished. If there were such a need, it would be inappropriate to use the conventional designation "spontaneously present and uncompounded." And it would follow that dharmakaya was subject to destruction, because it would be compounded, and this because it would be created by causes and conditions. *The Perfect Dynamic Energy of the Lion* states:

> Given that one is never beyond the ultimate meaning of what
>   is unborn,
> one does not awaken to buddhahood by upholding samaya.
> Given that mandalas abide timelessly and naturally,
> one does not behold deities by drawing mandalas.
> Given that the mudra that seals one's practice is timelessly perfect,
>   not brought about by transformation,
> using mudras in an effortful way only dissipates spiritual
>   attainment.
> Given that the heart essence is timelessly and naturally lucid,[44]
> one's potential is spoiled by the recitation of essence mantras.
> Given that the immeasurable mansion is timelessly and
>   naturally perfect,
> natural manifestation is undermined by the visualization
>   of immeasurable mansions.
> Given that rays of responsiveness arise naturally,
> the benefit for oneself dissipates with meditation on
>   the deity's characteristics.
> Given what is spontaneously perfect, without being
>   deliberately developed,
> there is no need for the stage of development or that of inviting
>   the deity.
> Deities are not delighted with offerings and praises[45] that
>   involve effort.
> Given that dharmakaya does not entail reification and is
>   unobstructed,

what has ultimate meaning is not found through meditation
  on the characteristics of things.

And *The All-Creating Monarch* states:

I have revealed that there is no view to cultivate in meditation.
I have revealed that there is no samaya to uphold.
I have revealed that there is no enlightened activity
  involving effort.[46]
I have revealed that there are no paths to traverse.
I have revealed that there are no levels of realization
  to determine.[47]
Timeless awareness does not entail concepts and involves
  no specific conduct.[48]
The true nature of phenomena, just as it is, cannot be
  contrived. [57b]

Now, the meaning of the preceding points can be summarized as the
transcendence of cause and effect, effort and achievement:

Therefore, within the essence of ultimate basic space,
causality is transcended and the ten attributes do not pertain.
Mind itself, the ultimate meaning of genuine being, involves no
  effort or achievement.
Please understand this in order to pacify all conceptual
  elaborations of existence and nonexistence!

Because your fundamentally unconditioned nature—naturally oc-
cur-ring timeless awareness—has never existed as anything whatsoever,
the process of cause and effect, effort and achievement, involved in the
ten attributes can do nothing to improve it, and the phenomena of samsara can do nothing to detract from it. Those of the very highest acumen
will understand the essence—like[49] space, free of the elaborations of
existence and nonexistence—that abides as the unique sphere of being.
The All-Creating Monarch states:

Countless eons ago,
those who had faith in me, all-creating enlightenment—
those yogins with suitable karma and good fortune—
had no view to cultivate in meditation, no samaya to uphold,
no activity involving effort,[50] no paths to traverse,

no levels of realization on which to train, no causal framework,
no twofold division into ultimate and relative,
nothing to cultivate in meditation or to achieve,
no motivation to arouse, and no antidotes.
So that they might perceive the nature of all-creating mind,
I revealed it for just this purpose.

And *Naturally Arising Awareness* states:

Everything is perfect in my enlightened form.
Everything displays itself in my enlightened speech.
Everything is realized in my enlightened mind.
My enlightened qualities manifest as anything at all.
My enlightened activity is found without being sought. [58a]
My view is the kaya of the sphere of being.
My meditation is free of ordinary consciousness.
My conduct is beyond any finite scope.
My fruition is the state of oneness.
My samaya is nothing to be upheld.[51]
My empowerment is neither bestowed nor received.[52]
I am the supreme charnel ground,
the tomb of all buddhas and ordinary beings.
From my supreme blessings
come all buddhas of the three times.

This is the commentary on the fifth section of *The Precious Treasury of the Basic Space of Phenomena*, demonstrating the transcendence of effort and achievement, cause and effect.

6

All-Inclusive Awakened Mind

In showing that all phenomena are thus subsumed within awareness, pure in its very essence, it can be demonstrated initially that all things, alike in suchness—their true nature—are subsumed within the context of being unborn:

> Just as all light is subsumed within the sun as its source,
> all phenomena are subsumed within awakened mind as
>   their source—
> even the impurity and confusion in the universe of appearances
>   and possibilities.
> Whatever occurs, by examining basic space as its matrix
>   and abode
> you find that it has no foundation, but is subsumed within
>   the timeless freedom of mind.
> Beyond labels and their meanings, confusion and its absence
>   are subsumed
> within the true nature of phenomena—the timeless expanse,
>   a supremely spacious state.

Just as rays of sunlight are subsumed within the orb of the sun, all phenomena of the universe of appearances and possibilities are subsumed within their source, awakened mind. Suppose we then investigate this, examining the place from which samsara and nirvana (whose very essence is that of a dream) come, the place in which they abide, and the place to which they go. Since samsara and nirvana have never existed, they have never existed in any mode of coming, abiding, or going;

[58b] or, conversely, since none of these three modes has ever existed, samsara and nirvana have never existed. And so, given that even what is termed "awakened mind as the supportive ground" or "awakened mind as basic space" has never existed as something with an identifiable essence, all things are none other than their true nature, which is like space; this is conventionally referred to as "things being subsumed within the true nature of phenomena." But it should be understood that subsuming and what is subsumed are without foundation or support. *The All-Creating Monarch* states:

> I am explained as being the heart essence, since I subsume
>   all phenomena, however they manifest.
> I am the seed, since I give rise to all phenomena, however
>   they manifest.
> I am also the cause, since from me come all phenomena,
>   however they manifest.
> I am the trunk, since from me come the branches of all
>   phenomena, however they manifest.
> I am the ground, since within my scope all phenomena abide,
>   however they manifest.
> I am explained as being the root, since all phenomena, however
>   they manifest, are in fact me.
> . . . .
> This is the ultimate distillation of enlightened intent:
> given the nature of the all-creating monarch,
> it can be shown that all things are unborn,
> just as, given that all phenomena[1] are unborn,
> it can be shown that they are subsumed within their
>   unborn nature.

And *Naturally Arising Awareness* states:

> All phenomena, by nature free of any objective frame
>   of reference,
> are subsumed within the basic space of timeless awareness,
> which is not the ordinary seeking mind.[2]

It can be shown that objects of the phenomenal world, however they manifest, are subsumed within the scope of awareness, just as dreams are subsumed within the scope of sleep:

Even the marvelous display of awareness's own pure
    manifestations—
the kayas, pure realms, timeless awareness, and enlightened
    activities— [59a]
is subsumed within the naturally occurring state that is not
    made or unmade.
Awakened mind subsumes the universe of appearances and
    possibilities, all of samsara and nirvana.
Lucid and uncompounded, it can be compared to the sun
    shining in the empty sky.
Occurring primordially and naturally, it is a spacious,
    timeless expanse.

Because everything—a buddha's pure perceptions and an ordinary being's impure perceptions based on confusion—is subsumed within the scope of each one's awareness, there is no phenomenon that is not subsumed within awareness, that is, within awakened mind. That awareness can be compared to the sun in that it is spontaneously present and utterly lucid by its very nature, and to the sky in that it is empty and without identity. It is termed "naturally occurring timeless awareness," "primordial dharmakaya," or "buddhahood, just as it is." *The All-Creating Monarch* states:

The true nature of phenomena that transcends everything
    is awakened mind.
Awakened mind is the very heart of all phenomena.
Awakened mind is the very source of all phenomena.
Being the very source, it also subsumes all that has
    ultimate meaning.

. . . .

I am the true nature of all phenomena.
There is nothing other than my nature.
The teachers—the three kayas—are my nature.
Buddhas throughout the three times are my nature.
Bodhisattvas are my nature.
The four levels of yoga are my nature.
Even the three realms—of desire, form, and formlessness—
are shown to be the nature of me, the all-creating one.
The five elements are also my nature.
Beings in the six realms are my nature.

All sensory appearances are my nature. [59b]
All of conditioned existence is my nature.
The entire universe[3] is my nature.
Since there is nothing other than my nature,
the source of all phenomena is subsumed within me.

The vast expanse of being can be shown to be the nature of mind:

Mind itself is an unchanging, vast expanse, the realm of space.
Its display, the dynamic energy of awakened mind, is
   indeterminate.
In that it entails mastery over samsara, nirvana, and all
   spiritual approaches,
this unique state, in which nothing need be done, outshines
   everything else.
There is no context anywhere that constitutes an extreme.
There is no straying at all from the true nature of phenomena,
   awakened mind.

In being the matrix and basic space of the entire universe of appearances and possibilities, the expanse of space entails mastery in that it provides an open avenue for everything. Similarly, the true nature of phenomena—awakened mind—also entails mastery in that it is the ultimate womb, or basic space, of all samsara and nirvana. Everything is such that it does not stray at all from this infinite expanse, which precedes everything and abides timelessly as the expanse of the spacious nature of phenomena. *Naturally Arising Awareness* states:

Before there was space,
there were never any characteristics of space.
Before there was the true nature of phenomena,
there were not even names for characteristics of objects
   in the phenomenal world.
Before there was buddhahood,
there was never anything to characterize an ordinary being.
Before there was nirvana,
there was never anything that could be called[4] "samsara."
Therefore, I am the most holy one,
foremost and most venerable[5] among all buddhas.
I myself am greater than the five elements.

Indeed, I came about before the elements. [60a]
Furthermore, I awakened to buddhahood before the buddhas.
I am the kaya of authentic bliss.
Everything is perfect within my realm.[6]

And *The All-Creating Monarch* states:

The heart essence—the spacious, spontaneously present nature
    of phenomena—
has not wavered, does not waver, and will not waver.
The expanse that is the true nature of phenomena,
subsuming the entire universe of appearances and possibilities,
is spontaneously present, free of all plans and actions.

A fitting metaphor can be found for the fact that, in subsuming everything, awareness does not waver:

Given that everything is wholly positive, arising as a single
    state of spontaneous presence,
that which is sublime and without rival—
the greatest of the great, within which everything without
    exception is subsumed—
is the wholly positive basic space of phenomena.
Since everything is united within it as though under a monarch,
it entails mastery over all samsara and nirvana and does not
    waver at all.

Just as all the subjects in a realm are under the dominion of a monarch
who does not leave his or her own palace, so all samsara and nirvana is
subsumed within the scope of awareness, which does not stray from the
true nature of phenomena. *The Universal Theme of Perfection* states:

All phenomena without exception are subsumed
within the vast expanse of awakened mind, equal to space.
It is like a monarch,
unwavering and with mastery over all.
It is the expanse of equalness.
Naturally occurring timeless awareness is forever without
    transition or change.

Although everything is created by awakened mind and arises from
mind, it can be shown that mind itself is not created by anyone or any-

thing and in fact need not be, for it is beyond all plans and actions. *The All-Creating Monarch* states:

> Awakened mind, which creates everything, is unique in not being
> created. [60b]
> All-creative—naturally creative through enlightenment itself—
> what is unique in not being created need not be created.

It can be shown that all phenomena, being equal by nature, are neither good nor bad and entail no effort or achievement:

> **Since everything is wholly positive, with not a single thing that
> is not positive,**
> **all things are identical within the wholly positive state, in
> which there is neither good nor bad.**
> **Since everything—whatever is or is not the case—is of the same
> basic space,**
> **all things are identical within the unwavering, spontaneously
> present state of equalness.**

Given that all phenomena are a display of what by nature are equal expressions of emptiness, they are identical in being neither good nor bad and entailing no effort or achievement. Given that they are equally empty, without basis and pure like space, they are identical in being neither good nor bad and entailing no acceptance or rejection. And given that they are equal within the scope of naturally occurring time-less awareness, they are identical in being neither good nor bad and not being subject to any extreme or division. *The Supreme "Mother"* states:

> Since all phenomena are equal,
> the perfection of sublime knowing is a state of equalness.

And *The All-Creating Monarch* states:

> The characteristic of all phenomena is that of space;
> the characteristic of space is that of suchness itself.
> The characteristic of the three kayas is that of abiding
> in suchness.
> Everything abides in suchness itself.
> However they appear, all phenomena[7] are just as they are;
> they cannot be contrived.

They are neither good nor bad and entail no acceptance
  or rejection.

It can be shown that due to the very fact that things arise from basic
space, they are beyond effort and achievement:

> The single state from which everything without exception
>   arises is the basic space of phenomena.
> There is nothing to achieve or to seek[8] within the context
>   in which nothing need be done. [61a]
> Since effort and achievement are not other than their natural
>   state of basic space,
> whence could effort come? To what achievement could it lead?

Although the effort and achievement in dreams seem so exhausting,
they are pointless, for you do not move from the single place in which
you sleep and nothing at all that you seem to have done is actually done
or finished. The effort and achievement in which you are engaged at
present—trying to apply antidotes in order to abandon certain things—
are just like that. Given that there is nothing other than simply the scope
of awareness, nothing in the least is ever done or finished, for there is
no straying from what is simply the scope of awareness itself. To invest
what is clearly apparent yet nonexistent with some ultimate meaning is
nothing but confusion, like the scope of Dawa Gyaltsen's mind;[9] this
does not bring you one bit closer to your true nature.

Therefore, nothing need be done by way of effort or achievement
concerning mind itself, which is like space, because it cannot be altered
by causes or effects. Since naturally occurring timeless awareness abides
as the ground of everything, all phenomena arise from it, although it itself is beyond the extremes of positive and negative. *The Reverberation
of Sound* states:

> If such a mode as this—the way in which things abide and
>   are present—
> were explained to shravakas and pratyekabuddhas,
> they would be completely terrified and would faint.
> Therefore, it should be kept most secret.
> Since phenomena, which cannot be labeled,[10]
> have no place of origin, it is called "the ground."

Since it has no location, it does not abide in any finite way at all,
as either substance or emptiness.
It cannot possibly come from either illumination or darkness,
because there is no possibility of any extreme, no coming
    or going.
Since there is no bondage due to striving and effort,
it simply is what it is, without deviation. [61b]
Because it is neither restricted nor localized,
and because both virtue and harm are removed,
it has never existed as anything, whether positive or negative.
Because the empty nature of phenomena is all-pervasive—
since it does not abide in samsara or nirvana—
it abides as the very essence of timeless awareness,
inseparable from it in three ways.

And *The Perfect Dynamic Energy of the Lion* states:

Since self-knowing awareness is timelessly unchanging,
I am not obscured by either virtue or harm.
Given that this awareness occurs naturally,[11] without causes
    or conditions,
there is no need for structured spiritual practice.

For these reasons, cause and effect, effort and achievement, are transcended:

**Since there is no object to seek, nothing to perceive in
    meditation,
no state to achieve, nothing that comes from anywhere else,
and no coming or going, there is equalness—dharmakaya.
This spontaneous perfection is found within the basic space of
    the supreme sphere of being.**

Mind itself, the essence of which is like space, is the unique sphere,
basic space. Given that all phenomena are subsumed within its scope,
there is nothing to seek through factors like the ten attributes, for the
basic space of phenomena is free of limitation. *The All-Creating Monarch* states:

The heart essence of everything—this awakened mind,
timelessly and spontaneously present by its nature—
need not be sought[12] or achieved through the ten attributes.

My nature is like space, the universal metaphor.
In[13] pure space, all is such that it entails no effort.[14]
While everyone seeks something in pure space,
space is entirely beyond all effort and achievement.[15] [62a]
So too is the all-creating heart essence, awakened mind.
Because I transcend the entire range of finite experience,
in me there is no point of view to hold or anything ever
    to cultivate in meditation.
Likewise, the nature of the ten attributes is such that
concerning me, the transcendent one, nothing need be done.
Those who follow spiritual approaches based on either causes
    or results
seek me through the ten attributes,
wishing to behold me and my nature.
As though stepping out into space and falling to earth,
they will fail in their attempts to progress by using these
    ten attributes.
My nature shows itself to be authentic.
Because I transcend the entire range of finite experience,
there is no view to cultivate in meditation.
Similarly, the ten attributes do not ultimately exist,
so do not think that they do.
Since I am not an object to be seen by looking,
do not try to look—rest in suchness itself.

Now, it can be shown that all spiritual approaches are subsumed within
awareness—that is, awakened mind. First, there is the way in which the
three lower approaches are subsumed:

> The transmissions of shravakas, pratyekabuddhas, and
>   bodhisattvas
> are decisive concerning the nonexistence of both the self
>   and what pertains to it,
> and so they are identical in their intent, a spacelike state free
>   of elaboration.
> The transmission of supreme yoga—the sublime secret of ati—
> is that of resting in genuine being, just as it is—naturally
>   occurring timeless awareness—
> within the spacious state in which there is no distinction
>   between self and other.

> So the ultimate meaning of the enlightened perspectives of all
>   three lower approaches
> is subsumed within this sublime heart essence.

In the view of shravakas, all external and internal phenomena [62b]
are like space, in which no personal identity exists. In that of pratyekabuddhas, this view is extended to a partial realization of the nonexistence of phenomena that are reified as objects. In that of bodhisattvas,
the nature of both the individual personality and phenomena—that is,
of what are reified as a subject and as objects—is that of space in that it
lacks identity. *The Discourse of the Ever-Turning Wheel* states:

> Even though this is not recognized, all phenomena—
> like space—have no characteristics.

Such realization, moreover, is subsumed within the enlightened intent of great perfection, naturally occurring timeless awareness. This
is because this intent embraces the suchness of all phenomena, for they
are subsumed within the spacelike essence itself of naturally occurring
timeless awareness, empty yet lucid. *The All-Creating Monarch* states:

> Everything without exception is subsumed
> within the nature of all-creating awakened mind
> and is free of elaboration, like space.

The three intermediate approaches are also subsumed:

> The three approaches of kriya, upa, and yoga, moreover,
> which employ oneself, deity, meditative absorption, and clouds
>   of offerings,
> are identical in holding that spiritual attainment comes from
>   the complete purification of body, speech, and mind.
> However, according to the secret and most majestic
>   transmission of the vajra pinnacle,
> appearances, sounds, and awareness are completely pure—
>   timelessly the deity.
> Spiritual attainment is fully evident as the complete purity of
>   body, speech, and mind,
> and so the enlightened perspectives of all these approaches are
>   subsumed within this sublime heart essence.

The tradition of kriya tantra (the tantra of action) holds that spiritual attainment comes from thinking of oneself as a servant, and the

deity as a master, while making offerings, praising, and so forth. That of upa tantra (the tantra of conduct) holds that spiritual attainment comes from visualizing the deity as the expression of timeless awareness [63a] in front of oneself as the commitment aspect. And that of yoga tantra (the tantra of union) holds that spiritual attainment comes from dissolving the deity as the expression of timeless awareness into the mandala as the commitment aspect and then making offerings, praising, and so forth.

These approaches are identical in that they purify distortions of body, speech, and mind and ensure spiritual attainment. Their enlightened perspectives are subsumed within the approach in which all phenomena, pure and equal within the scope of buddhahood as the mandala, are understood to be awakened mind. *The All-Creating Monarch* states:

> Within the mandala of the sublime, naturally occurring
>   heart essence,
> if body, speech, and mind rest in a relaxed state, just as they are,
> they are spontaneously present as[16] the enlightened intent of me,
>   the all-creating one.

The three higher approaches are also complete:

> In the three stages of maha, anu, and ati, moreover,
> the universe of appearances and possibilities is a pure realm
>   of masculine and feminine deities.
> These stages hold that the unwavering nature of phenomena
>   is naturally occurring timeless awareness,
> for basic space and timeless awareness are inseparable in their
>   total purity.
> Given that everything is completely pure within this sublime,
>   excellent secret,
> the immeasurable mansion, without being created, is a blissful
>   realm, a timeless expanse.
> Within this infinite and all-pervasive state, which cannot
>   be divided into outer and inner,
> there is nothing to characterize in light of your value judgments.
> With everything timelessly infinite—the spacious expanse
>   of[17] dharmakaya—
> the enlightened perspectives of all these approaches are
>   subsumed within the heart essence of the supreme secret.

In the two approaches of mahayoga tantra (the tantra of the father principle of supreme yoga) and anuyoga tantra (the tantra of the mother principle, that of the yogini), awareness is the ground aspect of the mandala, and the universe—clearly visualized as deities and the immeasurable mansion—is the path aspect of the mandala. [63b] It is held that, since basic space and timeless awareness constitute the unity, beyond union or separation, of skillful means and sublime knowing, through practical implementation of this path one attains the fruition, the mandala of sublime enlightenment.

However, in ati, great perfection, everything is understood always to be the mandala of buddhahood, and so it is held that awareness "arrives" at the ground of being in all its immediacy by not straying from its true nature—that is, from uncontrived, unadulterated enlightened intent that involves no acceptance or rejection. It is the ultimate approach of the supreme secret, because the ultimate heart essence is subsumed within it. *The Perfect Dynamic Energy of the Lion* states:

> However many mandalas of enlightened form there are,
> they are all, without exception, clearly apparent as
>   sensory appearances.
> However many mandalas of enlightened speech there are,
> they are all, without exception, revealed in what is audible.
> However many mandalas of enlightened mind there are,
> they are all, without exception, unsullied by concepts.
> Enlightened form, speech, and vajra mind—
> from what is not manifest, everything manifests.

And *The All-Creating Monarch* states:

> . . . the threefold mandala of resting without contrivance
>   in genuine being,
> not deliberately arranged, but perfect all at once.
> With this realization, one enters into the ultimate meaning
>   of the spontaneously present heart essence.

Now, the point that everything is subsumed and perfect within awakened mind is summarized:

> **Perfection in one, perfection in everything—**
> **the expanse within which all phenomena are subsumed**
> **is itself subsumed within the supreme state of spontaneous presence,**
> **a timeless and naturally lucid state of utter relaxation.**

Everything is the perfection of awakened mind. Furthermore, there is perfection in oneness, in that everything is perfect within the scope of awareness. There is perfection in duality, in that there is perfection in the creations of ordinary mind. And there is perfection in everything, [64a] in that there is perfection in abundance, since anything can and does manifest. *The All-Creating Monarch* states:

> In this there is no lack of perfection at all.
> Since there is perfection in one, perfection in two, perfection
>   in everything,
> there is ease in the abundance of fresh possibilities.
> There is perfection in one—perfection in awakened mind.
> There is perfection in two—perfection in what is created
>   by ordinary mind.
> There is perfection in everything—perfection in abundance.
> According to this transmission concerning the perfection in one,
> the enlightened intent of buddhahood abides herein.
> The significance of perfection in everything
> is that complete abundance is ensured.

A yogin who comes to such a realization is to be praised. *The Perfect Dynamic Energy of the Lion* states:

> If the truth of buddhahood is perceived, one is an heir
>   to victorious ones.
> If realization is mastered thoroughly, there is always bliss.

And *The All-Creating Monarch* continues:

> Although they who dwell in this state, in which nothing need
>   be done,
> may look like ordinary individuals, such as gods and humans,
> their enlightened intent is in accord with the true nature of
>   phenomena—they are buddhas.

This is the commentary on the sixth section of *The Precious Treasury of the Basic Space of Phenomena,* demonstrating that everything is subsumed within awakened mind.

7

Spontaneously Present Awareness

It can be shown that, in being subsumed within awakened mind, all phenomena "are spontaneously present":

> The transmission of awakened mind, spontaneously present
>   by nature,
> is the summit of the most majestic mountain, not created
>   yet ensuring all that has ultimate meaning.
> Exalted above all, it is the supreme and most majestic
>   spiritual approach.

Like the most majestic mountain, which rises to sublime heights in the midst of the four continents, [64b] ati—the spiritual approach of the vajra heart essence—is explained to be the pinnacle, exalted above all other approaches. *Naturally Arising Awareness* states:

> The very pinnacle of all views
> is explained to be ati, great perfection.

There is a metaphor showing it to be the pinnacle of everything:

> Once one has reached the summit of a majestic mountain,
> one can see the valleys below all at once,
> while from the valleys one cannot see what it is like at the
>   summit.
> Similarly, ati, the vajra heart essence,
> is the pinnacle spiritual approach and sees what is meaningful
>   in all others,

> while the lower approaches cannot see its ultimate meaning.
> Therefore, it is the pinnacle,[1] the peak experience, which is
> spontaneously present.

While the valleys below can be seen all at once from the summit of a mountain, the perspective from the summit cannot be seen from the valleys. Likewise, all that is meaningful in lower spiritual approaches can be seen all at once from ati, yet the meaning of this approach cannot be seen by lesser ones, because these lower levels cannot reconcile themselves with the higher one. As is explained in *The Gathering of Secrets:*

> Therefore, this is the pinnacle, the peak experience.

A further explanation can be given regarding the distinction between the higher approach and lower ones and the superiority of the former:

> It is like a great wish-fulfilling gem that, if prayed to,
> ensures all that is wished for as a matter of course.
> Such is not the case for ordinary things.
> Since the vajra heart essence is the spontaneous presence
>   of the three kayas,
> buddhahood is ensured, in and of itself, within the basic space
>   of natural rest.
> It does not require effort or achievement—that is its superiority.
> Although those in lower approaches strive through acceptance
>   and rejection,
> they accomplish nothing for eons—what a great debility!

If one prays to a wish-fulfilling gem, [65a] it ensures all that is wished for. This, however, is only within the domain of those with good fortune. Likewise, it is only within the domain of those of the very highest level to rest at ease and without effort, having realized that enlightened qualities are spontaneously present in naturally occurring timeless awareness. Some people, inspired by the fact that there is a gem that grants all wishes, pray to a wooden replica of the gem, but their wishes are not fulfilled. They are like those who believe that buddhahood comes about due to the effort and achievement of lower spiritual approaches. As can be shown, though, this leads to nothing but debility and fatigue. *The All-Creating Monarch* states:

The purpose is as follows:
If all beings throughout the three realms
came to perceive natural mind as suchness,
they would attain the level of atiyoga in that very instant,
since buddhahood does not abide on the level of words.
But even if people with little good fortune and no suitable karma
were taught explicitly and without reservation, they would not
   gain realization.
Those who desire a precious gem will not obtain it by
   polishing wood.
Accordingly, fortunate yogins of ati with suitable karma
have no view, samaya, activity, paths, levels of realization,
deliberate motivation, meditation and practice based on causality,
   or antidotes.

. . . .

Eagerly trying to arouse the bliss that requires no effort—
there is no greater debility than this.

Now, since it can be shown that awareness, which involves no concerted effort, is the three kayas, the enlightened intent of naturally settled dharmakaya is as follows:

Awakened mind—timelessly spontaneous and uniform
   awareness—
the spacious nature of phenomena, just as it is, the naturally
   settled state,
is dharmakaya by nature, the expanse of primordial
   equalness. [65b]
It is present in everyone but within the reach of only
   a fortunate few.
If left just as it is, it is innately ensured within that
   context.

The essence of awareness—empty, lucid, and free of elaboration— is the ultimate meaning of dharmakaya. It is not within everyone's reach, but rather is perceived by the few who have realized mind itself to be settled in its own place, because its mode, a supreme equalness free of extremes, is the essence of vajra basic space. *The Perfect Dynamic Energy of the Lion* states:

> As I, Samantabhadrā, nonconceptual dharmakaya,
> regard the "object"—the true nature of phenomena, lucid
>   awareness—
> I inwardly perceive this awareness, free of diversity.
> As I regard self-knowing awareness, evident in the multiplicity
>   of objects,
> I inwardly discover nonconceptual, supreme dharmakaya.

And *Naturally Arising Awareness* states:

> As for[2] the vajra mandala, empty yet lucid,
> dharmakaya is nonconceptual and unobstructed,[3]
> free of the contrived limitations of reification.
> It entails no opinions about phenomena, which are
>   beyond extremes.

The enlightened intent of naturally settled sambhogakaya is as follows:

> **Sambhogakaya—infinitely pervasive, naturally lucid, and**
> **   spontaneously present—**
> **is present in everyone, but the perception of it is within the**
> **   reach of only a few.**
> **If you rest naturally with whatever manifests, without**
> **   conscious striving,[4] it is evident.**

Even as sense objects arise continuously in your perception, naturally lucid awareness—the nature of being as sambhogakaya—is perfectly clear in that these objects are vividly apparent without reification ensuing. *The Perfect Dynamic Energy of the Lion* states:

> Timeless awareness as sambhogakaya displays itself completely
>   on a vast scale.[5]
> Naturally lucid,[6] it is spontaneously present without involving
>   deliberate plans or actions.

The nirmanakaya aspect of enlightened intent is as follows:

> **The continuous display is the infinite expanse of**
> **   nirmanakaya. [66a]**
> **It is present in everything, clear in the arising of things.**
> **It is the pure expanse of self-knowing awareness.**

The miraculous display of wish-fulfilling qualities and
    activities, moreover, is nowhere else.
Like turbid water when the sediment settles, it becomes clear[7]
    if you rest in the naturally pristine state.

That quality, pure and simple in all its nakedness, of things seeming
to arise within the scope of naturally abiding awareness is nirmanakaya.
Given that it expresses itself timelessly as enlightened qualities and activity, within the context that entails no effort, no acceptance or rejection, reflections of sublime levels of insight and states of perception arise
like the vivid reflections that become clear in turbid water once the sediment has settled. *The All-Creating Monarch* states:

> Abiding timelessly like the ocean,
> it serves as the source of myriad phenomena.
> Its enlightened qualities are equal in extent to the far reaches
>   of space,
> yet have no specific place where they are brought together.
> The supreme and most majestic state of meditative absorption
> occurs instantaneously within the very heart of enlightenment.
> Sensory appearances are as vast as a great ocean.
> Involving no concepts, they are as vast as the far reaches of space.

Thus, it can be shown that the enlightened intent of the three kayas is a
single basic space beyond any concerted effort:

The truth of primordial purity is not found by being sought.
Enlightenment—buddhahood—is evident within the naturally
    occurring expanse.
Since it has already been accomplished, there is no need to
    achieve it anew.
This naturally abiding greatness is enlightened intent,
    the expanse that is the true nature of phenomena.
Make no effort concerning what is unchanging and
    spontaneously present!

Given that mind itself, just as it is, is already ensured as a natural
attribute—the essence of dharmakaya— [66b] I can advise you that
there is no need to engage in any effort or achievement, as stated in *The
All-Creating Monarch*:

One can, moreover, trust that everything is awakened mind.
In always trusting that it is awakened mind,
one can trust that mind is dharmakaya without searching for it,
and in trusting that this effortless state has always been
   dharmakaya,[8]
one abides in effortless, supreme bliss.

It can be shown that such awareness is a single state of natural abiding:

**The timeless ground, the innately abiding ground, is the
   ground that is at the very heart of enlightenment.
Since it does not stray at all from the context that is its nature,
do not stray from the lucid expanse that is the ultimate
   meaning of awareness!**

Awareness in its very essence has never existed as anything whatsoever and thus entails no proliferation or resolution, so if you wish to realize and make evident its ultimate meaning, it is very important not to
stray from meditative stability—consciousness settled in its own place—
and its naked, unobstructed quality. This is because the true nature of
phenomena—which is free of anything that could cause it to stray—and
deviation into all-consuming concepts about objects are mutually exclusive. *The Perfect Dynamic Energy of the Lion* states:

In dharmakaya, the source of everything,
the spacious expanse that entails no object is explained to be
   the essence.[9]
If nothing is discarded or adopted, there is sublime
   meditative absorption.[10]

And *The All-Creating Monarch* states:

Abiding in the fundamental nature spontaneously ensures
   the absence of straying.

**The reason that everything is ensured by being left as it is
lies in the unchanging, ever-present state of sovereign mastery—
   the five aspects of timeless awareness. [67a]
The state of original buddhahood—the five aspects each of
   enlightened form, enlightened speech, enlightened mind,
   enlightened qualities, and enlightened activity—**

is spontaneously present within the beginningless and
  endless expanse.
Do not seek it elsewhere, for by nature it is timelessly ensured.

Since the essence of awareness is without transition or change, there
are five aspects of enlightened form, including unchanging vajrakaya.
Since the essence of awareness is inexpressible, there are five aspects of
enlightened speech, including enlightenment as the true nature of phenomena. Since the essence of awareness is free of elaboration, there are
five aspects of enlightened mind, including naturally occurring timeless
awareness. Since the essence of awareness ensures all that is wished for
in its natural perfection, there are five aspects of enlightened qualities,
including the ground in which everything is perfect. And since the four
kinds of enlightened activity are ensured within the essence of awareness, which is ensured as timeless awareness that is the equalness and
purity of things, there are five aspects of enlightened activity, including
the totally pure nature of phenomena.

The perfection of these twenty-five aspects constitutes the enlightenment of Samantabhadra, original buddhahood. Since they are already
timelessly ensured within the essence of awareness, there is no need to
seek them elsewhere. *The Heart Essence of Secrets* states:

> Perfect buddhahood is not to be found
> anywhere in the ten directions or four times.
> Since mind itself is perfectly awakened as buddhahood,
> do not seek buddhahood elsewhere!
> Even if victorious ones were to seek it, they would not find it.

And *The All-Creating Monarch* states:

> Due to the nature of me, all-creating enlightenment,
> the three kayas—the heart essence of all victorious ones—
> are naturally and spontaneously present without having
>   to be sought.
> My uncontrived nature is ensured as dharmakaya, [67b]
> my uncontrived essence as sambhogakaya,
> and my fully evident responsiveness as nirmanakaya.
> I do not reveal these three to be results ensured by
>   being sought.
> They are spontaneously present in supreme bliss without
>   having to be sought.[11]

And *The Perfect Dynamic Energy of the Lion* states:

> In great perfection, the essence of awareness,
> the qualities of buddhahood are perfect without having
>   to be sought.[12]

Given that samsara and nirvana occur within awareness, dharmakaya is nowhere other than mind itself:

> Moreover, enlightenment—dharmakaya as experienced
>   by all buddhas—
> is none other than the ultimate meaning of unchanging
>   equalness.
> And since it is spontaneously present within that naturally
>   occurring context,
> do not seek it, do not try to achieve it.
> Completely let go of hope and fear!

Buddhahood—the discovery of dharmakaya—is nothing other than the uncontrived and unadulterated essence of awareness becoming evident. And because awareness is present in everyone without transition or change, I advise you to rest in the spontaneous presence of your uncontrived awareness. *The Pearl Garland* states:

> Perfect buddhahood is self-knowing awareness itself.[13]

And *The All-Creating Monarch* states:

> For me, all-creating awakened mind,
> unborn and free of dualistic perception,
> "unborn dharmakaya" is just a label.

It can be shown that there is no need to abandon samsaric mind, since mind itself is ensured as dharmakaya:

> Even the naturally occurring timeless awareness of all
>   ordinary beings
> is unmade and unsought, and spontaneously present
>   as dharmakaya,
> so do not react with rejection or acceptance, but rest in this
>   context of basic space!

Even for those called "ordinary beings," there is nothing other than the context of awareness. [68a] Thus, since awareness itself is such that it cannot be separated into samsara and nirvana, there is no need for beings to exert themselves or try to achieve something else. *The Perfect Dynamic Energy of the Lion* states:

> For ordinary beings and buddhas, awareness is not different.

And *Naturally Arising Awareness* states:

> An ordinary being's awareness is true buddhahood.[14]

It can be shown that awareness does not waver and is beyond effort:

> **Within the essence of being—spontaneous and uniform,**
> **unwavering and beyond deliberation—**
> **lies the spacious expanse of the ground of being, not created**
> **yet ensuring all that has ultimate meaning.**

Dharmakaya is spontaneously present as the essence of awareness, and so it abides as this uncreated essence, ensuring all that has ultimate meaning; it constitutes timeless awareness, amazing and marvelous. This can be shown to be the ground of being as the basic space of phenomena, free of limitation. *The Reverberation of Sound* states:

> Timeless awareness, amazing and marvelous,
> was ineffable in the past and will be ineffable in the future,
>   for it is primordially ineffable.
> Right now, it is beyond the realm of the imagination.
> Free of limitation, its very nature is emptiness.
> Beyond words, surpassing ordinary consciousness,
>   and essentially empty,
> that nature is not in any way divisible
> and so entails no manifestation of responsiveness in actions.
> Due to the third, manifest aspect of timeless awareness,
> knowledge deriving from conceptual consciousness
>   is misconstrued,
> leading to a state of confusion.[15]
> But it has no limited frame of reference.
> It is ineffable, and within its marvelous display
> the fruition state of all buddhas is discovered.

Inside and out, everything is the basic space of phenomena,
which has no manifest form whatsoever.

It can be shown that spontaneous presence, the continuous flow of empowerment, is timelessly complete within the scope of awareness:

Unchanging and ever-present, the embodiment of the kayas
   and timeless awareness [68b]
is the conferral of the supreme, naturally occurring
   empowerment, like the investiture of a royal heir.
Since the universe of appearances and possibilities is
   timelessly[16] and spontaneously present,
there is no need for concerted effort,[17] for it is spontaneously
   present by nature.
Everything is ensured, unfolding as a supreme state of
   spontaneous presence.

Since awareness is timelessly perfect as the essence of the three spontaneously present kayas, complete empowerment is already ensured as
naturally occurring timeless awareness, and so does not now depend on
concerted effort or empowerment rituals. *The Perfect Dynamic Energy
of the Lion* states:

The empowerment of supreme, naturally manifest
   timeless awareness[18]
abides thus within the ground of being.

And *The All-Creating Monarch* states:

The most majestic state of awareness holds mastery over lucidity
and so does not depend on the power of ordinary bliss.
Realizing this, rest just as intended in the ultimate
   nonconceptual state.
Within awareness—the receiving of the all-creating monarch's
   empowerment—
things constantly arise, just as they are, without being contrived.
Without causes or conditions, the path of sublime peace
is that of resting in the ground of being,
and however one rests is the realm of suchness.
The supreme skillful means of the all-creating monarch is
   the empowerment of realization.

If all beings were to enter the realm of what simply is,
they would understand that flaws and positive qualities are equal
and so would completely transcend the question of whether they
    had entered or not.
The enlightened intent of gaining mastery through
    all-creating awareness
cannot be expressed verbally and is beyond the scope
    of speculation.
Deliberate recollection is pacified and there is no
    conceptual elaboration.
Pervasive like space, it has absolutely no bias.
Empowerment consists of realization that cuts through hope
    and fear.
A yogin who engages in this with certainty
receives the transmission of atiyoga, beyond causality. [69a]
The all-creating monarch, uncontrived timeless awareness,
does not in any way proclaim, "Rest in such-and-such a way!"

That is to say, from the standpoint of the essence of awareness, which
has never existed as anything whatsoever, there are neither empowerments, stages of development and completion, nor other such factors. If
you have not come to this decision, you have not come to a final resolution concerning view. So from now on you should realize that from the
standpoint of awareness, samsara and nirvana, acceptance and rejection, plans and actions, view and meditation, and so forth are all like
space, nonexistent as objects. *The Pearl Garland* states:

All duality comes from the differentiation of a single ground,[19]
but a unique state free of elaboration abides as enlightened intent.
By nature it is the sphere of supremely blissful being.
It is the single mandala of all buddhas.
Its very essence is original purity,
while its very nature is spontaneous presence.
It transcends levels, extremes, and biases.
It is neither existent, nonexistent, nor even apparent at all.
It is not within the range of language or logic.[20]
It is not one or two or anything that can be enumerated.
It is ensured as supreme emptiness by its innate nature.
It is not within the range of scriptural authority or reasoning.
It cannot be portrayed by tantras or pith instructions.

One will not come to understand its ultimate implications
through view, meditation, or conduct.
Its ultimate meaning cannot be established as some fruition.
Phenomena obscure suchness.
It is not ensured by being contemplated.
It cannot be analyzed by sublime knowing.
Suchness is free of any harm or any benefit
brought about by generosity, discipline, or patience.
It [21] cannot be perceived even if one examines it thoroughly
by listening to teachings, contemplating, and meditating.
It has no mandala. [69b]
There is no deity, no seed syllable to visualize.
What effect could mantras and mudras have?
There is no need for elaborations such as making offerings.
How could there be empowerment or samaya?
There are no stages of approach and accomplishment.
There is no process of light shining from the chakras.
There is no protection or anything to be protected.
It is beyond any context of negative influence or harm.
It is me and it is ordinary beings.
It is mind and it is what occurs due to mind.
It is manifold and it is unique.
Samsara and nirvana are me.
I am mandalas and other developmental processes.
I am phenomena and what manifests as phenomena.
I am stillness and movement. [22]
I am sitting, lying down, and moving about.
I am also life force, as well as its termination.
The three worlds are born from this suchness.
It manifests as deities, mantras, and mudras.
It appears as virtue and its results.
It is also the ten perfections.
Levels of realization and enlightened qualities, moreover,
    all come from it.
Conduct, meditation, view, and so forth all come from it as well.
All greater and lesser spiritual approaches come from it.
In brief, all phenomena that manifest as they do come from it. [23]

In essence, awareness has never existed as anything whatsoever, and
so you decide that it is timelessly empty, like space. The way things arise

within its context is such that anything at all can and does manifest, and so you come to a decisive experience of the spontaneous presence of everything. And since these two aspects are one and the same as awareness, you recognize that they are free of the extremes of existence and nonexistence. Since this is the perspective of the great perfection, [70a] you should understand the nature of awareness to be that supreme, nondual spontaneous presence—manifest yet not established as something that exists, empty yet not nothing.

This is the commentary on the seventh section of *The Precious Treasury of the Basic Space of Phenomena,* demonstrating that everything is timelessly and spontaneously present within awakened mind.

8

Nonduality
Within Awakened Mind

Thus, all things are pure by nature and spontaneously present. Their nature can be further characterized as nondual, for the fact that they arise within a single basic space signifies that even in arising they do not, in their very essence, exist separate from one another:

> Within naturally occurring timeless awareness, a single
> basic space,
> all things are present in such a way that they are in essence
> nondual.
> Continuous dualistic perceptions arise as a display due to
> the dynamic energy of awareness.
> In what is called "awakened mind," there is no duality
> of sensory appearances and what the mind imputes
> about them.

Reflections arising on the surface of a mirror are such that whatever appears is nothing other than the mirror. Similarly, since all phenomena arise within the scope of awareness, they are nothing other than awareness. The myriad dreams that arise during a single night's sleep are nothing other than that state of sleep. Similarly, samsara and nirvana are nothing other than the display of awareness. Because waves, whether big or small, all form on a single river, they are nothing other than that river. Similarly, all phenomena manifest by arising in such a way that they do not exist as anything whatsoever; they simply manifest clearly without truly existing. There is only this, and so there is no dichotomy between awareness, whose nature is emptiness, and the emptiness of phenomena. By relying on these three cases of inferential reasoning, you come to the decision that no phenomenon exists within a dualistic framework. [70b]

You also realize that all phenomena constitute a supreme state of nondual equalness, by considering four points: there is equalness in that they have never existed, in that they are unceasing, in that by simply manifesting within the essence of awareness they are capable of performing their respective functions, and in that their manifestation is simply a matter of what arises due to interdependent conditions. *The Most Majestic State of Meditative Absorption* states, for example:

> Anything born of conditions is therefore unborn
> in the sense that by nature it does not come into being.
> I have said that whatever depends on conditions is empty.

No duality is possible within the essence of samsara and nirvana, which arise as manifestations of the dynamic energy of awareness. There appears to be a duality between a dream image and the person perceiving it, but there is no duality, because neither ultimately exists: there is simply the specific arising, at a single moment during a single state of sleep, of a single clear manifestation that does not truly exist. *The Ornament of Manifest Realization* states:

> Just as a dream and its perceiver
> are not seen in a dualistic light,
> so phenomena can be realized[1]
> to be nondual in a single instant.

In this way, all phenomena that manifest do so clearly without truly existing. Even one's own ordinary consciousness, awareness, body, and so forth manifest clearly without truly existing. Though phenomena can manifest as anything at all, they are simply clearly apparent without truly existing, for they do not exist in the least as phenomena in their own right, whether as one thing or separate things. Therefore, you should understand that, although all phenomena of the universe of appearances and possibilities, whether of samsara or nirvana, do manifest in light of awareness, [71a] none of them "exists within a dualistic framework." Because these phenomena, which arise in light of awareness, arise within the context of basic space, they come from awareness itself and so are conventionally said to be "simply magical expressions of awareness." *The Pearl Garland* states:

Moreover, earth, water, fire, and air—
these great elements come from this.
Gods, demigods, human beings,
hell beings, animals, and pretas
truly come from this greatness.
Desire and attachment, aversion, ignorance,
pride, jealousy, and so forth
come about as its magical expression.
The ordinary mind based on the nonrecognition of awareness,
conceptual consciousness, mind-body aggregates,
components of ordinary experience, sense fields,
avenues of ordinary consciousness,
and the five sense faculties come about as well.
Sounds, odors, tastes, tactile sensations,
and other sense pleasures come about as its adornment.
As well, what has life force,[2] is superficial, and without
    true essence
comes about as its display and dynamic energy.
The ground of all ordinary experience and what it
    perpetuates—
flesh, blood, lymph, bones, skin, hair,
and the physical bodies made of these—come from it.
Body, speech, and mind,
as well as myriad mental events[3]
all come from my essence.
Men, women, horses, cattle, and other physical forms
all come from it.
Eating, sleeping, sitting,
and all manner of other activities come from it.

And *The All-Creating Monarch* states:

Ah, great and courageous one, realize my nature! [71b]
I am the nature of awakened mind.
Awakened mind is the all-creating monarch.
The nature of the all-creating monarch is enlightened form,
    speech, and mind.
There is not a single thing that is not created by enlightened form,
    speech, and mind.
Buddhas of the three times are created by enlightened form,
    speech, and mind.

> The bodies, speech, and minds of ordinary beings in the three
>   realms—these three factors
> are also created by the enlightened form, speech, and mind of me,
>   the all-creating one.[4]
> Moreover, all that is subsumed within the universe of
>   appearances and possibilities
> is, in its uncontrived nature, just as it is,
> created by the enlightened form, speech, and mind of me,
>   the all-creating one.

At this point, you should avoid any association with the opinions of deluded people who misinterpret conventional expressions. Some blithering idiots, who lack the advantage of having heard teachings, hold that "sensory appearances manifesting outwardly in all their variety are awakened mind" and "it is one's own mind that manifests thus." But the difference between such assertions and my present argument, that things are of the same essence within the expanse of awakened mind, is as vast as that between heaven and earth. Deluded people assert that these manifestations are "awakened mind" or "one's own mind," while I am asserting here that phenomena arise within the scope of awakened mind, but due to a dynamic process by which they are reified as having identity. I am further asserting that, even as they arise, they are nothing more than the display of this dynamic energy, simply conditioned appearances manifesting due to interdependence—that is, specific phenomena that have never existed either as mind or as anything other than mind and that manifest clearly without truly existing anywhere, outwardly or inwardly. [72a]

It is simply the case that the emptiness of these myriad external phenomena (sensory appearances that are based on confusion, have no basis, and have never known existence) and the emptiness of mind itself cannot be separated from one another. From the perspective of the true nature of phenomena, these are not mutually exclusive, so in our tradition we say that "all phenomena included in what is external and internal are of one taste—awakened mind." But we do not assert that things that simply appear on the conventional level are identical to one's own mind. We make this distinction for the following reasons: There is a categorical difference between sensory appearances and mind. No correspondence can be proved between what is self and what is other, between what remains part of one's experience and what is left behind, or between what exists and what does not. Several further distinctions apply to phenomena, such as that between sensory appearances in general and one's individual perception of sense objects. For these reasons, you should realize that my assertion bears no similarity to the position of deluded people.

In general, moreover, it is the method of all Buddhist schools to differentiate things on the relative level of truth—sensory appearances as distinct from mind, confusion as distinct from its absence, samsara as distinct from nirvana, and so forth. Given that this is so, which of these misguided methods is used has as much significance as whether a dog or a fox is leaping, for in my approach no classification is to be made concerning things as they are conventionally designated, the parameters of the spiritual path, or what is pure versus what is impure. And since nothing has ever existed as anything whatsoever, given the fundamentally unconditioned nature of ultimate reality, someone who held that everything is mind would definitely be confused. Such a person would be upholding the biases of those who assert this, such as certain proponents of the Mind Only school who accept sense data as valid or those who are influenced by holders of extreme views. For this reason, there is nothing to do but refrain from relying on their methods.

The explanation that "everything is mind" found in the Category of Mind [72b] is not the same as the position of these people. When that figure of speech is used in this category, what is being said is that everything comes from *awakened mind* and arises as a display due to its dynamic energy. Using the threefold classification of dynamic energy, display, and awakened mind, a definitive conclusion is reached concerning phenomena. Awakened mind here is comparable to space in that it has never existed as anything whatsoever, yet serves as the matrix for anything at all. Its dynamic energy is a continuous mode of arising comparable to the surface of a highly polished mirror. The display is the arising of phenomena in all their variety, likened to the eight metaphors for illusoriness.

Furthermore, from the point of view of their emptiness, these three are not separate from one another, for they have never existed as anything whatsoever. From the point of view of how they manifest, they do so as this triad of awakened mind, dynamic energy, and display—by nature without underlying basis in the very process of arising one from the other (which, for the sake of analogy, can be compared to consciousness, sleep, and the dream state). Though from the point of view of their essence, they are beyond being one thing or separate things, from the point of view of how things manifest they can be described in terms of these three conventional designations. According to these designations, it does not follow that the display and awakened mind are identical. And so, from the point of view of phenomena being aspects of the display, they can be distinguished as either sensory appearances in general or one's individual perception of them as sense objects. Using one of the eight metaphors for illusoriness, they are understood to be reflections that manifest clearly without existing anywhere, outwardly or inwardly. And so regardless of how things are labeled—as general or specific phenomena, and so forth—in my tradition of the great perfection, it is held that they constitute the supreme state of what is clearly apparent without truly existing, [73a] and so you should realize them as such.

Once you understand how things can be explained in this way, you find that this philosophical system is more exalted than any other, for it offers a many-faceted approach that includes a spacious overview as well as thoroughness, precision, and differentiation, such as that between samsara and nirvana. Nowadays, only in our tradition is it understood how to explain all this thoroughly.

Now, all phenomena that arise within naturally occurring timeless awareness abide in a supreme state of undifferentiated equalness. They are perceived by yogins as expressions of emptiness that manifest clearly without truly existing, so the certainty that such yogins feel when this realization arises in their own experience is praiseworthy:

> Within enlightenment—awareness without transition or change—
> the universe of appearances and possibilities, whether
>   of samsara or nirvana,
> arises with nothing to renounce or attain.
> In the experience of yogins who do not perceive things
>   dualistically,
> the fact that things manifest without truly existing is
>   so amazing they burst into laughter.

Someone who sees through a magician's illusions, and realizes that what manifests does not exist, has no sense that they have any truth, but rather perceives them as comical; but while they have never existed as anything good or bad, to be accepted or rejected, they still arise continuously. Similarly, all phenomena of samsara and nirvana are understood to be a display that manifests clearly without truly existing. It can be shown that yogins who have realized the very essence that is the single state of equalness and purity are not caught up in the framework of either samsara or nirvana. *The Perfect Dynamic Energy of the Lion* states:

> Samsara and nirvana are perfect in a single awareness.
> Without reification, awareness's own manifestations are beyond
>   one's experience of ordinary phenomena. [73b]

And *The Array of Inlaid Gems* states:

> . . . not some object that manifests or that causes manifestation,
> nor something that is not manifest, but the total purity of
>   all phenomena.[5]

All phenomena[6] arise yet do not exist, for they are nonexistent in the very moment they manifest, and so it can be shown that they are simply reflections, expressions of emptiness, manifesting clearly without truly existing:

> **Although sensory appearances do not exist, they manifest**
>   **in all their variety.**
> **Although emptiness does not exist, it extends infinitely,**
>   **reaching everywhere.**
> **Although dualistic perception does not exist, there is still**
>   **fixation on things having individual identity.**
> **Although they have no basis, a continual succession of lifetimes**
>   **manifests.**
> **Although nothing exists that can be refuted or proved, pleasure**
>   **is accepted and pain is rejected.**

If you reflect on the significance of the true nature of phenomena, the manifestation of objects of the phenomenal world is simply an amazing arising of things. For even though they are in essence beyond being existent or nonexistent, the way they manifest in all their variety is to appear as awareness's own manifestations. This is similar to the fact that in dreams there are self and others, pleasure and pain, wealth and property, good and bad, emotional reactions of acceptance and rejection, past and future lifetimes, and so forth. Though none of these actually exist, within that context one's mind is completely consumed by afflictive emotions, for one reifies things as existent. This is referred to as "indulging in perceptions based on confusion," due to the very fact that one reifies what is clearly apparent yet nonexistent, investing it with identity. *The Exalted Discourse of the Rare and Sublime Meteor* states:

> All phenomena are similar to the Sugata.
> Those whose minds are undeveloped—who reify things in terms
>   of their characteristics—
> are involved with the phenomena of their world, which do not
>   truly exist.

Now, that which is not born of either external or internal phenomena is pure and equal to space. Given that this is so, there are two steps in determining how to realize it. [74a] Initially, a definitive conclusion can be reached concerning what manifests as external sense objects—that these appearances are expressions of emptiness, illusory and without foundation:

> Looking around, I find the perception of beings to be
>   truly amazing.
> They fixate on what is not real as real, so that it certainly
>   seems real.
> They fixate on confusion where there is no confusion, so that
>   there certainly seems to be confusion.
> They reify what is indeterminate as determinate, so that
>   it certainly seems determinate.
> They reify what is not so as being so, so that it certainly seems so.
> They reify what is untenable as tenable, so that it certainly
>   seems tenable.

Though it is the nature of sensory appearances to manifest outwardly, in their very essence they are simply natural expressions of emptiness. But spiritually undeveloped people, who do not understand suchness itself, fixate on them as having characteristics and some ultimate meaning, reifying phenomena as external or internal. They reify what is not real as real, what is not a state of confusion as a state of confusion, what is indeterminate as determinate, what is beyond being this or that as this or that, and what is untenable as tenable. And so:

Ordinary mind is seduced[7] by trivial sense objects in all their variety.
One's useless focus moment by moment extends into a continuum,
as days, months, years, whole lives go by.
Beings are deceived by misconstruing what is not dualistic
    as dualistic.

Unable to recognize the very essence of awareness in the moment, one perpetuates the process of reifying things out of confusion, and so time passes. After a number of such moments, one has been confused for a short while; these short periods stretch into days, days into months, and months into years during which one has been confused. Beings remain confused because of this relentless pattern, for while awareness—dharmakaya, pure like space—has no underlying basis and abides naturally within them, [74b] their failure to recognize this allows what is merely an adventitious condition to come about. As *The Pearl Garland* states:

Dharmakaya is like the sky,
obscured by clouds of adventitious concepts.[8]
Although the true nature of phenomena is without confusion,
a mode of confusion manifests as ordinary consciousness.[9]
Entailing causes and conditions, this occurs moment by moment.

And *The Garland of Jewels* states:

The threefold path has no beginning, middle, or end.
The cycle of samsara—with causal circumstances circling
    interdependently—
is like a whirling firebrand.

Thus, sensory appearances that manifest to ordinary beings—who in their confusion believe that what they perceive exists in its own right—manifest to a yogin as simply the play of illusion. This is due to the key point that confusion has no basis or foundation.

That is to say, given that the very essence of awareness is a pristine state of original purity, like space—beyond any question of whether or not there is confusion—its own enlightened perspective is that of dharmakaya, pure as natural lucidity in all its nakedness. This is referred to as "the enlightened perspective of a supreme state of total purity that has no underlying basis." In essence, nothing whatsoever has ever existed, whether as the recognition or nonrecognition of awareness, as nirvana or samsara, or as anything else. A yogin realizes this just as it is in the present moment, in and of itself. Those who do not lose sight of this context perceive external sense objects, which are based on confusion, as illusory expressions of emptiness—the ground of being manifesting as sensory appearances, pristine within the expanse that is their true nature. And so such people are referred to as "yogins who are pure like space, for whom even the name 'samsara' does not exist." *The Pearl Garland* states:

> Although sense objects manifest as they do,
> in original purity—purity from the very beginning—
> not even the concept "confusion" can be expressed. [75a]
> Similarly, how could there be a lack of confusion?
> Therefore, confusion is primordially pure.
> In the supreme manifestation of the ground of being
>   as sensory appearances,
> there is nothing to be labeled[10] "nonrecognition,"
> so confusion has never existed.
> Since what is termed "ordinary consciousness" is not something
>   to be labeled in any way,
> not even the term "confusing distortions" exists.
> Since there are no sequences of words or syllables,
> the confusion of labeling does not exist.
> Since nothing can be labeled[11] a "phenomenon,"
> not even the expression "confusion due to mental labeling" exists.
> Since nothing has ever existed as ordinary mind or consciousness,
> there is inevitably no confusion that stirs the mind.
> Since there are neither coarse nor subtle distortions,
> there is inevitably no self-perpetuating confusion.
> Since there is neither anything to do nor the doing of it,
> how could there be confusion that reifies objects?
> Since there are neither sense objects nor sense faculties,
> there is no confusion due to dualistic perception.[12]

And *The Reverberation of Sound* states:

> Given that "confusion" is originally pure,
> there is nothing to be improved by changing it to some
>   unconfused state.
> One perceives that things manifest without existing.
> There naturally ceases to be any concept that these nonexistent
>   phenomena

have been created by, or come from, anything.
This is not perception based on some confused frame
  of reference.
Since the nature of being is a timeless, unwavering radiance,
all phenomena are of one taste in equalness.
With freedom from reifying concepts,[13] buddhahood
  is timeless.
It cannot be improved or changed.

Once you realize that external sense objects do not exist, your experience of their true nature, entailing no reification of objects, becomes pure like space. Then, you reach the definitive conclusion that the reification of an inner perceiver has no support or basis:

As a yogin with a pure mind looks inward, [75b]
awareness, without underlying support or basis, is free
  of labels.
It cannot be perceived in any way that can be characterized
  or described—
structured view and meditation are done away with.
Given this state of infinite evenness, open, relaxed, and
  spacious,
there is no sense of spiritual practice, for there is no distinction
  between formal sessions and the periods in between.
Everything is unrestricted, completely equal, and
  uninterrupted.

Thus, looking at your own mind, you find that in essence it is not limited to being something identifiable; like space, it is pristine by nature and without support. Its true nature, the natural purity underlying ordinary consciousness, is referred to as "dharmakaya free of the extremes of existence and nonexistence." *The Reverberation of Sound* states:

All phenomena are without basis,
and there is no possibility that any of them has a foundation.
Without desire and free of conditioned existence,
mind is by nature uncontrived and beyond description.
Concepts based on the confusion of plans and actions fall away.
There are no phenomena, no buddhas, no ordinary beings,
no "I," no identity, and no dualistic perceptions.

This cannot be expressed with words.
"Mind" cannot even be located.
Because the manifestations of emptiness do not exist,
one's ordinary consciousness of them is undermined.
The truly amazing thing is that,
given that the true nature of phenomena is not created,
nothing occurs.
The truly amazing thing is that,
given that dharmakaya is not something that occurs,
nothing comes or goes.[14]
Given that awareness is not a context for samsara,
its true nature has no origin.

Awareness—realization of the nonduality underlying dualistic perception—is a supreme state of spontaneous presence not subject to extremes.
Thus:

With no reference point—whether body or sense object
   or perception—
there is infinite evenness within the undifferentiated, vast
   expanse of space, [76a]
and so there is no inner agent that can be held to have identity.

Awareness entails the realization that nothing can be reified as an
object or a subject, and its essence is conventionally termed "naturally
occurring timeless awareness." However, I am not positing what those
of the Mind Only school call "naturally lucid self-awareness." This is
so for the following reasons: Since outer and inner do not exist, nothing has ever existed as an inner mind. Since self and other do not exist,
nothing has ever existed simply as self-awareness. Since object and subject have never known existence, nothing has ever existed as freedom
from that duality. Since nothing exists as an object of sensation or of
awareness, nothing has ever existed as a nondual state of experience.
Since mind and mental events do not exist, nothing has ever existed as
"one's own mind." And since whether or not there is lucidity is irrelevant,
nothing has ever existed as natural lucidity.
   That which cannot even be labeled "awareness," since it is beyond
any question of there being awareness or not, is nevertheless referred to

as "great and total perfection free of limitation." It may be referred to by such designations as "naturally occurring timeless awareness," "awakened mind," "dharmakaya," "basic space as supreme spontaneous presence," and "naturally lucid self-knowing awareness in all its nakedness." However, you should realize that in its very essence it is supremely indescribable, for such labels are simply applied to facilitate understanding. If you fixate on these terms as referring to some ultimate "thing," I consider you to be no different from those of the Mind Only school who posit that consciousness without the duality of object and subject is some "thing" that they term "naturally lucid self-awareness."

Those who have not refined their intellects babble on about their position concerning this issue; taking the two preceding assertions to be the same, they claim, "We understand self-knowing awareness!" [76b] But this claim amounts to nothing but a declaration of their outright arrogance.

The methods of evaluating reality that are used in the system of natural great perfection—for example, determining it to be free of limitation—are largely in accord with those of the syllogistic Prasangika approach in the Middle Way school. But the Middle Way school takes as its working basis sheer emptiness that is like space, while this system takes as its basis awareness, pure and simple—originally pure in all its nakedness and unceasing, though it has never existed as anything—so that awareness and the phenomena that arise within its scope are judged to be free of limitation, like space. *The Reverberation of Sound* states:

> Since multiplicity is eliminated, awareness is free of conventional
> designations.
> Since it has never existed as any one thing, it is pure by nature.
> Since it is pure by nature, all that has ultimate meaning is ensured.
> It is free of such expressions as "pure nature," "foundation,"
> "the basis of samsara and nirvana,"[15]
> "hollow,"[16] "without true essence," and "superficial."
>
> . . . .
>
> Since nothing need be done, it is devoid of characteristics.
> Since there ceases to be any basis for description, it does not abide
> in any extreme.
> Because all that is subject to degeneration has come to an end,
> it is not material.[17]

There cease to be any underpinnings[18] of consciousness—
    its essence is lucidity.
Lucid awareness is not thought, which is subject to the
    limitations of sense objects.
Because it is beyond language—there are no true words for it—
all basis for speculation has come to an end.

And *The Array of Inlaid Gems* states:

Within the basic space of phenomena, conduct is irrelevant.
Given its timeless original purity, its spacelike quality,
dharmakaya itself has no substance or characteristics.[19]
Supremely spacious, without division into outer and inner,
the spacious nature of phenomena is free of limitation
    and has no substance.
As for the view of great perfection, this sacred converging
    of secrets, [77a]
there are a great[20] many variations in spiritual approaches,
but there is nothing other than this single nature[21]—the definitive
    meaning of all that is secret.
The spacious mandala of the true nature of phenomena is without
    characteristics.[22]

Now, once yogins have realized that both object and subject are of the
nature of space—having never known existence—they experience all
phenomena within a supreme state of total freedom, with no reference
point. Thus, as a sign that the inner subject has been cleared away, it can
be shown that outer objects constitute a panoramic state of freedom:

As you look outward at sense objects manifesting externally,
everything is unobstructed, vivid yet ephemeral,
random, without any reference point.
You perceive, hear, think, are aware, experience, and feel as
    never before.
"What is this? Are my perceptions by nature those of a lunatic?
    Am I in a dream?"[23]
You burst out laughing at yourself!

At this stage, when you have definitely gained realization, you are
capable of realizing the vision of all yogins. You are like someone who,
with the wisdom of experience, perceives a magical display as having no

true existence and, by extension, understands the perceptions of others who are also privy to such knowledge.

Before, you perceived outer manifestations—sense objects—as existing in their own right. But now that you have realization, the very essence that you have certainty of is such that your holding to things as having true existence is overturned. So you think, "I perceive all these reified sense objects as though dream images, or the reflection of the moon in water, or forms in mirages—they are unobstructed, vivid yet ephemeral." Whatever manifests arises as awareness's own manifestation, randomly and without any particular reference point, leaving you wondering whether any of it exists or not. [77b]

You might wonder whether the conduct and character of ordinary beings are different from what they were before. As things seem to manifest with no reference point, you might think, "Does everyone realize this?" With all reference points fading away in emptiness, you experience, feel, think, and are aware as never before, so that you experience awareness as an infinite evenness. You might wonder how you have ended up in such a state in which thoughts never arise, for your consciousness is completely open and your ordinary experiences are naturally pristine,[24] inherently pure. Occasionally you may burst out laughing at the way your behavior and all that you see and hear are continually without any frame of reference. You may become aware of thoughts like "Am I crazy? Is everyone else crazy? Is this a dream or the intermediate state after death?" The thought may occur to you: "This awareness, bursting forth in all its nakedness, in which all reference points fade away, is present in everyone. What, then, is the problem in realizing it? It's right here!" With your unconditional compassion arising unchecked, you also speak of these things to others, sing vajra songs, and act without inhibition, all of which show that your awareness has no fixation. All sensory appearances manifest unobstructedly in the moment.

At this point, dharmakaya, in which dualistic perception is naturally overturned, arises from within—a process that is referred to as "purifying the objects of fixation that are misconstrued as having identity." *The Pearl Garland* states:

> Since phenomena, awareness's own manifestations,
> are without distortion, any division of them into coarse and
>   subtle is overturned.
> Since they entail no dualistic perception, confusion is overturned.

Since they involve no mental stirring, the subtle energy of karma
    is overturned. [78a]
Since they are unobstructed, substantiality is overturned.
Because they entail lucidity, nothingness is overturned.
Since they are timelessly perfect, the stage of development
    is overturned.
Since they involve no effort, conduct is overturned.
Since they are established without being sought, meditation
    is overturned.
Since they are naturally free, sensory appearances are overturned.
Since they manifest directly, view is overturned.
Since they entail no terms or words, conventional designations
    are overturned.
Since they have never known existence, fixation is overturned.
Since they have never known nonexistence, dependence on other
    factors is overturned.
Since they cannot be reified as objects, imputation is overturned.
Since they constitute a oneness, limitations imposed by
    enumeration are overturned.

And *The Six Expanses* states:

Within mind itself, in which the six avenues of
    consciousness manifest,
ordinary thought patterns are pure in their own place.
Within mind itself, in which terms and words manifest,
conventional labels are pure in their own place.
Within mind itself, in which things manifest on a coarse level,
the four elements as conditions are pure in their own place.
Within mind itself, in which dualistic perception manifests,
the reification of identity that binds the mind is pure in its
    own place.
Within mind itself, in which things seem to exist,
things are pure in their own place.
Within mind itself, in which things seem not to exist,
as aspects of emptiness they are pure in their own place.
Within mind itself, in which things seem to be existent
    or nonexistent,
philosophical systems[25] are pure in their own place.
Within mind itself, in which things manifest as phenomena,[26]
their characteristics are pure in their own place.

Within mind itself, in which there are nonmanifest phenomena,
states of confusion are pure in their own place. [78b]
Within mind itself, in which antidotes manifest,
distortions are pure in their own place.
Within mind itself, which is innately so,
the supreme, indwelling ground of being is pure in its own place.

It can further be shown that such realization, an experience that arises from within, has no reference point:

You are free of any notion of enemy or friend, attachment
or aversion, near or far.
Since there is a unique evenness in that everything is equal,
without any distinction between day and night,
samsara—the reifying of characteristics and reference points—
is cleared away.
Since you have no concepts about "the scope of naturally
occurring timeless awareness,"
you have transcended the cage of acceptance and rejection,
of what is an antidote and what is to be abandoned.
With such realization, there is nondual timeless awareness.
You have arrived at enlightened intent, naturally occurring
and wholly positive.
You have arrived at the point of resolution, with no chance
of falling back.

At this point, your realization extends throughout day and night, arising as a supreme, ongoing state. Since you do not hold anything at a distance out of aversion, considering it a threat, thoughts that occur during the night are cleared away within their true nature. And since you are not deeply attached to anything out of a fondness for something supportive, all-consuming thoughts that occur during the day are cleared away within basic space. Since the samsaric process of dualistic perception is cleared away day and night, awareness abides within the scope of dharmakaya. Furthermore, since there is freedom from ordinary thinking that reifies antidotes as something absolute, cognitive distortions are free in their own place. And since there are no distinctions between things—as supportive and so to be accepted, or threatening and so to be rejected—the obscuring effect of afflictive emotions is naturally free and pure. You have arrived at enlightened intent, naturally occurring and wholly positive. This is referred to as "reaching the point at which phenomena resolve." The tradition of the great perfection, [79a] moreover, establishes the true measure of the spiritual path through[27] either emptiness or manifestation—that is, through resolution that occurs by means of either trekchö or *tögal* [surpassing ordinary experience].

In the practice of tögal, the visions of utter lucidity resolve in the immediacy of what has always been; a state like the cloudless sky signifies the resolution of visionary manifestations within their true nature. At that point, since all afflictive emotions and corporeality are resolved inwardly, the indications that one has awakened to buddhahood in this lifetime reach full expression.

For those whose realization comes solely through the method of trekchö, originally pure awareness bursts forth in all its nakedness, and so its dynamic energy—all fixated thinking, whether positive or negative, concerning samsara or nirvana—is pure. So, regardless of how the mind functions, concepts and afflictive emotions are unborn, cleared away in the freedom of the ground of being. This is referred to as "resolution within the true nature of emptiness."

When the sun rises at daybreak, darkness cannot be found even if sought. Similarly, dualistic perception has been cleared away, free within the ground of being and free of any restrictions. In this very lifetime, you have arrived at the state of original purity in which phenomena resolve, and you are known as "a yogin who is free of the restrictions of samsara and nirvana." This is what the great lord of yogins Dhekevajra intended when he said:

> For a yogin who is free of restrictions, it is like the sun rising
>   at daybreak.
> This is the vision of dharmakaya—how marvelous!

At this point, since you abide within the enlightened intent of infinite evenness—spacious and pervasive perfection—you are fully aware that all afflictive emotions are free within their true nature. It may seem to others that yogins have afflictive emotions and ordinary experiences, such as recalling things and expressing themselves verbally, [79b] but such yogins are not encumbered by any of this. So, just as nothing material can attach itself to space, no flaw or distortion can sully these yogins, and there is no question of their being bound or free, for they are beyond the extremes of positive and negative. *The Pearl Garland* states:

Since phenomena are completely pervasive, they do not come
  from somewhere else.
Since they arise naturally, darkness is cleared away.
Since they are the heart essence, they are pervasive within
  dharmakaya.
Since they manifest within lucidity, they unfold as sambhogakaya.
Since mother and son have reunited, they occur as nirmanakaya.
Since they are present within one's realization,[28] they serve as
  skillful means.
Since they are beyond imagination, ordinary consciousness is
  cleared away.
Since they can be neither affirmed nor denied, all philosophical
  systems are finished with.
Since they are distilled as the vital essence, awareness is lucid.

And *The Six Expanses* states:

Within mind itself, in all its supreme, innate immediacy,
sensory appearances are patently pure in their own place.
Within mind itself, which seems to be something,
falsehoods are pure in their own place.
Within mind itself, which seems to be nothing,
stealing is pure in its own place.
Within mind itself, which is both something and nothing at all,
unchaste behavior is pure in its own place.
Within mind itself, which involves no impropriety,
idle gossip is pure in its own place.
Within mind itself, in which sense objects manifest,
slanderous words are pure in their own place.
Within mind itself, in which mental stirring manifests,
sexual misconduct is pure in its own place.
Within mind itself, which is originally pure,
even the act of taking life is pure in its own place.
Within mind itself, in which conditions manifest,
covetous attitudes are pure in their own place.
Within mind itself, in which results manifest, [80a]
attitudes of ill will are pure in their own place.
Within mind itself, in which sound manifests,
what is audible is pure in its own place.
Within mind itself, in which forms manifest,

these reified aspects are pure in their own place.
Within mind itself, in which odors manifest,
states of consciousness are pure in their own place.
Within mind itself, in which flavors manifest,
the consciousness responsible for taste is pure in its own place.
Within mind itself, in which what is tangible manifests,
tactile consciousness is pure in its own place.
Within mind itself, in which ideas manifest,
reification of these as abstract or particular is pure in its own place.
Within mind itself, in which sensory appearances manifest as
    having identity,
states of fixated consciousness are pure in their own place.
Within mind itself, in which sensory appearances manifest
    without identity,
things are free of fragmentation, pure in their own place.

Any mere approximation of this, being contrived and superficial, is to be avoided:

> **Without any realization of equalness in its naturally**
>   **occurring state,**
> **you may obsess on the word "nonduality"**
> **and place your confidence in some state that you speculate**
>   **has no frame of reference whatsoever.**
> **This is truly a mistaken notion—the dark realm in which**
>   **awareness is not recognized.**

Those who have no realization of awareness in all its nakedness instead think, "It is unborn like space, beyond the extremes of positive and negative." They speak off the tops of their heads, using enormously potent words to discuss ultimate reality without basing what they say on personal experience, and since they place confidence in such speculation, their behavior remains crude. They are referred to as "individuals with mistaken notions pretending to be yogins." You should be aware that the majority of them have been seduced by maras. While they may, for example, gather many followers, [80b] they guide these people along a path that leads in the wrong direction, and so are certainly not aware that they themselves are also headed that way. They can turn away from that fate and follow the correct path by ridding themselves of their retinues and other encumbrances, relying on authentic gurus, and applying themselves to spiritual practice that focuses on the significance of one-ness, the true nature of phenomena. *Naturally Arising Awareness* states:

> Otherwise,[29] there may be indications that one has not gained deep realization but is just paying lip service. Further, if one acts like a mad person, this means one has encountered an obstructive mara and should perform an extensive ganachakra feast and pursue spiritual practice!

There are a great many people like this nowadays.

Now, those with good fortune are advised to gain realization of their very essence within the state of perfect equalness, the spacious expanse of the ground of being:

> Therefore, it is in the naturally occurring state without
>   transition or change
> that the most majestic perfection of goals is experienced
>   as nonduality.[30]
> The total freedom of the three realms—the ultimate meaning
>   of the nonduality of samsara and nirvana—
> is the fortress of dharmakaya, the nature of being that arises
>   inherently from within,
> such that it is completely pure like space, yet is in fact beyond
>   all metaphors.

Given that the true nature of phenomena and mind itself are insepa-rable, on the strength of your becoming familiar with this and refining it in your own experience, a state of realization that is like space arises naturally from within; this is referred to as "building the vajra fortress of dharmakaya"—that is, this realization is spontaneously present as great perfection beyond limitation. You definitely experience it in three ways: as dharmakaya, the essence free of limitation; as the supreme continuum of natural freedom underlying concepts; and as the totally pure and nat-urally awakened fruition. [81a] These three are discussed successively in the following scriptural sources. *The Reverberation of Sound* states:

> Since nothing ever need be done, there is freedom,
> and[31] since nothing occurs, nothing remains.
> Since there is no going, the ongoing process of coming comes
>   to an end.

There is no single thing or duality that occurs by being created.[32]
Conventional designations do not exist even in the state of confusion.
Their nature is devoid of existence, nonexistence, and
    the karmic process.
The fruition is timelessly free of ordinary consciousness.
It is beyond all description, imagination, or expression.

And *The Pearl Garland* states:

Since awareness occurs naturally, it is "free."
Since it abides, it is "pervasive."
Since it cannot be characterized, it is "empty."
Since it never sets, it "arises."
Since it has no solidity, it is "unobstructed."
Since it abides as freedom, it "returns to its nature."
Since it manifests in myriad ways, it is "radiance."[33]
Since it is nondual, it is "oneness."
Since it gives rise to everything, it is the "cause."
Since it is the perfection of everything without exception,
    it is the "fruition" itself.
Since its frame of reference is pure, it is the "path."
Since it resolves confusion, it is also "explanatory commentary."
Since it abides in and of itself,[34] it is a "continuum."
Since it can be pointed out, it is "pith instruction."
Since it defies[35] enumeration, it is "calculation."

And *The Six Expanses* states:

Within mind itself, in which things manifest within frames
    of reference,
whatever establishes these frameworks[36] is pure in its own place.
Within mind itself, in which patterns of ordinary consciousness
    manifest,
sensations are pure in their own place.
Within mind itself, in which conceptual consciousness manifests,
whatever promotes examination[37] is pure in its own place.
Within mind itself, in which forms manifest, [81b]
the combinations of the elements are pure in their own place.
Within mind itself, in which consciousness manifests,
causes and conditions are pure in their own place.
Within mind itself, in which sensations manifest,
experiences of them are pure in their own place.

NONDUALITY WITHIN AWAKENED MIND 173

Within mind itself, in which ideas manifest,
all instances of dualistic perception are pure in their own place.
Within mind itself, in which predispositions manifest,[38]
all kinds of afflictive emotions are pure in their own place.
Within mind itself, in which the reification of concepts manifests,
objects of one's attention are pure in their own place.

Now, realization, which involves no reification or fixation, can be summarized as the single ultimate heart essence within the spacious expanse
of space:

As long as you remain fixated on individual things, on "this"
  or "that,"
you remain caught in dualism—the cage of confusion entailing
  self and other.
When you make no biased distinction—of "this"—
everything is the same in the state of equalness, with no frame
  of reference,
and so Vajrasattva declares, "Nonduality is realized!"

Whether or not someone has realized awareness to be the ultimate
meaning of dharmakaya is determined by whether or not awareness
is experienced as entailing an element of reification or fixation. This is
similar to basing a distinction between a clear and an unclear sky on
whether or not clouds, mist, and haze are present.

In this respect, as long as yogins fixate on their own view, meditation, and so forth, or make distinctions between things to abandon and
antidotes to rely on, it is certain that the realization of nonduality is not
present in their mindstreams. This is because they are not free of their
fixation on duality as existing in and of itself. My holy guru, the lord
of dharma Kumararaja, the glorious protector who gained spiritual accomplishment of the ultimate meaning of suchness, [82a] said, "You
know whether or not you have gained realization of the way of abiding
by whether or not you are free of fixations." This is similar to what is
said in a song of realization:

There is an end to suffering ever being aroused,
even pain as insignificant as a sesame husk.

Those who do not use their ordinary consciousness to establish ab-
solutes by fixating and reifying, by accepting or rejecting things, may be

skilled in determining what is spiritual or not. But if they do not reify in the slightest their own or others' philosophy, view, meditation, conduct, or fruition, then Vajrasattva declares that they are "yogins of natural great perfection." *The Array of Inlaid Gems* states:

> Supreme emptiness is dharmakaya.
> It cannot be illustrated by symbols or expressed within frames
>   of reference.
> Self-knowing awareness is without cause or condition.
> It is beyond the extremes of being empty and not empty.[39]

And *The Reverberation of Sound* states:

> Since ultimate reality is free of ordinary consciousness,
> the sense faculties are free[40] all at once,
> and so the key point of direct perception[41]
> ensures that one's personal philosophy breaks down.
> Thus, without fixating on or reifying anything,
> one savors the taste of the authentic nature of phenomena.
> Without any grounds for falling back into the three realms,[42]
> this is like space itself dissolving into space—
> the most sublime yoga.

This is the commentary on the eighth section of *The Precious Treasury of the Basic Space of Phenomena,* demonstrating nonduality within awakened mind. [82b]

9

The Decisive Experience

You come to the decisive experience of this nondual awakened mind within the spacious expanse that transcends ordinary consciousness:

> Within the single expanse, supremely spacious by nature,
> awakened mind, equal to space, is pivotal.
> Focus on this key point and distill it to its vital essence;
> it is the greatest of the great—wholly positive and spacious
>   enlightened mind.
> In its very essence, it thoroughly shatters the outer confines
>   of reality.
> Within this single vast expanse, there is no duality of
>   realization versus its lack,
> of freedom versus its lack, but a supreme state of equalness.

At this point, in order to come to the decisive experience of awareness as the source of all phenomena, you come to a decisive experience of the essence of awareness as supremely spacious—equal to space itself—nondual and not subject to extremes. Mind is pivotal—a space-like, vast expanse; you can identify it by focusing directly on awareness, which is without origination or cessation—naked, unobstructed, free of ordinary consciousness that engages in thinking in terms of identity, and not restricted or localized in any way whatsoever. You thus perceive dharmakaya in all its nakedness, unsullied by the distorted speculations of ordinary consciousness. According to the great perfection approach, the very essence of original purity is supremely unobstructed dharmakaya. There is no other point to arrive at, no other decisive experience to come to. *Vajrasattva: Mirror of the Heart* states:

Understand all aspects of awareness to be free of ordinary consciousness, which involves concepts about identity. Similarly, bring this understanding to the point of understanding that all phenomena are continuous. Bring the understanding of what is continuous to the point of understanding that it manifests in any way at all. Bring the understanding of what manifests in any way at all to the point of understanding that it is unborn.[1] [83a] Bring the understanding of what is unborn to the point of understanding that it does not come or go. Bring the understanding of what does not come or go to the point of understanding that it is nondual. Bring the understanding of what is nondual to the point of understanding that it is supreme lucidity without limitation. Similarly, bring this understanding to the point of not conceptualizing or thinking about any phenomenon in any way. Bring this understanding of all phenomena to the point of experiencing their essence clearly and without distraction.

This citation shows that it is necessary here to understand dharmakaya—the originally pure, naked state in which phenomena resolve—as the final point to which one is led, the point at which one comes to this decisive experience. If this is not understood, someone might teach that the stage of completion concerns what is unborn and beyond imagination or expression, leading someone else to then think, "It is inconceivable and inexpressible." But this would mean that the concepts of inconceivability and inexpressibility had become objectified, as though one were naming the unnameable, and there would be no chance of recognizing the very essence of mind itself. *Naturally Arising Awareness* states:

If one does not understand that dharmakaya is unobstructed,[2]
then even though one accepts that the stage of completion is the
   experience of what is unborn,
that is like pretending that a fox or a monkey is a lion.

At this point, there are two ways to identify awareness in all its nakedness by focusing on it directly. The first is to be directly introduced to it without reliance on some key point. This bare consciousness, an uninterrupted openness, is present at all times without indulging in any conceptual elaboration directed outwardly, without reifying anything inwardly, without settling somewhere in between, without being ordinary contriving consciousness, and without stirring in thought. When master and student share that for even a brief moment, through the master's blessing it is directly introduced as it arises in all its nakedness, and so is perceived by the student in and of itself, in all its nakedness. It is crucial to maintain the certainty that this awareness is itself dharma-kaya, [83b] neither meditating on it deliberately nor becoming distracted.

Second, there are six ways to introduce awareness directly by relying on key points:

Direct introduction to awareness with the mind focused: Have the student sit cross-legged, breathing gently, with eyes wide open and mind resting without concepts. At that point, have the student disregard both the clarity and stability that are present when one abides in an extremely clear state of mind (for these are but meditative experiences), and directly introduce the naked wakefulness of awareness as dharmakaya.

Direct introduction to awareness with the mind at rest: Without any focusing of his or her mind, but while it is very present and settled in its own place, have the student let go of its abiding quality, and directly introduce lucid wakefulness as dharmakaya.

Direct introduction to awareness by getting to the root of the matter: Have the student direct his or her attention inwardly, examining specifically where the mind comes from or is located. When (without anything actually being found) the mind becomes lucid in all its nakedness, have the student let go of the tendency to fall into some entirely nonconceptual state, and directly introduce naked wakefulness, beyond any label or meaning, as dharmakaya.

Direct introduction to awareness through elimination of the sense that anything is real: When the student's mind is lost in response to sense objects, have the student eliminate any sense of ordinary mind relating in some way to those objects—for example, by reducing them to their components. When he or she is thus abiding in pristine emptiness, which is inexpressible and in which there is no sense of either objects or mind, have the student let go of that sense of abiding, in which there is no tendency whatsoever for thoughts to proliferate or resolve, and directly introduce the quality of awareness in all its pristine nakedness as dharmakaya.

Direct introduction to awareness in the gap between sense objects and consciousness of them: Have the student rest contentedly while remaining conscious of a sense object. Then, without directing attention outwardly to the object [84a] or inwardly to the mind, he or she arrives at a seamless state of bare perception. Have the student let go of the sense of dwelling in that bare state, and directly introduce bare awareness, vivid and lucid, as dharmakaya.

Direct introduction to awareness by inducing distraction: Have the student spend a short time being idle; then deliberately cause him or her to become distracted by talking or whatever. At that point you might say, "What does 'hasaraki'* mean? Tell me! Tell me!" Having no idea what it means, the student will experience mild astonishment and wonder. Then, have him or her let go of the sense of dwelling on that astonishment, and directly introduce the lucid wakefulness that is thus exposed as dharmakaya. Alternatively, you might say "Stay put!" when the student is on the point of going, or say "Go away!" only to say "Come back!" once he or she has gone a short distance. Then, have the student let go of what he or she experiences in turning back—consciousness that is clear and involves no proliferation of thoughts—and directly introduce the wakefulness thus exposed as dharmakaya.

In brief, you may employ methods that entail mind when it is thinking or when it is at rest—methods that may involve the subtle channels, energies, and bindu or any other appropriate methods. But regardless of which you employ, once awareness, clear and pure like a crystal globe, has been elicited in all its nakedness—free of ordinary consciousness, so that it entails no view or meditation and no antidote—directly introduce that awareness as supremely unobstructed dharmakaya.

A distinction must be made between this and a meditative experience of clarity. A meditative experience of clarity is a clear state of mind at rest, but dharmakaya is the unity of lucidity and awareness, free of any sense of being at rest. It is that naked, aware quality that is not colored by any sense of being appearance, emptiness, clarity, bliss, or some nonconceptual state. This being so, the distinction here has to do with whether or not the experience has an unobstructed quality and whether there is a quality of awareness rather than one of abiding, and so there is no possibility of mistaking one for the other. Regarding these key points, [84b] *The Reverberation of Sound* states:

> These are focusing the mind, letting it rest,
>   getting to the root of the matter, eliminating the sense that
>   anything is real,

* A nonsense word.

seeking in the gap between sense objects and consciousness
      of them,
and inducing distraction.

You come to the decisive experience of unobstructed awareness in all
its nakedness that is not cultivated in meditation. In essence, it is free of
the three phases of origination, cessation, and duration. It can be identified in a number of ways—for example, as a supremely indescribable,
inconceivable, and inexpressible state; as a supreme state that is beyond
labels and in which phenomena resolve; as a state beyond virtue or
harm, positive qualities or faults; or as supreme original purity that has
been so from the very beginning. But it is not held to be a blank void
similar to space, so the method of direct introduction differs from that
of other approaches.

In the Middle Way school and other such approaches, the focus of
attention is the true nature that applies universally to all phenomena yet
has never existed as anything whatsoever. It is determined to be without
origination or cessation and so forth. In the majority of approaches in
the Categories of Mind and Expanse, one's consciousness and the sense
objects one perceives are all judged to be a single state of evenness that,
for example, has never known nonexistence or existence. So there is a
great potential for flaw and error, for losing sight of what is fundamental.

In the present approach, while any number of methods can be used
to indicate what is intended, they all have in common a unique freedom
from elaboration, for the essence of being is elicited unobstructedly in
all its nakedness. Since you reach a decision without any obscuration or
any potential for error, you come to the decisive experience within the
state that is beyond labels and in which phenomena resolve, without any
possibility of mistaking that essence.

It can be shown that for a yogin with such realization, who abides in the
genuine, ongoing flow of realization, samsara is cleared away without
even its name remaining:

> A garuda whose wings have grown within the egg [85a]
> abides in the expanse of the sky once it breaks out of the egg.
> It overwhelms nagas and crosses directly over abysses.
> So also, a fortunate yogin who has realized the vajra heart
>   essence, just as it is,

the pinnacle of all spiritual approaches,
outshines those following lower approaches and crosses
   directly over the abyss of samsara.

The garuda, the most powerful of birds, whose wings form fully within the egg, hatches out of the confining egg at the appropriate time, whereupon it soars into the vault of the sky, immediately capable of overwhelming nagas and crossing directly over abysses. Similarly, a yogin of natural great perfection who has in this lifetime realized awareness to be dharmakaya (having been introduced directly to it by a guru), yet has not yet passed away, is like a garuda whose wings have grown within the egg. But in that the yogin no longer experiences awareness as having fixed dimensions, he or she is also like a garuda that has hatched out of the confining egg and soars into the sky. Such a yogin is immediately capable of outshining those who follow lower spiritual approaches, overwhelming afflictive emotional patterns, and crossing directly over the abyss of samsara. *The All-Creating Monarch* states:

> It is like a great garuda soaring in space.
> There is no proliferation or resolution of thoughts.

An alternative interpretation takes into account the fact that, while the threefold dynamic energy of one's realization may have reached full expression in this present life, one has not become free of the confining shell of this illusory body. Once one has passed beyond its confines, one will instantly become free in original purity. This is similar to a garuda hatching out of its confining egg and soaring into the sky. At that point, while soaring in the sky of dharmakaya (that is, awareness), [85b] the garuda (that is, rupakaya) acts to ensure both kinds of benefit for those to be guided, thus outshining those who follow lower spiritual approaches and crossing directly over the abyss of samsara. *The Perfect Dynamic Energy of the Lion* states:

> In the very bodies of all ordinary beings
> abides the essence[3] of pure timeless awareness,
> but it cannot break through its confines.
> For example, what is confined within a womb or an egg
> is not evident, but hidden.
> Once its natural energy is perfected, however, it emerges.
> Similarly, as soon as this body born of concepts has been
>   cast aside,

one encounters the realm of awareness's own manifestations.
Self-knowing awareness, abiding timelessly,
perceives its essence nonconceptually.
The pure perspective of timeless awareness
and the truth of buddhahood are perceived.
In essence, timeless awareness's own manifestations
do not entail the ordinary mind's conceptual process.
Sense objects in the past and sense objects in the future—
sensory appearances are directly cut through.

You come to the decisive experience of the essence of awareness being
beyond causality:

**The freedom of everything—abiding in a supreme state of
equalness—
is unacceptable to those involved in cause and effect, effort
and achievement,
but in the most sublime approach it makes perfect sense as
the ultimate meaning of unwavering equalness.**

Since there is nothing to add to or remove from the essence of awareness, it is beyond cause and effect, effort and achievement, and involves
no acceptance of any positive quality or rejection of any flaw. Although
this is unacceptable to those in lower spiritual approaches, who are
alarmed or even terrified by this, it makes perfect sense to true yogins of
the highest caliber. *The All-Creating Monarch* states:

I, the all-creating one, do not reveal this transmission
to those who follow spiritual approaches based on either causes
or results.
If I were to reveal this transmission definitively, [86a]
they would claim, "Positive and negative actions entail
causality,"
exaggerating or underestimating me, the truth,
and so they would not encounter the truth that I am[4]
for a long time.

. . . .

Without trying to abide, without thinking, without needing[5]
anything whatsoever,
abide naturally in a nonconceptual state of equalness.

> The ordinary mind of effort does not pertain to what is
>   timelessly ensured.
> Those who abide in supreme bliss
> embody the very essence of all phenomena.

At this point, avoid any incorrect notions that repudiate the intended meaning because the metaphors involved are contradictory. On the one hand, some claim that "causality is definitely responsible for things coming about, as, for example, a sprout comes from a seed." But they also claim that "mind itself is like space." These two metaphors imply that in order for buddhahood to be accomplished due to the essence of mind, the process is at the same time composite and noncomposite. Because of this contradiction, the good fortune to attain buddhahood swiftly is lacking in ordinary spiritual approaches. Why is this so? Given that they consider substantial things to be something "other," anything thus brought about by cause and effect, effort and achievement, would amount to something "other"—that is, a perception based on confusion. It is fundamentally contradictory for what is in essence unconfused to be attained through confusion.

As well, everyone is in agreement that mind itself is like space; therefore, a metaphor that involves causality is meaningless in this regard and unacceptable, because there is a contradiction between that metaphor and the intended meaning. If mind itself is explained to be spontaneously present, this stands in contradiction to its "being produced through causes and conditions"; [86b] there is thus an internal contradiction between such a statement and one found in a scripture of the ordinary spiritual approaches: that it is "uncompounded and spontaneously present."[6] Furthermore, given that mind itself is like space, there is an enormous contradiction in proving that underlying meaning by using a metaphor that concerns the mundane process of origination. This cannot be the case. *The All-Creating Monarch* states:

> Because great perfection is timelessly beyond causality,
> the state in which nothing need be done is not accomplished
>   by being sought or achieved.
> Teachers who view things in terms of causality issue
>   pronouncements.
> They take phenomena with ordinary characteristics as
>   their standard
> and try to accomplish results through causality.

Mind does not entail causes, and so never any results.
Because awakened mind is not born,
do not take ordinary phenomena—which are born—to be
    metaphors for it
and misinterpret it as something that comes into being
    and then decays.
Without realizing[7] that it occurs naturally, beyond causality,
such teachers take phenomena with ordinary characteristics as
    their standard
and rely on causes, claiming that results come from them.
This is the provisional transmission of spiritual approaches based
    on causality.
Not dependent on causes, incomparable timeless awareness
gives rise to everything, and so there is no other source
    of phenomena.
To seek it, taking ordinary phenomena (whether causes or effects)
    as the standard
will not bring about what has never existed as a result.
Because awakened mind occurs without causes or conditions,[8]
do not take ordinary phenomena, which originate and cease,
    as the standard.
Because awakened mind is not created by conditions,
do not take ordinary phenomena, which are created by
    conditions, to be metaphors for it. [87a]

Therefore, since the essence of awakened mind is not created by anything whatsoever, but occurs naturally and is without transition or change, there is no context within which it can be sought through causes and conditions—it is like space. Given that awakened mind is the ground from which phenomena come about, there is no need for these in turn to create it, for that would be a mistaken notion about the process of creation, in that awakened mind has never existed as anything to be created. Therefore, it is ensured without your having to seek it, for you clearly experience its spontaneous presence when you abide within the state in which nothing need be done. The same source states:

Abiding in the fundamental nature spontaneously ensures
    the absence of straying.
With natural abiding, there is nothing for anyone to contrive.
To abide in what simply is, without its being sought,[9]

means that nothing need be done—this is revealed to be the most
   sublime activity.
Having realized the ultimate meaning of this, do not act.
In not acting, abide in suchness.
Whoever abides in suchness ensures that there is no error
   or contrivance.

Such awareness—beyond cause and effect, effort and achievement—
is definitely an authentic sign of the culmination of realization:

Everything is supreme bliss, equal to space itself—
   the expanse of dharmakaya.
There is nothing that is not free within the expanse of
   dharmakaya.
The true nature of everything is experienced intuitively[10]
   as the kaya of the vajra heart essence.
The dynamic energy of this heart essence is perfect within
   the body born of habitual patterns.
Once the body of conditioned existence between birth
   and death is cast off,
awareness is experienced as a oneness, in no way divisible.
Once one has "gained the empire" on the level of
   spontaneous presence,
emanations occur without restriction [87b]
and one can engage in every situation without impediment.
Such is the domain of a yogin who "is effortlessly borne
   on the wind."
While this is unacceptable to anyone involved in lower spiritual
   approaches,
it is shown by the ati approach to make perfect sense—it is the
   key point of the fruition.

In this regard, there are three possibilities. One with diligence and
the greatest fortune is freed like mist, with the restrictions of the body
vanishing naturally. One with a middling degree of these qualities is
freed like the space inside a vase. And one with a lesser degree is freed
like the sun and moon on the fifteenth day of the lunar month.

For one of the highest order, the indications of success reach full
measure through the four visions as they occur in the path of trekchö,
in the reverse of the usual sequence. That is to say, first one recognizes

the very essence of being in the vision termed "the resolution of phenomena"—awareness as naked original purity. While one maintains
this most majestic enlightened intent of dharmakaya, such that there is
no coming together with or falling away from it, there is the full expression of unobstructed awareness as freedom from the extremes of being
one thing and being many. As one maintains this experience—within
which all circumstances that manifest outwardly or inwardly are free in
their true nature—without losing sight of it, any attempts at suppression
or indulgence, afflictive emotions, and concepts are inherently pure and
so resolve naturally. Meditative experiences arise naturally without one
reacting to them, such that they are free of restriction, just as they are,
without being reified. Finally, these transitory meditative experiences
resolve and awareness "reaches" the fundamental ground of being. At
that point, the vision termed "the direct perception of the true nature
of phenomena" arises in a straightforward way, and one abides in this
fundamental state of original purity in all its nakedness and immediacy.

It is in this context that the terms "leaving phenomena behind," "the
resolution of phenomena," and "transcending phenomena" are used.
While nothing has ever existed as anything, there occur ten indications
that one of the highest order has gained supernormal powers and perception, as well as mastery over the elements, [88a] which can no longer harm one. One cannot be crushed by earth, carried away by water,
burned by fire, or moved by wind. One can fly in the sky like a bird. One
can transform material objects and transport them over long distances
to places like mountaintops and buildings. One can ensure benefit for
beings through the interdependence of all that arises in various ways.
One can perceive the very atoms of one's body. One gains clairvoyance
and other supernormal powers of perception. And one achieves miraculous powers and levels of insight. *The Heaped Jewels* states:

> When anyone rests in the natural state without concentration,
> understanding manifests in that individual's mind,
> without someone having to teach all the words
> by which the mind understands these meanings.[11]
> As this understanding dawns in the mind,
> all that is nonmanifest and all sensory appearances,
> which themselves entail no concepts, are seen to be
>   naturally pure.
> Thus, in an unobstructed way, everything

becomes an expression of the supreme unity of emptiness
and lucidity.
Each of the four elements—earth, water, fire, and air—
dissipates into space like mist
without its specific potential manifesting.
Regardless of the complexity with which confused fixation
is experienced,
these aspects of dualistic perception naturally cease
in that they have never been born, so nothing manifests.
Because this resolution happens naturally,
an illuminating experience like one's own can be so for all beings.

One with a middling degree of accomplishment is freed like the space inside a vase. Once one has become familiar with this approach, one's body at the time of death can be compared to a vase, while the mind is like the space within that vase. The instant the bond between body and mind is loosened, [88b] self-knowing awareness—dharmakaya as original purity—merges with and becomes indistinguishable from supreme space—dharmakaya as the ground of being. In other words, awareness, elicited in its naked oneness, "awakens" to buddhahood, in every way inseparable from the true nature of phenomena. When one realizes that self-knowing awareness is unobstructed (in that there is no longer any division into outer and inner, just as there is no division in space once a vase is shattered), dharmakaya holds to its natural place, while rupakaya and the enlightened activities it entails arise spontaneously, like stars and planets appearing naturally in the sky. This is what *The Conjunction of Sun and Moon* refers to in the following line:

Trying to fragment space, which is nonmanifest . . .[12]

Though awareness is illustrated by this metaphor of space, do not take it literally to mean that awareness is reduced to some state of voidness, because metaphors illustrate things partially, but not entirely. That is to say, the lack of differentiation between outer and inner space illustrates that awareness is atemporal, but it is definitely not the case that one's awareness somehow dissolves into some universal basic space. This metaphor merely illustrates the fact that this oneness of awareness, being freed from its confines at the point of death, is elicited in all its nakedness and, holding to its natural place of dharmakaya, simply rests without transition or change.

One with a lesser degree of accomplishment is likened to the sun setting and the moon rising on the fifteenth day of the lunar month. Analogous to the sun setting on the fifteenth day, at the time of death one is ushered out by the unimpaired realization of the scope of naked awareness. Analogous to the moon rising, one is guided by the arising of naturally present timeless awareness in the intermediate state, in which one encounters one's true nature. Without anything intervening between these two events, one awakens to buddhahood inseparable from the realization of awareness that is present as dharmakaya in all its nakedness. [89a]

That is to say, awareness as originally pure dharmakaya—utter lucidity free of elaboration—arises the instant one's inner respiration stops and consciousness issues into space. Of the five aspects of subtle energy, the four energies of earth, water, fire, and air dissolve, while the energy of space enters into a state of utter lucidity. So as his or her awareness is about to leave the body, a yogin enters into the basic space of original purity, transferring consciousness as enlightened intent that is borne by subtle energy. Saying "Hik!" one projects one's awareness from the heart up through the aperture at the crown of the head, where one imagines one's root guru, a *Hum*, or a vajra, and so in an instant passes directly upward to dharmakaya.

To merge with the kayas and timeless awareness, one lies in the sleeping lion posture, focusing one's awareness on one's gaze. By transferring consciousness while focusing that gaze on the unity of basic space and awareness in the space in front, one awakens to buddhahood in an instant, without any intermediate state ensuing.

These are very important key points—teachings specific to this great perfection approach. They are further stated in *The Conjunction of Sun and Moon*:

> Having been borne on the four subtle energies in succession,
> one is stirred by a single great energy.[13]
> Regarding that moment, I reveal how to merge with the object
>   and environment
> and how to merge with the kayas and timeless awareness.
>
> Concerning how to merge with the pure object
>   and environment,[14]
> my advice is to transfer from one state to another.

> One should train the consciousness in conjunction with the subtle
>   energy on which it is borne.
> Furthermore, it is crucial to have become proficient previously.
> It is crucial to focus and project one's awareness.
> Moreover, one should project it upward with "Hik!" [89b]
> It reaches the presence of the guru.
>
> Concerning how to merge with the kayas and timeless awareness,
> one should direct one's awareness in the following way:
> with the body in the sleeping lion posture,
> one focuses one's awareness on one's gaze.
> One should use the space in front as the path for a short time.
> If one's experience of basic space and awareness does not change,
> one will, without doubt, awaken to buddhahood
> without any intermediate state ensuing.

These two methods of transference are taught for the benefit of two kinds of yogins, respectively—those who practice trekchö and those who practice tögal.

Thus, having become free in the state of original purity, one benefits from having reached the ongoing state of most majestic being—dharmakaya—within the secret embrace of precious spontaneous presence. And as the rupakaya arises within that context, throughout all worlds of those to be guided, emanations issue forth without hindrance, restriction, or bias. So the spontaneous accomplishment of these two kinds of benefit is ensured. This is missing in lower approaches but is present in this one—such is the superiority of this most majestic spiritual approach, the spontaneously present vajra heart essence. I will give the scriptural citations for these points in the last chapter, on fruition.

It can be shown that awareness is beyond causes and conditions:

> **Since the magical illusion of origination occurs within what
>   has no origin,
> it is the ordinary confused mind that characterizes things as
>   involving causality.
> What the ati approach reveals as the absence of causes or
>   conditions
> makes eminently perfect sense, although it is unacceptable in
>   lower approaches.**

The dynamic energy and display that arise as a miraculous expression of origination do so within the scope of the essence of being, which has no origin and is beyond cause and effect. Such a perspective is unacceptable in spiritual approaches concerned with causality, but makes perfect sense in this approach. [90a] What it entails is similar to a miraculous display in space, unborn yet arising continuously. *The All-Creating Monarch* states:

> The heart essence of everything—this awakened mind,
> timelessly and spontaneously present by its nature—
> need not be sought or achieved through the ten attributes.
> My nature is like space, the universal metaphor.
> In pure space, all is such that it entails no effort.
> While everyone seeks something in pure space,
> the nature of space is beyond all effort and achievement.[15]

You come to the decisive experience of samsara and nirvana as inseparable, supremely equal and perfect within the scope of awareness:

> **The intent and conduct of buddhas and ordinary beings**
>   **are not separate,**
> **so it is the ordinary confused mind[16] that holds samsara**
>   **and nirvana to be a duality.**
> **What the ati approach reveals as nondual**
> **makes eminently perfect sense, although it is unacceptable**
>   **in lower approaches.**

Just as experiences of samsara and nirvana in your dreams are identical within your own mind, samsara and nirvana are identical within the scope of awareness, and so are beyond the extremes of acceptance and rejection, hope and fear. *The Perfect Dynamic Energy of the Lion* states:

> Samsara and nirvana are self-knowing awareness itself.
> They are not separate, but nondual.[17]

You come to the decisive experience of it being irrelevant whether or not one has realization:

> **Given the freedom in which it is irrelevant whether or not**
>   **one has realization,**

> to believe that freedom comes about through realization is
>   the enemy of equalness.[18]
> What the ati approach reveals as a single state of equalness
> makes eminently perfect sense, although it is unacceptable
>   in lower approaches.

Since all phenomena are timelessly free, nothing need be done to free them anew through realization. [90b] If they were not timelessly free, realization could not free them, and if they are already free there is no need to make them so. Therefore, do not treat their essence, which has nothing to do with whether or not there is realization, as a case of bondage versus freedom.

Even the thought that freedom comes about through direct introduction is deluded. One strives to free this essence from whatever binds it, but nothing need be done to free it, for unobstructed awareness, which has never existed as anything whatsoever, does not entail any duality of something to be realized and someone to realize it. There is equalness, because nothing is improved by realization or worsened by its absence, and so there is no need for any adventitious realization. And because there has never existed anything to realize—for the ultimate nature of phenomena is beyond ordinary consciousness—to speak of "realization" on even the relative level is nothing but deluded. What can be shown at this point is the transcendence of view and meditation, in which nothing need be done regarding realization, nothing need be directly introduced, and no state of meditation need be cultivated. So there is the expression "it is irrelevant whether or not one has realization." *The Great Garuda* states:

> Conceptual consciousness that labels and speculates about[19]
>   the heart essence has come to an end.
> Resting imperturbably, free of obscuration, is the
>   uncorrupted path.
> Intangible and without parallel, timeless awareness is
>   the actuality of everything.

And *The Reverberation of Sound* states:

> "Freedom" is just a conventional designation.
> To whom or what does realization or its absence apply?
> What in this case can be thought of as "freedom"?
> How could there be involvement in the three realms?

It is the nature of phenomena that they are free of the limitations
of conditioned existence.

You come to the decisive experience that does not rely on the key points
of skillful means and sublime knowing:

> To hold that one cannot realize the inexpressible [91a]
> without relying on specific means to characterize it is
> a fool's attitude.
> What the ati approach reveals as inseparability from
> the ultimate[20]
> makes eminently perfect sense, although it is unacceptable
> in lower approaches.

Lower spiritual approaches hold that one cannot perceive the ultimate meaning of mind itself without relying on their respective means—
methods such as those involving the subtle channels, subtle energies,
and bindu or the two accumulations. In this case, what makes perfect
sense in the ati approach is the superior realization whereby one directly
experiences the unobstructed state in all its nakedness, without relying
on anything whatsoever. Since one does not experience separation from
the essence of awareness even for an instant, to say that it is realized or
perceived is merely to use a conventional expression. *The Great Garuda*
states:

> Holding the breath and closing the eyes bind one's mind.
> In the state that has no underlying basis, uncontrived and free of
> anything to rely on,
> assuming specific postures and trying to relax in lucidity bind
> one to sensory appearances.
> If one's mind is not impartial and free of extremes,
> mental analysis and speculation[21] prevent one from experiencing
> the way of abiding.
> Without the confidence that comes from resting naturally
> in timeless freedom,
> in which nothing need be done,
> realization is constrained by wishful thinking and fleeting
> meditative experiences.
> Without the key point of its resting in its own place, which need
> not be sought,

awareness is bound[22] by one's relying on teachings that
concern causality.

You come to a decisive experience that is beyond imagination, transcending what is boundless:

> Although great perfection is timeless and infinite, without fixed
>   depth or extent,
> to claim that it is "unfathomable" is a fool's attitude.[23]
> What the ati approach reveals as a boundless, unique state
> makes eminently perfect sense, although it is unacceptable
>   in lower approaches.

Followers of lower spiritual approaches—and even some who follow the Categories of Mind and Expanse—hold that because the ultimate essence, this great perfection, [91b] has no center or limit, no fixed
depth or extent, it is some boundless void state, which they call "beyond
the scope of awareness." Here, on the other hand, unique, unobstructed
awareness is revealed in all its nakedness, and so does not lie within the
scope of ordinary mind or consciousness or any frame of reference. To
perceive it within the scope of one's individual self-knowing awareness
is to realize it through the key point of distinguishing between ordinary
mind and timeless awareness. *Samantabhadra: Mirror of Enlightened
Mind* states:

> Uncontrived view is unobstructed timeless awareness.
> Uncontrived meditation is lucid and without reification.
> Uncontrived conduct is naturally occurring relaxation itself.
> Uncontrived fruition is the scope of naturally manifest awareness.[24]
> Uncontrived samaya is the unwavering true nature of
>   phenomena.[25]
> Uncontrived empowerments constitute empowerment into
>   the dynamic energy of awareness.
> Uncontrived faith is the expanse of unchanging space.[26]
> Those of the most sublime acumen, who have such realization,
> abide in an unwavering state of equalness on the level of
>   supreme bliss.

You come to the decisive experience of awareness—the unique sphere of
being—as dharmakaya in all its nakedness:

The usual order of things is reversed within the single sphere
of being,
and so hope and fear concerning the fruition are cut
through—a state equal to space.
So vast, so supreme, the enlightened mind of victorious ones
is equal to space.
There is no renunciation or attainment—the expanse of
the single sphere.
This is timeless freedom; it is irrelevant whether or not
one has realization.
A yogin is content on the path equal to space, with nothing
needing to be done.

Given that all phenomena of samsara and nirvana fundamentally arise within the scope of awareness—the unique sphere of being—there is a reversal of the usual way in which interdependent factors cause the universe of appearances and possibilities to occur in all its variety. That is to say, you trace them back to the place from which they originally came, [92a] and so get to the heart of awareness. Once you have realized that samsara and nirvana are miraculous expressions of awareness, there is no hope of attaining some higher state of buddhahood, for you have decided that no buddhahood exists aside from what arises due to awareness itself. There is no fear of falling into samsara, for you have decided that fundamentally appearances are nothing other than the perceptions of unconfused awareness. By realizing that awareness itself, like space, cannot be identified, you come to the decisive experience of supremely spacious spontaneous presence as a great state of timeless freedom beyond labels. You are brought to the point where samsara and nirvana resolve, which is to arrive at the enlightened intent of Samantabhadra. *Samantabhadra: Mirror of Enlightened Mind* states:

The infinite expanse of enlightenment is unobscured and
totally pure.
Since buddhahood does not exist, there is not even the
label "buddha."[27]
Since reification does not exist, there is not even the label[28]
"ordinary being."
Since conceptualization does not exist, there is no confusion
due to nonrecognition.
Since fixation does not exist, there are no concepts or objects.[29]

Since attachment does not exist, there are no habitual patterns
    of ordinary mind.
Since the past does not exist, there is not even the label "future."
Since the present does not exist, there is not even the label
    "afflictive emotion."
Since the teachings do not exist, there is not even the label
    "teacher."
This yoga—the spacious realization of the single sphere
    of being[30]—
is one of abiding definitively and without change on a level
    from which there is no regression,[31]
is spontaneously present and without change in the state
    of supreme bliss,
and is the unobscured, clearly evident fruition in the
    nonconceptual state.

You come to the decisive experience of confusion as a supreme state beyond labels:

**This timelessly awakened awareness that entails no object
does not wander in samsara, for it is beyond all basis for
    confusion. [92b]
No one at all is confused, for there is no context for confusion.
Everything lies within the scope of the basic space of
    phenomena, a single lucid expanse.
With no time frame, this spaciousness is equal to space itself.
Samsara is primordially pure, a timeless and spontaneously
    present state of utter relaxation.**

Consider the fact that while dreams do not stray from the context of sleep, sleep does not stray from the context of awareness and awareness in turn does not stray from the context of the basic space of phenomena. If you analyze and examine this, you see that no one has ever experienced falling into samsara. Samsara itself is already and forever pure, for it is by nature clearly apparent without truly existing—the very essence of what a dream is, manifest yet without an independent nature. These expressions of emptiness are furthermore pure in dharmakaya, which is without underlying basis or foundation. So the causes of confusion, confusion itself, perceptions based on confusion, and the one experiencing confusion have never known existence. One has not been confused in the past, does not experience confusion in the present, and cannot possibly be confused in the future, because there is already and forever a total purity as the very essence of space, which is without underlying basis. *The Great Garuda* states:

> There is no name for, let alone the possibility of, confusion
> or nonrecognition for anyone.[32]
> Therefore, since nothing has ever been freed, freeing later on
> is a fallacy.

And *The Pearl Garland* states:

> The unconfused ground that abides thus
> is self-knowing awareness, so utterly lucid!
> The three kayas are timelessly perfect without being created.
> The fruition abides naturally and timelessly.
> Phenomena never affect it.
> Philosophical tenets are timelessly beyond being maintained.
> There is never any sullying due to the five poisons.
> Where, then, is samsara? Where is confusion?[33] [93a]

You come to the decisive experience of the nonduality of samsara and nirvana:

> One does not enter a state of freedom or attain nirvana.
> The unchanging vast expanse—samsara and nirvana have
>   never known existence.
> Here there is no frame of reference for renunciation or
>   attainment, hope or fear,
> but rather a supremely spacious expanse that is the
>   primordially enlightened ground of being.
> All things are mere labels, for in actuality they are beyond
>   characterization or expression.
> Having decisively experienced that samsara is not confusion
>   and nirvana is not freedom,
> let no one make any effort!
> Let no one try to meddle with or alter this!

That is to say, given that self-knowing awareness is timelessly empty and pure like space, samsara is pure in that bondage does not exist and nirvana is totally pure in that freedom does not exist. Since self-knowing awareness is beyond the extremes of existence and nonexistence, you come to a decision that it entails no effort or achievement, no hope or fear. *The Tantra Without Letters* states:

> The ultimate essence, awareness itself,[34] is not created.
> How could there be a creator?
> It is not contrived; there is no one to contrive it.
> It is not samsara or nirvana, not bondage or freedom,[35]
> not a specific point of view, but free of any point from which
>   to view.
> It is not ordinary seeing, but a totally pure[36] way of seeing.

You come to the decisive experience of freedom from limitation as a supremely spacious expanse:

> **Awareness, with no breadth or depth,**
> **is not subject to restrictions or extremes, so give up any frame**
> **of reference.**
> **Awareness, involving no plans or actions, no coming or going,**
> **entails no time frame or antidote, so drop reification and effort.**
> **If there is a deliberate frame of reference, it is a cause of**
> **bondage.**
> **Do not rely on any fixed construct whatsoever—let go**
> **in evenness!**

You should understand that, in essence, awareness is not subject to restrictions or extremes, [93b] involves no time frame, no renunciation or antidotes, no plans or actions, no coming or going, no view, meditation, conduct, or fruition, no question of what it is or is not, and no effort or achievement. It transcends the effort and achievement involved in the ten attributes. It is a supremely spacious expanse, free of limitation and all-pervasive, yet it has never existed as anything whatsoever. *The All-Creating Monarch* states:

> My nature shows itself to be authentic.
> Because I transcend the entire range of finite experience,
> there is no view to cultivate in meditation.
> Similarly, the ten attributes do not ultimately exist,
> so do not think that they do.
> Since I am not an object to be seen by looking,
> do not try to look—rest in suchness itself.

Since there is no causal factor separating one from the unborn
    state free of elaboration,
there is no need to observe vows or spiritual disciplines.
Because the heart essence is timelessly and spontaneously present,
there is no need for effort or achievement.
Because naturally occurring timeless awareness is unobscured,
this awareness, this timeless awareness, cannot be made
    more lucid.
Because everything abides on my level,
there are no levels of realization to train on or traverse.
Because I abide all-pervasively,
there is no path that leads to me.
Because I am timelessly free of dualistic perception,
there is nothing that could even be labeled "subtle."
Because my form is all-pervasive,
"duality" has never existed.
Since I have always been naturally occurring timeless awareness,
there is no definitive conclusion about me for others to reach.
Since I am the very heart of everyone's enlightenment,
there is no secret source of pith instructions elsewhere. [94a]
Because I am beyond all misinterpretation,
I have decisively experienced all phenomena.
Since there is no object, only me,
I have also decisively experienced that there is no view to cultivate
    in meditation.
Because there is nothing to uphold, only me,
I have also decisively experienced that there is no samaya
    to uphold.
Because there is nothing to seek, only me,
I have also decisively experienced that there is no enlightened
    activity to seek.[37]
Because there is nowhere to abide, only me,
I have also decisively experienced that there are no levels of
    realization on which to train.
Because obscurations are timelessly absent in me,
I have also decisively experienced that I am naturally occurring
    timeless awareness.
Because I am unborn—the true nature of phenomena—
I have also decisively experienced that I am that subtle nature.
Because there is nowhere to journey, only me,

> I have also decisively experienced that there are no paths
>   to traverse.
> Because buddhas, ordinary beings, and the universe of
>   appearances and possibilities
> all occur due to me—enlightenment, the heart essence—
> I have also decisively experienced timeless nonduality.
> Because I epitomize naturally occurring timeless awareness,
> I have also decisively experienced that I am the supreme
>   lightning transmission.
> Because all phenomena are none other than me,
> I, the all-creating one, am the decisive experience of everything.

Now, since your realization is as vast as space, you come to the decisive experience of a supreme state in which nothing need be done about phenomena. In doing so, with the fundamentally unconditioned quality of this state becoming fully evident, you come to the decisive experience of a supreme state beyond ordinary consciousness, in which phenomena resolve:

> **It is of no concern whether or not all phenomena are
>   timelessly free.**
> **It is of no concern whether or not the way of abiding is
>   pure by nature. [94b]**
> **It is of no concern whether or not mind itself is free of
>   elaboration.**
> **It is of no concern whether or not anything has ever existed
>   within the fundamentally unconditioned, genuine state.**

The essence of awareness is this exposed state—bare and without any underlying basis—in which phenomena resolve. *The Pearl Garland* states:

> Since one has already arrived without taking a step,
> the very path to follow has already been traversed.
> Since there is nothing to describe with the spoken word,
> the realm of expression and imagination is forever transcended.
> Since the proliferation and resolution of thoughts[38] are
>   timelessly empty,
> there is timeless abiding in supreme meditative stability.
> Since distortions are naturally pure,
> there is abiding in a supremely unobstructed, undistorted state.

With realization that goes beyond the ordinary mind of hope and fear, you come to the decisive experience of a contented mind that is supremely and profoundly spacious:

> It is of no concern whether or not samsara and nirvana are
> by nature a duality.
> It is of no concern whether or not all thoughts and expressions
> are transcended.
> It is of no concern whether or not confused attempts at proof
> and refutation are demolished.
> It is of no concern whether or not the view to be realized has
> been realized.

Since there is nothing to plan or to do concerning awareness in the immediate moment, there is only this bare state in all its nakedness, in which nothing need be done and which can in no way be affected by phenomena. *The Natural Freedom of Awareness* states:

> In essence, true awareness
> is not awareness that entails plans or actions.[39]
> Reification is the very cause of going astray,
> so the path does not entail refuting or proving anything.
> Awareness is not in any way dependent.[40]
> It does not perceive[41] in terms of restrictions or extremes.

And *The Pearl Garland* states:

> Since nothing is created and nothing happens,[42]
> there has been freedom from plans and actions
> from the very beginning.

Having realized the state in which there is nothing to conceive of as the supreme state of timeless resolution, you come to the decisive experience that is beyond the proliferation and resolution of ordinary mind's conceptual frameworks:

> It is of no concern whether or not you meditate on the ultimate
> meaning of the true nature of phenomena. [95a]
> It is of no concern whether or not you engage in examination,[43]
> since there is nothing to accept or reject.
> It is of no concern whether or not the way of abiding has ever
> existed as the fruition.
> It is of no concern whether or not you have traversed the paths
> and levels of realization.

Having realized that the essence of awareness is empty, pristine, and unsullied by phenomena, do not examine it for any reference point, thinking, "That's it!" *The Tantra Without Letters* states:

> Not something that makes things manifest, it is free of any
>   tendency to manifest.
> Not something that obscures, it is beyond anything
>   obscuring it.[44]
> Not something that diminishes, it pervades the ten directions
>   without impediment.
> Not involving effort, it is beyond effort and achievement.
> Not one thing, it is nevertheless free of being many.

And *The All-Creating Monarch* states:

> The uncontrived genuine state is the true nature of everything.
> There is no buddhahood apart from this nature.
> To use the term "buddhahood" is simply to use an arbitrary
>   designation.
> This true nature requires nothing other than itself—natural mind.
> Natural mind, uncontrived, is defined as dharmakaya.
> In being uncontrived, it is timelessly unborn,
> so in the ultimate sense of its being unborn, there is nothing
>   to seek or achieve.
> That which requires no action will not be accomplished
>   by attempts to seek or achieve it.

Having realized unobscured awareness, pure and simple, you come to the decisive experience of there being nothing to become free of and nothing to attain:

> It is of no concern whether or not you are free of all
>   obscurations.
> It is of no concern whether or not the development and
>   completion stages perfect your true nature.
> It is of no concern whether or not the fruition of liberation
>   is attained.
> It is of no concern whether or not you wander in the six states
>   of samsara.

Since the essence of awareness has nothing to do with renunciation or attainment, or with freedom versus confusion, you now have no expectation of attaining buddhahood as some higher state, [95b] so do not meditate on teachings concerning the development and completion stages, thinking they are the path leading to such a state. You have no fear of wandering in samsara as some lower state, so do not practice confession and other techniques to refine away obscurations and the effects of harmful actions, thinking they are its causes. Since karma is exhausted within the state in which nothing need be done and phenomena do not exist, you are content without having to renounce samsara or attain nirvana. *The Pearl Garland* states:

> Since there is only the ground of being—no phenomenon that
>   exists as something else—
> this is the unique, naturally occurring primordial state.
> Since attempts to evaluate things as a unity or as dualities have
>   fallen away,
> the sphere of being is unparalleled.
> Since the darkness of ignorance is primordially and totally pure,
> manifestations of awareness are pervaded by utter lucidity.
> Since samsara, which is without cause, has already ceased,
> there has always been the level of natural buddhahood.[45]
> Since things that can be characterized are pristinely empty,
> the mind that reifies their identity falls away timelessly.

Having realized this resolution of phenomena to be an unfettered state of infinite evenness, you come to the decisive experience in this naturally expansive state that entails no evaluation whatsoever:

> **It is of no concern whether or not the nature of being is**
>   **spontaneous presence.**
> **It is of no concern whether or not you are bound by dualistic**
>   **perceptions of affirmation and denial.**
> **It is of no concern whether or not you have arrived at the**
>   **enlightened intent of the true nature of phenomena.**
> **It is of no concern whether or not you follow in the footsteps**
>   **of masters of the past.**

Now, there are no distinctions to be made on the basis of this awareness. Nothing need be done about phenomena, and even if you were to try to do something, nothing exists as a phenomenon. Existence and nonexistence are extremes. "Is" and "is not" are ordinary consciousness.

View and meditation are fetters. The true nature of phenomena is a potential point of error. Samsara and nirvana are awareness, awareness is unobstructed, and this unobstructed quality is naked. What remains is consciousness that is naturally expansive openness, unfettered and seamless.

If it is thought about, there are concepts. If it is meditated on, there is ordinary consciousness. If it is described, [96a] there are words. If it is looked at, there is dualistic perception. If it is left alone, there is the true nature of phenomena, while if anything is done, there is samsara. If anything occurs, it arises naturally. What remains is consciousness settled in its own place, open like the sky, joyous, and blissfully spacious.

It is not so by being made so. It is not seen by being searched for. It is not freedom that is cultivated in meditation. It is not ensured by being sought. It is not freedom that comes from relaxing. It is not ensured by being reified. What remains is bare consciousness in all its nakedness—the state that is beyond labels and in which phenomena resolve.

Nothing stands between samsara and nirvana. The unobstructed state leaves no trace. In what naturally arises, there is no bias. In natural freedom, there are no phenomena. In the resolution of phenomena, there are no labels. In view and meditation, there is no evaluation. In self-knowing awareness, there is no ordinary mind. In openness, there is no bias. There is no basis for origination or cessation. What remains is naturally lucid, uninterrupted consciousness that is immediate and without bias.

It is free even in arising, empty even in manifesting, and evanescent even in stirring. It "is" even as it "is not," while it "is not" even as it "is." It is nonexistent even in being present, while it is nonetheless present even in being nonexistent. It stirs even in abiding, while it abides even in stirring. What remains is meditative stability as the ongoing flow of natural, seamless consciousness.

You may meditate on it as existent, but it is impossible to affirm. You may meditate on it as nonexistent, but it is impossible to deny. You may view it as both existent and nonexistent, but it is not subject to such extremes. You may think of it as both or neither of these, but it is not subject to such bias. It may manifest as pleasure or pain, but these leave no trace in their wake. It exhibits a pristine quality as the true nature of phenomena, but ordinary consciousness does not ensue. There is uninterrupted freedom, but you do not maintain some fundamentally unconditioned state. What remains is unconstrained and unbiased consciousness that has free rein.

Let it exist, let it not exist. Let it manifest, let it be empty. Let it be, [96b] let it not be. Let it be good, let it be bad. Let it be realized, let it not be realized. What remains is a naturally pristine, naked state—consciousness that is empty and evanescent, an all-embracing open dimension in which no traces remain.

There has never been freedom, for there is no basis for it. There is no recognition of the very essence of being, for there is no duality. You do not engage in view and meditation, for nothing need be done. You do not maintain the way of abiding, for it is not some "state." You do not try to settle naturally, for there is no abiding. Freedom does not lie in some "natural state," for it has no support. There is nothing that is timelessly pristine, for there is no basic space. In the final analysis there is no bias, for you are beyond perceiving or attaining anything. What remains is naked consciousness, in which there are no phenomena and nothing need be done.

Do not bind this in the trap of view and meditation. Do not force it into some empty framework as the true nature of phenomena. Do not maintain it within the context of the way of abiding. Do not try to elicit it as an unobstructed state in all its nakedness. Do not rush headlong into the narrow confines of things simultaneously arising and being freed. Do not abandon yourself to a state of evenness in which things fade naturally. Do not act with the aim of gaining natural freedom. Do not consign yourself to an inexpressible experience of the fundamentally unconditioned state. Since there can be a strong counterproductive tendency to waste time on the innate clarity of your experience, in letting awareness, which has no reference point, rest evenly with no focus, do not meditate on phenomena, do not change your ordinary consciousness, do not anticipate anything, do not follow after anything that has passed, and do not try to hold on to the present. Without your having to maintain its unobstructed quality, what remains is naturally unfolding awareness, which cannot be evaluated, as a supremely spacious expanse free of limitation.

Now, whatever manifests is pristine in that it is not subject to restrictions and so transcends any evaluation of whether it "is" or "is not." This point, which you come to in all its immediacy, is described in *The Pearl Garland*:

Whatever is said or planned or done
is conduct that expresses the lucidity of emptiness
and awareness.
Concepts of good and bad
are the vast expanse of the ongoing flow of meditation.
Opinions that wrong views are correct [97a]
are the view of unbiased yoga.
All reification involving hope and fear
is fruition that occurs without obstruction.

The nature of these states of realization can be clearly explained:

No matter what arises, even if heaven and earth change places,
there is a bare state of relaxed openness, without any
underlying basis.
Without any reference point—nebulous, ephemeral, and
evanescent—
this is the mode of a lunatic, free of the duality of hope and fear.
With unbiased view and meditation, ordinary consciousness
that is caught up in reification collapses.
Without the entanglements of wishful thinking, there is no
"thing" to strive for or achieve.

How is this so? you ask. Since enlightened intent does not stray from the true nature of phenomena, there is freedom in the state that is beyond labels and in which phenomena resolve. Therefore, you perceive whatever manifests to be the display of naturally occurring timeless awareness and realize that it is like the reflection of your face in a mirror. So what you perceive outwardly—the display of awareness—is nothing more than an expression of emptiness that has no origin. Since its true nature is pure like space, you perceive that there is no duality between it and the true nature of your awareness. Whatever manifests, then, is an expression of emptiness, the display of awareness. Whatever stirs in the mind is timelessly pristine and leaves no trace. Since its true nature is one of equalness throughout the three times, there is freedom in the supreme state beyond ordinary consciousness, in which nothing need be done. Therefore, the teachings refer to "the time when phenomena, which involve acceptance and rejection, resolve." *The Reverberation of Sound* states:

There is no straying from this single enlightened intent.
Sensory appearances are clearly evident in the immediacy
    of their manifesting,
like a face in a mirror.
So freedom is that, and that itself is freedom.
Since these are naturally occurring, empty objects,[46]
there is no separation in awareness between perception
    and consciousness of them. [97b]
That itself is freedom in all its immediacy.
Because everything is free[47] when this single point is understood,
all attempts to quantify it as two or three fail.
Nothing that manifests can be conceived of or reified as an object.
Mental stirring and reification are timelessly empty.
Given the perfection of the lucid enlightened intent of emptiness,
all attempts to quantify myriad things fail.

It can be shown that for yogins, for whom realization has arisen from within, whatever arises is free within its true nature, without any possible alternative:

Let whatever happens happen and whatever manifests manifest.
Let whatever occurs occur and whatever is be.
Let whatever is anything at all be nothing at all.

That is to say, there are no distinctions whatsoever to be made from the perspective of awareness. Since things arise within the scope of a single awareness, no quality of "better" or "worse" affects the ground of being. Since all that arises is nothing other than the dynamic energy of awareness, no quality of "better" or "worse" affects the essence of that dynamic energy. Because things are already free in arising, if they are not reified they are understood to be identical in that they are naturally evanescent, so no quality of "better" or "worse" affects their essence. Whatever arises, whatever manifests is already empty, for it is a non-existent manifestation within the ground of being. Since there is no concern that it has ever existed, there is no need for ordinary consciousness to reify what—like water in a mirage—manifests clearly without existing. Therefore, yogins never have to choose between accepting or rejecting any of their thoughts or the sense objects they perceive. Because these are all understood to be identical within the state that is beyond labels and in which phenomena resolve, and which has no underlying basis, they are conventionally described as being "beyond extremes." *The Natural Freedom of Awareness* states:

> Sensory appearances are devoid of substance.
> Emptiness transcends all characterization.
> Transcendence is inexpressible. [98a]

For yogins who have gained realization in total freedom without any reference point, conduct is unpredictable, and they experience sensory appearances in a naturally settled, "ordinary" state:

> With your conduct unpredictable, you make the final leap
>   into awareness
> without the slightest basis for determining what is spiritual
>   or not,
> and so this bare state with no reference point is beyond the cage
>   of philosophy.
> Whether eating, moving around, lying down, or sitting, day
>   and night you rest in infinite evenness,
> so that you experience the true nature of phenomena as
>   their equalness.
> There are no gods to worship, no demons to exorcise,
> nothing to cultivate in meditation—this is the completely
>   "ordinary" state.
> With this single state of evenness—the uncontrived ruler that
>   has no pride—
> there is oneness, a relaxed and unstructured[48] openness.
> How delightful—things are timelessly ensured without having
>   to be done,
> and being free of effort and achievement, you are content.

Regarding this, you might think, "Individuals involved in spiritual teachings and the spiritual path turn away from what is ordinary and spend their days and nights in various burdensome kinds of formal religious practice, so what is accomplished by abiding in an 'ordinary' state? Is there no difference between worldly people and yogins?" But you should understand the following: The former are just worldly people who have never trained their minds in spiritual ways, and because they do not think about this they deprive themselves of spiritual intentions and actions. The latter enjoy the contentment that comes of realizing that spirituality is already and forever ensured without being made so. Because spirituality is already ensured for them, they have cast it away or transcended it. So there is nothing spiritual for them to do and they perceive things in a naturally settled, "ordinary" state. In the same vein, you should also understand that the minds of worldly people get caught up in the entanglements of the world, but this is not the case for yogins, [98b] who are thus not similar to ordinary worldly people.

If they were similar, it would mean that just as ordinary people go through the cycle of samsara, so too are yogins in a state of confusion. But since, for the latter, nothing need be done—physically, verbally, or mentally—there are no factors that contribute to confusion, and since they appear to be "ordinary," having awakened into an unobstructed state, they are not subject to bondage. They are free of karma and its inevitable consequences. To give an example, when a hemp rope is burned in a fire it still seems to be a rope, but it cannot perform its function of binding. Similarly, since their minds are unobstructed, yogins may seem to deny or affirm things with ordinary consciousness and may appear to be concerned with food, clothing, and possessions, but they are not bound by these things, because they are not fixated on them, having realized they are dreamlike, without any basis. This is not the case for worldly people, however, and so their minds are bound by fixations that seem entirely legitimate; just as though the rope was not burned in the fire, there is bondage due to the usual denial or affirmation of the mind inwardly or sensory appearances outwardly. It is for these reasons that one powerful lord of yogins said:

> Whatever you fixate on, cast it aside!
> If you are to gain realization, that is everything.
> No one will ever gain understanding by any other means.

He also gave the following advice:

> You are bound not by sensory appearances, but by fixation
>   on them,
> so cut through fixation, Naropa!

Wrong thinking concerning this "ordinary" state can be refuted. Those whose merit and good fortune are minimal—whose minds cannot face the implications of this realization and the enormity of these teachings—might object by saying, "But in the context of realizing the way of abiding, it must be appropriate to carry out the spiritual activities that need to be done! Don't you accept the fact that happiness is gained as a result?" [99a]

My response to this is as follows: Be careful! You are making arbitrary distinctions between good and bad, even though all phenomena arise equally in light of awareness. With phenomena manifesting as if dreams, I do not reject some and accept others, for to engage in rejection and acceptance, effort and achievement, is contradictory for a yogin. It is said that a yogin of natural great perfection does not place hope in any goal, whereas those who place hope in effort and achievement, cause and effect, are not suitable candidates for this approach and so apply themselves to the more commonplace teachings of lower spiritual approaches intended for less mature people. *The All-Creating Monarch* states:

> To be unaware of this and to engage in effort and achievement
> conflicts with the ultimate meaning of transcending causality—
> and so one will not encounter the supreme bliss in which nothing
>   need be done.
> Owing to the diseases of effort and achievement, awareness has
>   already gone unrecognized.
> Therefore, great perfection beyond causality
> is not within the reach of those who lack good fortune,
> so they should avail themselves of[49] teachings on causality.

Since this distinction occurs in our own scriptural sources, I do not contradict it.

Those who have little good fortune may further say, "It may be true that nothing need be done deliberately, since everything is equal in awareness, but it must still be necessary to do something, because accomplishment comes about from something being done but does not if nothing is done." To them I say: If something is not so, trying will not make it so, while if it is so, there is no need to try to make it so. Though effort and achievement pertain to a relative perspective, from the ultimate perspective of mind itself nothing whatsoever need be done. And given that dharmakaya is already ensured in mind itself, it becomes evident if you leave it as it is, but it is not ensured by your doing anything, just as a reflection in limpid water will not be clear if the water is disturbed. [99b] The same tantra states:

> Buddhahood does not happen by being made to happen.
> It is unsought and naturally indwelling, and so is
>   spontaneously present.
> Rest nonconceptually in this effortless, naturally abiding state.

Therefore, just as effort and achievement are hindrances to enlightenment and the need to rest is extolled, it is a great flaw to try to do anything about mind itself, about which nothing need be done, for doing so would mean there was some incongruity between cause and effect, between the ground and the path, and nothing would come of it. *The All-Creating Monarch* states:

> There is no greater hindrance to enlightenment
> than being unaware of what is already ensured, beyond effort
>   and achievement,
> and instead viewing it as being ensured by meditation involving
> plans and actions, effort and achievement.

Someone might object, "This may indeed be the case, but something still needs to be done, for I have not yet reached that level." My answer is as follows: Alas, unfortunate one. This is not a case of going from one place to another. Since there is no going, there is nowhere to arrive. You are truly astonishing—going to look for yourself when you already are yourself! Our scriptural sources show that someone like you is beyond the pale and therefore in a deplorable condition. The same tantra states:

> In wishing for happiness, one turns one's back on happiness.
> One has experienced some happiness, yet because of that
>   happiness one seeks more.
> To be confused about enlightenment is to try too hard at
>   spiritual practice.
> Someone who perceives in this way will not behold buddhahood.

I advise those of future generations to keep this secret from such people. The same tantra also states:

> Since they do not perceive my nature,
> I, the all-creating one, do not reveal my spiritual approach
>   to them.

Those who lack the good fortune to appreciate the ultimate
    meaning of great perfection [100a]
are enmeshed in[50] provisional teachings that deal with causality.
If I revealed the timeless transcendence beyond finite experience
to those without good fortune who delight in causality,
    they would misinterpret it.
If I revealed it, they would thus belittle their own minds
and would be reborn in one of the six classes of beings, to remain
    forever in samsara.

I have stopped engaging in spiritual plans and actions and instead experience the naturally settled, "ordinary" state. Nevertheless, from my perspective—that of fundamentally unconditioned immediacy in the essence of awareness—I am no different from those who apply effort and achievement to spiritual practice. In fact, the spiritual practice I engage in is similar to their ordinary plans and actions. All the conduct of yogins is already experienced as spiritual; it is spontaneously present as the display of their true nature. The *Pearl Garland* states:

For one who sincerely wishes to experience mahamudra,
    the supreme seal,
eating and drinking are the stage of approach,
while lying down and sitting are that of accomplishment.
One's predispositions are consecrations.
Yawning and coughing ensure the accomplishment of
    the mandala.
Rain and mist anoint the entire three-thousand-fold universe
    as the mandala.
The orderly paths one follows are the layout.
The footprints one leaves are the designs rendered in
    colored powders.
One's desire to move about constitutes ritual stances.
The movements of one's limbs are ritual gestures.
Whatever one says is mantra syllables.
One's thoughts are the stage of development.
Thoughts that stir in one's mind are offerings.
All that manifests as form is the enlightened form of the deity.
Speaking aloud is music itself.
One's own body is the ritual vase itself,
the hair on one's head constitutes the ornamental leaves
    and petals adorning its mouth, [100b]

and one's blood and lymph are the fluids
that fill one's heart and other organs as ritual substances.
Sensory appearances manifesting to one's awareness are
    the empowerments granted;
without having to be conferred, they are complete.
The desire for transcendence is samaya,
but the desire to uphold something is bondage itself.
The desire for freedom is impairment,
while one who affirms its nonexistence is a sublime sage.
One's perceptions are indications of the seals of practice,
while attachment to them is meditative experience.
Lucid awareness is spiritual instruction,
while the coming together of sense objects and mind is
    the context for its application.
Birth, aging, illness, and death are the key points of
    familiarization.
The six open avenues of consciousness constitute realization.

And *The All-Creating Monarch* states:

Desire-attachment, aversion, and ignorance
derive from the path of supreme enlightenment.
The five enlightened qualities of conduct
are called "the adornment of basic space, the true nature
    of phenomena."

View and meditation can be shown to be spacious, involving no objects:

**Given that there is no basis for the view or specific context
    for meditation,
there is no factor of conduct or fruition to accomplish.**[51]
Since everything is infinitely uniform[52] **in undifferentiated
    equalness, there is no need for concerted effort.**[53]
In the absence of any fixed dimension, you are content.

What does this mean? All reification of phenomena is transcended, because phenomena resolve with the realization of naked, unobstructed awareness. *The Six Expanses* states:

I, Samantabhadra, have no view.
Since I have no view, ordinary perception has come to an end.
Likewise, I have no meditation.

Since I have no meditation, deliberate attention has ceased.
There is nothing that can be described as "conduct."
Since there is no conduct, the body's elements resolve. [101a]

It can be shown that universal freedom is a supreme state of spaciousness:

**Since there is no speculation, ordinary ideas of achievement
come to an end.
Since there is nothing to abandon, antidotes—constricting
fixations—are transcended.
There is not the slightest sense of there being anything,
or everything, or even something that "is" or "is not,"
and so whatever manifests, whatever arises, is inevitably free.**

Here, there is no sense of rejection or acceptance, of "is" or "is not,"
within the very essence of awareness, and so your perceptions and consciousness are all imbued with the confidence born of "the four modes
of freedom." *The Reverberation of Sound* states:

Since self-knowing awareness is free of all concepts,
it is imbued with the four modes of freedom.
Due to the confidence of freedom derived from these four
key points,
awareness does not abide in either samsara or nirvana.
It does not come about and is not created.[54]
It has no underlying basis or foundation.

That is to say, in this regard the very essence of these four modes of freedom can be shown in general, and freedom can be explained in particular to be a state of confidence.

The four modes of freedom are as follows: Due to the key point that awareness is free in all its nakedness, sensory appearances and consciousness arise unobstructedly, and you gain confidence about everything within your experience of naturally occurring timeless awareness. Due to the key point that they come into being simultaneously in the same indivisible instant, they arise naturally within the state of freedom that is their true nature and that occurs in the moment without depending on any succeeding moment. Given that sensory appearances and consciousness are expressions of emptiness that have no basis, exertion

and constricting fixations are transcended due to the key point of imperturbable rest, a natural settling in which nothing need be done. And
due to the key point that all phenomena are naturally empty and beyond
any attempt to do anything about them, you gain confidence in their inherent condition, in which they resolve in all their nakedness, naturally
evanescent.

As for the way in which you rely on this sense of confidence, just as
a bird with full-fledged wings has the confidence [101b] to soar in the
vault of the sky and pass directly over abysses, so a yogin who has realized that all phenomena are timelessly free has the confidence born of
understanding that there is no need to free them anew through effort.
You remain without doing anything whatsoever and realize that all phenomena are naturally freed in and of themselves, like a knot in a snake,
so that there is a profound spaciousness that need not rely on anything
else as an antidote. With the realization that all phenomena, however
they manifest, are free in the immediacy of that context, what is perceived is evanescent and without reference point. And with all phenomena being in this completely open state of total freedom, you realize they
constitute a seamless, supreme state of equalness, and you are content
without making any effort whatsoever. Once you have perceived the key
point in this way, you do away with efforts spent on antidotes. You are
beyond the point where there is any object to abandon. There are none
of the constraining fixations of ordinary thinking. The stronghold of
denial and affirmation topples. You come to the decisive experience of
a supremely spacious state of equalness, and so experience the expanse
of spacelike awareness in which phenomena and ordinary consciousness resolve. Someone for whom everything comes together as a single
blissful expanse within the spacious state of contentment is known as "a
yogin of natural great perfection."

At this point all phenomena, which involve rejection or acceptance,
and in fact all dualistic perceptions are naturally free without being
deliberately abandoned, and so are pure, being naturally cleared away
and leaving no trace. This is similar to last night's darkness vanishing
without a trace when the sun rises at daybreak, although there is nothing that departs or anywhere that it has gone. Though phenomena have
never actually known existence, they arise as though they do in fact
exist as something to accept or reject, due merely to the fabrications of
ordinary consciousness. Once you realize the ultimate meaning of this,

[102a] ordinary consciousness with its plans and actions fades away, so that the phenomena it fabricates also fade away. Since they are nonexistent, "natural freedom" is referred to in a purely conventional way as the pristine state of their nonexistence; however, this is really a case of awareness—empty yet lucid and without underlying basis or foundation—"abiding in its natural place of rest." *The Reverberation of Sound* states:

> What is called "the freedom of natural mind"
> is not a case of passing from one state to another.
> Mind, which is not freed by anything,
> is fundamentally perfect, so it does not come or go.
> It is not found by investigation, and so has no underlying cause.
> It has no underlying basis or foundation,
> and so abides as the unity of emptiness and lucidity.[55]
> Mind abides as natural lucidity,
> and due to this key point it is free, not subject to limitation or bias.
> It is free of time, and so has no underlying basis.
> It is effortlessly free, and so involves no exertion.[56]
> It is free due to confidence, and so involves no effort;
> this is explained as "freedom through confidence."
> Its freedom is timeless, and so has no basis for being
> reestablished.[57]
> It is naturally free in and of itself, and so there are no antidotes.
> It is freedom that lies in immediate perception, and so things fade
> at the point where they are seen.
> It is totally free, and so involves no effort.

Now, you come to a final resolution within the infinite state equal to space, in which phenomena do not exist:

> **Phenomena are ineffable—they do not exist as timelessly free,**
> **naturally free, or not free—**
> **and so the single state of evenness with no reference point**
> **is beyond being any phenomenon that could be decisively**
> **experienced.**

Even if you come to a decisive experience of the timeless equalness of all phenomena in the supreme state of total freedom, no phenomenon that could be decisively experienced exists, no context exists in which to come to such an experience, and no one who could come to such an experience exists. Thus, there is no reference point whatsoever that can be determined, either in name or in actuality, and so there is not the slightest sense of your being somewhere or of some final point to which you are led. [102b] *The Natural Freedom of Awareness* states:

> Even given the reification involved in speculative views,
> phenomena cannot be characterized, but are free in their
>   own place,
> and so are conventionally referred to as "naturally occurring."
> All phenomena defined dualistically—
> whether in terms of the extreme of existence or of nonexistence—
> are free of being viewed that way in actuality.

And *The All-Creating Monarch* states:

> In mind there is no definitive conclusion to reach regarding the
>   certainty of one's release.[58]
> Since it is beyond value judgments, there are no pith instructions
>   for coming to some decisive experience.

The meaning of all this can be summarized as enlightened intent, in which one's purpose is accomplished without anything having been done:

> Within the spacious expanse, the spacious expanse,
>   the spacious vast expanse,
> I, Longchen Rabjam, for whom the lucid expanse of being
>   is infinite,
> experience everything as embraced within a blissful expanse,
>   a single nondual expanse.
> I, Natsok Rangdrol, have reached the point of natural freedom
>   where phenomena resolve.
> Unchanging spontaneous presence is the pinnacle of my
>   excellent counsel.

Outwardly, the expanse of sensory appearances is spacious as a supreme and timelessly empty state without any underlying basis. Inwardly, the expanse of mental activity is spacious as a supreme and naturally pristine state in which thoughts leave no trace. Secretly, the expanse of awakened mind is spacious as a naked, unobstructed state.

These three abide as an uncreated spontaneous presence. I, Longchen Rabjam [The Entire Range of the Vast Expanse], a yogin of the sublime spiritual approach, have realized this in all its nakedness and natural lucidity. With the arising of a supreme state of infinite spaciousness—the expanse of samsara, originally pure without having to be abandoned, and nirvana, spontaneously present without having to be accomplished—everything is embraced within the blissful expanse of my realization that samsara and nirvana are nondual within the single expanse of awareness. I, Natsok Rangdrol [The Natural Freedom of the Myriad Display], a yogin for whom myriad phenomena are inherently free in their true nature, [103a] have reached dharmakaya, enlightened intent beyond ordinary consciousness. And so my realization has reached full expression at the point where phenomena resolve in their true nature. Thus, since I have gained the ongoing state of authentic being, the most majestic state of dharmakaya, in this present life, I would say that I have reached the summit of the most excellent endeavor. *The Heaped Jewels* states:

> The complete, ultimate meaning of natural great perfection
> penetrates to the core of the ordinary mind.
> The thought that this does not manifest or exist as an object[59]
>   is not cut through deliberately.
> Rather, it is cut through in its own place.
> The root of the nonrecognition of awareness, without having
>   to be examined,
> is determined never to involve confusion.

And therefore *The Six Expanses* states:

> Spiritual people who have such appreciation
> awaken to buddhahood before there is buddhahood and
> become foremost among those who hold all mantras of awareness.[60]
> For them—"masters of the glorious gathering"—
> the empowerments of the heruka are complete.
> They are universal monarchs and are called "exceptional."
> All buddhas in the past have proclaimed,
> "These people have transcended the three lower states of existence."

This is my advice to you fortunate ones who follow my example and do just as I have done:

Moreover, you who follow my example[61]—
bring everything together thus within the timeless range
of a single vast expanse.
In this way, you will gain the ongoing state of authentic being
on the level of Samantabhadra.

You students whose good fortune is similar to my own and who train by following my example, as well as you fortunate ones who will enter this path generation after generation into the future—bring all phenomena together as a single expanse within enlightened intent, wherein everything is already ensured without anything needing to be done, and put this into practice. As general supports, consult authentic scriptural sources, pith instructions, [103b] and my own works, and master their contents. Having gained the ongoing state of authentic being on the majestic level of the true nature of phenomena, you will discover enlightenment—buddhahood—within yourselves. As *The All-Creating Monarch* states:

Ah! Yogins who have followed this path and meditated
abide henceforth on the level of victorious ones.[62]

And as *The Six Expanses* states:

Those with the fortune of being familiar with this
attain the enlightened dimension, which does not entail concepts.
Appreciating[63] the radiance of my responsiveness,
they share equal fortune with me.
They are my core and my retinue as well.

In this chapter are found many of the practical techniques, the treasury of spiritual attainments, the key points, and the unifying themes of the great perfection. And so it is my profound advice that you consult and contemplate it thoroughly and ensure that you become familiar with these pith instructions in your personal experience.

This is the commentary on the ninth section of *The Precious Treasury of the Basic Space of Phenomena*, demonstrating the decisive experience that one comes to concerning all phenomena within the expanse of awakened mind.

10

Natural Meditative Stability

The decisive experience that you come to—the way of abiding as awareness—is itself shown to be implemented through naturally settled meditative stability. To begin with, you come in a general way to a definitive conclusion about the essence of being:

> Awakened mind is by nature primordially pure.
> The true nature of phenomena is such that there is nothing
>   to discard or adopt,
> nothing that comes or goes, nothing to achieve by trying.
> Rather, the sun and moon of utter lucidity arise
> when one rests naturally in the spacious expanse that is the true
>   nature of phenomena.

That is, it is a special feature of this approach that utter lucidity abides as a natural attribute when you rest [104a] without discarding or adopting anything so that pure, naked awareness is settled in its own place. The commentary in this chapter is presented in three parts—my advice that you put this into practice, the distinction between meditation and true meditative stability, and the actual way you can put this into practice.

You should put this into practice because you must immediately delineate the boundary between samsara and nirvana. If you practice diligently, you can attain enlightenment in this very lifetime, but if you do not, then when you need such practice, there will be no benefit in having been directly introduced to awareness once or in having valued spiritual teachings only sporadically. For if you have not meditated, you will have to wander forever in samsara. *The Reverberation of Sound* states:

The flaws of not having meditated are as follows:
The characteristics of samsara predominate,
so that there is self and other—that is, sense objects and
    consciousness of them.
One is involved with words—that is, with biased points of view.
Sense objects entail frames of reference,
and afflictive emotions are bound up with one's sense of self.
The path to buddhahood is lost,
one does not understand the nature of the fruition,
one is deprived of the ground within which all phenomena
    are equal,
self-knowing awareness is confined within the three realms,
and one falls, caught up in concepts.

This point is also found in more ordinary spiritual approaches, as
The Avatamsaka states:

A practitioner who has not meditated
is just like a deaf musician who cannot hear himself play,
even though he delights others. [104b]
A practitioner who has not meditated
is just like a skillful ferryman who dies in the water
even though he has brought many people to freedom.
A practitioner who has not meditated
is just like those parched with thirst
whose torment is not assuaged by the sight and sound of water.

And as *The Treasury of Higher Teachings* states:

Because meditation is the foremost factor in becoming
    detached, . . .

As for the distinction between meditation and true meditative stability, many developmental frameworks are spoken of in more ordinary
spiritual approaches in general and, even in this approach, as methods
for instructing those of lesser acumen. Briefly, all meditation techniques
are subsumed under two headings, based on whether or not their frame
of reference involves a support. Techniques that involve a support consist of focusing one's mind without distraction on an appropriate object
perceived outwardly—a form (such as the image of a deity, a symbolic
implement, a twig, or a pebble), a sound, an odor, a taste, or a tactile

sensation. Techniques that involve no outer support are the province of mind. Some involve mental images and are held to elicit nonconceptual states of awareness through focus on specific visualizations entailing the subtle channels, subtle energies, and bindu. Others involve focusing on syllables, spheres of light, or chakras in the subtle channels, visualizations of fire in the practice of chandali, and so forth. A technique that involves no mental image is to sit cross-legged, gaze straight ahead, and settle one's mind without distraction in a completely nonconceptual state; this, therefore, takes the state of pristine emptiness as its nonconceptual frame of reference. The preceding points are subsumed within the general explanation that such frames of reference are of two kinds—those involving concepts and those that are nonconceptual. [105a]

To summarize, everyone holds that "meditation" refers to some state with a single reference point, positing that it is essentially a state of mind at rest, that its purpose lies in some hoped-for goal that can be reached through stabilization, and that its function is to arrest dualistic perception. *The Reverberation of Sound* states:

> "Meditation" is mind at rest,
> cutting through mental stirring, whether directed outwardly
>   or inwardly;
> it is the cessation of dualistic perception.
>
> . . . .
>
> Subtle channels, subtle energies, and bindu,
> physical postures, visualizations, and emptiness—
> these are held to be "meditation."

These verses show that the very idea that subject–object dualism is to be arrested already involves a subject (an ordinary state of consciousness) perceiving an object (a frame of reference). And so these are simply methods by which one begins to approach the profound aspects of spiritual teachings, not the actual practice of profound yoga.

True meditative stability is a particular feature of the great perfection approach. Just as heat is present as a natural attribute the moment there is fire, and wetness is naturally present in water, naturally settled meditative stability is present in awareness. Once you have been directly introduced to awareness, you abide in that naturally settled meditative stability, so that even though you do not deliberately cultivate meditative experiences of bliss, lucidity, and nonconceptual awareness, they arise naturally. This is similar to the fact that meditative stability, being present as a natural attribute of awareness, arises naturally in the intermediate state after death.

Once you forge the spiritual path using ordinary mind, it is in the very nature of the process that you either have the experience of meditating when you strive or lose it when you do not. But as soon as you forge the path using awareness—timeless awareness— [105b] you abide in the ongoing flow of naturally settled meditative stability, so that you abide at all times in that state in which enlightened qualities come about as a matter of course and there is no possibility of its being lost.

There is a similarity between the way a great meditator achieves a nonconceptual state of ordinary mind and the way a yogin recognizes awareness in all its nakedness to be nonconceptual. But while there is a similarity in that both are nonconceptual states, there is a difference in that the nonconceptual state of ordinary mind is lost if physical posture and other factors are let go, for awareness has not been elicited in all its nakedness. Nonconceptual awareness has nothing to do with such factors, and therein lies a vast difference.

Forging the path with ordinary mind entails using antidotes to refine away concepts, so that these incidental concepts seem to vanish without a trace, whereas in experiencing awareness one is unfettered by concepts. These two situations are similar in that ordinary recollection and thinking vanish into a state in which there is no fixation. But those who follow the former approach do not cut through the very root of the problem, and so conceptual reification and fixation can arise at random and one might think to oneself, "Being unborn, these arise continuously." In the latter approach, one cuts through that root, so there is nowhere and no way for them to arise. Rather, the continuous inner glow that is the dynamic energy of responsiveness becomes fully evident, manifesting reflexively like images in a mirror. There is a vast difference here, since one perceives what arises outwardly from responsiveness to be like rays shining from the sun.

Furthermore, both the state of ordinary mind resting naturally and the innate abiding of awareness resting naturally have a vivid quality. These states are similar insofar as they are lucid yet nonconceptual, but the aspect of ordinary mind remains anchored in dualistic perception, so that any quality of abiding entails an element of fixation. There is a vast difference here, in that in the latter case there is no interruption of awareness, which is unobstructed.

In addition, [106a] sense objects manifest within the limpidity of awareness, so there is a continuous aspect of clarity, and thought processes arise as the ordinary mind's response to external sense objects. These two situations are similar, for in both there is conscious perception of sense objects. But awareness does not focus on external objects, for even though they manifest to it, it is unencumbered by them, so the root of ordinary thinking has been cut through. The focus of ordinary mind shifts outward in response to sense objects, so the root has not been cut through and ordinary thinking takes place. Therein lies the difference. *The Six Expanses* states:

> Self-knowing awareness without concepts
> and one's ordinary mind without any sullying elements—
> these two are similar, so similar that this could lead to quite
>   an error.
> The manifestations of unobscured, profound lucidity
> and beings' fixated thought patterns—
> these two are similar, so similar that this could lead to quite
>   an error.
> Meditation as an unsought state of rest
> and the ease that comes from the subtle channels and energies
>   and ordinary mind—
> these two are similar, so similar that this could lead to quite
>   an error.
> Sense objects manifesting to awareness without any thought
>   concerning them
> and beings of the six classes thinking about them in confusion—
> these two situations are similar, so similar that this could lead to
>   quite an error.

In brief, meditation with ordinary mind, which involves some frame of reference, is anchored in dualistic perception, while awareness—naturally settled meditative stability—is the ongoing and naturally settled state that is the true nature of phenomena. And so there is a difference between achieving those worldly states of ordinary mind that lead to the higher realms (and perpetuate samsara) and abiding in your own natural state within the enlightened intent of buddhahood (which actually connects you with the liberation of nirvana). *The Reverberation of Sound* states:

> What occurs in the state of settling naturally
> is said to be pure meditative stability.
>
> . . . .
>
> The way of abiding is an uncontrived state of natural rest; [106b]
> in no way does that change.
> It is the enlightened intent of buddhas.

There are five specific ways in which the path of the heart drop teachings is superior to an ordinary path forged with meditation: Since you come to a realization of awareness in all its nakedness, it is of no consequence whether your intellect is sharp or dull. Since you directly realize with your own faculties that awareness is unobstructed, you do not rely on sublime knowing that involves conceptualization and analysis. Since you realize that awareness beyond words is unobstructed, you no longer entertain hope that ordinary thought patterns or explanations have ultimate significance. Since you realize that whatever you perceive is the manifestation of the three kayas as your spiritual path, rather than merely the manifestation of a better or worse state of confusion, you do not place your confidence in deeply ingrained fixation on sensory appearances. And since awareness is unobstructed in all its nakedness, you see that view, meditation, conduct, and fruition are factors that obscure awareness.

This approach is particularly superior in that you do not rely on calm abiding and profound insight to find ease through an abiding state of mind. *The Reverberation of Sound* states:

> In the definitive experience of the heart drop,
> intellectual capacities, whether sharp or dull, are of
>   no consequence.
> Since the limitations of speculative words have been exhausted,
> this experience is not just a sublime form of knowing, but direct
>   perception with one's faculties.[1]
> Since the true nature of phenomena is not perceived through words,

ordinary spiritual approaches do not serve any ultimate purpose.
Because the three kayas manifest as the path,
one who perceives that they do will not revert to the three realms.
Since all phenomena are of one taste in their equalness,
there is reliance on ground, path, and fruition.[2]

How amazing! The difference between this spiritual approach and others is greater than that between heaven and earth. But even though this is demonstrated, it is not realized, and even though explained, [107a] it is not understood. Those who have only a slight inclination toward these teachings, and who accept some rudimentary interpretation of direct introduction, lack a karmic connection with the secret heart drop approach of natural great perfection. Regardless of what they have done, they have not come the slightest bit closer to buddhahood. How incredible—this is as depressing as it is ludicrous.

Now, the method by which this special path is put into practice can be shown:

> **Without sense objects being blocked or mind being reified,**
> **if there is no straying from the natural state of spontaneous**
> **   equalness[3]**
> **you arrive at the enlightened intent of supreme spaciousness,**
> **   Samantabhadra.**

This is by way of a general remark. *The Tantra Without Letters* states:

> The naturally occurring state of resting imperturbably has never
>   been contrived.
> It is not altered by sensory appearances or fabricated by ordinary
>   consciousness.
> If one abides in "space"—the true nature of phenomena—
>   it reveals itself to be enlightened intent.

Inwardly, there is no straying from the essence of awareness, elicited in all its nakedness as the unobstructed unity of lucidity and emptiness. There is no fascination with sense objects that manifest outwardly, no proliferation of thoughts in the ordinary mind inwardly, and no nondual process of meditation restricting awareness in between these two options. Rather, awareness abides freely and unobstructedly, settled in its own place. Through the four methods of resting and the three aspects of meditative absorption, you "narrow it down" to awareness. The four methods of resting are resting imperturbably like a mountain, resting imperturbably like an ocean, resting imperturbably in awareness, and resting in the immediate perception of sensory appearances. The three aspects of meditative absorption are meditative absorption as the supreme state of natural abiding, meditative absorption as the supreme, innate state of immediacy, and meditative absorption as the supreme application of the all-embracing seal. [107b] I will discuss the four methods of resting imperturbably as they occur when you put them into practice.

The Four Methods of Resting

First, it can be shown that you begin by resting imperturbably like an ocean:

> Without the arising and subsiding of thoughts, there is
>   a naturally limpid, pristine state,
> like the unwavering evenness[4] of a limpid ocean.
> Free of the occurrence of or involvement in thoughts, free of
>   hope or fear,
> you abide within the state of naturally occurring timeless
>   awareness, the true nature of which is profoundly lucid.

Even as reflections of planets and stars appear in an ocean undisturbed by wind, they are not other than the water, yet are not affected by it. Similarly, even as perceptions of sense objects arise continuously within awareness, which, being unobstructed, is immaculate, they are not tainted by reification, and so you rest without straying from that limpid, pristine state of awareness. *The Tantra Without Letters* states:

> The pure enlightened intent of resting imperturbably
>   like an ocean
> is not the ordinary perception of sensory appearances,
>   nor does it cause them to manifest.
> It is not empty or something that exists as emptiness.
> It is not mere clarity, but is the realm of supreme lucidity.
> It is not mental laxity, and agitation is automatically absent.

It has never wavered, does not waver, and will never waver.
It has never varied, does not vary, and is beyond all variation.[5]
Behold the supreme method of resting, which is not brought
    about deliberately.
Do not try to complicate or simplify it.
This unique state of resting imperturbably
is not one of maintaining stillness, yet there is no going
    beyond it.
Rest in the timeless, spontaneous vastness of immutable
    basic space,
in secret timeless awareness, which is like an ocean.
In this great ocean, whose depths are hard to fathom,
behold the pinnacle of the victory banner that never falls.
In the ineffability of mind, which is empty, lies the supremely
    uncontrived kaya.
Not produced, it is victorious over all attempts to produce it.
The uncontrived state of resting imperturbably has never come
    into being.[6] [108a]
It is not altered by sensory appearances or fabricated by ordinary
    consciousness.
If one abides in "space"—the true nature of phenomena—
    it reveals itself to be enlightened intent.
Timeless awareness—dharmakaya—is the total renunciation
    of ordinary thinking,
so if nothing causes one's mind to stir, there is the enlightened
    intent of meditation.
If one does not indulge in extremes, with sense objects as a frame
    of reference,
then, like planets and stars being reflected as though in the
    ocean's depths,
lucidity is continuous without being reified.
Such is the way in which enlightened intent is present.

In this regard, some deluded people who are not learned in the tantras, but just speak off the tops of their heads, take as a final statement
the incomplete treatment given in some texts and so think, "These four
ways of resting imperturbably are methods of resting used only in tögal." This is an indication that they have not developed their connection
with these teachings and do not understand how to apply them in prac-

tice. While one application is outlined in the preceding citation from the "Blossoming Lotus" section of *The Tantra Without Letters*, in general these four methods can be applied in a number of ways, as outlined in *The Precious Detailed Instructions Concerning Perception,* where it is said that they are applied in all situations. Whether your approach is that of trekchö or tögal, fundamentally you should understand how to elicit unobstructed awareness in all its nakedness. If you do not understand this, these ways of resting will be of no benefit, however you apply them.

If you adulterate the trekchö approach with the spiritual path of every deluded meditative "adept," you will squander your life on what are very minor means of focusing the ordinary mind, and so will not transcend samsara. And if, in tögal, you fixate on things as real and invest them with characteristics, you will err and take rebirth in the form realm. So at this point it is very important to recognize bare consciousness in all its nakedness. [108b] But it is not enough simply to understand this—you must maintain an ongoing state of authentic being.

To that end, it is very important not to stray from that state, and so numerous methods of resting are spoken of as skillful means. Initially, you must establish your natural place of rest to be the enlightened intent of resting imperturbably like an ocean, so it is crucial to become proficient in doing so. This involves a developmental process of cutting through potential errors, as *The Reverberation of Sound* states:

> In meditation that consists of abiding without going astray,
> the avenues of the senses are lucid,
> though concepts do not stir in the mind.
> Mind that investigates consciousness itself
> is truly ineffable and is not lost to externals.[7]
> It is neither clarity that fragments one's experience,
> nor preoccupation with emptiness,
> nor the sustaining of bliss,
> nor impartiality that becomes apathy.
> Contrived relaxation in the clarity of mindful awareness,
> a path that leads to incorrect training,
> fixation on the arousal of inner bliss,
> reification of clearly evident attributes,
> manipulation of visualized colors and syllables—
> if one does not succumb to such limitations,
> meditation consists of abiding without going astray.

Here the phrase "reification of clearly evident attributes" refers to engaging in thoughts of "this" or "that" concerning the manifest quality of external sensory appearances. The phrase "manipulation of visualized colors and syllables" refers to the reification involved in conceptualizing and analyzing the inner experience of mind at rest. The rest of the citation is easy to understand.

As for resting imperturbably in awareness:

> Without the compulsions of ordinary mind,
> there is an unfeigned state—a natural settling, uncontrived
>   and unadulterated—
> though it cannot be characterized with words.
> This absorption in the expanse of being, the true nature
>   of which cannot be characterized,
> involves neither meditation nor something to meditate on,
> and so laxity and agitation dissipate naturally, and enlightened
>   intent occurs naturally. [109a]

As for resting imperturbably in awareness, in tögal this consists of resting in the continuum that is the radiance of awareness. But in trekchö, the utterly profound key point is to rest right in actual awareness, naked and unobstructed. While abiding within the limpid ocean of awareness, you identify its wakeful, pristine quality in all its nakedness and ensure that you do not stray from it. And so it arises as the true nature of phenomena, without any discontinuity or division into outer and inner. *The Tantra Without Letters* states:

> The pith instruction for resting imperturbably in awareness—
> this is the point at which one touches on the secret.
> . . . .
> The enlightened intent of the single decisive point concerning
>   sensory appearances
> is to seek a means of resting in awareness itself.[8]
> This is the supreme secret of secrets.
> On the strength of one's perceptions of sensory appearances,
>   one is liberated to the far shore.
> One is not bound by attachment, for these are awareness's
>   own manifestations.

This is referred to as "eliciting the unobstructed, unique sphere of being in all its nakedness." The same tantra states:

> The unique sphere of being is without elaboration.
> It transcends verbal expression and analysis by
>   ordinary consciousness.[9]

As for resting in the immediate perception of sensory appearances:

> **All-consuming thought patterns cannot be abandoned by being**
>   **renounced, for they are the dynamic energy of awareness.**
> **Their true nature is such that there are no distinctions, nothing**
>   **to differentiate or exclude,**
> **so that nature is not ensured by achievement, but arises as**
>   **basic space.**
> **Without rejecting samsara, you perceive it to be naturally**
>   **occurring timeless awareness**
> **through the pure yoga of the dynamic energy of the vast**
>   **expanse of being.**

As apparent sense objects arise continuously within the limpidity of awareness (which is like a mirror), the dynamic energy of responsiveness is continuous within that awareness, and so you are vividly aware of these sense objects and feel as though you are "encountering" them. Although in essence sense objects do not entail concepts, their specific manifestation makes it seem as though they do. [109b] But even as they arise, you do not try to block them, deliberately focus on them, or leave them alone as a compromise. Rather, as you allow them to settle in their own place, they do not stray from the context of their true nature. Since limpid awareness is the ground for the arising of all sensory appearances, if the five kinds of sense objects arise they are naturally evident as the masculine buddhas of the five families. If the five elements arise they are naturally the five feminine aspects. If the five emotional poisons arise they arise within basic space as supreme timeless awareness. This being the case, whatever manifests is nothing other than the context of awareness itself. Since awareness itself abides unobstructedly as dharmakaya, if you do not reify it, you understand it to be unsullied. This is termed "the enlightened intent of Vajrasattva, dharmakaya that can be neither illuminated nor obscured." *The Tantra Without Letters* states:

The supreme skillful means of awareness[10]—
resting in the immediate perception of sensory appearances—
is the ground underlying all great visions.
The five minor elements are buddhas manifesting on the path.
The five great elements are clearly evident manifestations
      of the mothers.[11]
Rest without distraction in the supreme state that is
      without reification!
In the supreme secret mantra approach, timeless awareness
      has five great aspects.
Rest in basic space, unaffected by the five great elements!
Resting in the immediacy of[12] Vajrasattva's awareness
reveals the entire perspective of dharmakaya.[13]
As the pure visions of timeless awareness manifest in all
      their immediacy,
the secret method of resting[14] is to rest in the immediate
      perception of them.
Given that the five elements, manifestations of the kayas,
      have not been abandoned,
there is no renunciation—rest in your own ultimate nature!

This method ensures that awareness is not obscured by any circumstances. It is a pith instruction for ensuring that conditioned appearances arise such that they clarify your experience of awareness, and it is valuable to three kinds of people—beginners, intermediate practitioners, and those who have gained some degree of stability. [110a] For the first kind, the harm that circumstances can cause is transformed into the spiritual path. For the second, circumstances arise as though in a mirror and constitute further training on the path. For the third, they arise naturally and without impediment as means to enrich spiritual practice.

Your recognition of awareness is challenged when you perceive objects manifesting to your five senses or when denial or affirmation, ingrained fixations, or strong afflictive emotions occur in your mind. These can be eliminated by distilling the limpid lucidity of awareness and eliciting its unobstructed essence in all its nakedness. *The Heaped Jewels* discusses this way of practicing in detail:

When objects of the phenomenal world manifest with
      characteristics,
they are natural manifestations of my enlightened qualities,

so do not accept or reject any of them.
While beings experience suffering, my bliss arises naturally.
In the lack of separation between happiness and suffering
    at such times
lies the perfection of my enlightened qualities.
When the bodies of hell beings, animals, and tormented spirits
manifest as sense objects,
they display themselves as my enlightened embodiment.
Someone for whom this holds no terror
is in touch with my enlightened embodiment.
Whenever strong passions occur—
ignorance, aversion, or desire—
they are my nonconceptual awareness.
Since this awareness is naturally free in and of itself,
it looks through my eyes.[15]
When directed outward, the mind's attention
is my naturally pure sublime knowing.
If there is no further analysis[16] of it,
it hears my sounds.
When ordinary thought patterns form,
that is my noble, nonconceptual state of meditative absorption.
If ordinary consciousness does not fixate on this, it smells
    my scents.
When ordinary consciousness engages obvious forms,[17] [110b]
that is the arising of meditative experience—my awareness's
    own manifestation.[18]
If union and duality are finished with,
it tastes my flavors.
Thus, all that appears, all that is audible,
arises as the display of me, Samantabhadra.
Since what causes this display to arise is unceasing,
it occurs as my enlightened qualities.
Given that all this simply ensures[19] that my qualities manifest,
it will not come to an end, for it is inexhaustible.
Therefore, this is the pure realm that symbolically expresses
    the three kayas.

In this case, you put into practice the fact that sensory appearances and consciousness of them are of one taste in nondual unity. But it is crucial not to mix this up with ordinary techniques. If you just "look at" whatever arises, you will compound the confusion of conceptual thinking. If you just experience some sort of "letting go," you will cultivate a dull state of meditation in which you fail to recognize your true nature. If you cut through the proliferating meditative experiences that engage you, but then seek some subtle limpid quality of mind in the aftermath, you will be led to make distinctions based on acceptance and rejection. With such approaches, you will fail to grasp the key point that awareness arises naturally. You will be like a dog that is indifferent when it sees felt cloth being cut up!

In this regard, let me define precisely a secret key point specific to the heart drop approach. When appearances manifest, when thoughts arise, or at any other time, you recognize bare awareness in all its nakedness, and so you need not rely on any other factor whatsoever. In that context, the bare state of awareness in all its nakedness (which cuts through mental ties to the three times) is spontaneously present as a supreme state of equalness that is utterly lucid, for it arises naturally as the enlightened intent of naturally settled dharmakaya. No matter what arises in this state, do not reflect back on what has passed, do not think ahead about what is yet to come, and do not analyze the present moment in between. Rather, ensure that you do not stray from the recognition of bare awareness in all its nakedness. [111a] *The Six Expanses* states:

> For anyone who does not hold on to traces of the past or anticipate the future, but lets consciousness rest moment by moment in its natural place, all consciousness blends as one,[20] without any distinction of earlier or later, in what I call "the single unifying essence."[21] This is the yoga of knowing[22] the equalness of the three times.
>
> Through the skillful means of allowing focused attention to resolve naturally, samsara and nirvana blend in nonduality. One who brings an end to recollections of the past, curbs anticipations of the future, and allows consideration[23] of the present to fade naturally is what I call "a yogin who knows the equalness of the three times."
>
> In not fixating on previous states of mind, not relying on future states of mind, and not paying attention to present states of mind, one is a yogin who realizes the equalness of the three times.
>
> If one does not give the slightest credence to nonrecognition of awareness in the past, invite nonrecognition in the future, or

associate intimately with nonrecognition in the present, one is a yogin who knows the equalness of the three times.

If one is not attached to past aversion, does not usher in future aversion, and does not hone present aversion, that is said to be "the yoga of realizing the equalness of the three times."

If one does not gather clouds of past ignorance, till the soil of future ignorance, or bring down a rain of present ignorance, that is said to be "the yoga of realizing the equalness of the three times."

One who does not acknowledge buddhahood in the past, invest buddhahood in the future with significance, or devote energy to buddhahood[24] in the present [111b] is said to be "a yogin of the equalness of the three times."

One who does not try to renounce past desires and attachments, is not resigned to future desires and attachments, and does not banish present desires and attachments is a yogin of the equalness of the three times.[25]

One who does not cling to past envy, focus on future envy, or dwell on present envy is a yogin who realizes the equalness of the three times. Then one is known as "a[26] yogin who realizes the nonduality of samsara and nirvana."

In this citation, "buddhahood" refers to awareness, in which the continuity of the three times is cut through and there is no contrivance.

You might think, "Isn't the explanation that, in arising, consciousness has enlightened qualities that are its natural dynamic energy at odds with the approach of resting without conceptualization or analysis?" But in fact these two are strongly connected. When something such as an afflictive emotion arises vividly, in letting it arise you recognize awareness, elicited in all its nakedness. As you rest without contrivance and do not stray from that recognition, thus cutting through the continuity of the three times, enlightened intent arises naturally as meditative stability that does not stray from the true nature of phenomena.

As for resting imperturbably like a mountain:

**In the timeless unity of sensory appearances and mind—
the naturally settled state that is the true nature of phenomena—**

meditative absorption is experienced as an unwavering,
    ongoing flow.
Thus, the vajra pinnacle, the most excellent enlightened mind
    of Samantabhadra,
is the most sublime, spacious state, equal to space.
The most sublime meditation of all involves no differentiation
    or exclusion.
It is spontaneously present as the superb, timelessly infinite
    monarch.

Once the three other methods of resting have been perfected, the
state of resting imperturbably like a mountain occurs as a matter of
course. Just as there is no transition or change in the most majestic
mountain, you discover the confidence of enlightened intent that does
not stray from the true nature of phenomena. [112a] That is to say, once
yogins realize the essence of awareness, timelessly without transition or
change, and abide within it, they do not stray from it, regardless of what
circumstances manifest. Given that circumstances themselves arise
within that enlightened intent, they serve to clarify one's experience of
awareness; this is like heaping more wood on a fire. *The Tantra Without
Letters* states:

Resting imperturbably like a mountain is the secret view itself.
There is no doubt, and mental stirring[27] is automatically absent.

The Three Aspects of Meditative Absorption

The three aspects of meditative absorption are auxiliary to the four
methods of resting. As for meditative absorption as the supreme application of the all-embracing seal:

The ongoing flow of utter lucidity, timeless and omnipresent,
    is spontaneously present within this context, in which nothing
        is discarded or adopted,
    and so it is the most sublime enlightened intent—the basic
        space of phenomena, the nature of samsara and nirvana.
This vast expanse, unwavering, indescribable, and equal
    to space,
is timelessly and innately present in all beings.

Awareness pervades all of samsara and nirvana, and natural meditative stability permeates awareness, so enlightened intent is present without interruption in all beings, although this is not realized. As *The All-Creating Monarch* states:

> The completely nonconceptual heart essence
> is neither hidden within the mindstream of anyone
> nor deliberately evoked.
> It is naturally present at all times
> for those who seek enlightenment.

As for the means to cultivate this meditative absorption, sit cross-legged, direct your gaze to the space in front of you, and rest in the essence of bare self-knowing awareness, vivid and striking, without thoughts proliferating and resolving in your consciousness. In this way, you apply the natural seal to all outer sensory appearances and inner mental stirring, so that your recognition of awareness does not fall under the sway of the duality of sense objects and mind. [112b] *The Six Expanses* states:

> Those who wish to cultivate meditative absorption
> as the supreme application of the all-embracing seal
> should—in order to focus on the unchangeability that is
>   the key point—
> take the sitting posture as their support[28]
> and project their awareness into the vault of space.
> Likewise, with their eyes focused on the space in front
> using the "elephant's gaze,"
> they rest without deliberate mindfulness
> in the supreme application of the all-embracing seal.

To remove any constraints on this state of meditative absorption:

> It is the ordinary confused mind that perceives
> sensory appearances to be something other than oneself.
> It is the ordinary confused mind that believes in meditation
>   and making an effort.
> The true nature of confusion is the realm of equalness,
>   the natural state of rest—
> the natural expanse that is unwavering and primordially pure.

There is nothing to do and no effort to make[29]**—whether or not
you are resting is irrelevant.**

It is not as though there is anything to renounce or accept by resting
in awareness as the supreme application of the all-embracing seal—in
fact, it is confused thinking to hold that there is. By bringing that confusion back to its natural state of rest—the expanse of the vajra heart
essence that is beyond being improved or harmed—you will certainly
realize the nondual state in which whether or not you are resting is irrelevant. *The Natural Freedom of Awareness* states:

> In essence, true awareness
> is not awareness that entails plans or actions.
> Reification is the very cause of going astray.

Meditative absorption as the supreme state of natural abiding is illustrated by four topics—view, meditation, conduct, and fruition that transcend any schema of view, meditation, conduct, and fruition. As for the
first topic:

> **Given the unchanging, spontaneously present nature of
> phenomena,
> if you look again and again with self-knowing awareness,
> free of any complicating conceptual framework,** [113a]
> **you will see that there is nothing to look at.
> Nothing to look at—this is the view of omnipresent awareness.**

In this case, you "look" without distraction to what has ultimate
meaning—the essence of bare awareness in all its nakedness, beyond
anything to look at or anyone to look. *The All-Creating Monarch* states:

> Ah! The all-creating monarch, teacher of teachers,
> has proclaimed the ultimate meaning of unerring enlightened
> intent.
> In the ultimate heart essence, beyond all exaggeration or
> underestimation,
> making an issue of whether or not there is meditation is like
> arguing with space.
> Not to waver from the ultimate meaning of realization is
> enlightened intent.

It is not anything with substance or without substance.
It is neither subject to nor beyond extremes,
so do not confine yourself to the bias of whether or not
    there is meditation.
If you realize the ultimate meaning of the view that cannot be
    cultivated in meditation,
you realize that it is spontaneously present as the most majestic,
    uncontrived state of equalness.[30]

As for meditation, it does not involve meditating and is beyond it:

**Given awareness, which is not cultivated in meditation and
    in which nothing is discarded or adopted,
if you meditate again and again, you will see that there is
    nothing to cultivate in meditation.
Nothing to cultivate in meditation—this is the meditation
    of omnipresent awareness.**

The essence is naked awareness. *The Reverberation of Sound* states:

As for how the characteristics of meditation manifest,
it is characterized as empty yet lucid awareness,
its nature unadulterated by anything whatsoever.
The extremes of dualistic perception are resolved,
and the true nature of phenomena is pure in its very essence.
Given the unconfused way in which this is perceived,
along with the pure nature of causes and conditions,
what is tangible or intangible is naturally pure,
and so fixation on objects of the five senses is pure,
the coarse elements are pure,
and the unfolding vision is revealed through pure
    timeless awareness.
Therein lies the true nature in which phenomena resolve. [113b]

The way to meditate is stated in *The All-Creating Monarch:*

Since there is no duality of meditation and something to meditate
on in the state of enlightenment—the true nature of phenomena
that cannot be cultivated in meditation—there is meditation if
one rests naturally without deliberately meditating.

As for conduct, it is the supreme lucid expanse—the true nature of phenomena, which is beyond any conduct to enact and anyone to enact it:

> Given the way of abiding, nondual and free of acceptance
>   and rejection,
> if you engage in conduct again and again,
> you will see that there is no conduct to enact.
> No conduct to enact—this is the conduct of omnipresent
>   awareness.

Since the essence of awareness is free of plans and actions, regardless of what arises within that context—sensory appearances or states of mind—rest your body, speech, and mind in a relaxed way. *The All-Creating Monarch* states:

> Ah! Mind is the essence of what simply is.
> What simply is has never been contrived.
> This naturally occurring state is free of all causes and conditions.
> Rest your three avenues of body, speech, and mind in
>   effortless relaxation!

As for the fruition, it cannot be achieved, for it occurs timelessly:

> Given spontaneous presence, timelessly ensured and free of
>   hope and fear,
> if you strive to achieve again and again,
> you will see that there is nothing to achieve.
> Nothing to achieve—this is the fruition of omnipresent
>   awareness.

Bare awareness itself, naked and stable, is the spontaneously present fruition—dharmakaya. *The All-Creating Monarch* states:

> Ah! O courageous one, Excellent Vajra, meditate on me!
> Since the ultimate meaning of their unborn total purity is evident,
> do not view sensory appearances as real.
> Do not try to do away with them.
> Since sensory appearances are naturally free in that they
>   are unborn,
> do not meditate on them as empty.
> Freedom comes from realizing what simply is.
> Ah! I, the all-creating monarch, the teacher of teachers, [114a]

have proclaimed that all phenomena, however they appear,
are unborn and totally pure.
Realize that this is the heart essence of how things are born.
Ah! Since I reveal that the three kayas come from me,
everyone acknowledges that "mind itself is unborn."
But while everyone strives to understand[31] the significance of its
    having no independent nature,
no one has yet[32] realized that it is unborn.
Therefore, other than coming to understand this transmission
    from the all-creating monarch
and abiding in it without distraction,
do not make an effort.
Do not train your mind with antidotes.
Do not focus on[33] objects.
Do not concentrate your mind with ordinary attention.
Since whatever occurs is the ultimate meaning of suchness,
enter into the ultimate meaning of me, the all-creating one.
Ah! The all-creating monarch, the teacher of teachers,
has passed this transmission on to the retinue, uncontrived mind.
You yogins who have realized that everything without exception
    is unborn[34]—
do not strive through the ten attributes.
Given the nature of all-creating awakened mind,
consciousness does not function dualistically and so need not
    be renounced.
Through your gaining mastery by realizing this and abiding
    in its ultimate meaning,
it is spontaneously present as the enlightened intent of the
    all-creating monarch.

Thus, meditative absorption, the supreme state of natural abiding, is beyond view, meditation, conduct, and fruition. The meaning of these four topics is subsumed within the single state of bare awareness, immaculate in all its nakedness. Thoughts about sensory appearances perceived outwardly do not proliferate in your mind, and since appearances that arise do not transcend being its natural adornment, there is an unobstructed quality of consciousness in which they vanish naturally, leaving no trace. Your mind does not think about its inner stirring, and since you understand that to be a continuous radiance—the dynamic energy of responsiveness— [114b] you experience the spaciously expansive quality of the limpid ocean of the naturally pristine state. You do not deliberately cultivate some state of equalness or nonduality that falls between these alternatives, and so you ensure that you do not stray from this most majestic abiding state of bare awareness, for it arises as meditative stability whose abiding quality is one of settling naturally. The six avenues of consciousness are relaxed, unsullied by antidotes that involve efforts at reification. *The Six Expanses* states:

> Meditative absorption is the naturally abiding state
>   of resting imperturbably.
> The avenues of the senses are not blocked,
> and one does not engage in physical activity.
> Even sleep is not abandoned.
> There is none of the ordinary mind's analytical division.
> In brief, one's body and speech are in their natural state,
> and the stirring of one's conceptual consciousness is not lost
>   to things outwardly.
> Moreover, the alert, analytical conceptual consciousness
> does not stir in response to the objects of the six senses.
> Lucid yet nonconceptual meditative experience is born
> from[35] the supreme, nonconceptual realm of awareness's
>   own manifestations.

Concerning meditative absorption as the supreme, innate state of immediacy:

> Within the state of equalness, there are no thoughts about
>   sense objects and no reification of ordinary mind,
> so the occurrence of and involvement in hope and fear
>   are pacified.
> Abiding in the equalness of sense objects and mind
> means that, as a matter of course, there is no straying from
>   the expanse that is the true nature of phenomena.[36]
> One abides in an omnipresent state in which what are
>   characterized as sense objects do not exist as objects.
> Since there is omnipresent awareness, timeless and nondual,
> within the state of great perfection—the indivisibility of
>   samsara and nirvana—
> everything is in a state of infinite evenness, without acceptance
>   or rejection.

In this case, the meaning of an "innate state of immediacy" is that of awareness resting in the direct experience of its sense objects. To reiterate, there are two aspects to consider—the very essence of being, abiding as natural meditative stability, and recognition of the manifestations of its dynamic energy when they arise as sense objects in all their immediacy. [115a]

The naturally settled state is the abiding aspect that occurs when you abide so that you are very present, without any occurrence of or involvement in hope and fear; since this is true meditative stability, you rest in it. Having directly identified that immaculate, wakeful state, you maintain its continuity. *The Tantra Without Letters* states:

> There is no division between outer and inner, so lucidity is neither external nor internal.
> Not entailing a specific point of view, it transcends both affirmation and denial.
> Since there is no view, there is nothing to be viewed.
> There is no straying from this ultimate meaning so, as a matter of course, there is no view.
> None of this exists, yet one abides within the context of it.[37]

And *The All-Creating Monarch* states:

> Ah! In supreme bliss—just as it is, effortless—
> do not make any effort with body, speech, or mind.
> Do not contrive or create constructs.
> Do not conceptualize.
> Do not be influenced by the characteristics of things.
> Rest in the ultimate experience of bliss, naturally occurring timeless awareness.
> This is the enlightened intent of naturally occurring utter lucidity.
> This is the active expression of the all-creating monarch's enlightened intent.

When the dynamic energy of awareness seems to arise from the limpid clarity of awareness in direct response to sense objects, the relentless tendency of thoughts to proliferate in the mind is just the arousal of thoughts due to subtle energy, so let them go. There is an aspect of awareness in that quality, so identify that aspect very precisely. Then, when you just let the proliferating quality go where it will, it naturally vanishes. *The All-Creating Monarch* states:

Do not adopt postures, suppress your senses,
or restrict your speech, for there is nothing to do or to seek.
Moreover, let your mind go where it will, and rest in an
    unwavering state.
. . . .
Ultimate reality, the meaning underlying everything, is unborn.
With the awareness that concepts and characteristics are
    likewise unborn,
not a single thought process stirring in the mind [115b]
ever diverges from its unborn state.
If one understands that there is meditation regardless of what
    thoughts occur,
then no matter what takes place, there is no distraction, even if
    one does not try to meditate.

As for the key points here, having identified the essence of awareness, which you have elicited in all its nakedness, do not investigate the stirring or proliferating quality of thoughts, do not try to look at their essence, and do not try to settle naturally. These are extremely important, the key points crucial to trekchö. If you don't understand this, you will become lost, either by compounding the confusion of thoughts themselves, by using antidotes in a haphazard process of renunciation, by settling in dualistic perception, or by remaining in an ordinary state.

It can be shown that neither of these two contexts—natural abiding or natural arising—is better or worse than the other:

> What is tangible and what is intangible are equal in basic space,
> buddhas and ordinary beings are equal in basic space,
> relative reality and ultimate reality are equal in basic space,
> flaws and positive qualities are equal in basic space,
> and all directions—above, below, and in between—are equal
>   in basic space.
> Therefore, whatever display arises from that naturally
>   occurring state,
> even as it arises, things arise equally, none being better
>   or worse.
> What need is there to accept or reject them by applying
>   antidotes?

> When things abide, they abide equally, none being better
> or worse.
> Whatever is now taking place in your mind, rest in
> natural peace.[38]
> When things are free, they are equally free, none being better
> or worse.
> In the wake of being conscious of them, do not continue to
> suppress or indulge in them.

To take an example, still water and water that moves in waves are neither better nor worse than one another, for both are equally water. Similarly, neither of the two contexts of awareness—as it abides in its natural place of rest or as it arises—is better or worse than the other, because in neither is there any straying from awareness itself, [116a] only the mere fact that awareness is either abiding or arising. *The Vajra Pavilion* states:

> As long as thoughts proliferate in the ordinary mind,
> there is the very embodiment of the protector—
> are water and waves different from one another?

In the same way, all things—the tangible and the intangible, buddhas and ordinary beings, relative reality and ultimate reality, flaws and positive qualities—are equal in that they are all unborn within the basic space of awareness. They are equal in that they simply manifest continuously. And they are equal in that, even as they manifest, they are nonexistent, being clearly apparent expressions of emptiness. This is similar to the fact that, while you can distinguish among directions—above, below, cardinal, intermediate—they are equal in the realm of space.

Therefore, since there is no distinction of better or worse when things initially arise, do not accept or reject them. Since things are equal in the interim, let them remain in the naturally peaceful state. And since they are equal in the final outcome, given that they are freed by vanishing naturally, do not try to anticipate or follow after them. *The All-Creating Monarch* demonstrates that you should not settle deliberately or focus on any frame of reference:

> The unborn nature of everything without exception is completely
> pure meditative absorption.
> Whether one is meditating or not does not depend on
> circumstances.

What one meditates on is all phenomena, however they
    manifest.
If one rests[39] in the natural state without seeking anything,
    without any specific method concerning how or when to rest—
    that is meditation.

Now, the ultimate meaning of the preceding points can be summarized
as the supreme state of equalness that is the true nature of phenomena:

**Within awakened mind itself—the expanse of the ground
    of being—
the way in which everything arises as its dynamic energy
    and display is unpredictable. [116b]
Even as things arise equally, they arise within that primordial
    expanse.
Even as they arise unequally, they arise within the basic space
    of their equalness.
Even as they abide equally, their true nature is a natural state
    of rest.
Even as they abide unequally, they abide within the basic space
    of their equalness.
Even as they are freed equally, this constitutes the expanse
    of naturally occurring timeless awareness.
Even as they are freed unequally, they are freed within the basic
    space of their equalness.**

Within this state of awareness, like space, the entire display in all its
variety arises naturally through an open avenue by which the dynamic
energy of responsiveness expresses itself. Things manifest in such a way
that they appear to be better or worse, higher or lower—as the five emotional poisons and other aspects of samsara, timeless awareness and
other aspects of nirvana, and spiritual approaches. They are all pure in
that their very essence is that of the dream state, so in actuality nothing is better or worse than anything else, nothing is to be accepted or
rejected. Within the vast palace of the basic space of phenomena, everything is subsumed within a single unborn state of equalness and perfection. This is similar to the fact that the sun, moon, planets, and stars are
subsumed within the realm of space. *The Natural Freedom of Awareness* states:

Just as, for example, the sun and moon are subsumed
within the realm of empty space,
so the myriad display of timeless awareness is subsumed[40]
within the spacious palace of phenomena.
Awareness—timeless awareness as emptiness—
    is subsumed
within the spacious expanse of ultimate reality.

Let me reiterate more concisely what it is to directly determine in your immediate experience the equal significance of natural abiding and natural arising. Train in this, as is stated in *The Six Expanses:*

In meditative absorption as a supreme, innate state of immediacy,
one's body is, as it were, completely ordinary,
one's speech is free of spoken words,[41] [117a]
and one's mind is not tightly bound.

Twenty-Two Topics That Identify Key Points

Having thus discussed the methods of resting that are beyond deliberate meditation, as well as the auxiliary aspects of meditative absorption, in order to discern the implications of these I will now offer a concise overview based on twenty-two topics that identify key points specific to this approach.

Six Implications Concerning Freedom

One implication to be discerned is that there is a supremely spacious state of timeless equalness within basic space:

Given[42] naturally occurring awareness, the timeless equalness
    of everything,
arising and nonarising are timelessly nonexistent in basic space,
abiding and nonabiding are timelessly nonexistent in basic space,
and freedom and the absence of freedom are timelessly
    nonexistent in basic space.

Awareness, its dynamic energy, and the display of sensory appearances and ordinary mind are all such that they have never known existence or nonexistence, have never known manifestation or emptiness, and have never known samsara or nirvana, but rather are already pure like space, without any underlying basis. The implication concerning everything that manifests or that stirs in the mind—that it has never known existence—can be discerned within the state in which phenomena resolve. By completely letting go within the expanse that entails no conceptualization whatsoever, you embrace the larger scope of there being no origination. *The Great Garuda* states:

> Abandon the desire for bliss, for it harms the mind.
> Rely on the state of resting naturally, and you are free of needing
>   to do anything about samsara or nirvana.
> As for the miraculous expressions of mind and sensory
>   appearances—"This is self, this is other"[43]—
> the hindrances of mental stirring, perceiving, thinking,
>   and fixating are dispelled,
> and so there is imperturbable rest that defies all attempts
>   at verbal expression.
> The implication that whatever manifests is the miraculous
>   expression of ordinary conceptual mind
> can be discerned in the "interval" between the state free of
>   phenomena and the mind's conceptual process.[44] [117b]

NATURAL FREEDOM

Another implication to be discerned is that things are naturally freed and vanish naturally, like a knot in a snake:

> **Within awareness, a supreme state of unwavering equalness,**
> **even as things arise, they arise naturally, holding to their**
> **   own place.**
> **Even as they abide, they abide naturally, holding to their**
> **   own place.**
> **Even as they are freed, they are freed naturally, holding to their**
> **   own place.**

The three phases of things arising, abiding, and being freed do not take place anywhere other than within the immediacy of awareness, so the expression "their own place" refers to bare awareness abiding as naked original purity within the natural basic space of dharmakaya. The expression "holding to their own place" refers to recognition of this. Even as things arise naturally, the implication discerned is that they are freed within naked awareness, the place from which they arise. Even as they abide naturally, the implication discerned is that naked awareness is the place in which they abide. And as for their natural freedom, even as they vanish, the implication discerned is that naked awareness is the place to which they go. *The Great Garuda* states:

> Without cause, naturally free, and not relying on conditions,
> the unbiased, naturally pure view does not exist as some "thing."
> The three hindrances that involve the limitations of ingrained
>   opinions are dispelled.
> The implication that sensory appearances and consciousness
> constitute a supreme, naturally occurring state of
>   innate immediacy
> can be discerned within[45] the "interval" between cause and effect,
>   which arises naturally and is free of elaboration.

TIMELESS FREEDOM

Another implication to be discerned is that things are timelessly free in that they are free of any basis:

> **Given that awareness is unchanging and free of elaboration,**
> **everything is of the nature of space—what arises, arises**
> **   timelessly;**
> **what abides, abides timelessly; and what is free is free**
> **   timelessly.**

Even though there is the appearance of water in a mirage, it is already free in not being water, for it has never existed as water. Similarly, all phenomena, having no independent nature, are timelessly empty and without identity, and so are timelessly free of having substance or characteristics. In this way, whatever sensory appearances manifest outwardly and whatever states of consciousness arise inwardly, [118a] all of them are initially devoid of anything that could bring them into being, and so they have definitely never known existence, even as they seem to come into being or arise. What seems at present to abide in light of consciousness is devoid of any essence as something that could abide, and so is free of any constraint, being clearly apparent without truly existing.

Finally, what seems to cease is devoid of any essence as something that could cease. Because things are unborn, they do not abide, and the fact that they have never existed as anything that could cease makes thinking about them in such terms similar to thinking that the water in a mirage has vanished or ceased to be. This is simply a case of mistaken perception, since nothing actually ceases, and so you come to the decisive experience that nothing has ever existed as anything that could cease to be. You should understand that since things are already free in that they have never known existence, there is no need for anything that arises in light of ordinary consciousness to be freed by applying antidotes. *The Pearl Garland* states:

> Freedom is not due to effort;
> rather, one abides timelessly in freedom.

The actual way to discern the implication of this key point and put it into practice is as follows: Even as sense objects manifest in light of consciousness, you understand that they have no basis and so release them into openness without contriving or tampering with them in any way. Even as sensory appearances arise directly in, and are directly encountered by, your consciousness, they have no basis and so are released into a state of bare experience, which is the direct encounter with awareness. Your consciousness of sensory appearances is continuous, yet it does not reify or analyze them. Rather, you maintain what is simply an undistracted identification of naked awareness itself, pristine in its openness. *The Great Garuda* states:

> The ground of being is total freedom, the timeless purity
>   underlying characteristics.
> The hindrances of ordinary consciousness are dispelled
>   effortlessly, with nothing needing to be done.
> The implication that the threefold direct encounter is the display
>   that manifests as sense objects [118b]
> can be discerned within the "interval" between objects and mind,
>   without distraction, regardless of what arises.

As this quotation indicates, even as you are conscious of sensory appearances, you identify bare awareness arising in the "interval" of resting imperturbably. I have focused on this point and explained it extensively because it is so crucial.

FREEDOM IN IMMEDIATE PERCEPTION

Another implication to be discerned is that freedom in immediate perception is a supreme state in which ordinary perception vanishes:

> Thoughts arise, abide, and are freed.
> Their simultaneous arising and being freed is uninterrupted.
> Since it is uninterrupted, there is no separation into cause
>   and effect.
> Since there is no cause and effect, the abyss of samsara
>   has been crossed.
> Since there is no longer an abyss, where could one go astray?

That is to say, since awareness is uninterrupted, its dynamic energy is continuous. Even as you seem to be conscious of sense objects, thoughts do not go beyond any of their three phases—arising, abiding, or being freed (which is to say, vanishing). Given that they can be likened to the flow of water, there is no opportunity for cause and effect to be reinforced in any single moment. Thoughts arise and vanish simultaneously, and so are like patterns drawn on water. Ordinary consciousness perceives these two phases, as well as that of abiding, to be aspects of awareness. When even occasionally you experience thoughts simultaneously arising and being freed, you realize that it is impossible for any causal process to exist. With your naked realization of this, the cause of samsara is exhausted. Since its result—remaining within the three realms and the six states of samsara—is impossible, your mind is at ease.

This key point leaves no room for any obscuration or potential for error. Due to the purity that lies in the simultaneous arising and freeing of thoughts, error and obscuration are cut through in the context of their true nature. This is what is meant by "crossing over the abyss of hope and fear."

The way to discern the implication of this key point and put it into practice is as follows: It makes no difference what arises where—whether ordinary consciousness manifesting in response to sense objects, or sense objects manifesting to ordinary consciousness—for the moment you rest in the immediate perception of the context in which thoughts arise, [119a] it is impossible for there not to be a pristine state in which they vanish naturally, leaving no trace. At that point, by resting in the wake of their vanishing, you identify the presence of a bare state of lucid, pure awareness, its limpid quality intense and enormously potent.

While everyone else cultivates a nonconceptual state of meditation—a pristine state in which everything fades away—I hold this to be calm abiding (that is, the abiding quality of awareness), which will not help you understand the key point here. I must emphasize the need to identify bare, unobstructed awareness in all its nakedness under any circumstances, a tenet that is unique to the great perfection approach. The implication of freedom in immediate perception is discerned by identifying awareness in the "interval" between sense objects manifesting outwardly and consciousness—aware yet empty—arising inwardly. *The Great Garuda* states:

> Freedom in immediate perception is naturally pure, boundless,
> completely perfect, and free of limitation.
> Any dualism is[46] naturally dispelled.
> The implication that the vast expanse is a supreme state that need
>   not be sought
> and is free of anything needing to be done
> can be discerned within[47] the "interval" between sensory
>   appearances and emptiness,
> in which nothing need be said or done.

FREEDOM FROM LIMITATION

Another implication to be discerned is that there is freedom from limitation, beyond imagination or expression:

> **The expanse of Samantabhadra is timelessly unchanging.**
> **The expanse of Vajrasattva is without transition or change.**
> **The term "buddhahood" is nothing more than a label**
> **for what is simply recognition of the very essence of being—**
>   **the way of abiding.**

Since nothing has ever existed within the essence of awareness, that essence is Samantabhadra—"wholly positive." Since it is the unobstructed unity of emptiness and lucidity, it is the spacious expanse of Vajrasattva—"immutable being." To identify this is called "finding buddhahood within yourself," for even if you were to search elsewhere, [119b] you would not find it. *The Web of Magic* states:

> Perfect buddhahood is not to be found
> anywhere in the ten directions or four times.
> Since mind itself is perfectly awakened as buddhahood,
> do not seek buddhahood elsewhere!

And *The Exalted Discourse on Transcendent Timeless Awareness* states:

> Since mind itself is perfect buddhahood,
> do not seek buddhahood elsewhere!

If you put this into practice, it makes no difference whether thoughts arise, or indeed what takes place. Do not direct your thoughts outwardly to sense objects, think inwardly about your ordinary mind, or settle into some unborn state between these alternatives as the "natural state." Rather, identify unobstructed awareness in your immediate perception of it. In the very instant you do so, you abide in enlightened intent that is like space—beyond elaboration, imagination, or expression—a state free of limitation in which nothing has been deliberately rejected but which is not experienced in light of your ordinary consciousness.

Here the phrase "is not experienced in light of your ordinary consciousness" is used because there is no proliferation and resolution of thoughts. Since you do not think about the sense objects you perceive, it is said that "nothing can be characterized as real." When both seemingly real sense objects and the proliferation and resolution of thoughts are absent, there are no other modes by which samsara and nirvana can be evaluated and reified, and so there is "one's own awareness"—that is, timeless awareness as one's individual experience of self-knowing awareness, indescribable, inconceivable, and inexpressible. *The Pearl Garland* states:

> Since it is freedom from limitation, the four alternatives have
> ceased to be.

And *The Great Garuda* states:

> Rely on the state of resting naturally, and you are free of needing
> to do anything about samsara or nirvana.
> As for the miraculous expressions of mind and sensory
> appearances—"This is self, this is other"[48]—
> the hindrances of mental stirring, perceiving, thinking, and
> fixating are dispelled, [120a]

and so there is imperturbable rest that defies all attempts
    at verbal expression.
The implication that whatever manifests is the miraculous
    expression of ordinary conceptual mind
can be discerned in the "interval" between the mind free
    of phenomena and its conceptual process.

This key point is the great universal path adhered to by those who are spiritually advanced and by those who follow them. This has been stated in passages such as the following:

Indescribable, inconceivable, and inexpressible, the perfection
    of sublime knowing
is unborn and unceasing—the very essence of space.
It is the domain of each individual's self-knowing timeless
    awareness.
I pay homage to the mother of victorious ones of the three times.

And in *The Precious Unborn Treasury:*

Do not think of anything, do not think of anything at all!
Do not contrive, but relax naturally and gently!
The uncontrived state is the precious unborn treasury.
It is the path blazed by all victorious ones of the three times.

And in *Engaging in the Conduct of a Bodhisattva:*

When the tangible and intangible
are not experienced in light of ordinary consciousness,
since there are no other alternatives at this point
there is utter peace without any frame of reference.

Freedom from limitation is praised as the ultimate meaning of the true nature of phenomena:

With the realization of this, there are no phenomena to accept
    or reject,
so all things are in a state of infinite evenness that is their sole
    true nature.
As on the Isle of Gold, there is no division or exclusion.
This nature is not subject to limitation, for error and
    obscuration have been seen through.

> Within awakened mind itself, in which there are no pitfalls,
> the three kayas, involving no effort, are spontaneously perfect,
> so the phrase "beyond imagination or expression" is a mere
>   figure of speech. [120b]

Having realized that all phenomena, like space, are without basis, you perceive them in their equalness: no phenomena exist that are good or bad, that are to be accepted or rejected. On the Isle of Gold, all things are equally gold, so whatever forms manifest, they are neither good nor bad; there are no ordinary rocks or stones to be found, for everything is made of gold. Similarly, all phenomena constitute a state of infinite evenness within the great perfection that is free of limitation, so the labels "error," "obscuration," "samsara," and "nirvana" are irrelevant. Furthermore, the statement that the three kayas abide as a spontaneous presence, given their true nature as a supremely spacious state of evenness and equalness, is simply a figure of speech. In actuality, you have cut through limitations by going beyond what can be characterized or described, so that enlightened intent is spontaneously present as a supreme state beyond ordinary consciousness. *The Natural Freedom of Awareness* states:

> It is beyond limitation or distortion.
> The distortions of the four extremes are naturally
>   cleared away.
> It is free of the biases of reification.

FREEDOM IN ONENESS

Since there is nothing comparable to freedom in oneness, the implication to be discerned is that it is a bare state in all its nakedness:

> Sensory appearances are unrestricted;
> awareness is evident and naturally occurring.
> Since the genuine state of uncontrived rest is unobscured
>   and unobstructed, with no division into outer and inner,
> it is evident as the supreme nature of phenomena.
> Let your mind and body relax deeply in a carefree state.
> With an easygoing attitude, like a person who has nothing
>   more to do,

let your mind and body rest in whatever way is comfortable,
neither tense nor loose.

People have individual awareness. Given that no one has two or
more awarenesses, there is freedom in oneness, since in this context
whether there is bondage or freedom must be evaluated on the basis of
this sole awareness. Given that this sole awareness is the unique sphere
of dharmakaya, [121a] it is also fitting to refer to "freedom in oneness,"
because everything is freed through one's realization of awareness. Furthermore, when unobstructed awareness arises in the context of sensory appearances that are not subject to restriction, without thinking
in terms of sensory appearances as distinct from mind, you identify that
sole state of bare awareness, and so the true nature of phenomena becomes evident in its own right. This is the spiritual instruction in which
the profound experience of spaciousness in a natural carefree state is likened to that of a person who has finished a task.

In putting this into practice, when three factors—consciousness (the
dynamic energy of bare awareness), sense objects, and the perception of
them—come together, you are conscious of sense objects but you do not
think of this as a duality; instead, you identify the sole state of awareness. With this, you are free of the restrictions imposed by the duality
of sense objects and ordinary mind. This is similar to an entire pack
load being freed of its restraints when the single peg that holds the ropes
binding the load is pulled out.

In addition, the conventional expressions "all-consuming thought
patterns" and "the phenomena of samsara" are used to refer to the
three factors of sense objects, consciousness of them, and the process
of ideation. Once you have identified the sole state of awareness, all
three are cleared away so that you are free of their restrictions. This is
naturally occurring timeless awareness, the true nature of which is such
that words and ordinary consciousness fall away. Reifying samsara as
something to renounce, and nirvana as something to accept, entails this
triad of object, consciousness, and ideation, so you should discern the
implication that bare awareness arises in the "interval" that is free of ordinary consciousness, which involves renunciation using antidotes. To
summarize this thoroughly, the implication you discern is that the sole
state of bare consciousness is found in the "interval" in which the duality of outer sensory appearances and inner consciousness is put aside
and dismissed in its entirety. *The Great Garuda* states:

Timeless awareness, not manifest yet free of being a void,
is not reified, not relinquished,[49] and not corrupted, but is
   the natural state— [121b]
it is the one factor that applies to three.
It is neither false nor true, but a magnificent means of
   abiding.
. . . .

With the falling away of karma, the sense faculties, words,
   and ordinary consciousness,
the[50] corrupting and contriving hindrances of skillful means
   and sublime knowing are dispelled.
There is no need to posit some fruition state that relies on
   the absence of phenomena,
and rather than one becoming bound by more opinions,
the implication of meditative "warmth"—relaxed, fresh,
   and genuine—
is laid bare in its natural state, discerned within[51] the "interval"
   between samsara and nirvana.

The logical consistency of freedom in oneness can be established:

**However things stay, they stay within their fundamental
   nature.**
**However they dwell, they dwell within their fundamental
   nature.**
**However they move, they move within their fundamental
   nature.**
**Fundamentally, there is no coming or going within the basic
   space of enlightenment.**
The enlightened forms of victorious ones do not come or go.

All the appearances of moving, staying, or dwelling that manifest in
dreams do so within a single state of sleep, but it is not the sleep that
moves, stays, or dwells. Similarly, nothing—neither the universe of appearances and possibilities, whether of samsara or nirvana, nor any
of the myriad beings who manifest as moving, staying, or dwelling
therein—strays from the sole state of awareness; rather, everything is
clearly apparent without truly existing, the ground of being manifesting
as sensory appearances. The essence of awareness is such that it does

not stray from the dharmakaya of the victorious ones—the epitome of what entails no coming or going—which abides in its natural place of rest. *The All-Creating Monarch* states:

> The suchness of the universe of appearances and possibilities,
>   whether of samsara or nirvana,[52]
> does not stray from awakened mind.
> There is peace, for nothing strays from awakened mind.

Since no description or expression falls outside the context of inexpressible awareness, [122a] it can be shown that in actuality there is nothing to be expressed:

> **However description occurs, it occurs within its fundamental
>   nature.**
> **However expression occurs, it occurs within its fundamental
>   nature.**
> **Fundamentally, there is no description or expression within
>   awakened mind.**
> **The enlightened speech of the victorious ones of the three times
>   is indescribable and inexpressible.**

The speech that takes place in dreams does not stray from the state of sleep. Similarly, none of the sounds in your present waking state exist as something "other," outside the context of awareness, and awareness is pure, inexpressible, and equal to space. *The Six Expanses* states:

> Words based on concepts like the two levels of truth
> are understood, even in our ordinary consciousness,
> to be like words heard in[53] a dream.

Since consciousness does not stray from awakened mind, it can be shown that in actuality thoughts are without any basis or foundation—that, even as they manifest in your consciousness, they have never known existence:

> **However thinking occurs, it occurs within its fundamental
>   nature.**
> **However conceptualization[54] occurs, it occurs within its
>   fundamental nature.**

> There is never any thinking or conceptualizing within
>   awakened mind.
> The enlightened mind of the victorious ones of the three times
>   is free of thinking and conceptualizing.

What arises as consciousness, even in arising, has never known existence as consciousness but is like the thoughts that take place in a dream. But insofar as ordinary beings hold what does not exist to be existent, they are said to "engage in concepts based on confusion." Although in actuality concepts do not stray from the scope of awareness, awareness is beyond the scope of ordinary thought and so is completely nonconceptual timeless awareness. This is the enlightened mind of the buddhas, which abides free of the limitations of ordinary thought. [122b] *The Array of Inlaid Gems* states:

> The enlightened mind of buddhahood is free of the extreme of
> conceiving in terms of identity, and so is inconceivable timeless
> awareness itself.[55]

When yogins realize the ultimate meaning of this, they discover self-knowing awareness—original buddhahood—within themselves as a supreme, unobstructed state, and so samsara, formed of perceptions based on confusion, is emptied. *The Six Expanses* states:

> Born of nonconceptual timeless awareness,
> original buddhahood, timelessly present, is discovered
> through the pith instruction on resting without trying to do so.
> At this point, confused perception is pure.[56]
> As a sign of this purity, phenomena resolve.
> With this resolution, samsara is emptied.

Thus, just as all appearances, sounds, and thoughts occur within the oneness of awareness, not being anything "other," it can also be shown that the three kayas and their pure realms constitute the oneness of self-knowing awareness:

> Since what is nonexistent can occur in any way at all, there is
>   nirmanakaya.
> Since the richness of being enjoys itself, there is sambhogakaya.

**Since no substantial basis for these two exists, there is
dharmakaya.
The fruition is the expanse within which the three kayas
are spontaneously present.**

Since the essence of awareness is beyond characterization or expression, it is dharmakaya—which is to say, there is no basis for awareness ever having existed as something real or characterizable. Once you have realized it to be unobstructed, in the context of that realization you enjoy this selfsame awareness as a state of spontaneous presence. Since awareness abides in its natural place of rest, it is sambhogakaya—that is, the ground of natural lucidity—without being any specific "thing." Its aspect as the continuous way in which responsiveness arises due to that pristine lucidity is nirmanakaya. Thus, the three kayas are not anything other than awareness itself. This is naturally occurring timeless awareness. *The Secret Web of Magic* states:

> Nor do the marvelous kayas and pure realms of
>   buddhahood [123a]
> exist elsewhere—this is the state of naturally occurring
>   timeless awareness.

Thus, since samsara and nirvana do not stray from the single state of awareness, if this single awareness is free, then all samsara and nirvana is free. This key point can be shown to be utterly profound.

The Pearl Garland gives a synopsis and examples of these five modes of freedom:

> Within unceasing awareness,
>   there is nothing to be confused about, so there is no regression.[57]
> Since it is timeless freedom, it is exalted above everything.[58]
> Since it is natural freedom, sense objects as conditions of one's
>   experience resolve.
> Since it is freedom in immediate perception, one's perception
>   of sensory appearances is pure.
> Since it is freedom from limitation, the four alternatives have
>   ceased to be.
> Since it is freedom in oneness, it is devoid of any sense
>   of multiplicity.
> Since circumstances are freed by circumstances,

I do not rely on constructs.
Since sense objects are freed by sense objects,
I do not rely on dualistic perception.
Since causes themselves are freed by causes,
I do not rely on either samsara or nirvana.
Since phenomena are freed by phenomena,
I do not rely on conventional descriptions.
Since mind itself is freed by mind,
I do not rely on characterization by the intellect.
Just as impurities can be cleansed with impurities,
in the same way purity is freed by purity.
Just as poison is used to counteract poison,
iron to cut iron,
stone to shatter stone,
and wood to burn wood,
things serve as their own undoing.
Freedom does not come from incompatibility.

The preceding discussions have dealt with six themes that concern the five modes of freedom [123b] and the very essence that underlies them.

Three Methods of Resting That Relate to Essence, Nature, and Responsiveness

Now, the spiritual instruction that the expanse of enlightened intent is the true nature of phenomena is given in stages. The larger scope to be embraced is that this expanse is equal to space, beyond imagination or description:

Within the very state that is the vast expanse of awakened mind,
the concepts of ordinary thinking do not occur.
If the characteristics of ordinary consciousness do not stir in
   the mind,
that itself is enlightened intent, the unique state of buddhahood.

Among the three aspects of awakened mind—essence, nature, and responsiveness—let us first define the context of the essence. It is mind itself—resting in a state of infinite evenness within basic space that involves no recollection or thinking—free of the occurrence of or involvement in thoughts, free of hope and fear. *The Great Garuda* states:

> On the level of resting without meditating, self-knowing
>   awareness[59]
> is free of labels and ordinary consciousness, for it is the
>   transcendent field of everything.
> What involves constructs is, in fact, the natural state itself—
>   what need is there to contrive it?[60]

And *The All-Creating Monarch* states:

> In the state of enlightenment—the true nature of phenomena—
>   which involves no acceptance or rejection,
> one abides like space, so body and mind cannot be contrived.
> Since there are no deeply ingrained concepts, there is nothing
>   to meditate on.
> In utter peace, like space, free of all sullying factors,
> there is no involvement with sense objects, only enlightened
>   intent free of entangling frameworks.

The implication to be embraced is that awareness is the supreme unity of lucidity and emptiness:

> **The nature of enlightenment is similar to the spacious vault
>   of the sky.**
> **The most sublime form of meditation involves no recollection
>   or thinking.**
> **One's nature is unwavering and uncontrived.**
> **Unplanned and completely free of the formation of ideas,**
>   **the true nature of phenomena, the naturally settled state,**
> **is without transition or change throughout the three times.**
> **The most sublime form of meditation involves no stirring or
>   proliferation of all-consuming thoughts.**

The nature of awareness is utter lucidity, comparable to the sun and moon [124a] when they shine unobscured in the sky. Without the proliferation and resolution of thoughts, rest with alertness in that state of natural lucidity, elicited in all its nakedness. Then spontaneous presence becomes evident in its own right. *The Great Garuda* states:

> The key point is that timeless awareness, experienced in a relaxed
>   and uncontrived way, is not cultivated in meditation.[61]

> Without cause and free of conditions, awareness's own
>   manifestations are unobscured.
> Free of effort, unique, and not created by anyone or anything,
> the timelessly perfect heart essence expresses itself in the
>   spontaneous presence of sense objects.

In this regard, because concepts are in direct contradiction to this innately limpid state and are endless, so that there is no respite from them,
you should abide in the natural limpidity of the nature of being—the
naked, inherently pristine state that is free of concepts. *The All-Creating
Monarch* states:

> Concepts that enumerate the characteristics of sense objects
>   are countless.
> Nothing is what it is by being produced,[62] and concepts only
>   undermine concepts.
> The spiritually undeveloped are deceived, and are like water that
>   has become sullied.

As well, the indivisibility of things arising and simultaneously being
freed is embraced in all its nakedness:

> Any abiding in suchness is the sacred state of mind—
> the unique state of buddhahood, free of all
>   characterization.
> It is the unwavering basic space of phenomena, a state
>   of evenness that transcends reifying concepts.
> This is the expanse of the enlightened intent of the
>   victorious ones,
> the sublime, spacious nature of being.
> When the bonds of physical and mental contrivance are
>   abandoned,
> there is unfeigned relaxation.
> No matter what recollection stirs in the mind,
> if you do not waver from the context of the true nature of
>   phenomena—that of resting in the ground of being—
> everything is the spacious expanse of the enlightened intent
>   of Samantabhadra.

Although thoughts arise continuously within the limpidity of awareness, stirring and proliferating as they arise, they are, like water and

its waves, neither better nor worse than one another. [124b] So when you let them go, having identified unobstructed awareness as a supreme state of equalness, the arising of thoughts and their being freed are simultaneous. By recognizing the hidden weakness—that in their very stirring thoughts occur only to cease—you allow whatever arises to do so as it will. This is a very crucial point. Since you do not think about or corrupt the experience by using some technique to identify where thoughts arise, freedom is ensured without antidotes being used to abandon anything. *The Great Garuda* states:

> With abiding, thoughts cease, while with mental stirring, they are
>   pure in their natural state.
> With the perception of ineffability, there is no renunciation;
> within the essence of being, there is nothing to be cleared away.
> One abides in this state, which is not some level, and relates
>   to sense objects as they are.
> There is no arriving at some distant shore.

And *The All-Creating Monarch* states:

> Since conceptualization and analysis[63] are transcended,
>   do not indulge in them!
> Do not meddle with the uncontrived state, just as it is!
> Let go of all plans and do not think about the true nature
>   of anything that manifests.
> Resting naturally is revealed to be freedom.

At this point, you might ask, "Isn't there a contradiction between not regarding the onset of mental stirring as a flaw and the earlier explanation of the absence of concepts?" How very amazing! Since you speak of such a difference, you still don't understand. Suppose that I said, "You unfortunate person, you're a stupid pig whose immense delusion is running rampant!" How would you like that? In any case, let me explain this clearly. When thoughts stir and proliferate, having arisen due to the dynamic energy of responsiveness, that proliferation is a matter of thoughts riding on the mount of subtle energy. So you rest imperturbably, without prolonging their duration or looking at their essence, and having identified unobstructed, naked awareness, you continue to experience it as a supreme, uninterrupted state of pristine lucidity in all its simplicity, nakedness, and purity.

The preceding points boil down to the methods of resting that relate to the three aspects of essence, nature, and responsiveness. [125a]

Five Themes Concerning the Dispelling of Constraints

Now, constraints are dispelled within the spacious state of enlightened intent that is the true nature of phenomena. To begin with, without interfering with the way the dynamic energy and display of awareness arise, you dispel constraints within the unique state of equalness and purity, beyond ordinary consciousness:

> Since nothing is reified or discarded, there is none of the tension
>   or laxity of the compulsive mind.
> The unrestricted state of natural settling, just as it is, is ensured
>   as a matter of course.
> Unwavering, infinite evenness is an expanse with no fixed
>   dimension.
> If all ordinary thinking occurs naturally and is pacified
>   naturally,
> that is the skylike enlightened intent of Vajrasattva.

This verse says, in effect, "If you are not distracted from the essence of awareness as the unity of emptiness and lucidity, there is no problem even if its dynamic energy expresses itself without restriction." This is illustrated by the fact that as long as a crystal remains in place, there is nothing contradictory about five-colored light scattering from it in all directions. It is not as though you hold your consciousness, which arises without restriction, within a single context. Rather, you ensure a simple, unobstructed state in which you are not distracted from bare awareness, the ground from which consciousness arises.

"Well," you might think, "wouldn't one be distracted by allowing proliferating thoughts to scatter however they will?" But here distraction is not possible. As subtle energy moves outward, awareness remains focused within, and as its radiance turns back inward, its dynamic energy is freed as it is absorbed into the ground of being, because it is never separate from the unified sphere that is the bare essence of awareness. *The All-Creating Monarch* states:

> Given the oneness within the basic space of phenomena,
>   there is nothing to traverse.

Given intimate contact with the meaning of the heart essence,
    there is no distraction.
Given the unified sphere of being, thoughts do not
    proliferate[64] anywhere.

Since realization or its lack inherently implies freedom versus bondage, the larger scope is one in which such constraints are dispelled:

If you maintain an undistracted state within the uncontrived
    expanse of being, [125b]
even engaging in thoughts concerning sense objects is within
    the scope of the true nature of phenomena.
As for that true nature, it is nonconceptual and as spacious
    as the sky,
but if you try to contrive it deliberately and compulsively,
    it becomes a cage of characteristics.
Though you may spend day and night in such meditation,
    that is the bondage of fixation, pure and simple.
The Victorious One stated that it resembles the meditative
    stability of the gods.
Therefore, it is extremely crucial that your mind—
which is undistracted and in which effort and striving have
    been eradicated—
settle naturally, beyond reifying effort.

If you have not fathomed this key point, it will be difficult for you to progress along the spiritual path. Even though you may meditate day and night with a one-pointed mind, if you are fixated on or attached to meditative experiences of bliss, clarity, or nonconceptual awareness, your meditation will be identical to the meditative stability of the gods and will not be able to lift you the slightest bit farther out of samsara. *The Chapter on the Sacred Collections of Meditative Absorption* states:

Even though meditative absorption may be thoroughly stabilized,
if one indulges in overt fixation on it,
one is said to be on "the level of a fool's entertainment."
This will not lead to actual nirvana.

When yogins come to a realization of bare awareness, even though, due to its dynamic energy, they are conscious of sense objects, this energy does not fall outside the scope of its essence—the true nature of phenomena—and so they have not strayed from the spontaneously present enlightened intent of dharmakaya. *The All-Creating Monarch* states:

> Given the view that concepts are free in their own place,
> when one rests naturally and without distraction, there is nothing
>   to do or to seek.[65]
> Everything, moreover, occurs naturally and is free in its own
>   place.

Let me summarize the significant points here. Even though deliberately contrived view and meditation involving a framework are taught, you should understand that they are within the realm of ordinary characteristics. As for what is completely "ordinary" and uncontrived, [126a] you should understand that consciousness failing to realize awareness in its bare state and being lost in response to sense objects is the thinking process in samsara. When the distortions of hope and fear do not intrude on the state of unobstructed awareness, all the "sharp edges" of concepts are worn away. You should understand that if there is no distraction from the context of that realization, there is a nondual state, which is the enlightened intent of the victorious ones. The same tantra states:

> Ah! The essence of the teacher is the all-creating monarch.
> While the true nature of phenomena entails no meditation
>   or ordinary thinking,
> to abide in some vague state without thinking is samsara,
>   pure and simple.
> To seek[66] something and meditate on it is the path of concepts
>   and characteristics.
> Therefore, the all-creating one does not proclaim that freedom
> lies in abiding in meditative absorption that involves hope and fear.
> When realization severs the bonds of these two,
> one abides in the meaning of equalness, the absence of opposites,
> and so the enlightened intent of me, the all-creating one,
>   is spontaneously accomplished.
> . . . .
> Thus, the pith instruction is to focus one's undistracted attention
> on the heart essence, which cannot be cultivated in meditation.

Having dispelled constraints within the essence of enlightened intent, which is beyond ordinary consciousness, you can embrace that intent as the transcendence of the proliferation and resolution of thought and recollection:

> Since naturally occurring timeless awareness is without
>   limitation or bias,
> it cannot be characterized as some "thing," for all elaboration
>   naturally subsides.
> Therefore, give up creating more concepts.
> Train in the ultimate meaning of supreme spaciousness free
>   of any foundation.

Since the essence of awareness is free of the limitations imposed by elaboration, it is crucial that the spiritual path of yogins who desire enlightenment not deviate from that essence, because the fruition will not be attained [126b] if the ground and path are at cross-purposes. Therefore, there can be no deliberate process of meditation using some reference point; there is simply no straying from the naturally pure state, the realization of bare awareness. This is the enlightened intent of naturally occurring timeless awareness. It is free as the supreme state of total perfection in which nothing is rejected. *The Great Garuda* states:

> Responsiveness, which by nature expresses itself continuously
>   in sense objects,
> is free in that these empty objects rest in their natural state
>   without being analyzed.
> The very absence of extremes purifies the avenues to rebirth
>   in higher realms.

And *The All-Creating Monarch* states:

> Ah! Having proclaimed the enlightened intent of the
>   all-creating one
> to the fortunate, who engage all at once in yoga,
> one should further proclaim that there is nothing to cultivate
>   in meditation or to engage in,
> only attention to and familiarization with the expanse[67]
>   of realization.

Given that awareness is a unique state free of elaboration, regardless of what labels are applied to it, the larger scope is one of constraints being dispelled:

> The unique nature of phenomena is naturally occurring
>   timeless awareness.
> The unique view is freedom from the limitations of elaboration.
> In the unique meditation, nothing is discarded or adopted,
>   nothing comes or goes.
> In the unique conduct, there is no duality of acceptance
>   and rejection.[68]
> The unique fruition is free of the duality of renunciation
>   and attainment.
> This is the enlightened intent of naturally occurring
>   spontaneous presence.

The unobstructed essence of awareness—the unique sphere of being—can be analyzed from a purely conventional perspective: Since this essence is unobstructed, it is unique dharmakaya. From the standpoint of its being free of the limitations imposed by elaboration, it is great perfection, the view free of limitation. Within the context of your realizing this same essence to be your own true nature, your consciousness is limpid and nonconceptual, [127a] with no proliferation or resolution of thoughts, no coming or going, and so this is the unique state of utterly lucid meditation. Since this essence does not involve the duality of acceptance and rejection, one of its qualities is that acceptance and rejection are naturally cleared away—this is the unique state of nondual conduct. And since samsara and nirvana do not exist within this essence, there is no renunciation or attainment, no hope or fear, and so this is the unique fruition state. *The Perfect Dynamic Energy of the Lion* states:

> Conduct is beyond the dualities[69] of reifying attachment.
> Meditation is beyond the duality of discarding and adopting.
> View is beyond extremes and bias.
> Fruition is beyond the dualistic extremes of renunciation
>   and attainment.[70]

Since everything is free of constraints within naturally occurring timeless awareness, it is embraced as the supremely spacious, uniform ground:

> The true nature of all phenomena in their entirety—
> the universe of appearances and possibilities,
> whether of samsara or nirvana—is the primordial state.
> Since it does not stray from naturally occurring timeless
> awareness itself,
> understand it to be enlightened intent, with everything at rest
> in the ground of being.

When myriad dream images manifest, even though months and years—even eons—seem to pass, none of them has ever existed, for they simply manifest as they do without straying from self-knowing awareness as their place of rest. Similarly, you should understand that even though everything seems to manifest at present as the universe of appearances and possibilities, whether of samsara or nirvana, and to endure for a long time, none of it strays from the basic space that is its essence, and so it is without transition or change within this primordial state. *The Scriptural Transmission of Supreme Dynamic Energy: The Perfection of Enlightened Qualities* states:

> Primordially, the context of phenomena in their entirety—
> the universe of appearances and possibilities, whether
> of samsara or nirvana—
> is that of naturally occurring timeless awareness,
> from which they have not strayed, being its supreme,
> spontaneously perfect dynamic energy. [127b]
> Free of any substance, they are natural expressions
> of emptiness.

The preceding five themes concern ways in which you are freed from the constraints of doubt and conceptual limitation.

Three Ways of Coming to a Decisive Experience of Awareness

Now, to come to a decisive experience of the naturally limpid "ocean" within the pristine state of utter lucidity, you hold to your own place as a supreme, unwavering state of equalness:

> Concerning phenomena that manifest[71] as myriad
> sense objects,
> without thinking in any way, "This is how to rest,"

> rest spontaneously in the naturally settled state, free of the
>   proliferation and resolution of thoughts.
> Abide as a matter of course within the expanse of equalness,
>   the true nature of phenomena.

When you experience the very essence of awareness in all its limpidity, the way in which things manifest is continuous and vivid. Within this context, you experience self-knowing awareness resting in its true nature, which does not involve any proliferation or resolution of thoughts. *The Great Garuda* states:

> Since all phenomena are unsullied and free of elaboration,
> this key point—that they are not created and are free in their
>   natural state—is[72] supreme.
> The key point concerning the cessation of causes, the fading away
>   of conditions, and the falling away of results
> is that the expanse of being itself is the single factor that ensures
>   freedom without relying on anything at all.

And *The All-Creating Monarch* states:

> Resting in the natural state without seeking anything,
> without any specific method concerning how or when to rest—
>   that is meditation.

You also hold to your own place as the unobstructed state of natural lucidity in all its nakedness:

> Neither focusing your senses on, nor letting your gaze
>   wander to,
> the manifestations of sensory appearances in all their variety,
> neither thinking of "self" nor conceiving of "other,"
> rest, naturally lucid,[73] in the supremely spacious state
>   of complete openness.

The metaphor is that of reflections arising in a limpid ocean. Your body is unmoving, your legs crossed in vajra posture. Your gaze does not waver, but is clear and rests straight ahead. You do not block sense objects, and they manifest clearly in all their variety. [128a] You are in a nonconceptual state of mind, for the proliferation and resolution of thoughts are naturally cut through. You rest in unobstructed awareness. *The Array of Inlaid Gems* states:

The metaphor for abiding continuously and unobstructedly
    in the essence of awareness
is that of the reflection[74] of planets and stars in a limpid
    ocean.
One abides in the supremely unobstructed state of things
    in all their variety
without this ever being just a latent potential.

Freedom from restrictions is extolled as an infinitely even state of spaciousness:

Given the enlightened intent of naturally occurring timeless
    awareness, in which everything is equal—
expansive and elevated mind free of the proliferation and
    resolution of thoughts—
the experience of blending with space, without any division
    into outer and inner or in between,
arises as meditative absorption that is blissful, clear, and free
    of elaboration.

This is simply a case of identification, without cultivating some reference point in meditation. Hold your upper body erect. Let your gaze rest openly by focusing your eyes on the space in front or on the far distance (you can alternate between these). Allow your awareness to expand. Let your five senses remain naturally expansive. By meditating in this way, you pass into an openness in which there is no division into outer and inner or in between. Meditative experiences arise—of your physical body blending with space, of states of bliss, clarity, and non-conceptual awareness, or of a supreme, unobstructed state of naked awareness. You may feel that all sensory appearances become transparent, or that your consciousness becomes unobstructed and completely open, with no trace of thoughts remaining, or that anything can and does arise within a state that is nothing whatsoever in itself, since you have experienced everything decisively as empty, free of restriction, and unobstructed. You may feel that no matter how you analyze and contemplate, you cannot find any thoughts by searching for them, that it is now impossible for them to occur, that they never did occur, [128b] and that no one has them at present. You may ask yourself, "What is all this talk about 'so many thoughts'?"

Meditative experiences of unobstructed awareness arise in a way that cannot be expressed with words. *The Perfect Dynamic Energy of the Lion* states:

> The natural abiding of enlightened intent is meditative absorption
>   as a state of resting imperturbably.
> Awareness's own manifestations have no actual substance
>   but are the foremost[75] of all mandalas.
> The unchanging, inherently pristine nature of phenomena
>   is the universal environment.
> Awareness's own manifestations abide, vividly present,
>   in nonconceptual oneness.[76]
> To be free of the concepts of intellectual speculation
> is the great, ultimate "logical argument"[77] of the secret
>   mantra approach.

The preceding points deal with three ways of coming to a decisive experience of awareness within the context that cannot be cultivated in meditation.

Five Major Ways of Making Clear Distinctions

Now, there are some major criteria for making clear distinctions in order to dispel the limitations imposed by conceptual doubts. One such clear distinction to be made concerns resting within naturally occurring enlightened intent as the method for purifying samsara—that is, perceptions based on confusion:

> **Given the enlightened intent of the true nature of phenomena,[78]**
>   **which never strays from a state of rest, the ground of being,**
> **there is no division into outer and inner, for that nature is free**
>   **of the elaborations of dualistic perception.**
> **There is no ordinary mind fixating on something "other"—**
>   **a "sense object"—**
> **so nothing is reified as an object, and your perceptions of the**
>   **universe are free of fixation.**
> **No context exists for taking rebirth in samsara—this is similar**
>   **to space.**

The essence of self-knowing awareness is not reified as an object, and even though it manifests as a display, that display is not reified and so awareness is not sullied by external sensory appearances.

Now, given that no context exists for taking rebirth in samsara:

> There is no inner concept of mind as "self,"
> so nothing is reified as a subject, and the all-consuming
>   thought patterns of conditioned existence are stilled.
> The potential for rebirth in samsara is cut through at the root.
> At that point, you have arrived at the enlightened intent of
>   dharmakaya,
> like space, in which there is no division into outer and
>   inner and no frame of reference for phenomena based on
>   confusion. [129a]
> You have touched on the point of resolution, and since there
>   is no coming or going,
> everything is an infinite expanse, the pure realm of
>   Samantabhadra.
> You have reached the sublime palace of dharmakaya.

Inwardly, you do not reify what arises within mind due to its dynamic energy, and so it is emptied of karma and afflictive emotions. There is nothing that could cause you to take rebirth in samsara or fall into confusion, and so you are freed from the reification of mind and sensory appearances. The stronghold of dualistic perception crumbles. Awareness becomes fully evident as an unobstructed state devoid of confused perception and reification. Then you are said to have "arrived at the point of resolution," to have "reached the pure realm of Samantabhadra," to have "gained the most majestic ongoing state of authentic being, dharmakaya."

When you experience awareness free of ordinary mind, implicitly it is also free of ordinary mind's confused perception. So there is no place to "go," only the unique state of buddhahood. This is because the essence that is buddhahood, being free of anything that could obscure it, becomes fully evident. When awareness is involved with ordinary mind, we speak of an "ordinary being," and when it is free of ordinary mind, we speak of a "buddha." *The Pearl Garland* states:

Wise people should know
the distinction between ordinary mind and timeless awareness.
Ordinary mind is the ground of all habitual patterns.
It is the distortion common to ordinary beings.
It is the reification of objects and mind.[79]
Therefore, it is the very nature of samsara.
If there is freedom from ordinary mind, that is awakening
   to buddhahood.
The distortions common to all ordinary beings have
   been exhausted.
Beings are driven by ordinary mind,
for without it they would not go on being driven.
Therefore, beings appear as if in a magic show.

That is to say, due to the ordinary mind that reifies things, perceived objects, though they lack true existence, appear clearly, manifesting in five ways— [129b] as forms, sounds, odors, tastes, and tactile sensations. Due to the ordinary mind that reifies itself, karma and its inevitable consequences, as well as afflictive emotions, manifest in countless ways. Samsara—the reification of objects where none exist and the reification of mind where none exists—manifests to ordinary beings like a dream, due to the arising of the expressions of dualistic mind. *The Perfect Dynamic Energy of the Lion* states:

By their very nature, ignorant and spiritually undeveloped people
try persistently to tie space into knots.
They reify their perceptions of sense objects, even though these
   objects do not exist.
Though nothing exists as self or other,
out of confusion they reify things[80] as self and other.

Thus, forging the spiritual path with unique timeless awareness—awareness in which ordinary mind does not exist—is the key point for ensuring the attainment of dharmakaya, free of ordinary mind, in this lifetime. Forging the path with ordinary mind entails other approaches that do not transcend the state of ordinary beings and afford no opportunity to attain buddhahood. You may ask, "Doesn't one forge the path with what arises continuously in the mind—that is, with an aspect of responsiveness, the simultaneous arising and freeing of thoughts?" Though you are in fact forging the path with an "aspect of responsiveness," here this refers to bare awareness—the ground for the arising of thoughts—not wavering from its natural place of rest. You absolutely do not forge the path from the perspective of thoughts—that is, with what has already arisen in the mind due to the dynamic energy of responsiveness. I have already explained, again and again, that when you rest in the essence of awareness, you let go of ordinary mind so that it vanishes naturally.

Therefore, understand that ordinary confused mind—which is rooted in the nonrecognition of awareness, reifies sense objects as having identity, and is unable to "stay in one place" without being caught up in sense objects—is a confined space. And so forge the path with unobstructed, nonconceptual timeless awareness, [130a] free of ordinary consciousness that engages in thinking in terms of identity. *The Perfect Dynamic Energy of the Lion* states:

> Such duality occurs in the minds of ordinary beings.
> As for the perceptions of ordinary mind and the nonrecognition
>   of awareness,
> they are reinforced by the reification of sense objects where
>   none exist.
> As for the perspective of awareness—timeless awareness—
> it is free of concepts, which invest things with identity.
> There is no hope that something "is"
> and doubts vanish that something "is not."

This key point alone is understood to be extremely important, as stated in *The Exalted Amassing of the Rare and Sublime*:

> Though there is freedom from ordinary mind, from conceptual mind, from ordinary consciousness, still the experience of meditative absorption is not forsaken. This is the inconceivable secret of enlightened mind of those who have gone to suchness.

And in *Clear Words*:

> The flow of the elaborations of ordinary mind and mental events is interrupted.

And in *The Entrance into the Middle Way*:

> The kayas make the cessation of ordinary mind fully evident.

Since the subject matter of these scriptural citations is not something that untutored minds can comprehend nowadays, people have no idea what such sources are talking about. In explaining them here, as though opening people's eyes for them, I am providing what I call "the treasury of the most majestic spiritual approach."

By making a clear distinction concerning awareness in its natural state of rest, you can differentiate it from a one-pointed state of calm abiding:

> If awareness in the moment does not stray from the ground
>   of being,
> familiarization with that experience negates any furthering
>   of conditioned existence.
> You are free of the karma and habitual patterns that perpetuate
>   rebirth.
> You have come to the decisive experience of causality, described
>   as the equalness of samsara and nirvana.
> You have arrived at the heart essence of enlightenment, which
>   does not abide in conditioned existence or the state of
>   peace. [130b]
> It is crucial that you distinguish between this and a one-pointed
>   state of calm abiding.
> This is the enlightened intent of natural great perfection.

Awareness abiding in its natural state of rest has the quality of being naked, unobstructed awareness. This can be differentiated from a one-pointed state of calm abiding, the quality of abiding without thoughts proliferating. As you become familiar with that state of awareness, the karma and habitual patterns that perpetuate rebirth fall away by virtue of the cessation of ordinary mind. Your present familiarity with awareness, free of ordinary mind, ultimately makes dharmakaya, which is also free of ordinary mind, fully evident. All moments in which you experience awareness free of ordinary mind are identical, in that awareness does not stray from the ground of being, and so the auspicious circumstances for the fruition becoming fully evident arise as you extend the flow of awareness moment by moment.

In the context of samsara and nirvana arising as a display due to the dynamic energy of the ground of being manifesting as sensory appearances, samsara and nirvana are equal in that they are clearly apparent without truly existing, manifesting as a display of energy within that ground. In the context of awareness being free of ordinary mind, they are equal in that they have never existed in essence, and so it is explained that "samsara and nirvana are nondual and equal within awareness." *The Perfect Dynamic Energy of the Lion* states:

> Samsara and nirvana—
> how could these be imputed to be a duality?

And *The Commentary on the Awakening Mind* states:

> There is not the slightest distinction
> between samsara and nirvana.

And *The Ornament of Manifest Realization* states:

> Conditioned existence and peace are nondual.

A clear distinction can be made between the ground of all ordinary experience and dharmakaya:

> **If you stray from your fundamental nature, the functioning of**
>   **conceptual mind is samsara, pure and simple.**
> **It involves cause and effect—you have not come to the decisive**
>   **experience. [131a]**
> **A person who makes this mistake falls lower and lower.**
> **Therefore, the sublime secret—great perfection—does not**
>   **stray from basic space,**
> **and the expressions of dynamic energy resolve within the**
>   **ground of being.**
> **Enlightened intent abides as an unwavering state of equalness.**

The very essence of awareness can be likened to a mirror, and its dynamic energy to the mirror's clarity; due to that energy, awareness's display arises like reflections in a mirror. In this context, the essence of awareness is dharmakaya, for it does not stray from the state of abiding as dharmakaya.

The "ground of all ordinary experience" is a nonconceptual, neutral state in which there is no realization of bare awareness. If you remain in that state, you encounter blocks to true meditative stability, for you reinforce karma for rebirth in higher realms. Within that state, there is an aspect referred to as "consciousness as the ground of all ordinary experience." As well, there are the six avenues of sense consciousness that arise in response to objects, so that these consciousnesses based on the sense faculties extend outward toward objects. This reinforces the karma that perpetuates samsara, pure and simple. In short, all phenomena of samsara are contingent on this ground of all ordinary experience.

If you yogins do not differentiate between dharmakaya and the ground of all ordinary experience, you will not cut through the root of samsara and nirvana, and all the spiritual practice you undertake will serve to perpetuate samsara. I am explaining this so that you will turn away from it.

Dharmakaya is bare awareness elicited in all its nakedness, free of elaboration, empty yet lucid. So awareness is not a support for karma and habitual patterns. It abides as dharmakaya, since it is empty in essence; as sambhogakaya, since it is lucid by nature; and as nirmanakaya, since it is the unceasing ground for the arising of things.

The essence of the ground of all ordinary experience is a state of ignorance, nonconceptual and neutral, comparable to the consciousness of beings in the formless realm. Its nature is the aspect of consciousness as the ground of all ordinary experience, serving as the basis for the arising of the sense consciousnesses. [131b] Instead of responsiveness, there are the six avenues of consciousness and the reification of sense objects. These factors reinforce the diverse karma that perpetuates samsara. Furthermore, the possibility of erring into the formless realm opens up primarily if you are habituated to the context of the ground of all ordinary experience, into the form realm if you are habituated to the context of consciousness as the ground of all ordinary experience, and into the desire realm due to the six avenues of consciousness. Nowadays, in their meditation people either focus on the ground of all ordinary experience, or focus on consciousness as the ground of all ordinary experience (that is, consciousness that is merely limpid and nonconceptual), or maintain the experience of freeing, upon their arising, thoughts based on the six avenues of consciousness. But none of these methods goes beyond the three realms.

In this approach, having identified unobstructed awareness, you gain the fundamental state of dharmakaya. Since you have no expectation that a nonconceptual state of calm abiding is meditation, the ground of all ordinary experience is undermined. Since your spiritual path is not forged with a merely limpid state of meditation, consciousness as the ground of all ordinary experience is undermined. And since your path is not forged with the arising of thoughts directed outward, the six avenues of consciousness are undermined. You abide constantly in timeless awareness as the three kayas—dharmakaya, sambhogakaya, and nirmanakaya. Since awareness, which in essence has never existed as anything whatsoever, abides innately as emptiness, it is timeless awareness as dharmakaya. Since it has a quality of unobstructed lucidity, it is timeless awareness as sambhogakaya. And since there is realization of bare awareness as the unceasing ground for the arising of things, it is timeless awareness as nirmanakaya. This is the key point—the necessity at all times of eliciting unobstructed awareness in all its nakedness. If it is not elicited in its bare state, you are not free of the consciousness found in the three realms, so you have not risen the slightest bit out of samsara. Therefore, you must distinguish between the ground of all ordinary experience and dharmakaya. [132a]

In essence, the ground of all ordinary experience serves as a repository for habitual patterns. As for the derivation of the term, the "ground of all ordinary experience" refers to the phenomena of samsara. Since it is the ground of these, it is called the ground of all ordinary experience. For the sake of analysis, it is threefold: The "ground of all ordinary experience as it applies to physical embodiment" constitutes the beginningless habitual patterns that bring about the manifestation of a body and, deriving from that, all that serves as the basis for the amassing of one's individual body. The "ultimate ground of all ordinary experience as a process of involvement" constitutes the nonrecognition of awareness that is the basis for reinforcing all the karmic factors that perpetuate involvement in conditioned existence, such as the mind-body aggregates. The "ultimate timeless ground of all ordinary experience" constitutes the beginningless nonrecognition of awareness that is the pervasive support for the phenomena of samsara.

The essence of dharmakaya is unobstructed awareness, free of elaboration. As for the derivation of the term, "dharma" refers to what is authentic, the ultimate essence of being, and "kaya" refers to what supports it. Upon analysis, it is found to be threefold, for it abides as the qualities of the three kayas—essence, nature, and responsiveness. *The Reverberation of Sound* states:

> These are the key points concerning the ground of all ordinary
> experience and dharmakaya.

Of these, I will now explain the ground of all ordinary experience.
It is the ground of all that is or is not in any given case.
There is its[81] essence, the derivation of the term, and the
      analysis of it.
In essence it functions as a repository for habitual patterns.
It is analyzed with respect to physical embodiment,[82]
involvement, myriad variety, and the timeless ground.
As for the derivation of the term, "all" means inclusive
and "ground" refers to what amasses and reinforces.
Dharmakaya is free of elaboration.
It has none of the characteristics of the usual process of reification.
While in essence it is the inseparability of emptiness and lucidity,
distinctions arise through a threefold division
into dharmakaya, sambhogakaya, and nirmanakaya.
As for the derivation of the term, "dharma" means the
      authentic path,
and "kaya" means that accomplishment comes from it. [132b]

And *The Pearl Garland* states:

There is the ground of all ordinary experience because there is
      reinforcement.
There is dharmakaya because what is subject to degeneration has
      fallen away;
though it is empty it is lucid and, being lucid, it is pervasive.
It is not defiled by ordinary thinking, for recollection disappears.
It is free of elaboration itself.
Like space, it is pervasive and empty.
It is naturally pure and free of all characterization.
The ground of all ordinary experience, involving causes
      and conditions,
is like a reservoir, because habitual patterns are amassed.
Dharmakaya is free of habitual patterns.
From the consolidation of conceptual consciousness, ordinary
      mind, and other factors,
the ground of all ordinary experience manifests to beings
      in myriad ways.
Since dharmakaya is free of conceptual consciousness
      and the like,
the many forms that manifest have no corporeality.

You will find a detailed treatment of this topic in *The Precious Treasury of Utter Lucidity*.

As for the key points concerning ordinary mind versus timeless awareness: The essence of ordinary mind is thinking based on confusion. As for the derivation of the term, it is "ordinary mind" since it "minds" sense objects. Upon analysis, we find that there is pure ordinary mind—nonconceptual states and the impulse toward liberation—and impure ordinary mind—the thinking process within samsara.

The essence of timeless awareness is identified as the facet of consciousness that is due to the aspect of dharmakaya. As for the derivation of the term, it is "timeless awareness" because it is awareness that abides thus as dharmakaya, timelessly. Upon analysis, we find that timeless awareness as it abides as the ground of being has three aspects—essence, nature, and responsiveness. Timeless awareness as it is endowed with attributes has five aspects—timeless awareness as the basic space of phenomena and so forth. Timeless awareness as it permeates all sense objects has two aspects—timeless awareness just as it is and timeless awareness of all that there is.

The Reverberation of Sound states:

> These are the key points concerning ordinary mind and
> timeless awareness:
> "Ordinary mind" refers to what in essence engages in
> and permeates confused thinking,
> and it is the foundation of recollection and thinking. [133a]
> A distinction can be made between its pure and impure
> aspects.
> As for the derivation of the term, it refers to thought that
> gives rise to objects of attention—
> what is "minded," what does the "minding,"
> what "minding" is, and why things are "minded."
> Timeless awareness is not ordinary thinking.
> Its essence is natural lucidity, the ultimate meaning
> of the heart essence.
> Its divisions are held to be three.
> As for the derivation of the term, it carries the meaning
> of abiding timelessly;
> and since awareness does so, it is timeless awareness.

And *The Pearl Garland* states:

> Because ordinary mind comes about through consolidation
>   and reinforcement,
> it is distorted and defiled,
> so the ground of all ordinary experience, the consolidating mind,
>   and so forth
> are variations of this distortion.
> Wise people should know
> the distinction between ordinary mind and timeless awareness.
> Ordinary mind is the ground of all habitual patterns.
> It is the distortion common to ordinary beings.
> It is the reification of objects and mind.[83]
> Therefore, it is the very nature of samsara.
> If there is freedom from ordinary mind, that is the level
>   of[84] buddhahood.
> The distortions common to all ordinary beings have been
>   exhausted.
> Beings are driven by ordinary mind,
> for without it they would not go on being driven.
> Therefore, beings appear as if in a magic show.
> Enlightened mind is free of all vacillation,
> but it is not like some inanimate thing.
> It is conscious and aware, exhibiting an illuminating quality.
> It incinerates all concepts,
> for it is timeless awareness itself, consuming like fire.
> It is analogous to space itself.
> It is empty yet lucid, as well as aware.
> Therefore, timeless awareness reveals itself in one's perceptions.
> Arising naturally, undifferentiated responsiveness
> is pervasive, is connected with everything, and is the perfection
>   of all phenomena.
> As for recollection, there is no recollection;
> timeless awareness is free of the very basis of recollection. [133b]
> Timeless awareness itself is as follows:
> it is pure timeless awareness as it abides as the ground of being,
> as it is endowed with attributes, and as it permeates the domain
>   of the senses.

A more detailed treatment of these distinctions can be found in my presentation in *The Precious Treasury of the Sublime Spiritual Approach*.

In the heart drop teachings of the great perfection approach, a very important key point in making clear distinctions is to differentiate the ground of all ordinary experience from dharmakaya and to differentiate ordinary mind from timeless awareness.

As the foregoing implies, another clear distinction lies in gaining certainty about causality. This can be shown as follows:

> Within this context, there is no cause and effect, no concerted effort.[85]
> View, for example, cannot be cultivated in meditation.
> Although the mode of cessation is described as having neither center nor limit,
> when dynamic energy itself deviates from this natural state,
> the myriad display arises as the multiplicity of the universe of appearances and possibilities.
> So never say categorically, "There is no cause and effect."

Given that dharmakaya abides as the essence of unobstructed timeless awareness in all its nakedness, from the perspective of ultimate truth it can be shown that the ten attributes—which entail cause and effect, renunciation and acceptance, and conscious striving—do not exist. However, diverse states of consciousness arise from the ground of all ordinary experience and its dynamic energy, and to say that the phenomena of samsara (which manifest in all their variety) and the attendant all-consuming concepts have no causes or effects and so forth is to profess a nihilistic view like that of the Charvaka philosophy. The relative phenomena of samsara manifest through the force of the illusion-like interdependence of causes and conditions.

You might ask, "How do these appearances manifest?"

> Interdependence ensures that conditioned, composite phenomena are beyond enumeration and imagination. [134a]
> Confused perception in samsara, and even states of peace and bliss, are beyond enumeration and imagination.
> All of this constitutes the very process of interdependence, which is the coming together of causes and conditions.

Bliss and pure realms, as well as suffering and impure realms—all that is pervasive and equal in extent to space—consist of illusion-like sensory appearances that manifest due to the interdependence of their respective causes and conditions. Although these are empty since in essence they do not exist, they manifest in specific forms through the force of interdependence. They are analogous to horses or oxen that manifest through a magician's spells and power substances. *The Exalted Discourse That Completely Consolidates Precious Enlightened Qualities* states:

> It is the nature of the space element that it is without any
> furthest limit.
> The sublime knowing that guides the world is also without any
> furthest limit.
> It is the nature of the realms of ordinary beings that they are also
> without any furthest limit.

And *The Most Majestic State of Meditative Absorption* states:

> The karma reinforced by one's actions never becomes nonexistent.
> In samsara, moreover, positive and negative effects come
> to maturity.

And *The Amassing of the Rare and Sublime* states:

> From virtuous karma come states of happiness,
> and one perceives the many boundless buddha realms.
> From nonvirtuous karma come forms of suffering,
> and one experiences lower destinies, inferior states of rebirth,
> and blazing hot environments.

A clear distinction can be made by coming to a decisive experience concerning causality:

> **If you evaluate your fundamentally unconditioned nature,**
> **you find it has never existed as anything whatsoever.**
> **So too, in taking this as your path, you have no frame of**
> **reference whatsoever**
> **for straying from that fundamentally unconditioned nature**
> **in all its immediacy.**
> **Rather, you appreciate it within the context of enlightened intent.**

> Having reached the ultimate state in the immediacy of your
> fundamentally unconditioned nature,
> you are not sullied by anything at all. [134b]

Within the specific context of the enlightened intent of abiding in the immediacy of dharmakaya—that is, of ultimate timeless awareness itself—nothing whatsoever has ever existed, whether as samsara or nirvana, cause or effect, and so forth, because all elaboration has thoroughly subsided and there is nothing to add or remove. Samsara is arrested, since there is no karma with respect to your fundamentally unconditioned nature itself. Similarly, to ensure that you never stray from this nature is to come to a decisive experience of causality within great perfection. This is referred to as "going beyond virtuous and harmful causes and effects"; but under other circumstances you make errors concerning causality and samsara ensues, even though you do not want it to. This is like a seedling growing when a seed is planted in conjunction with warmth and moisture. If some element of confusion diverges from your fundamentally unconditioned nature, then without question you are not engaged in yoga. Therefore, until you have gained an ongoing state of authentic being, it is important that your recognition of awareness not be seduced by negative influences and it is imperative that the dynamic energy of unobstructed awareness be refined through training. *The Pearl Garland* states:

> This is the level of completely perfect buddhahood.
> There is no straying from the very essence of being.

And *The Perfect Dynamic Energy of the Lion* states:

> Dharmakaya is the nonconceptual, naturally pristine state
>   of meditation.
> It is not an objective construct, and if one realizes the ultimate
>   meaning of this,
> one experiences it as the supreme state of meditative stability
>   that is not made or unmade.

The preceding points constitute five major ways of making clear distinctions in order to dispel errors, obscurations, and flaws.

Thus, three definitive groupings that are crucial to this approach—the four methods of resting, the three aspects of meditative absorption, and the twenty-two topics, which constitute a total of twenty-nine sections—have been presented so that there will be no mistake concerning its key points. [135a]

Now, the ultimate meaning of all these sections can be summarized as the true nature of phenomena, which is beyond causality and conscious striving:

> Afflictive emotions, karma, and habitual patterns have
>   no support
> within this vast expanse, but are the playing out of magical
>   games of illusion.
> You must be liberated from this, so please come to a decisive
>   experience of causality.
> As a means of doing so, there is nothing superior to this approach.
> Therefore, it is crucial not to stray from the enlightened intent
>   of the true nature of phenomena.[86]
> This is the expanse of my profound and heartfelt advice.
> It is crucial to go beyond what everything is or is not,
>   transcending "is" and "is not."

You need to become free right now from samsara, from the confused state of causality that is like a dream. In this regard, if you come to a decisive experience of its cause (karma) and its conditions (afflictive emotions), the effect (samsara) will not come about, just as if there is no seed, the seedling that would be its result will not grow. Because an effect follows in the wake of its cause, everyone agrees that for samsara to be eliminated, its cause must cease. Take, for example, the well-known scriptural passage that begins:

> All phenomena come from causes.
> The Tathagata has spoken of those causes.
> Whatever brings about the cessation of those causes . . .

As for the means of arresting the perverse process of causality, there is no approach more profound than that of natural great perfection, and its method is that of not straying from naturally occurring timeless awareness, the enlightened intent of the true nature of phenomena. In this regard, it is imperative to go beyond the extremes of hope and fear, as well as reification. *The All-Creating Monarch* states:

Desiring happiness is the illness of attachment.
It is through an absence of desire that one gains happiness.
Buddhahood does not happen by being made to happen. [135b]
It is unsought and naturally indwelling, and so is
    spontaneously present.
Rest nonconceptually in this effortless, naturally abiding state.

This chapter contains a very important summary, for it brings together the definitive key points for putting this approach into practice.

This is the commentary on the tenth section of *The Precious Treasury of the Basic Space of Phenomena*, demonstrating that enlightened intent does not deviate from the true nature of phenomena.

11

Resting in Uncontrived Conduct

As a support to the preceding discussion of enlightened intent as a supreme state of resting in genuine being, there is a valuable instruction concerning manifest circumstances—they are pure in that they are naturally evanescent. A major pivotal point is that sensory appearances are free in their own place even as they are directly encountered:

> Within the oneness of everything as awakened mind, equal
>   to space,
> dualistic perception draws you into confusion—conditioned
>   existence and causality.
> Since sensory appearances based on confusion are illusory
>   and have no true support,
> when you encounter them directly, maintain the experience
>   of their leaving no trace, free of evaluation.

In the direct encounter between your consciousness and sense objects, you identify consciousness as a bare state of resting naturally. As I indicated earlier, in letting go—by resting imperturbably, resting in the immediacy of perception, resting naturally—you gain natural freedom, the natural state of naked dharmakaya. *The Pearl Garland* states:

> The true nature of phenomena is unchanging and utterly stable.
> Its domain is awareness's own naturally free manifestations.
> Its radiance is by nature inherently pure.
> It is imperturbable rest, rest in the immediacy of perception,
>   natural rest.

Another major pivotal point is that negative circumstances provide training in the recognition of awareness:

> When something unwanted falls into your lap, you have
>   a negative reaction,
> such as anger, dislike, envy, upset, irritation, anxiety,
> depression, mental anguish, or fear of death and
>   rebirth. [136a]
> When such reactions arise as a display due to dynamic energy,
>   identify them as such.
> Do not renounce them, indulge in them, refine them away,
>   transform them, look at them, or meditate on them.
> Rather, rest spontaneously in the single, naturally settled state
>   of evenness,
> free of the proliferation and resolution of conceptual
>   frameworks.[1]
> Mind as a pure[2] expanse of space, in which things vanish
>   naturally and leave no trace,
> arises with intensity from within, pristinely lucid.

When you experience displeasure, and a strong reaction, such as anger, upset, or aversion, takes place in your mind, do not renounce it, following the shravaka approach. Do not refine it away with antidotes, following the bodhisattva approach. Do not transform it into timeless awareness, following the approach of the outer and inner tantras. Do not deliberately encourage it, following the approach of some adherents of the Category of Mind, or look at its essence as would some other adherents, or meditate on it as would still others. Rather, in that context identify bare awareness in its pristine nakedness, so that the displeasure fades naturally and lucid, unobstructed awareness arises with greater clarity. *The Heaped Jewels* states:

> While beings experience suffering, my bliss arises naturally.
> In the lack of separation between happiness and suffering
>   at such times
> lies the perfection of my enlightened qualities.

Another pivotal point is that anything that manifests is freed in your direct encounter with it, so antidotes that employ renunciation are cleared away within the ground of being:

Within unconstrained awareness, which neither "is" nor
   "is not,"
sensory appearances are not fixated on as anything, but rather
   are encountered directly.
This brings about natural rest in the state that cannot be reified
   as anything,
and suppression and indulgence, which are not anything
   that can be freed in some way,
fade without leaving a trace. [136b]
An experience without fixation wells up from within.
This itself—just as it is—is the timelessly spacious expanse
   of enlightened intent.

However your consciousness reacts to the sense objects it perceives, whether indulging in or suppressing them, do not look at the essence of these feelings, meditate on them, or seek some alternative, for by your simply identifying bare awareness, they are free in their true nature. That is to say, there has never been any state of bondage, so while the conventional label "freedom" can be applied, things are free in their bare state once you perceive the key point—that bare state. They are free in the sense of being timelessly free once you perceive their timelessly pure essence. They are free in their own place once you rest directly in the natural state of rest. They are free in the sense of being free in your immediate perception of them, for they fade away directly in the context in which they manifest. They are free in the sense of being completely free once you have realized they have no basis—there is nothing that is not free. And they are free in the very moment, for they occur in such a way that they are free even as they arise. Regardless of what circumstance manifests—no matter what appears or arises—it is awareness's own manifestation and poses no threat to yogins of the great perfection. Once you perceive this key point, freedom occurs when you experience decisively that there is no turning back from the true nature of phenomena. *The Reverberation of Sound* states:

Furthermore, I will explain the true nature of freedom.
With freedom due to the key point, exertion falls away.
Freedom is timeless, so there is no need to create it anew.
Freedom is natural, so there are no antidotes.
There is freedom in immediate perception, so things fade
   at the point where they are seen.

There is total freedom, so there is natural purity.
Freedom is beyond time, so becoming familiar with it
    is unnecessary.
Since the nature of being is free, it is uncontrived.

The supremely joyful state of natural freedom is another pivotal point, which can be discerned in your unobstructed experience of ordinary consciousness and things:

Similarly, you may experience what is desirable and brings joy
    to the mind— [137a]
things accomplished with ease, friends, pleasant news, wealth
    to be enjoyed, and attractive places and regions.
With anything attractive, there arises a state of mind that is
    naturally enriched by joy.
When you identify this and rest imperturbably, settling
    naturally,
you experience it as uncontrived and spontaneously present
    in primordial basic space.

When joy is deeply aroused by anything at all, that is the limpid clarity of awareness, so rest without straying from a very natural identification of bare awareness. *The Heaped Jewels* states:

When directed outward, the mind's attention
is my naturally pure sublime knowing.
If there is no further analysis[3] of it,
it hears my sounds.

Another pivotal point is that consciousness—which involves the proliferation and resolution of thoughts—is, in its natural place of rest, free within the nondual state that is its true nature:

You may have a neutral attitude—when you are going about
    or sitting or resting quite indifferently—
that is neither pleasant nor unpleasant.
Regardless of what arises, identify its nature as it arises,
    without reacting positively or negatively.
Thus, the true nature of phenomena, the naturally settled state
    without differentiation or exclusion,
is called "ignorance free as supreme utter lucidity."

In any context in which your consciousness is drawn to and becomes aware of a sense object in a way that is neither pleasant nor unpleasant, do not look at the context of that experience but identify the bare state that is the ground from which it arises. With this, there is a simultaneous occurrence of freedom in the immediacy of your perception of sensory appearances (without rejecting these outer appearances) and freedom in the immediacy of your mind stirring (without eliminating this inner stirring). This is similar to the loads being loosened on both sides of a pack animal's back when the peg holding them is pulled out. The quality of this neutral state of consciousness being free is termed "ignorance free as empty utter lucidity." [137b] When the very essence of awareness is experienced in all its nakedness, all the expressions of its dynamic energy—the whole spectrum of sensory appearances that manifest as its naturally pristine display—are by necessity also free. Having no basis and unaffected by thoughts, they are free in their own place, abiding timelessly within their true nature.

In brief, there is bondage if ordinary consciousness reifies things, freedom if it lets go, and "transcendence of the extremes of bondage and freedom" when freedom has no relevance at all. *The Pearl Garland* states:

> Given that what occurs is indeterminate,
> mind itself, in which things appear to be determinate, is free.
> All[4] sensory appearances that manifest as forms
> are free within the state in which they have no
>   independent nature.
> Formless states are free of substance.
> Given that phenomena are freed by phenomena,
> what is nonexistent is free of nonexistence.
> Given that the one is free of the one,
> what manifest as two are both free.

Another pivotal point, concerning the dream state and sleep, is that ignorance is experienced as utter lucidity:

> **At night and other times when you are overtaken by sleep,**
> **as you lie in a naturally settled state free of the proliferation**
> **and resolution of thoughts,**
> **sensory appearances that manifest in obvious ways disappear,**
> **so reification of them disappears as well.**

> With the disappearance of even what is subtle or very subtle,
>   together with the reification of it,
> the mind that is aware in a uniform, nonconceptual state
> abides naturally, free of the occurrence of and involvement
>   in thoughts, as well as hope and fear.
> This is the context in which all-consuming concepts are free
>   within the basic space of phenomena
> and so is described as "samsara being free as nirvana."

Sleep is the mind imploding helplessly, entering into a state of ignorance. Since the subtle karmic tendencies of the dream state accumulate as latent potentials, some texts present techniques for incorporating them into the spiritual path in order to refine them away. Other texts demonstrate more elaborate techniques, such as the recognition, control, [138a] transformation, and cessation of dreams. Here, these karmic tendencies are refined away through the single key point of their true nature, which is without elaboration.

Assuming the sleeping lion posture, you focus without distraction on the essence of bare consciousness. With this, you draw the attention you would otherwise pay to dream images (which seem external to you) inward. When thoughts become increasingly subtle and you make sure that you are not distracted from the continuous radiance of awareness, subtle energy and mind enter the central channel and there ensues a completely nonconceptual state. This blends with the unobstructed awareness you have identified. Since subtle energy and mind do not proliferate outwardly, you abide in the unique context of utter lucidity, without dreaming. Once you are familiar with this, though you still see and hear incidental sensory appearances, a quality of lucidity that does not involve thoughts about them is unified with this nonconceptual state. A third factor, naturally indwelling bliss, arises in conjunction with these two. *The Reverberation of Sound* states:

> Body, speech, and mind are focused intently,
> and the supreme state of utter lucidity blends with sleep.

My holy guru placed great emphasis on this point. In this regard, though your dreams will be numerous at first, eventually they will cease. In the very best of cases, dreams will cease after the whole issue of dreaming has been left behind; in middling cases, after they have become very clear; and in the least of cases, after they have become virtuous. This range of experience refers to the very best, middling, or lesser extent to which the mind remains aware of its limpid clarity at the point of going to sleep. The same tantra states:

> For them, dreams are numerous at first.
> In the very best of cases, they finally cease in that one leaves
>   them behind.
> in middling cases, after having become extremely clear,
> and in the least of cases, due to being known for what they are.
> In the last of these, they are not clear, but do improve. [138b]
> In these ways, the practice reaches full expression.

It can be shown that sleep is naturally occurring timeless awareness:

> **Even sleep is the primordial vast expanse, occurring naturally.**
> **Expressions of dynamic energy are absorbed into the ground**
> **   of being, into the basic space that is its essence,**
> **so that all the elaborations perceived as a display subside**
> **   as a matter of course.**
> **This is the enlightened intent of naturally occurring timeless**
> **   awareness, in which nothing need be done.**

In waking consciousness, what arises as a display due to dynamic energy arises outwardly from naturally occurring timeless awareness as an externalization of its utter lucidity. During the night, your fixated perception of the display dissolves into dynamic energy. This energy in turn dissolves into the ground of being, so that for a short time you abide in a state of utter lucidity that involves no concepts whatsoever. This is sleep as naturally occurring timeless awareness. It is referred to as "the context in which samsara is free as nirvana." *The Six Expanses* states:

> Not even sleep is abandoned.
> There is none of the ordinary mind's analytical division.
> In brief, one's body and speech are in their natural state
> and the stirrings in one's conceptual consciousness are not lost
>   to externals.
> Moreover, the alert and analytical mind does not go out to
>   the objects of the six senses.
> Lucid yet nonconceptual meditative experience is born
> within the supreme, nonconceptual realm of awareness's
>   own manifestations.

Concerning the fact that ignorance is pure by its very nature, *The Reverberation of Sound* states:

> Anyone who engages in the yoga of sleep
> thus uses ignorance as the path.

Another pivotal point is that afflictive emotions are free in their own place:

> **Thus, all desirable, undesirable, and neutral mental states,**
> **in which the three poisons arise as a display due to**
> **dynamic energy,**
> **occur within basic space, arising within the context of that**
> **space. [139a]**
> **Since they occur only within basic space, not straying from it**
> **in the least,**
> **without trying to anticipate[5] or manipulate them in any way,**
> **it is crucial to identify basic space itself, for as soon as you rest**
> **in that context,**
> **they will subside naturally, vanish naturally, and be freed**
> **naturally.[6]**

Since samsara and nirvana do not stray from the realm of basic space, they are merely natural expressions of emptiness that have no basis. As well, afflictive emotions have in essence never known existence. There is nothing that serves as their support. They do not come from some fundamental source. And so, solely by resting imperturbably in your natural state, you are freed of their restricting influence. When the essence of awareness is identified as unobstructed, afflictive emotions are naturally freed, pristine in their own place. This is similar to a pack load falling just where it is when the pin holding the restraining knot is pulled out.

If you do not understand this, you will not be able to abandon afflictive emotions even if you try, for they accompany you as naturally as your shadow does your body. You will not be able to refine them away even if you try, for what attempts the refining is no different from what is to be refined; this is like being unable to make a crystal more transparent than it already is. Your emotions will not change even if you try to change them, for mind cannot change mind, just as a piece of turquoise cannot change its color. You will not be able to still them by letting them become calm naturally, for they are none other than the thinking process involved in letting them go. They cannot be freed with antidotes, for that would be like wanting to make water clearer yet stirring it with a stick; antidotes themselves are just as much something to be abandoned as they are something used to abandon something else. Afflictive emotions in and of themselves are not your true nature—thinking that they are is no different from the thinking of a common fool, which cannot take you beyond samsara. *The Conjunction of Sun and Moon* states:

> "Are these afflictive emotions abandoned? Are they refined away? Are they transformed? Are they allowed to become calm naturally? [139b] Are they tamed by antidotes that are specific to each one? Does one let them play themselves out as they will? Are they in themselves one's true nature? Or are they naturally freed by themselves? O Teacher, I pray that you tell me."

Then Vajradhara issued this proclamation:
"Ah! Listen, great sage! Listen!
These are the words I have spoken:
These emotions dwell in the mindstreams of all ordinary beings.
They bind one to samsara.
If supreme bliss itself is obscured,
they have not been eliminated.
If they are not realized in their suchness,
they occur as naturally as the shadow that follows a yogin's body,
and so they cannot be abandoned even if one tries
    to abandon them.
Similarly, they cannot be refined away by one's attempts to do so.
Nor can they be changed by one's attempts to transform them.
One can only realize their unchanging heart essence;
one cannot refine away or change[7] them,
for they are like an outcropping of crystal or a piece of turquoise.
Yogins examine them to experience their innately pure nature.
Similarly, they are not a state of quiescence.
One can understand them only with profound insight through
    direct perception;
one cannot destroy them,
for they are like Sumeru, the most majestic mountain.
They cannot be freed with antidotes.

Without understanding the natural purity that is unsought,
it is as though one were stirring water while wanting to clarify it;
it will not become clearer and clearer.
These emotions, moreover, are not themselves one's true nature.
Without an understanding of the relaxed way in which
  awareness's own manifestations are perceived,
one's perceptions are like those of a common fool.
One's obsessions have not been eliminated."

That is to say, although efforts are made in other spiritual approaches, [140a] they are incapable of purifying afflictive emotions. In the ati approach, emotions are purified within basic space without being renounced, through the key point of realizing that self-knowing awareness is unobstructed. In this approach, freedom comes about through the effortful cultivation of the visions of tögal, which manifest in a natural state of rest. Alternatively, freedom comes about effortlessly through the realization of trekchö, the bare state of naturally free awareness. However, afflictive emotions are not freed by bare awareness—they themselves are freed by themselves, like a snake that has tied itself into a knot. This crucial point—that afflictive emotions are freed in and of themselves as they arise—comes down to not forgetting to realize bare awareness; and so, though it seems that awareness frees afflictive emotions, this is not actually the case. The same tantra states:

"Ah! Listen again, O sage!
People have two kinds of minds—
there are those who are involved in effort and those who are not.
Those involved in effort rest in their natural state.
The full measure of familiarity with visionary experience
ensures that the pure visions of timeless awareness
arise naturally everywhere, within and without.
These circumstances ensure that afflictive emotions do not occur.
Or as much as they do occur,
they are freed in their own place as one rests in the natural state.[8]
Therefore, these are the visions of a yogin.
The situation for those who are not involved in effort is as follows:
Naturally freed in and of themselves,
afflictive emotions are themselves naturally free just as they are.
Like iron cutting iron or stone breaking stone,
they are their own greatest antidote.

Anyone with such familiarity will,
having realized[9] natural great perfection,
discover its implications by resting without seeking
    anything. [140b]
Supreme bliss unfolds without being cultivated in meditation.
One directly experiences it as one's very nature.
Though someone who encounters it
may have committed harmful actions with immediate consequences,
that person will be freed by becoming familiar with it.
Of this there is no doubt—I swear it!"

Another pivotal point is that there is nothing good or bad, nothing to accept or reject:

Moreover, all afflictive emotions, karma, and habitual patterns
are magical expressions arising as a display due to
dynamic energy.
Antidotes that bring improvement—even the path to liberation—
are magical expressions arising as a display due to
    dynamic energy.
Since both arise timelessly as a display due to this energy,
it is crucial to rest without contrivance within the state
    of recognition.
They are equal in mode, equal in manner, and equal in stirring
    from the ground of being.
They occur circumstantially, are compounded, and do not
    transcend causality,
so it is essential that you transcend causality—resting naturally,
    resting imperturbably.

Whatever is to be abandoned—all-consuming concepts that arise in all their variety—and whatever causes them to be abandoned—positive concepts used as antidotes—are equal in arising as a display due to the dynamic energy of awareness. These two are equal, and so it is essential that you rest in a natural state in which neither of them is better or worse, neither of them is accepted or rejected. This is because both positive and negative concepts arise within the scope of awareness and are equal in being concepts about sense objects, and so there is no difference in the ways they seem to cease and vanish naturally. There is no difference between the two, since they manifest in the present moment within the scope of awareness, their natural state, reinforcing the sensory appearances that seem to manifest. And there is no difference between them in that, having initially stirred from the ground of being, [141a] they arise, or seem to come into being, becoming evident outwardly. It is essential that you come to a decisive experience of causality within the scope of awareness, through a supreme state of resting imperturbably in the natural freedom of concepts—both positive ones (which are characterized as antidotes) and negative ones (which are characterized as things to be abandoned).

All of these—positive concepts concerning view, meditation, conduct, and fruition, which are antidotes on the spiritual path, and negative concepts based on confusion, which are to be abandoned—lack any basis or foundation to begin with, so there is no limit to them even if you seek one. They manifest in the present moment without truly existing, so that if you examine them you find that they do not exist, but if you do not they are so countless as to defy imagination or description. And in the final analysis they neither come nor go, so in essence they are free of any such limit to be found. Because causes and effects are thus limitless, there is no limit that could be reached, and so there is no chance of establishing or realizing some limit—only a supreme state of resting imperturbably, resting naturally. *The Great Garuda* states:

> For anyone who posits a goal when it is said that "the path
>   has no basis,"
> the path to liberation[10] remains obscured precisely because
>   of this supposition.
> Emptiness (whether darkness or light), existence and
>   nonexistence,[11]
> affirmation and negation, cause and effect—there are no
>   such extremes as these four pairs of eight factors.
> This is analogous to the realm of space.
> Any positing of a limiting alternative to strive for
> is like a blind bird's search for the end of the sky—
>   nothing will be found.
> No one could possibly distort the ultimate meaning—
>   that nothing can be found.
> It is impossible for what is experienced as having no elaborations
>   ever to come to an end.

Another pivotal point to be shown is that the teachings of this most majestic spiritual approach are upheld by its lineage of succession and are kept secret from those of lesser aptitude:

> This is the very pinnacle of the sublime secret approach.
> Do not speak about it to those of lesser aptitude, but keep
>   it extremely secret. [141b]
> By being misinterpreted, the teachings concerning the heart
>   essence will be distorted.
> Exaggeration and underestimation are at odds with
>   enlightened intent.
> Those who violate the bounds of secrecy fall endlessly into
>   lower states.
> Therefore, the legacy of the most majestic and utterly secret
>   spiritual approach
> is taught and entrusted to holy people with good fortune.

This marvelous lineage of succession of the most majestic spiritual approach is kept secret from those who lack good fortune, but is revealed to the fortunate. Those with good fortune are entrusted with the most sublime vajra heart essence. As for those who lack such fortune, there are five considerations—their essence, their classification, the way in which secrecy is maintained, the faults of not maintaining secrecy, and the advantages of maintaining it.

In essence, those lacking good fortune consist of those who are not suitable recipients of these profound spiritual teachings because they have no claim to any share of them. They can be classified into three types—completely ordinary people with no karmic connection to spiritual teachings, small-minded people who are timid and apprehensive and who follow more common spiritual approaches, and individuals who have violated the bounds of secrecy by divulging secret teachings to unsuitable recipients or on inappropriate occasions. My advice is that, of all of these people, the meaning of these great secrets should be kept especially from those who have violated the bounds of secrecy. They encourage other small-minded people, who are unsuitable recipients, to cast aspersions on these teachings and thus to be reborn endlessly in lower states. The karma of this is far more serious than that of the five actions that carry immediate consequences after death. *The Highest Continuum* states:

> Those who associate again and again with evil companions,
>   bear ill will toward the sugatas,
> kill a parent or an arhat, commit unacceptable actions, or create
>   factions within the sublime assembly [142a]
> will, if they deeply contemplate the true nature of phenomena,
>   be swiftly liberated from that karma.
> But how can there be liberation for someone who always feels
>   aversion to spiritual teachings?

Immediately upon dying, those who violate the bounds of secrecy are reborn as beings in the hell of unceasing torment, where they face the risk of their tongues, which are then five hundred leagues long, being sliced open by ploughs of flaming iron. *The Perfect Dynamic Energy of the Lion* states:

> For those who violate secrecy,[12] moreover,
> their tongues, the organs of speech, are ploughed,
> and they experience great suffering.
> Therefore, keep this definitive meaning secret.

As for the way in which secrecy is maintained, there are three points—a general discussion of those to whom secrecy applies, an explanation of why maintaining such secrecy is faultless, and an explanation of the actual way to maintain secrecy.

The same tantra describes those to whom secrecy applies:

> Maintain complete secrecy toward those who lack realization
> and in fact toward all ordinary people.
> Various forms of advice have been given to maintain secrecy.

Some say that when people cannot understand the teachings, the timeless self-secrecy of those teachings is the means to ensure that, as long as such people do not lack faith, no secrets will be divulged. This is said to be similar to teaching birds and other creatures. But that is the impulsive babbling of idiots. It is contrary to the scriptural sources that are the words of the buddhas. Moreover, the rationale for maintaining secrecy is that, if the time is not right, the teachings must be kept secret even from those who are suitable recipients. This is similar to keeping *The Discourse Concerning Individual Liberation* and its ordination rituals and practical methods secret from novice monks who wish to take full ordination. These must be kept even more secret from ordinary people,

[142b] or else the greatness and blessings of these teachings will wane and one will suffer the consequences.

The reason that maintaining secrecy is faultless is stated in *The Perfect Dynamic Energy of the Lion*:

> The secret mantra approach is revealed by the application
> of skillful means.
> The secret mantra approach is not flawed.
> With their skillful means, the supremely compassionate ones
> enjoin secrecy because there are unsuitable recipients, those
> of dull aptitude,
> and those with negative karmic connections.

So the teachings are kept secret not because they are ignoble. Rather, they are kept secret to prevent others from reinforcing negative karma and to avoid impairing the dharma's greatness; there is no fault in maintaining secrecy. Another source states:

> As for the "secret" in secret mantra,
> it is not that the teachings are flawed.
> Rather, they are kept secret from those who are small-minded
> or who follow lower spiritual approaches.

The actual way to maintain secrecy applies to the three kinds of people discussed earlier—ordinary people, those who are small-minded, and those who divulge secrets. Do not disclose the terms, texts, key points, or even a partial discussion of the tenets of these teachings. When the time is not right, or in unsympathetic regions such as borderlands, do not breathe a word about your understanding of these teachings, or even of their existence or the fact that you have received them. Even if people who have heard rumors of them ask you, I would advise you to maintain secrecy and reply, "I'm not sure" or "Not having practiced them, I have no idea." *The Perfect Dynamic Energy of the Lion* states:

> Therefore, keep this definitive meaning secret.
> Do not disclose it even to the wind.

Since secrecy is spoken of again and again in this approach, [143a] it is a major point of samaya to ensure that the texts, physical postures, and so forth of these heart drop teachings are not disclosed. In particular, even if you had a vajra tongue, it would be inappropriate to explain or otherwise speak of the teachings without receiving someone's permission to do so. The same tantra states:

> The meaning of ati, the great perfection approach
>   of secret mantra,
> should not be spoken of to inferior people.
> Until one has received permission
> from a vajra master, a spiritual hero,
> one should not divulge secrets to others,
> even though one can speak as though with a vajra tongue.
> The meaning of supreme secrets is not explained
> to inferior people, those who have not received empowerment,
> or those who have a negative karmic connection.
> These are the implications of samaya.

As for the negative consequences of not maintaining secrecy, it will lead to misinterpretation, so that you and others will be reborn in lower states, the teachings of the heart essence will disappear, you will incur the punishment of the guardian deities, you will not accomplish your goals, and so on. *The Perfect Dynamic Energy of the Lion* states:

> Divulging this supreme secret[13] of ati, great perfection,
> to those of inferior aptitude
> would be, for example, like a stick creating fire by friction,[14]
> with the stick itself being consumed by flames
> and anything of worth also being incinerated.[15]
> The definitive meaning of the secret mantra approach
>   is like a fire.
> Those who have little good fortune, who lack wisdom,
> who harbor negative attitudes, or who are confused
>   about causality
> cast aspersions on the ultimate meaning of great perfection,
> and this sends them to the three lower states of existence.
> They suffer because they fail to realize the definitive meaning.

And *The All-Creating Monarch* states:

> If one does not observe what to accept or reject
> with respect to the ultimate meaning of the heart essence, [143b]
> nonhuman beings and spirits will cause obstacles,
> and in the case of both teacher and student,

powerful dakinis will bring about fear and untimely death.
Furthermore, due to misinterpretation the spiritual approach of
the heart essence will disappear.

The same tantra speaks of the nature of people who lack good fortune:

To discuss the perverse individuals who are unsuitable recipients:
They take delight in fame and mundane matters.
They are proud, do not venerate holy ones, have short attention
spans, and lose interest.
They act inappropriately and do not have the necessary ritual
articles or faith.
Their self-esteem and ambitious desire to further their practice
are at odds with the spread of the teachings as a whole,
and they boast about themselves and deprecate others, nurturing
an attitude of ill will.
Do not teach them, but maintain absolute secrecy.

And *Naturally Arising Awareness* states:

Showing no veneration or esteem,
they act so as to pervert the secret mantra approach.
Having no authentic spiritual affinity, they lack good character.
They have scant wisdom
and deny the kindness shown them.
They brag about their family origins,
adorn their bodies with fine ornaments,
and flaunt themselves in a meaningless way.
They are not considered students, but a master's enemies.
Do not explain the meaning of great perfection
to individuals who will not put it into practice.

As for the advantages of maintaining secrecy, everything that is excellent will be ensured for you and others, and the teachings will remain for a long time.

There are two considerations that have to do with teaching fortunate people—their characteristics and the way to examine them for suitability. [144a] The characteristics of a fortunate person are stated in *The Array of Inlaid Gems*:

This supreme mandala of secrets is not revealed to everyone.
It is revealed to the few who can maintain secrecy.

The kinds of people to whom these secret stages of the secret
    mantra approach
may be revealed are as follows:
They are revealed to those who are equal to the trust invested
    in them concerning secrecy,
who demonstrate enthusiasm for the meaning of what is secret,
who have great wisdom and very agile minds,
and who maintain their samaya and vows.

. . . .

It is said that the definitive meaning of the secret mantra approach
    is revealed
to those of the warrior class, the priestly class,
and also those of the merchant class,
as well as to especially great people.

And *Naturally Arising Awareness* states:

They have strong faith, great diligence,
and abundant wisdom, and are without clinging or attachment.
They show great respect and engage in the conduct of the secret
    mantra approach.
Their minds are free of concepts and distraction.
They uphold their samaya, are diligent in spiritual practice,
experience constant, deeply felt affection,
engage in clear, stable meditation,
act in accord with the master's words,
do not lapse into breaches of samaya,
act in harmony with others,
purify their minds through devotion,
and take each word they are taught to heart.
Thus acting in their own best spiritual interests,
they are worthy of being entrusted with what is secret.
Never straying from the ultimate meaning of vajra nature,
they rely on individuals of great learning.
They never go against their own best spiritual interests.
They speak gently without arrogant words [144b]
and act in harmony with others' minds.
They consider the master and the Tathagata
to be one—in no way different.
These are the characteristics of students.

Such students are said to be candidates
for the great perfection.

And *The All-Creating Monarch* states:

They have faith, great diligence, and compassion,
and uphold samaya.
They are steadfast, not discouraged or fickle.
They have no attachment whatsoever to their bodies, children,
spouses, servants, or possessions,
but rather offer them faithfully and joyfully.
Since these are signs of faith and samaya,
you should grant to such people the ultimately meaningful
experience of the[16] heart essence.
They give up arrogance,[17] are free of pride,
spare neither their bodies nor their lives for the sake of
the heart essence,
and do not go against spiritual commands.
To those who embody these signs
you should grant teachings on the unborn nature, which concern
the heart essence.

You should examine students before they receive spiritual teachings
to ascertain whether they are suitable recipients. You might impose a
difficult task, or criticize them with words that cut to the heart, or determine whether they lose faith when your conduct contradicts their expec-
tations, or say, "I want this or that possession" and see whether they are
able to relinquish it. If they are not suitable recipients, they will give up
because they lose their faith or are too fond of their possessions. Since
there is no possibility of their being benefited or being equal to the samaya involved, you should understand that it is best not to be connected
with such people.

If, on the other hand, they maintain their faith and are openhanded,
you can take these as signs that they have some karmic connection with
you from previous lives. So even though you have no need of their possessions, [145a] you should accept these in order to perfect their spiritual
development. The value of this lies in the auspicious connection between
master and student not going awry. *The All-Creating Monarch* states:

To free people from worldly attachments and to examine
their character,

a guru accepts everything—their bodies and their wealth—
and, having determined whether they are competent,
grants the ultimately meaningful experience of the heart
    essence—the all-creating monarch.

. . . .

Even if they do not need[18] something themselves,
holy ones will accept it and offer it to the Three Jewels.

As for conferring teachings on the fortunate, there are the qualifi-
cations of the master as the one conferring the teachings and those of
the student as the one receiving them. A master is learned and compassionate, has gained freedom, is imbued with blessings, is familiar with
the teachings, has experienced significant signs of successful practice,
makes meaningful connections with everyone, and shoulders the great
responsibility that comes with the teachings. As well, *Naturally Arising
Awareness* states:

Masters[19] who have gained realization of the vajra meaning
are of noble character and skilled in teaching.
They have received empowerment, apply the meaning of the
    secret mantra approach,
understand all outer and inner ritual activities,
and have become one with the chosen deity such that there is
    no coming together or separation.
They are not distracted from meditative absorption
and are learned in the secret tantras of the secret mantra approach
that hold the meaning of the pith instructions of the
    great perfection.
They can distinguish among all outer and inner methods
    of spiritual accomplishment.
They do not waver from the meaning of view
and have given up ordinary activities on the outer, inner,
    and secret levels.
Their qualities are like precious gems,
an inexhaustible treasure to be enjoyed.

The Reverberation of Sound states:

The great guru Vajradhara will explain the stages [145b]
    in detail:

"A completely qualified guru is a source of all enlightened
    qualities
and provides the basis for perfect enlightenment."

Naturally Arising Awareness speaks of fake masters who are mere
reflections of such a guru:

Although they use the words[20] of learned masters,
they lack understanding and are very proud.
They are foolish and deluded, interpret words too literally,
and do not contemplate the meaning of the secret mantra
    approach.
They speak arrogantly, disturb others' minds,
and lead them down wrong paths.
They have never beheld the mandalas of empowerment.
They violate samaya,
fail to respond to those who ask questions,
and have heard few teachings but harbor great pride.
They should not be considered masters, for they have a negative
    influence on students.
They are capable neither of revealing the secret mantra approach
nor of teaching ati, the great perfection.
Do not associate with them.

Accordingly, I advise you to avoid them.

Students who are qualified to receive these teachings show indications of a capacity to uphold them. This ensures that, once the very pinnacle of the heart essence has been entrusted to them, the teachings will
last for a long time, so that the tradition in which innumerable beings
of different kinds are led along the path to enlightenment will not be
impaired. All this is accomplished due to the special collective merit of
those beings. Furthermore, as *The Reverberation of Sound* states:

Those who uphold view and meditation
have most excellent faith and possess diligence.
They are capable of being generous and have devotion
    for their gurus.
They engage in uncontrived conduct, yet shun harmful
    actions. [146a]
They do not vacillate, but are utterly stable.
In addition, they are patient and relaxed

and have the easygoing manner of an innocent.
They have few concepts and are serene by nature.
They are free of physical and verbal busyness,
possess sublime knowing, and so can uphold the teachings.

And *The Array of Inlaid Gems* states:

They have powerful limbs, a dark complexion,
even, white, rounded teeth, slightly bloodshot eyes,
and hair of great quality, dark brown and curling clockwise.
They show little concern for their appearance,
and outwardly their conduct is quite ordinary.
These people speak forthrightly,
or else they echo all the words that others speak to them.
It is said that they are to be instructed in the great perfection.
If all these qualities are complete in anyone,
regardless of how low that person's status may be—
even if a butcher, a prostitute, a sweeper, or a hunter—
this vital essence of the secret pith instructions should
    be conferred.

Now, another pivotal point is that the definitive meaning of the pith instructions is subsumed within the supreme state of resting imperturbably, the true nature of phenomena:

In brief, whatever circumstance manifests—whether a sense
    object or state of mind—
do not apply antidotes or make an effort to abandon it,
for the key point of naturally settled awareness is to rest
    naturally, to rest imperturbably.

The fact that manifest circumstances are free in their own place is
due to the key point that naked awareness is a naturally settled state
of imperturbable rest. According to the distinctive principle of this approach, what binds an ordinary person arises as the path of freedom
for a yogin, [146b] for it arises from the ground of being. *The Great
Garuda* states:

Resting imperturbably, free of obscuration, is the uncorrupted path.
Intangible and without parallel, timeless awareness is
    the actuality of everything.

It does not rely on confusion, the reification of sense objects.
Responsiveness, which by nature expresses itself continuously
    in sense objects,
is free in that these empty objects rest in their natural state
    without being analyzed.

. . . .

The key point about the freedom of self-knowing awareness is
    that it is not corrupted by anything.
Although body, mind, and afflictive emotions are
    natural attributes
that manifest as fetters for those who are ignorant and
    spiritually undeveloped,
self-knowing awareness is the natural state of rest,
    genuine and uncontrived,
timeless natural freedom, which nothing can destroy.
Since it is free in its own place without having to be freed,
    what is the use of effort?
Timeless natural freedom is the very absence of any cause
    of being freed.
Given that there are harmful actions and their negative
    consequences, as well as great supports of bliss,
the key point of effortlessness is that these occur unsought
    and of their own accord.
They are free of any[21] basis, so how could virtue improve
    anything?
There is no buddha, and who creates the fetters that bind?
There is no name for, let alone the possibility of, confusion
    or nonrecognition for anyone.[22]
Therefore, since nothing has ever been freed, freeing later on
    is a fallacy.

When the meaning of this—the truth that is the true nature of phenomena—becomes familiar, ordinary mind is referred to as "the great
spectacle." *The Six Expanses* states:

A fortunate yogin who meditates authentically[23]
finds the gem that no one can find.
This is of inestimable value.
A person who encounters such inestimable wealth
sees the vision that no one can see.

This itself is self-knowing awareness—such a great spectacle!
A great spectacle thus takes place in the mind.[24]
The fragmentation of the phenomenal world is swept away.
Those who cut through this fragmentation [147a]
hold self-knowing awareness in their hands.
Spiritual people who have such appreciation
awaken to buddhahood before there is buddhahood and
those who are capable of beholding this mandala of bliss
become foremost among those who hold all mantras
    of awareness.[25]

The phrase "fragmentation of the phenomenal world" refers to whatever arises or manifests. Being "swept away" means coming to a realization of its underlying natural lucidity.

Another pivotal point is that pleasure and pain blend in equal taste:

Though all pleasure and pain are ways in which
    awareness arises,
you are bound to conditioned existence by reifying them
    dualistically as things to accept or eliminate.

If you react to two waves arising on the same body of water by accepting one and rejecting the other, you are being illogical. Similarly, it is illogical to react to states of consciousness that arise from a single awareness—perceiving what is pleasurable as something to accept, while perceiving pain as something to eliminate—because attachment and aversion are alike in being causes of samsara. *The Detailed Analysis of Empowerments* states:

In that all pleasure and pain are magical expressions
    of awareness,
how confused it is to reify them dualistically as things
    to accept or reject.

And *The All-Creating Monarch* states:

Do not pursue pleasure, do not reject pain.

If you ask why this is so:

Whatever appearances manifest are equal as sense objects—
    simply what is evident to the sense faculties.

Whatever thoughts arise are equal as mental events—
  simply conscious states that leave no trace.
Both are equal in the moment—simply the bonds of denial
  or affirmation.
In actuality, they are equal in the final analysis—nothing but
  appearances that have no basis.
Sense objects are equal in their distinctness—upon
  examination simply leaving no trace.
Ordinary states of consciousness are equal in essence—
  upon analysis nothing but space.
Objects and mind are nondual—simply pure open
  space. [147b]
Whoever understands things in this way is a descendant
  of Samantabhadra—
a sublime spiritual heir of the victorious ones, a master
  of awareness in the highest sense.

Thus, the states of consciousness that arise due to the dynamic energy of a single awareness—as pleasure or pain, good or bad, realization or the lack of it—all abide in a state of equalness, given that awareness is their true nature. That is to say, states of sensory consciousness, in which one is aware of objects, are equal in their underlying natural lucidity. In the very process of arising, thoughts occur, only to fade away, and so are equal, like ripples on water. The ordinary mind is bound when it is distracted by sense objects drawing it outward, so these objects are equally binding, like chains of gold and ropes of hemp. Since all of them are in actuality without basis or foundation—having never existed—they are equal in the final analysis. Since they end up vanishing naturally without a trace, they are of equal essence in that they are naturally freed. Since they have never known existence in actuality, they are equal in being fundamentally unconditioned. Since they arise from the same ground—awareness—they are equal as a display within naturally occurring timeless awareness. Since both objects and mind are equally definable as clear manifestations that do not truly exist, sense objects have never existed outwardly and mind has never existed inwardly.

Those who realize that objects and mind are of the nature of space ensure Samantabhadra's legacy and are said to be "fortunate masters of awareness, abiding on the level of the heart essence." This is because they perceive the key point and enjoy the blissful pure realm of self-knowing awareness. *The Heart Essence of Secrets* states:

Such is a master of sublime awareness—
considered by holy ones and sublime holy ones
to be their child or sibling, and so blessed by them,
honored by the leaders of the world and their retinues,
and abiding on the highest level, that of a master of awareness.

And *The Six Expanses* states:

Awareness is self-knowing by its own force;
no matter where in the three-thousand-fold universe
you may seek it, there is no place you will find it. [148a]
Its range is that of the entire universe.
In the nature of how sensory appearances manifest
lies the vision that no one can see—
the blissful pure realm of self-knowing awareness.
Being familiar with this,
yogins are fortunate ones who directly perceive
the enlightened embodiment of me, Samantabhadra.
Their fortune—self-knowing awareness—is equal to mine
    and they are free in[26] emptiness.
Those with the great fortune[27] of being familiar with this
attain the enlightened dimension, which does not entail concepts.
Appreciating the radiance of my responsiveness,
they share equal fortune with me.
They are my core and my retinue as well.
This radiant, precious gem,
this supreme secret of the buddhas
that no one can perceive—this I have revealed.
The responsiveness of me, Samantabhadra, who is
    without concepts,
manifests in ways that are continuous,[28]
and so the source of hope for ordinary beings
is this precious state of unsought rest.
Though it is not the province of everyone,
yogins who have realized this
are, among those with realization,[29] embodiments of
    victorious ones.
Homage is paid with a devoted mind to these powerful masters.[30]
Whoever is aware of and realizes
the mind of me, Samantabhadra,
shares a fortune equal to that of a thousand buddhas.

Fortunate spiritual individuals with dynamic aptitude
maintain an unwavering state of resting in equipoise.
They are masters in whom all mandalas converge.
Whoever is aware of and understands things in this way
encounters the significance of unsought rest.

Now, another pivotal point—that everything is equal within the supremely spacious state— [148b] can be applied to the pure nature of phenomena, the naturally settled state:

> Thus, phenomena are equally existent, equally nonexistent,
> equally apparent, equally empty, equally true, and equally false,
> so cast aside all antidotes that involve renunciation,
>> all concerted effort, all binding fixation.
> Expand into supreme equalness, in which sense objects
>> do not exist.
> Expand into supreme awareness, in which ordinary mind
>> does not exist.
> Expand into supreme purity and equality, in which flaws
>> do not exist.

All phenomena of samsara and nirvana—outer sensory appearances, inner states of consciousness, and so forth—are equal as manifestations that are clearly apparent without truly existing, and so there is a state of infinite evenness in which there are no antidotes that involve renunciation and no binding fixations. Phenomena are equal in being empty, pure within the ground of being, and so there is a state of infinite evenness that is like space, in which no sense objects exist. Phenomena are equal in arising naturally, whether they are imputed to be true or false, and so there is a state of infinite evenness that is the spacious expanse of awareness free of limitation. Samsara and nirvana are equally unconditioned in being timelessly empty and without basis, and so there is a state of infinite evenness that is the supreme purity and equality of positive and negative qualities. Awareness that is thus a state of infinite evenness is the supreme principle of this most majestic spiritual approach, and it abides within you. *Vajrasattva: Mirror of the Heart* states:

> It is great because it is the highest of all spiritual approaches.
> It is great because it is the way of abiding, with no distraction
>> from what has ultimate meaning.
> It is great because it is the pinnacle of all views.[31]

It is great because it is the pinnacle of all enlightened intent.[32]
It is great because it is the pinnacle of all conduct.[33]
It is great because it is the pinnacle of all fruition.[34]
It is great because it is unceasing lucidity in an
      unchanging context.
It is great because it is nonconceptual lucidity in a context
      without reification.
It is great because it is lucidity without fixation in a context
      without attachment. [149a]
It is great because it is supremely blissful lucidity in an
      inexpressible context.
It is great because it is the heart essence of infinite enlightenment.
It is great because it is awareness[35] free of conscious striving.
It is great because it is a state of equalness that does not stray
      from supreme bliss.
It is great because it is everywhere, yet is not some reified object.
It is great because it[36] cannot be definitively reduced to words
      and letters.

That is to say, although the essence of awareness—a state of infinite
evenness—is beyond view, meditation, conduct, and fruition, it is nonetheless the essence and supreme unifying principle of all these—view,
meditation, conduct, and fruition. Therefore, to analyze it briefly, *The
Six Expanses* states:

The heart essence of buddhahood[37] is the unsurpassable,
      sublime secret,
free of any terms that could describe it as "existing in this way."
Nevertheless, to illustrate it partially with mere words,
it is supremely illuminating self-knowing awareness, immaterial
      and immaculate.
One's conviction in it comes from deep within one's
      consciousness,
which is ordinarily involved with terms and names,
and so it is the supreme secret, the heart essence that crosses over
      the abyss of hope and fear.
The heart essence of all buddhas, it is the most sublime secret.
Even when examined partially according to the pith instructions
      concerning the meaning of enlightened intent,
self-knowing awareness, which lies at the very heart of the view,
      is found to be the lamp of timeless awareness,[38]

illuminating without restriction or bias in every direction.
For any spiritual person who is familiar with this, it is the realm[39]
    of nirvana.
This distills the implications that lie at the very heart of
    enlightened intent,
so that this rarest of meanings is indescribable, inconceivable,
    and inexpressible.
The secret distillation of timeless awareness[40] lies at the very
    heart of all meditation
 and so is the timeless integration of calm abiding and
    profound insight.
A yogin who meditates on this, the meaning of supreme
    equalness,
is foremost among all people in the world— [149b]
the most excellent, an object of reverence for gods and humans.
Bliss—supreme natural bliss—comes from grasping the three
    key points of resting in equipoise.
Within bliss itself arises the experience of nonconceptual
    timeless awareness,
so that all sensory appearances are a manifold display within
    that blissful expanse.
Therefore, it would be best, through the bliss of the body,[41]
    to grasp the key point of the three kayas.
It would be best, through the bliss of speech, to realize that all
    phenomena are inexpressible.
It would be best, through the bliss of mind, to blend samsara
    and nirvana in nonduality.
The blissful heart essence is the innermost heart essence of
    all buddhas.
The uncontrived heart essence ensures that everything falls into
    its genuine state.
The unceasing heart essence ensures that its own manifestations
    are cut through directly.
The unborn heart essence lifts one from the pit of samsara.
The naturally abiding heart essence ensures the delineation of
    spiritual approaches.[42]
The pervasive and extensive heart essence consolidates all aspects
    of the basic space of phenomena.
The supremely and timelessly pure heart essence levels
    all phenomena.

> The supremely empty heart essence tames the patterns of
>   afflictive emotions.[43]
> The supremely and naturally lucid heart essence turns back
>   the forces[44] of darkness.
> The supremely and timelessly perfect heart essence balances
>   all inequality.
> The secret,[45] nonconceptual heart essence undermines samsara
>   from its depths.
> The secret, innermost heart essence empties the realms of
>   ordinary beings. [150a]

Vajrasattva: Mirror of the Heart definitively states the full measure
of these factors:

> Since the three kayas never degenerate, great perfection is
>   endowed with the full measure of fruition.
> Since they are not subject to restriction or localization,
>   great perfection is endowed with the full measure of view.
> Since they are lucid, without involving concepts, great perfection
>   is endowed with the full measure of meditation.
> Since they occur naturally, uncontrived and unadulterated,[46]
>   great perfection is endowed with the full measure of conduct.

These citations, though, do not refer to anything like the common
system—which considers view to be the ground, meditation to be the
path, and conduct to be the supportive element, with some fruition
occurring eventually—because awareness is beyond view, meditation,
conduct, and fruition. *The Great Garuda* states:

> The meaning is free of conduct, is purified of meditation,
>   and is not to be viewed.

Therefore, if you analyze the facets of the very essence of awareness,
these four can all be distinguished simultaneously. View is the essence
of awareness, meditation is its nature, conduct is its responsiveness, and
the fruition is their inseparability, spontaneously accomplished.

This is the commentary on the eleventh section of *The Precious Treasury of the Basic Space of Phenomena,* demonstrating that manifest circumstances, equal to space in extent, are pure.

12

Timeless Freedom

Thus, the process of purifying manifest circumstances, the parameters of one's conduct, within basic space comes down to the key point that the fruition, timeless freedom, is present as a naturally abiding state. Therefore, in order to demonstrate that point in this chapter, it can be shown that basic space is an infinite state of timeless freedom:

All phenomena are timelessly free in awakened mind,
and so there is no phenomenon that is not free.

Images of men, women, horses, oxen, and so forth manifest due to the interdependence of such factors as substances and the power of magic spells, yet all of them are timelessly free within that context. [150b] So these horses and oxen, being mere manifestations that are clearly apparent without truly existing, do not actually exist in their own right. Similarly, all phenomena of the universe of appearances and possibilities, whether of samsara or nirvana, simply arise within the scope of awareness as magical expressions of the ground of being manifesting as sensory appearances. But they have never existed in essence, and so are referred to as "illusion in all its variety." Since sensory appearances manifest without having any independent nature, they are timelessly free within the scope of awareness. *The Great Garuda* states:

Timeless natural freedom is the very absence of any cause of
being freed.

This mode of freedom can be explained in detail. One way in which things are timelessly free is that they have no basis or foundation:

> Samsara is timelessly free, free in primordial purity.
> Nirvana is timelessly free, free in spontaneous perfection.
> Sensory appearances are timelessly free, free in having no basis
>   or foundation.
> Conditioned existence is timelessly free, free in the heart
>   essence of enlightenment.
> Elaboration is timelessly free, free in the absence of limiting
>   alternatives.
> Nonelaboration is timelessly free, free in unborn purity.

That is to say, it is the nature of phenomena that, even as they appear, they are found to be empty. This is conventionally described as "timeless freedom." In this sense, they are labeled from the point of view of their never having truly existed by nature, for what manifests as samsara and nirvana is simply the display, nominally bad or good, arising from awareness, the ground of being, as the manifest aspect of that ground. This is similar to good and bad dreams.

Concerning the sensory appearances of samsara, the outer aspect manifests as sense objects—both the animate and inanimate universe—and is referred to as "the universe of appearances and possibilities." This includes the inanimate universe of appearances, manifesting as expressions of the five elements, and the animate universe, which by nature consists of all possible life forms undergoing pleasure and pain due to karma and afflictive emotions. The inner aspect—what manifests as mind—includes mind in the desire realm, which involves conceptual elaboration, [151a] and mind in the higher realms, which constitutes states of meditative absorption that do not involve conceptual elaboration. All of these appearances are like dream images, for even though they manifest they have no ultimate validity, and so, timelessly, they are clearly apparent without truly existing. It can thus be shown that there is total freedom in the timeless emptiness of characteristics. *The Natural Freedom of Awareness* states:

> Similarly, all phenomena—states of ordinary consciousness
>   and things—
> are free in their very essence.

And *The Great Garuda* states:

> What are called "the six classes of beings" are empty, mere labels
>   that are applied.[1]

Due to the key point of emptiness and timeless freedom, nothing
    need be done,
and that itself is not some destination to arrive at, but a timelessly
    uncontrived state.

Since awareness's own manifestations arise as dream images and illusions, it can be shown that, having no basis, pleasure and pain are timelessly free in their equalness and purity:

Pleasure is timelessly free, free in the evenness that is
    the true nature of phenomena.
Pain is timelessly free, free in the uniform spaciousness
    of the ground of being.
Neutral sensations are timelessly free, free in dharmakaya,
    equal to space.
Purity is timelessly free, free in the emptiness of underlying
    purity.
Impurity is timelessly free, free in the supreme state of
    total freedom.

Within the very essence of this dream, pleasure, pain, indifference, the purity of the realms of buddhahood, and the impurity of beings' confused perception all abide in such a way that in essence they have no basis. And so they are timelessly free, for they are devoid of any causal factor that could initially bring them into being. Since they are continuous, being by nature mere sensory appearances, they arise as emptiness by the very fact of their manifesting like reflections. In the present moment, they are free in their abiding, for they are devoid of any abiding essence. Since they have a continuous manifest quality as the display of responsiveness, they lack any cause, and are free of any condition, that could lead to their cessation; thus, in the final analysis they arise as apparitions that come and go. They are free of limitation, for they are continuous and pure in accord with the eight metaphors for illusoriness. [151b] They are free as an illusory display, the unity of appearance and emptiness. *The Natural Freedom of Awareness* states:

Similarly, all phenomena with characteristics
are free within the state in which they cannot be characterized.
All phenomena, all compounded things,
are free within the empty state in which nothing need be done.

All phenomena, manifesting naturally without being reified,
are free within the empty state[2] of total purity.

And *The Great Garuda* states:

Material things cannot be supported in open space,
and mind is never subject to extremes.
To whom can samsara and lower states of rebirth appear ever to
have existed?
Without true existence—like dreams, magical illusions, and
castles in the air—
they are false appearances.
It is impossible for them to have the impact of truth.

In a similar vein, *The Exalted Discourse on the Most Majestic State of Meditative Absorption* states:

It is like conjurers of illusion emanating forms
before large crowds of people,
creating a variety of horses, elephants, chariots, and so forth.
If examined for what they are, they do not manifest as things
that exist.
Understand all phenomena to be thus.

And *The Intermediate-Length "Mother"* states:

O Subhuti, all phenomena are like dreams, like illusions. Even nirvana is like a dream, like an illusion. If there were any phenomenon greater even than nirvana, it would also be like a dream,
like an illusion.

What is "greater than nirvana" is naturally occurring timeless awareness, because it serves as the ground of nirvana or samsara, depending
on whether or not one has gained realization of its basic space. A song of
realization says:

Mind itself alone is the seed of everything.
Everything in conditioned existence and nirvana unfolds from it.
Homage to mind, which is like a wish-fulfilling gem [152a]
that grants the fruition of one's desires.

And *The All-Creating Monarch* states:

The very nature of awakened mind
is the heart essence of all phenomena without exception.

Unborn and totally pure, it is unobscured.
Free of any path to traverse, it has no potential for error.
Timelessly and spontaneously present, it is not something to seek.

Since the path to traverse is pure like space, it can be shown to be time-lessly free, beyond any conscious striving:

> Levels of realization and spiritual paths are timelessly free, free
>   in transcending the stages of development and completion.
> View and meditation are timelessly free, free in the absence of
>   renunciation and acceptance.
> Conduct is timelessly free, free in the wholly positive state.
> Fruition is timelessly free, free in the absence of hope and fear.
> Samaya is timelessly free, free in the supreme nature of
>   phenomena.
> Recitation and mantra repetition are timelessly free, free in
>   transcending verbal expression.
> Meditative absorption is timelessly free, free in transcending
>   the realm of thought.

Within the essence of awareness, nothing exists as levels of realiza-tion, spiritual paths, view, meditation, and so forth. So you should real-ize that these are timelessly free within the supreme context in which nothing need be done, for even if you tried to create them within the scope of awareness, your attempts would be substantially at odds with what you intended to accomplish. *The Pearl Garland* states:

> Not altered by conduct, sensory appearances are free.[3]
> Not sought[4] in meditation, objects of the phenomenal world
>   are free.
> With nothing posited through view, there is freedom from
>   affirmation and denial.
> Not fettered by any fruition, natural mind[5] is free.
> The timeless seal is applied to sensory appearances.

And *The Great Garuda* states:

> Due to the key point of emptiness and timeless freedom, nothing
>   need be done,
> and that itself is not some destination to arrive at, but a timelessly
>   uncontrived state.

> Given that the spontaneous vastness of the heart essence
>   manifests timelessly as sense objects, [152b]
> mantra repetition, ascetic practices, and states of meditative
>   stability obscure that very essence.
> The transformation of syllables, and virtuous physical
>   and verbal acts,
> contradict the key point—the naturally pure state of
>   timeless freedom.

And *The All-Creating Monarch* states:

> Awakened mind is like space.
> In mind itself—the true nature of phenomena—which is
>   like space,
> there is no view to cultivate in meditation, no samaya to uphold,
> nothing to seek[6] in enlightened activity, nothing to obscure
>   timeless awareness,
> no levels of realization on which to train, no paths to traverse,
> no subtle factors, no duality, and no interdependence.
> There is no definitive or conclusive statement concerning mind.
> Since it is beyond value judgments, there are no pith instructions
>   for coming to some decisive experience.
> This is the view of awakened mind, great perfection.

In this section, I consider both the larger scope of the decisive experiences you come to and the key points for discerning their implications. Dharmakaya is not to be sought or achieved elsewhere, since it abides within you, and such factors as view, meditation, conduct, and fruition obscure unobstructed awareness in all its nakedness. Therefore, you reach the definitive conclusion that self-knowing awareness, which transcends all phenomena, is like space. *The Perfect Dynamic Energy of the Lion* states:

> How marvelous!
> The enlightened forms of buddhas arise within self-knowing
>   awareness.[7]
> Since they do not exist even as abstract concepts, the true nature
>   of phenomena is a state of peace.[8]
> Unobstructed self-knowing awareness itself, the illumination
>   found within one,[9]
> does not involve any conceptual limitation, but is present as its
>   own radiance.[10]

Free of the ways that ordinary mind perceives,
it is the ultimate meaning of the true nature of phenomena
experiencing itself.
Do not complicate or oversimplify it, but look within the scope
of awareness.[11] [153a]
The true nature of phenomena, without finite depth or limit,
is wholly positive.
The two extremes of "is" and "is not" are completely eliminated,
for it is neither.[12]
Cut through concepts in the state that is unborn and does
not deteriorate.

Thus, once you have come to the decisive experience of enlightened intent that is the lucid expanse permeating all of space, no phenomenon that arises from awareness—no sensory appearance, no state of ordinary mind—can actually characterize or conclusively define awareness itself. It is uniquely, spontaneously present in its natural place of rest, in which nothing need be done. If phenomena could contrive, transform, or characterize awareness, this would erroneously imply that dharmakaya, great perfection, is not present within you. So it can be shown that the decisive experience you have come to transcends anything characterized by conscious striving. The same tantra states:

The meaning of timeless awareness is not found by being
thought about.
If the meaning of timeless awareness could be discovered by
being thought about,
naturally occurring timeless awareness would be a lie.
Dharmakaya is not perceived by being meditated upon.
If dharmakaya could be perceived by being meditated upon,
the true nature of awareness's own manifestations would be a lie.
The meaning of awareness is not realized by being looked at.
If the meaning of awareness could be realized by being looked at,
unceasing dharmakaya would be a lie.
Phenomena cannot be used to cut through the root
of nonrecognition.
If phenomena could be used to cut through the root
of nonrecognition,
originally pure timeless awareness would be a lie.
The meaning of buddhahood is not realized through
virtuous action.

If the meaning of buddhahood could be realized through
    virtuous action,
great perfection as the way of abiding would be a lie.
Harmful actions do not cause one to fall into samsara.
If harmful actions could cause one to fall into samsara,
the three instants would be a lie. [153b]
What has authentic meaning is not perceived through emptiness.
If what has authentic meaning could be perceived
    through emptiness,
utterly lucid timeless awareness[13] would be a lie.
The meaning of self-knowing awareness is not perceived
    through characteristics.
If the meaning of self-knowing awareness could be perceived
    through characteristics,
the inherently lucid[14] nature of phenomena would be a lie.
The meaning of spontaneous perfection is not found by any
    attempts to find it.
If the meaning of spontaneous perfection could be found by any
    attempts to find it,
the unchanging essence of being would be a lie.
Sensory appearances are not perceived by being reified.
If sensory appearances could be perceived by being reified,
the continuous nature of being would be a lie.
Conduct cannot liberate others.
If conduct could liberate others,
all-pervasive responsiveness would be a lie.

Thus, by making such clear distinctions, you come to a decisive experience of what has ultimate meaning; you also come to a decisive experience of the essence, the unchanging state. *Naturally Arising Awareness* states:

How marvelous! The totally pure mandala[15]
is free of both causes and conditions—
this is the ultimate meaning of timeless awareness, lucid
    and naturally occurring.
The six avenues of consciousness, sense objects, and conditions
are devoid of[16] reification.
If there are no reifying extremes, there is bliss—
complete liberation from any state in which "I" is reified.

There is the complete emptiness of phenomena, which are
   perceived as having identity.
There is freedom from sense objects being perceived
   as permanent.
Though it cannot be characterized, timeless awareness is
   perceived through its adornment.[17]
It is free of the dependent factors entailed in the spiritual path.
This, moreover, is the realization of the very meaning
   of awareness,
and with this realization one encounters the meaning
   of timeless awareness.
With this perception, there is no metaphor, only the actuality.
Incomparable, naturally occurring timeless awareness itself [18]
is unsullied by anything and is free of bias.
In a spiritual path based on words, there is speculation as to what
   is or is not transcendence,
but transcendence cannot be effected or contrived by[19]
   a spiritual path. [154a]
Timeless awareness itself, which involves no attachment,
is beyond the extremes of attachment and nonattachment,
beyond the words "transcended" and "not transcended."[20]

You come to a decisive experience of the supreme symbol, basic
space. *The Reverberation of Sound* states:

Furthermore, I will explain the view that is the subject
   under discussion.
If one does not take life, one does not awaken to buddhahood.
If the skylight is not blocked, darkness will not be dispelled.
The teacher of the buddhas, the King of Destiny in hell,
leads beings to the three lower realms through spiritual teachings.
One creates virtue by engaging in harmful actions.
The three realms of samsara come about through view,
all afflictive emotions and karma[21] are reinforced
   through meditation,
error and obscuration come about through conduct,
and the very cause of samsara comes about through fruition.

Furthermore, I will explain the connections between symbols,
   meanings, and words.
In the midst of an expanse of massing apocalyptic fire,

a person is not burned,
but explains the teachings of the three collections
and murders others as his activity.
What flourishing of virtue! How incredible!
If the iron house²² has no door,
the sun and moon can shine luminously
within the enveloping, unilluminated darkness,
but they are not seen by anyone.
They are clear objects to anyone's senses,
but are not seen. How incredible!

Furthermore, I will explain the view that reifies sense objects.
Since the ground of the three realms of samsara is empty,
nirvana, too, is swept away.
Since nonrecognition is exposed as the root of samsara,
the fruition, the three kayas, is uprooted.
With darkness, armor is donned and the sun has set. [154b]
When the skylight of lucidity opens, there is enveloping
    darkness.²³
The sharp edge cannot cut anything.
There is one thing that the vast, empty center cannot contain.
In the coming together of things in all their variety, there is one
    thing that is not found.
Concepts about the extremes of existence and nonexistence
    are dispelled.

Let me briefly explain the key points of these vajra words. You come to a decisive experience through "the view" of basic space, the "subject under discussion."

"If one does not take life" by cutting through dualistic perception, "one does not awaken to buddhahood," so you cut through to the supreme state of timeless emptiness free of any foundation.

"If the skylight" of ordinary consciousness looking at sensory appearances "is not blocked" by a pure and naturally settled state of imperturbable rest, the "darkness" of samsara "will not be dispelled," so rest without distraction in the naturally occurring state free of elaboration, in all its nakedness.

The king of the hells, which are the greatest torment in samsara, is "the teacher of the buddhas" of the three times because, when you perceive this torment, you feel disgusted and seek liberation. From the outset, it is crucial to turn your mind from samsara. In the interim, it is crucial that antidotes be freed in their own place, since these expressions of dynamic energy are to be abandoned and as such cannot lift you above samsara, including the lower realms.

Afflictive emotions, which arise as a display due to dynamic energy, are "harmful actions," but you experience them as pure in their true nature once you have realized they are naturally free in all their nakedness—this is the ultimate "virtue," the way of abiding. Finally, it is crucial to come to a decisive experience concerning causality.

"Through view" that involves dualism, you are not liberated from "the three realms." "Through meditation" that involves a frame of reference, "the karma" of the higher realms is "reinforced." "Through conduct" that involves acceptance and rejection, you are not liberated from the narrow impasse of "error and obscuration." A "fruition" that involves hope and fear perpetuates "samsara." For these reasons, [155a] it is crucial to realize that awareness is the resolution of phenomena.

You come to a decisive experience of ultimate enlightened intent, which occurs naturally. "A person" who has realized that awareness is unobstructed is not harmed even when sitting "in the midst" of the "fire" of samsara, which is the natural dynamic energy of that awareness. This person "explains the teachings" in that, for him or her, awareness arises freely in relation to sensory appearances that manifest without constraint. This person "murders" all-consuming thought patterns, cutting through them so that they are free of any foundation and the experience of naturally occurring timeless awareness "flourishes," which is "incredible," that is to say, amazing.

Although the timelessly and utterly lucid "sun and moon" of awareness are present in all beings—that is, in "the iron house" of samsara, which is in "darkness" due to karma and afflictive emotions—they do "not" have the power to make themselves "seen." In the context of "sense" consciousness—when you are consciously aware of sense "objects" and so forth—the sun and moon shine on and on as this quality of awareness, but are not recognized and so "are not seen." The crucial issue is that there is dust in the eye of self-knowing awareness. As *The Heaped Jewels* states:

As for self-identity and the objects of its reifying perceptions,[24]
from the very beginning, the true nature of all of them

has been such that they are awareness's own manifestations
in and of themselves,
but that timeless manifestation has not been understood.

Since factors to be abandoned are naturally eliminated, antidotes to them are also eliminated. You come to a decisive experience of the natural freeing of antidotes and what they address. The factors to be abandoned constitute "samsara"—the all-consuming thought patterns that are the natural dynamic energy of awareness, as well as their display. Given that these are "empty," their antidote—"nirvana," the aspect that comes from identifying awareness—is also nonexistent and so "is swept away."

When you cut through the root of "nonrecognition" to awareness itself, even that awareness, though labeled "the three kayas," cannot be reified, but is released into its timeless freedom and so "is uprooted."

The "darkness" of ordinary mind and mental events does not permit "the sun" of timeless awareness to be seen. [155b]

"When the skylight" of timeless awareness "opens"—that is, when awareness is elicited in all its nakedness—the "darkness" of ordinary mind and mental events is cleared away and originally pure timeless awareness, the true nature of phenomena, "envelops" you.

Even though "the sharp edge" of all-consuming thought patterns analyzes and examines, it "cannot cut" through to the root of naturally occurring timeless awareness, so instead thoughts proliferate outwardly.

In the "vast" range of apparent objects manifesting through the six avenues of consciousness, there is nothing that ultimately is the heart essence. Nothing is found to have true existence, and so the "center" is "empty," like that of a hollow reed.

Although sensory appearances may "come together" outside you as "things in all their variety," the "one thing" to be found—naturally occurring timeless awareness—"is not found" in the context of outwardly manifesting sense objects.

In effect, this tantra says: Inner basic space does not stray from the state of utter lucidity. Therefore, if you wish to perceive naturally occurring timeless awareness, put aside the proliferation and resolution of thoughts, which are the ordinary mind's way of being drawn out to apparent sense objects. Instead, look within to the ultimate meaning of uncontrived and natural lucidity and you will certainly discover it. As *The All-Creating Monarch* states:

Instantaneous timeless awareness, utterly unimaginable,
is like the precious gem that comes from all spiritual mentors.
Without any frame of reference and without depending on any
    changeable state,
it fulfills all one's hopes, since by its very nature it is excellent.
If one examines it, it proves to be nonexistent, but if one lets it be,
    it is supreme in that its occurrence is sublime.
There is no vacillation inwardly, no object to seek within.
Sense objects form outwardly, but there is no framework for
    elaborating on those objects.
Compassion—not arising from or engaging such objects,
    and without identity—
is not derived from anything else, nor will it ever be.
It abides timelessly.

The key points for discerning the implications at this stage are as follows:

Existence and nonexistence are timelessly free, for freedom lies
    in the transcendence of extremes. [156a]
Affirmation and denial are timelessly free, for freedom lies in
    the lack of any basis or foundation.
What is authentic is timelessly free, for freedom lies in the
    transcendence of conceptual frameworks.
What is not authentic is timelessly free, for freedom lies in the
    transcendence of conceptual bias.
Karma is timelessly free, for freedom lies in the absence of any
    sullying factors.
Afflictive emotions are timelessly free, for freedom lies in the
    absence of either bondage or freedom.
Habitual patterns are timelessly free, for freedom lies in the
    lack of any basis for supporting them.
The consequences of actions are timelessly free, for freedom
    lies in the lack of any basis for experiencing them.

With your realization of the essence of this sole awareness, everything is free and that freedom is the true nature of phenomena, the state
in which nothing has ever known existence. And so it makes perfect
sense that freedom comes with realization of this oneness. This is similar to the fact that if you yourself do not lose your footing, it is impossible for an illusory army to force you over a cliff, but if you do not realize

what is happening, you topple into the abyss. This example refers to an event in the past, when an illusory army was made to emanate near the edge of an abyss in Vaishali; those who failed to understand what it was were terrified and fled, falling over the cliff, while those who knew what was happening continued on leisurely and encountered no mishap.

Although one speaks of appearances as existent and substantial phenomena, and of emptiness as some nonexistent and nonsubstantial phenomenon, in fact the situation is beyond the extremes of existence and nonexistence, like the unity of appearances and emptiness in a dream. Naive affirmation amounts to positing that things are existent in being continuous and having identity. Nihilistic denial amounts to positing that things are nonexistent in being momentary by nature but divisible to the point where nothing remains. Neither of these positions is the case, because the fact that time has never existed means that neither a continuity nor a moment has ever existed, and the fact that no finite essence has ever existed also means that neither a continuity nor a moment has ever existed.

The virtuous path of liberation is considered authentic, while [156b] the nonvirtuous path of samsara is considered inauthentic. But neither of these has ever actually existed, for they have no independent nature, their very essence being like that of a dream. As for "karma," "afflictive emotions," "the consequences of actions," and "habitual patterns," it is impossible that these exist in actuality, for when your experience of them is pure they accord with the eight metaphors of illusoriness. You may assume they do exist in the mind, but if you examine the nature of their three phases—occurrence, duration, and disappearance—you cannot find either a mind as the support or an afflictive emotion as what it supports, and so they definitely do not exist. You may assume that they exist in the body, but if you investigate the body down to its irreducible subatomic particles, you will find neither a body as the support nor the consequences of actions as what it supports. None of these has ever existed, just as a flower in the sky has no place to grow or any finite essence of its own. *The Great Garuda* states:

> In this mind, about which it is fundamentally impossible
>   to posit anything,[25]
> habitual patterns and the consequences of actions have no basis,
>   so what could support them?

Just as a flower has no place to grow in the sky, having no support,[26] the body and mind have no location,[27] so there is no possible support for habitual patterns.

The fixating constraints involved in a spiritual path and antidotes are transcended:

Antidotes are timelessly free, free in the absence of anything to abandon.
There is neither renunciation nor acceptance, but freedom in expansiveness equal to space itself.
Freedom is timelessly free, free in the absence of bondage.
The lack of freedom is timelessly free, free in the absence of both bondage and freedom.
Relaxation is timelessly free, free in the absence of anything to be relaxed.
The state of resting imperturbably is timelessly free, free in the absence of anything to be brought to rest.

Antidotes are phenomena defined by what is to be abandoned, but in this context samsara does not exist as something to be abandoned, and so the spiritual path does not exist as an antidote for abandoning it. Both what is to be abandoned and its antidote [157a] are imputed in the mind, and since mind in essence does not exist, neither of these exists. Freedom is defined in relation to bondage, and given that there is no bondage, there is nothing to be freed. Even if there were a phenomenon called "nonfreedom," being a phenomenon entails a lack of independent nature, so again neither bondage nor freedom can exist. Through relaxation there is timeless freedom, but in fact there is no basis for anything to be relaxed. The state of resting imperturbably is timelessly free, because neither the process of resting, someone to make it happen, nor something to be brought to rest has ever known existence, so there is suchness itself, a timelessly nondual state. *The Perfect Dynamic Energy of the Lion* states:

As for view—the meaning of the enlightened intent of great perfection—
it does not fall into the bias of what is positive versus negative and so is beyond the dualistic extremes of[28] "is" and "is not."

> It has no duality of perfection versus imperfection.
> In great perfection, the essence of awareness,
> there is neither confusion nor its lack.

And *Naturally Arising Awareness* states:

> Completely beyond the realm of thought,[29]
> free of[30] the extremes of dualistic fixation,
> beyond the limitations of names and words, which characterize
>   things . . .

A definitive summary of these key points is as follows:

> **In brief, all phenomena that are appearances or possibilities,**
> **as well as what is neither an appearance nor a possibility**
> **   and is beyond ordinary phenomena—**
> **all these are already timelessly free in basic space,**
> **so there is no need now for anyone to make an effort to free**
> **   them anew.**

"All phenomena that are appearances or possibilities" refers to what can be objects of ordinary consciousness. "What is neither an appearance nor a possibility" refers to nirvana, which is never at any point an object of ordinary subjective consciousness, for as is said, "Ultimate reality is not the province of ordinary consciousness." [157b] In brief, then, all phenomena, whether of samsara or nirvana, are timelessly empty, beyond imagination or expression, and already free in primordial basic space. The fact that they are timelessly free means that there is no need to free them anew through effort, for they have no independent nature. *The Reverberation of Sound* states:

> Freedom is timeless, so there is no need to create it anew.

It is also pointless to make an effort or strive to prove the logic of the foregoing points:

> **Even though you might make an effort to do this, it would**
> **   be pointless,**
> **so don't! Don't! Do not strive or try to achieve!**
> **Don't look! Don't look! Do not look at the concepts in your mind!**
> **Don't meditate! Don't meditate! Do not meditate on**
> **   the phenomena of your ordinary consciousness!**

Don't analyze! Don't analyze! Do not analyze sense objects
  and ordinary mind! [31]
Don't try to achieve! Don't try to achieve! Do not try to achieve
  results out of hope and fear!
Don't reject! Don't reject! Do not reject afflictive emotions
  and karma!
Don't accept! Don't accept! Do not accept anything as true!
Don't bind! Don't bind! Do not bind your mindstream!

Given that the essence of awareness is unobstructed, it is in reference to that essence, which has never existed as anything, that the negative injunctions are repeated twice. This is to refute the dualistic process of reifying both object and subject. Within the essence of awareness, there is neither an object that can be reified as something to act on nor a subject that can be reified as some agent to take action, so I emphasize, "Don't! Don't!" with regard to both a planner making an effort and an action undertaken to achieve something. As *The Source of Precious Riches,* a manual on poetics, states:

When something is extremely meaningful,
  one should repeat the same word twice. [158a]

My advice to you is this: Within the essence of awareness, there is neither something to look at nor one who looks, so do not look with ordinary mind, using it to look at awareness as an object. Within awareness, there is neither something to meditate on nor one who meditates, so do not meditate. Similarly, do not get involved in conduct, achievement, renunciation or acceptance, constraints, or fixation. I give this advice because awareness is beyond existence and nonexistence, beyond dualistic perception. *Naturally Arising Awareness* states:

One is free of existence and nonexistence.
There is none of the distortion of ordinary dualistic mind.

Furthermore, the key points of the preceding statements are summed up in the following "sixteen essential factors," which, with their respective subdivisions, are another way of enumerating these spiritual teachings:

1. At the very heart of the pith instructions are three key points concerning awareness, which in essence is beyond confusion or the lack thereof—that is, its essence, nature, and responsiveness.

2. View entails three methods of resting—resting imperturbably on the outer level of sensory appearances, resting imperturbably on the inner level of mental stirring, and resting imperturbably on the secret level of awareness.

3. Conduct that is natural freedom without attachment has three key points—freedom in the immediate perception of sensory appearances, the natural freedom of mental stirring, and the timeless freedom of awareness.

4. Meditation that is timelessly present and uniquely decisive has four aspects—the outer level of sensory appearances, the inner level of consciousness, the secret level of awareness, and the level of suchness itself as the way of abiding. These aspects are free of any support based on recollection or thinking.

5. The perception of thoughts as naturally lucid has two secret vital points—the identification of self-knowing awareness as unobstructed when mind is at rest and when it is stirring.

6. The single nonconceptual state to which you are led—awareness settled in its own place—is naked original purity.

7. The spontaneously accomplished heart essence of awareness [158b] has two aspects—it abides in essence as original purity and by nature as spontaneous presence, and so is beyond affirmation or denial.

8. Three pith instructions on the spontaneously present fruition concern its emptiness, lucidity, and continuous quality.

9. The direct encounter has five aspects, which concern the naturally pure, naked essence of the five emotional poisons.

10. The limpid quality of enlightened intent, the unity of emptiness and lucidity, has six aspects—being timelessly empty, it involves no proliferation or resolution of thoughts; being naturally empty, it rests in its own place; being lucid yet empty, it allows for the continuous manifestation of sense objects; being empty in essence, it does not stray from its fundamental nature; being empty of existence, it cannot be thought of as being real or having characteristics; and being empty of nonexistence, it rests as the unceasing pristine quality of awareness.

11. The "place to which you are led" has eight aspects—you are led to original purity, which is beyond labels and in which phenomena resolve, a supremely spacious expanse that is free of eight extremes, for it cannot be reified as existent or nonexistent, manifest or empty, samsara or nirvana, bondage or freedom.

12. There are three mandalas—sensory appearances as the mandala of enlightened form, sounds as the mandala of enlightened speech, and consciousness as the mandala of enlightened mind. Having realized these to be so, you neither accept nor reject them.

13. There are twenty-one skillful methods—twenty-one methods of direct introduction for those of twenty-one different degrees of acumen. *The Tantra of Adornment Through Direct Introduction* states:

> There are twenty-one degrees of aptitude.
> Accordingly, those of the seven degrees of lesser intellect
>   are freed
> through seven stages of direct introduction
> to light and timeless awareness.
> Those of the seven middling degrees are benefited
> through seven stages of direct introduction
> to enlightened forms and tiglés.
> Those of the greater degrees are benefited [159a]
> through seven stages concerning awareness and basic space.

14. There are three things that "surpass"—the eight metaphors for illusoriness, which surpass ordinary perceptions; the "fresh breeze" of surrounding space, which surpasses ordinary consciousness, in that thoughts fade naturally, leaving no trace; and the unobstructed state, which surpasses awareness, being empty like space.

15. The heart essence has three aspects—the heart essence is empty, in that it is naked and timelessly free; lucid, in that it is naked and naturally free; and unceasing, in that it is naked and free as it abides.

16. There are three visions—that of five-colored light, which is the vision of radiance; that of pristine lucidity, which is the vision of awareness; and that of the resolution of phenomena, the transcendence of all reification, which is the vision of the fundamentally unconditioned nature of being.

Concerning these essential factors, *The Perfect Dynamic Energy of the Lion* states:

> In great perfection, the essence of awareness,
> there is neither confusion nor its lack.

> Thoughts in the minds of ordinary beings
> cannot be represented[32] by words and letters.
> It all comes down to three aspects at the very heart
>   of spiritual advice.

> Self-knowing awareness, the perspective of dharmakaya,
> will not be seen by one's looking for it.
> It all comes down to three essential methods of resting.

> Great perfection is unimpeded conduct itself.
> It does not come about by being made to happen.
> It all comes down to threefold natural freedom
>   without attachment.

> Great perfection is familiarity that is timelessly present.[33]
> It does not come about by being cultivated in meditation.
> It all comes down to four unwavering aspects that are free
>   of ordinary thinking.

> Since it is difficult to realize the twofold[34] significance
>   of great perfection,
> one cannot find words to describe it.
> It all comes down to two secret vital points of spiritual advice.

> Great perfection is nonconceptual awareness itself.
> It will not be realized through meditation.
> It all comes down to the single supreme state to which one is led.

> Great perfection is naturally occurring timeless awareness. [159b]
> It will not be accomplished by being achieved.
> It all comes down to two aspects of the definitive heart essence.

> Great perfection is the single decisive fruition.
> It is not perfected by being developed.
> Freedom from attachment comes down to three pith instructions.

> Great perfection is the direct encounter with sensory appearances.
> It will not be appreciated by being reified as an object.
> It all comes down to the totally pure fivefold essence.

Great perfection is the radiance of nonconceptual lucidity.
Its ultimate truth is not realized through attachment.
It all comes down to six ways in which it is what it is.

Great perfection is the perfect ground of distinct forms.[35]
One cannot fathom it through analysis.
It all comes down to eight ways in which there is no reification.

Great perfection is five unchanging paths.
One will not traverse these by training.
It all comes down to three mandalas.

Great perfection is the naturally pristine fruition state.
It will not be attained by being achieved.
It all comes down to twenty-one skillful methods.

Great perfection is the very essence of the secret mantra approach.
Spiritual attainment will not come about through offerings.
It all comes down to three things that surpass.

Great perfection is emptiness, timeless awareness itself.
Self-knowing awareness will not be perceived by being
    thought about.
It all comes down to three aspects of the heart essence
    of the teachings.

Great perfection is the clarity of natural illumination.
It will not be perceived by being conferred.
It all comes down to three ultimate visions.

These, then, bring one to the utmost extent of great perfection.
Such is my revelation of the nature of things.

There are "five paths" that describe the visions relating to the five aspects of timeless awareness. The path of timeless awareness as the basic space of phenomena is the vision that is "the resolution of phenomena in their true nature"—that is, the very essence of being, free of elaboration. From that [160a] comes the path of mirrorlike timeless awareness, the vision that is "the full expression of awareness"—the ongoing yoga of day and night that is the genuine state of the supremely lucid radiance of self-knowing awareness, not subject to restrictions or extremes. From that comes the path of timeless awareness as equalness, the vision that is "the enrichment of the enlightened qualities of meditative experience." Awareness's own manifestations, free of the limitations of fixating concepts about these meditative experiences, constitute the path of discerning timeless awareness, the vision that is "the direct experience of the true nature of phenomena." This reveals that self-knowing awareness does not deviate from the original ground of being. From that comes the path of timeless awareness as spontaneous fulfillment, in which awareness is free in its original purity, so that the true nature of phenomena, naked and unobstructed, abides as the very essence of being. In this context, that of trekchö, the order in which the visions are presented is the reverse of that found in tögal. This is what Vimalamitra meant in stating:

> Through the occurrence of these in the reverse order, moreover,
> one is brought to the original ground, self-knowing awareness.

Now, with the context of realization certain, you can get to the heart of the matter—the supreme state beyond labels, in which phenomena resolve:

> Since everything reverts to a state of evenness, with no object
>   whatsoever existing,
> there is no orderly process, there are no phenomena, there is
>   no identifiable frame of reference.
> The ground collapses, the path collapses, and any sense
>   of a fruition collapses,
> so you cannot conceive in the slightest of good or bad,
>   loss or injury.
> Your experience of evenness is decisive, timelessly so,
> and you feel certainty about the universe of appearances
>   and possibilities.
> The division between samsara and nirvana collapses—
>   not even basic space exists innately.[36]
> There is no reference point—no "How is it?" "What is it?"
>   "It is this!"
> What can any of you do? Where is the "I"?
> What can anyone do about what was so before but now is not?
> Ha! Ha! I burst out laughing at such a great marvel as this!

Within the supreme state in which phenomena resolve, unobstructed awareness is realized to be the fundamentally unconditioned nature of your awareness. [160b] Thus, the reification of all phenomena that manifest as the universe of appearances and possibilities, whether of samsara or nirvana—through which you misconstrue them as having true existence—reverts to a state of evenness. This experience arises due to the key point of realizing that phenomena, which do not truly exist as sense objects, are like space in the unity of their equalness and purity. It does not involve any orderly process of effort and achievement by which some things are renounced and others accepted, or anything to achieve through wishful thinking, or any entanglement due to the identification of things within a frame of reference.

Since these are absent, you turn away from any view in which a contrived ground fabricated by ordinary consciousness is assumed to constitute freedom from limitation. Instead, there is awareness—without any reference point and free of bias—which is beyond being an object that can be characterized or described. Since you are free of meditation that involves focusing the mind to produce calm abiding or profound insight, you are beyond any path involving some naturally calm or clear state. Any presumed division in the unlimited nature of phenomena collapses, so there is no interruption or discontinuity in enlightened intent, a spontaneously present and naturally settled state. Any fruition that involves dualistic perception based on hope and fear collapses, so awareness is elicited in all its nakedness as original purity in which phenomena resolve. Without your having to reach it, this state of resolution, naturally occurring timeless awareness, abides as the natural place of rest, and so a sense of well-being arises from deep within you. You cast aside the reification of phenomena as bad (and so to be renounced) or good (and so to be accepted), so you are beyond the narrow confines of loss or injury. Your understanding embraces sensory appearances and consciousness equally. You feel certain that, although vividly clear, they do not truly exist.

The division between samsara and nirvana collapses within the context of awareness. Not even a thought about "awareness, the ultimate meaning of the basic space of phenomena," exists within this natural state as some concept about the true nature of phenomena being unobstructed. Since there is no reference point as to how or what this is, any hint of its being this or that or something that can be identified is transcended. The ordinary mind that reifies sensory appearances outwardly is cast off, so sensory appearances that manifest as "other" are a great spectacle of empty forms. What is there for you to do? [161a] If the kind of ingrained fixation, involving plans and actions, that usually occurs does not, so much the better. The experience is a pleasant one, for you perceive sensory appearances to be dream images that have no basis. The "peg"—the internal reference point of ordinary mind, which rigidly reifies things—has been pulled out, so the "cord," the seeming continuity of what is reified as the "I," or self-identity, has been released.

Since the wild stallion of naturally expansive, unobstructed awareness cannot be found by being sought, I myself could not perceive it. There is no place about which I can say, "This is the place to which I have been brought, the place I have reached."

In my case, the concept I previously had—that naturally lucid dharmakaya in all its nakedness was some amazing "thing"—was left behind, leaving no trace of where it had gone. Thus, with any concept of "is" or "is not" or any reification of the way of abiding having now been cast aside, what previously seemed relevant did not exist in the natural place of rest that is the true nature of phenomena. So what was there for me to do about freedom or confusion or some fruition state of dharmakaya? As I looked outwardly at sensory appearances, they were unobstructed, vibrantly clear, ephemeral, and not to be reified. They did not fall within any extreme or division of being something or not, or of being located anywhere. As I looked inwardly at the conscious quality of self-knowing awareness in its natural place of rest, it could not be pinned down but faded into emptiness, indivisible, clear of concepts—a decisive experience that left no trace. Having merged with the empty space of openness that is my nature, if I am nothing whatsoever in the present moment, where does that leave all of you? Ha! Ha!

Here I have in mind the twelve kinds of vajra laughter, whose meaning awakens in one's mindstream. These twelve kinds of laughter are described extensively in *The Tantra of Heaped Jewels:*

> Then the teacher, Samantabhadra, the ornament of heaped jewels, seeing the way in which all phenomena arise continuously while being nothing whatsoever, marveled at himself. His own great shouts of laughter— [161b] laughter provoked by his amusement at himself—arose naturally from his throat.
>
> "O Vajra Heart Essence of the Speech of All Buddhas, behold the view, naturally occurring timeless awareness. How marvel-

ous—it is beyond positive or negative, beyond view or meditation. The immutable ground of being is free of any benefit or harm, regardless of what has been done or said. Ha! Ha!

"O Vajra Heart Essence of [37] Speech, behold the fundamentally unconditioned way in which things are present. [38] How marvelous—these manifestations undergo no change or alteration. Regardless of how one thinks of them, as pleasant or painful, in actuality they are unchanging. Ha! Ha!

"O Vajra of Speech, behold supreme emptiness, timeless awareness that is the source of everything. How marvelous—it arises as a display regardless of the many kinds of purposeful conduct undertaken. Regardless of what has been done, freedom is unceasing within the unborn expanse. Ha! Ha!

"O Vajra of Speech, behold the empty nature of phenomena, all-pervasive timeless awareness. How marvelous—it is unborn and abides timelessly, coemergent with being itself. Even if a person were to seize a sharp weapon and slay all beings at once, that person's mindstream would still be free of benefit or harm. Ha! Ha!

"O [39] Vajra of Speech, behold your empty awareness, timeless awareness within which everything manifests. How marvelous—all sensory appearances, however they manifest, arise as your allies. Manifesting in any way at all, they do not stray from their own ground. Ha! Ha!

"O Vajra Heart Essence of [40] Speech, behold empty awareness, the perspective within which everything is free. How marvelous—it constitutes its own greatest ally. Afflictive emotions are naturally freed in and of themselves. Ha! Ha!

"O Vajra of Speech, [162a] behold empty awareness, the essence of universal purity. How marvelous—the fruition is discovered naturally, effortlessly. With this single assurance, all of samsara and nirvana is pure in nonduality. Ha! Ha!

"O Vajra of Speech, behold the essence, supreme emptiness, the full expression of everything being at rest. How marvelous—the six classes of beings manifest as the three kayas. Beings awaken to buddhahood all at once without having meditated in the slightest. Ha! Ha!

"O Vajra of Speech, behold the three kayas as supreme emptiness, the timelessly perfect fruition. How marvelous—beyond union or separation, they are a unity[41] throughout the three times. Without one's engaging in the six perfections, the accumulations are completed in a single moment. Ha! Ha!

"O Vajra of Speech, behold the essence of resting in the immediacy of awareness—supreme emptiness, a state of universal equalness.[42] How marvelous—all plans and actions arise as adornment. All renunciation and acceptance are freed within the view. Ha! Ha!

"O Vajra of Speech, behold the emptiness of emptiness, supreme and timeless emptiness. How ironic—all buddhas find themselves on the edge of an abyss. Meditation involving plans and actions would cause them to plummet. Ha! Ha!

"O Vajra of Speech, behold the reification of emptiness as something that is not empty. How astonishing—some spiritual approaches misconstrue what is nonexistent as having identity. The unborn is attained through what seems to be born. Ha! Ha!"

With these words concerning this supreme marvel, Samantabhadra completely satisfied Vajra of Speech and others of the retinue. Since all sensory appearances arise naturally, manifest naturally, are freed naturally, and are attained naturally within this supreme marvel, [162b] they are in nondual union with the vajra of enlightened form.

Within this context, thoughts arise in an unrestricted way, so that their true nature is spontaneously present in the display of awareness's own manifestations:

> Since the perspective of confusion—the universe of
>   appearances and possibilities—collapses,
> day and night are timelessly pristine, naturally pristine,
>   pristine in space.
> Days and dates are pristine; months, years, and eons are
>   pristine.
> One thing is pristine; everything is pristine.
> The spiritual and the nonspiritual are pristine.
> Samsara, nirvana, and the ground of confusion are pristine
>   in primordial basic space.
> The term "basic space," a product of conventional mind,
>   is pristine.

However you strive, whatever effort you make, what now will
be of value?
The entanglements of the desiring mind resolve—the supreme
marvel of space!
The nature of this irreligious beggar resolved into such a state.

Since all reification and fixation concerning awareness have resolved,
your confused perception of the universe of appearances and possibilities collapses. All reifying fixation by which things are conventionally
misconstrued as having true existence—"This is confusion, this is not
confusion"—is cast aside, so all perceived sensory appearances become
free of restriction in a single seamless state of openness. Even things that
were previously valid—units of time such as a twenty-four-hour day, as
well as length and other defining parameters—are pristine in that you
perceive them to be unobstructed and without basis. They arise naturally in openness, like the carefree perceptions of a small child resting in
his or her own bed or of a cheerfully crazy person. Perceptions during
your daytime experience are naturally pristine, scintillatingly vivid. Perceptions during your nighttime experience are naturally pristine, tangible yet indistinct. Your perceptions of a twenty-four-hour period [163a]
are naturally pristine, the open ground of being. Your perceptions of
dates and months are pristine, a pristine state of evenness. Your perceptions of years and eons are pristine, a freeing of all restrictions. Since
the qualities of identity and separateness are pristine, things are limpid
in all their nakedness. Since the ground of confusion is pristine in primordial basic space, there is pristine emptiness. And since any final state
to which you might be led by reifying basic space is pristine, things are
unobstructed.

The absence of anything whatsoever to affirm is the "enclosure" of
emptiness. The absence of any effort whatsoever is the "valley" of the
true nature of phenomena. The resolution of any goal-oriented speculation is the wish-fulfilling gem. The absence of the mind's entangling
desires is the "sky" in which phenomena resolve. And the supremely
spacious state of uniform evenness is unobstructed openness.

Since you rest in infinite evenness, a state not subject to restrictions
or extremes, you experience a state of spontaneous presence within the
realm that is the true nature of phenomena—the "fourth time"—in
which conceptual elaboration is cut through. With this, there is pristine
evenness—your consciousness is naturally pristine, deliberate recollec-

tion resolves naturally, enlightened intent abides timelessly, and lucidity is uninterrupted. Everything is such that you perceive it as awareness's own manifestation and not something "other," so you feel that the enlightened intent of naturally arising actions has awakened in your mindstream. What is this? you ask. *The Six Expanses* describes it at length:

> At that point,[43] the enlightened deeds of a buddha are such that the entire universe is like a ripe sesame pod. Given that a buddha's[44] deeds arise naturally, manifest naturally, are naturally free, naturally expressive of awareness, and naturally accomplished, the consciousnesses of even gods, humans, and others who maintain the naturally occurring conduct of emptiness[45] are naturally pure within the expanse of equalness, just as it is. Their consciousnesses are naturally pristine, [163b] naturally awakened,[46] and naturally discovered, so the flow of deliberate recollection is simultaneously cut through for all of them. All their thoughts, moreover, are completely pure by nature, and their thought processes are naturally freed—whether instantaneously, gradually, developmentally, or by quantum leaps—for those processes are already timelessly pure, timelessly abiding, timelessly perfect, timelessly occurring, timelessly arrayed, and supremely and timelessly free.[47] One is amazed at oneself, one has conviction in oneself, one derives strength from oneself.

Now, I summarize the meaning of this. When you abide in the fortress of enlightened intent, in which phenomena resolve, it undergoes no transition or change throughout the three times:

> The fortresses of the foundation, of jewels, and of
>   surrounding space
> are spontaneously present within enlightened intent, which
>   is timelessly free in that it has no underlying basis,
> so the universe of the three states of conditioned existence is
>   free within the supreme state in which no sense objects exist.

Everything is primordially without origination, without location, and without cessation. So everything that is subsumed within the sensory appearances of the inanimate world (as a support) and the beings in the three states of conditioned existence (as what are supported) is already pure—timelessly ineffable, nonexistent as a sense object, and without any support. Therefore, within emptiness as the "fortress of space," whatever manifests or arises is grounded in the supremely and timelessly empty essence. Within unceasing lucidity as the "fortress of jewels," everything is naturally clear, a mere expression of emptiness, apparent without truly existing. Within awareness—the source of everything—as the "fortress of the foundation," everything is naturally one, the single basic space that is atemporal and in which nothing need be added or removed. And so all phenomena are spontaneously present within the infinite state of emptiness and equalness in which they resolve. [164a]

You have come to this decisive experience within the supremely spacious expanse that is free of limitation—enlightened intent that is not restricted or localized. It manifests naturally by your becoming aware that seven secret statements of wonderment arise naturally in your mindstream. What are they? you ask. *The Heaped Jewels* states:

> Then the teacher spontaneously proclaimed to itself these most majestic statements of wonderment:
>
> "How marvelous! You, Vajra Heart Essence of Speech, listen! Your awareness is itself free of birth and death. With this key point I, Samantabhadra, have shown that, in perceiving the essence of awareness,[48] there is not the slightest difference between an individual who has taken the lives of millions of beings and one who engages constantly in the ten perfections.
>
> "O Vajra of the Speech of All Buddhas, the true nature of phenomena entails no elaboration. With this key point I,[49] Samantabhadra, have shown that, regarding their awakening to buddhahood, there is not the slightest difference between two individuals, one a spiritual person whose familiarity with emptiness increases continually and the other a person who has never entertained the idea of emptiness for even an instant.
>
> "O Vajra of Speech, awareness itself is uncompounded. With this key point I, Samantabhadra, have shown that, regarding the opportunity to perfect the accumulations, there is not the slightest difference between two people, one with faith who has amassed immeasurable composite acts of virtue and another who is continually engaged in taking life.
>
> "O Vajra of Speech, awareness—timeless awareness—does not come or go. With this key point I, Samantabhadra, have shown that, regarding their perception of reality,[50] there is not

the slightest difference between two people, [164b] one a spiritual person who exhibits various physical and verbal signs of having realized the true nature of phenomena and the other an individual who has not trained his or her mind even for an instant by listening to and contemplating spiritual teachings.

"O Vajra of Speech, phenomena are by nature without origination or cessation. With this key point I, Samantabhadra, have shown that, regarding their access to avenues of realization, there is not the slightest difference between two people, one undergoing the agonies of heat or cold in a hell realm and another enjoying the bliss of buddhas.

"O Vajra of Speech, awareness is unchanging. With this key point I, Samantabhadra, have shown that, regarding realization of the essence of being,[51] there is not the slightest difference between two people, one a spiritual person who has cut through conceptual elaborations[52] and another who believes that things have permanent identity.

"O Vajra of Speech, dharmakaya is present within you. With this key point I, Samantabhadra, have shown that, regarding their attainment of the goal, there is not the slightest difference between two people, one who outwardly makes offerings, praises, and various prayers of supplication and another who simply sits without engaging in any action.

"O Vajra of Speech, it is for these reasons that a person who applies these statements about the supreme, naturally occurring state will discover the indwelling confidence to put them effortlessly into practice and will thereby awaken to buddhahood in the inseparability of sensory appearances and the three kayas."

Now, I advise you to dispel anything that would undermine the certainty of your realization:

> Those who bind themselves by holding to biases where none exist
> do not understand the nature of being.
> They themselves corrupt themselves. [165a]
> They themselves delude themselves.
> They are confused—so confused!
> They are confused by their perception of an abyss where
> no confusion exists.

Since all phenomena share an identical context in awakened mind, they are not subject to restrictions or extremes. But those of little merit who are involved in lesser spiritual paths and approaches, as well as beings who are spiritually undeveloped, construct and reinforce individual biases concerning such things as enemies and friends, self and other, philosophical systems, and view and meditation. Awareness is thus confined by their reification of the biases of self and other. Since they do not understand the nature of being, which, like space, is free of bias, they corrupt their recognition of awareness, so that even though self-knowing awareness is present as dharmakaya, they are deluded, not knowing that it is present within them.

How confused are those who experience phenomena in an ordinary way, as sensory appearances perceived in confusion. They are like children who fight and make a lot of effort—building playhouses, imitating people explaining or listening to spiritual teachings, and so forth—taking it all to be self-evidently true. Though confusion does not exist, these people invest things with identity and so exhaust themselves in their individual states of confusion, playing out the farce of reifying their sense of "I." This comes down to investing ultimately meaningless sensory appearances with identity. As Saraha states:

> What for me is play
> is exhausting for spiritually undeveloped people.

Since they are thus confused and distracted, samsara is confusion itself, like a dream. *The Perfect Dynamic Energy of the Lion* states:

> Ordinary beings, who are not like this,
> are distracted by the busyness of their concepts.[53]
> Just as children, whose minds are undeveloped, [165b]
> are distracted by many plans and actions,
> so too ordinary beings, who lack realization,
> are distracted by the mara of samsaric concepts.
> Let me show this, as follows:
> Some are distracted by reifying objects outwardly.
> Some are distracted by reifying a subject inwardly.
> Some are distracted by cultivating meditative stability.
> Some are distracted by engaging in plans and actions.
> Some are distracted by their attachments to[54] samsara.
> Thus, all ordinary beings are distracted

by the bonds of the five afflictive emotions.
They do not perceive that self-knowing awareness is the ultimate
     meaning of timeless awareness.
Fixated on these perceptions as true,
they do not behold the supremely pure vision.
Since ordinary beings—human and otherwise—
do not gain their own independence,
they remain in samsara for a long time.

Because investing what is nonexistent with identity thus brings confusion, I advise you to give up your deeply ingrained fixations:

Whether or not there is confusion, there is the expanse of
     awakened mind.
There is never any confusion or freedom in awakened mind.
You are bound by reifying what arises from it as a display.
In actuality, there is neither bondage nor freedom.[55]
Neither sense objects nor ordinary mind exist.
Do not be seduced into believing in the existence of what
     does not exist.[56]

Within the essence of awareness, samsara and nirvana have never existed, so there is no bondage or freedom, no confusion, no samsara. Still, due to the dynamic energy of that awareness a display arises as samsara and nirvana, manifesting according to the eight metaphors for illusoriness. You become bound by reinforcing the tendency to invest this with ultimate meaning. However, even as the display manifests, [166a] it has never existed as something with an ultimate essence. So it is of the nature of emptiness, in which there is never any bondage, for neither the specific forms of sense objects nor the mind that perceives them exist. In light of this, do not let your self-knowing awareness be seduced into believing that anything exists. In actuality, you remain confused in samsara because you reify both sensory appearances and ordinary mind—phenomena that arise automatically with your nonrecognition of the essence of mind itself. *The All-Creating Monarch* states:

In the absence of realization of the nature of me,
     the all-creating one,
the phenomena I have created are scrutinized
and sensory appearances are reinforced by the power
     of deeply rooted attachment.

Being impermanent and of the nature of illusions,
  they disintegrate.
To be unaware of this is to be by nature like someone
  born blind.

Thus, the root of confusion comes down to a process of reification, and that in turn comes down to a process of pursuing sense objects with concepts. This is the key point crucial to maintaining ongoing awareness so that you can become free upon directly encountering those objects such that they leave no trace.

There are many ways to eliminate confusion, but they can be subsumed under three headings:

Eliminating confusion in the context of the ground: Once you have identified the ground underlying confusion, confusion is naturally undermined. This is like finding thieves in your house and, after throwing them out, experiencing a sense of well-being. It is the method of natural great perfection.

Eliminating confusion in the context of the path: Since confusion is due to afflictive emotions, it is held that freedom comes from making emotions themselves the path. This is like losing one's way but finding it by turning around and retracing the same path. This constitutes the ordinary approaches of the secret mantra path.

Eliminating confusion in the context of the fruition: This is the dialectical spiritual approach based on causes. [166b] It holds that confusion and all that ensues from it are negated once buddhahood is attained. This is like a ruler taking control of his empire and then being able to conquer another region.

These methods involve different levels of mental energy and development, and so make use of different philosophical underpinnings and techniques of the spiritual path. While the lower approaches can be comprehended within the higher ones, the higher cannot be comprehended within the lower, so the definitive key points of the approach of natural great perfection should be kept secret. Otherwise, since lesser minds cannot accommodate these key points, the superior qualities of these teachings would be impaired and might instead lead those following lesser approaches to engage in harmful behavior. Therefore, they are imparted as a treasury of the most majestic secret. *The Heaped Jewels* states:

"Do not utter even a word of this among shravakas, pratyekabuddhas, and others! Why is this? you ask. On hearing all these
words, they will become frightened, terrified,[57] and will faint.
They will have no interest in the secret mantra approach and so
will repudiate it, and as the inevitable karmic consequence they
will undergo rebirth as beings in a vast hell realm. Therefore, you
should not even speak upwind of them, to say nothing of their
listening to you teach."

Vajra of Speech asked, "O transcendent and accomplished
conqueror, for what reason are all shravakas and others like this?"

The reply was: "It is because shravakas and pratyekabuddhas,
lacking good fortune, are small-minded and so are unsuitable to
receive the teachings of the secret mantra approach. [167a] Teaching them would be, for example, like trying to draw a bolt of
cloth through the eye of a needle even though it wouldn't fit and
there would be no chance of its going through."

If I advise you to give up reification, those of you who overanalyze
things might feel, "Anything and everything is reified, so how could one
give it all up?" In order to dispel doubts in your minds, I will explain
this in detail:

> Awareness is free in that it is timelessly awakened buddhahood.
> Do not confine it within the trap of the ordinary mind of
>   reifying fixation.
> The completely pure expanse in which objects never exist
> is the expanse of awakened mind, the supremely blissful
>   ground equal to space.
> Samsara is not possible within that context, which abides
>   primordially and innately.

The very essence of awareness is free of elaboration, so from the
point of view of awareness's completely pure nature, which abides as
timelessly awakened buddhahood, samsara is like space in that it has
never known existence. My advice to you is this: do not confine awareness within the trap of all-consuming, if adventitious, thought patterns.

Spiritual traps, which are major ways in which awareness is confined, have countless variations. However, they are said to be subsumed
under ten headings—the trap of fixating on conventional designations;
the trap of nonconceptual trance states; the trap of holding to concerted

effort; the trap of misconstruing sensory appearances as having true existence; the trap of seeking definitive meaning elsewhere; the trap of investing empty forms with characteristics; the trap of viewing emptiness in such a way that you lose sight of the fundamentally unconditioned state; the trap of babbling aimlessly about your realization; the trap of meditating on voidness, as though casting a stone in the dark; and the trap of enduring suffering because you lack the key point. [167b] *The Tantra of Heaped Jewels* states:

> Then the teacher majestically proclaimed the following
> with words that expressed his own greatness:
>
> "In not understanding the single taste of all phenomena,
>   someone who invests conventional designations with truth
>   is similar to one who carries a load the body cannot support.
>
> "In not understanding the nonduality of basic space
>   and awareness,
>   someone who meditates in a nonconceptual trance
>   is similar to one who reaches the lower slopes of a mountain.
>
> "In not knowing that the source of strength abides[58] naturally,
>   someone who believes in the effort involved in plans and actions
>   is similar to an artist falling in love with his or her painting.
>
> "In not understanding what is naturally occurring and continuous,
>   someone who assigns definitive truth to sensory appearances
>   is similar to one who deprives a tree of its life force.
>
> "In not understanding the timeless perfection of the three kayas,
>   someone who seeks some definitive transmission elsewhere
>   is similar to one who cannot locate an elephant's footprints.
>
> "In not understanding the vital point of the heart essence,
>   someone who represents things as the natural radiance
>   of awareness
>   is similar to one who catches a bird in a snare.
>
> "In not understanding the natural freedom of resting
>   imperturbably,
>   someone who claims to have gained realization of the view
>   is similar to a bastard pretending to be a king.
>
> "In not having physical and verbal signs of meditative
>   'warmth' unfold,

someone who asserts that he or she has realized what is unborn
is similar to the wind blowing in an empty valley.

"In not being familiar with the continuum of being,
someone who asserts that perceptions based on confusion
have ceased
is similar to one who points a finger in a dark room.

"In not understanding this unsurpassable continuum,
someone who claims to be applying it in a practical way
is similar to one who tries to follow a path that forks."

Let me unravel the meaning of these lines somewhat. All sensory appearances and states of ordinary mind [168a] are of one taste in that they are awareness's own unborn manifestations, having no basis within the scope of awareness. Without understanding this, you might hold that the way of abiding, mind itself, can be realized through developmental spiritual approaches and their many classifications of view and meditation, but you are bound by your perception of these conventions as having some ultimate meaning. This is similar to a traveler being burdened by a load. It would be best to cast aside such conventions.

Awareness is the timeless, nondual integration of emptiness and lucidity—naturally lucid and unobstructed awareness in all its nakedness, within the context of originally pure basic space that is free of elaboration. If you do not understand this, meditation in a one-pointed nonconceptual state of mind will not enable you to ascertain the true nature of phenomena, or to perceive the essence of the way of abiding, or to free yourself from the narrow confines of dualistic perception. You will be similar to a person who reaches a lower slope of Sumeru, believing it to be the summit. It would be best to uproot any focusing of your attention.

Awareness is natural meditative stability. If you fail to identify it as such, and instead hope to abide in meditation through some physical posture and key points of subtle energy and mind, you will have no chance of encountering the enlightened intent of the true nature of phenomena. Rather, you will be like an artist who falls in love with his or her own painting. So it would be best to give up spiritual paths involving effortful methods.

Empty forms, which arise as a display due to the dynamic energy of unobstructed awareness, simply are clearly apparent without truly existing. Without understanding this, some of you perceive sensory appearances to be your own mind, while some of you perceive them to be external—as something "other" with ultimate meaning. This is like leaves not growing on a tree whose heartwood has withered—it is meaningless to toil for the fruit. So it would be best to let go of all biased perceptions of sensory appearances as this or that.

In general, you perceive sensory appearances (which arise as a display due to dynamic energy) [168b] purely when you are purified of the tendency to reify them, but perceive them in confusion when you are not. Yet even as they manifest, they do not exist, having never existed as anything whatsoever, whether outwardly or inwardly, being simply a display. So they are only clearly apparent without truly existing—expressions of emptiness that have no basis, as I have already explained. The three aspects of awareness—essence, nature, and responsiveness—are the ultimate truth of the three kayas. Without understanding this, you might hold basic space to be ultimate truth, existing as some kind of empty state. This is similar to having an elephant living in your residence but, not knowing this, seeking its footprints elsewhere; though you search everywhere, you fail to find it. So it would be best to let go of any thought of searching for ultimate reality—the fundamentally unconditioned nature of being.

Awareness, limpid in all its nakedness, is the bare state in which phenomena resolve. Without understanding this, you might take the empty forms of outer sensory appearances—the radiance of awareness—to be awareness. This will not liberate you from the chains of dualistic perception. This is similar to tying a string on a bird; although it wants to fly, it cannot do so for more than a moment. So it would be best to let go of any concern regarding the freedom and purity of these radiant manifestations.

The ultimate significance of awareness lies in natural freedom, in resting imperturbably within the very context of that awareness. Without realizing this, you isolate specific experiences based on a general understanding of emptiness, bliss, lucidity, and the fact that nothing need be done. You thus assert that you have gained realization, thinking, "I have realized the view!" This is similar to a child with no legitimate claim feeling "I am the king!" just from having adopted the trappings. So it would be best to let go of any view based on intellectual speculation. As *The Source Verses on Sublime Knowing* states:

> So that all views would be renounced,
> you, Gautama, spoke what you did. [169a]

Placing your confidence in such patently arrogant intellectual speculation and boasting, "I have realized the view! There is nothing more to do!" has no connection with what has genuine meaning, so these are shameless words. Who but benighted idiots would utter them? Yet many people whose minds are closed and who proceed in entirely wrong directions hold these opinions. Wise people regard such opinions as completely worthless, because they contradict the sacred Buddhist teachings. Truly fathoming the meaning of what is unborn eliminates the confusion of fixating on things. One experiences physical and verbal signs of the "warmth" of gaining realization of the true nature of phenomena without fixating on these signs. Death holds no fear. One becomes supple and youthful, without gray hair or wrinkles. Claiming "I have come to a realization of what is unborn!" without any such indications is similar to the wind blowing in an empty valley. So it would be best to give up talking aimlessly about your realization and reifying it with intellectual speculation.

The very essence of awareness, the bare state in all its nakedness, is indeterminate in that it has never existed as some "thing," so its significance lies in the empty yet lucid continuum of being. Having no familiarity with this unobstructed experience, you might assert that your confused perception of samsara has ceased, along with any tendency to reify that confusion. This is similar to stumbling about in a dark room in which neither you nor anyone else can see anything—such factors of confused dualistic perception cannot purify your karma. So it would be best to give up meditation that requires your mind to have a frame of reference. [169b]

The natural key point—awareness in all its nakedness as the resolution of phenomena—is the unsurpassable continuum of being. Without recognizing this to be the very essence of being, you may deviate onto a path of error and obscuration. For no matter what methods you practice and what concerted effort you make, it might seem as though you have reached a decision for the moment, but you will not have taken it to its conclusion or gotten to the heart of the matter. So there are many places where your doubts and intellectual speculation can lead you astray. This is similar to someone wandering on a path that forks with no idea of which way to go. So it would be best to let go of any "direct introduction" to some benighted state of meditation on voidness. As the great teacher Garab Dorjé stated:

How emotionally biased is a view that holds to
    intellectual speculation.
How disappointing is meditation that relies on it.
How exhausting is conduct that engages in it.
How utterly confused is the hope of any fruition coming from it.

I advise you to be victorious over the maras, or deadening influences, of the dualistic state of samsara:

> Given that the unique sphere of being is without edges
>   or corners,
> to hold that things are the same or different is the confusion
>   of ordinary mind.
> Given that naturally occurring timeless awareness has neither
>   cause nor condition,
> perceiving[59] it to be involved in the samsaric process is
>   a hindrance to enlightenment.
> Given that unbiased spontaneous presence is free of limitation,
> fixation on the limitations of biased views is the mara that
>   creates complacency.
> Given that unceasing emptiness has neither substance nor
>   characteristics,
> labeling things as "existent," "nonexistent," "manifest," or
>   "empty" is the perversity of ordinary consciousness.
> Therefore, cast off the trap of whatever biases you hold
> and understand that unbiased spontaneous presence is
>   like space!

Given that unobstructed awareness is the unique sphere free of elaboration, holding that existence and nonexistence, appearance and emptiness, view and meditation, and so forth [170a] are in essence the same or that they are different—all such suppositions are concepts based on confusion, because naturally occurring timeless awareness has never existed as anything whatsoever. Moreover, holding that samsara and its sensory appearances can be found to exist in natural mind is a hindrance to your realization of what has ultimate meaning—the true nature of phenomena—because you are perceiving it as having substance and characteristics. Furthermore, the perception of anything as existing or not, as being something or not, arises as an adventitious state of ordinary consciousness that obscures the essence itself, which is free of elaboration. This is because such perceptions comprise a web of myriad conceptual elaborations.

Briefly, then, all thought and speech that reify within specific frames of reference constitute all-consuming and mistaken thought patterns. They are referred to as the "dark tunnel of samsara" that obscures your realization of the unobstructed essence of being. It can be shown that this is a case of investing things with characteristics, which is a mara that binds you. *The Great Garuda* states:

> To use one's body and speech in contrived ways and focus one's
>   mind on a reference point
> serves only to obscure the authentic nature of phenomena.
> What other "antidote" could be greater than this?

At this point, in order to become free of the constraints of maras, which are to be abandoned, it is crucial to understand them, so I will explain them a little. Maras in essence are confused thinking processes— that is, the nonrecognition of awareness and the dualistic perception it entails. As for the significance of the term "mara," it refers to something that obstructs liberation. In categorizing the maras, the most fundamental classification is that of the two poles of dualistic perception— object and subject. A secondary classification consists of four maras— the mara of the mind-body aggregates, the mara of "the lord of death," the mara of the afflictive emotions, and the mara of "the divine child." [170b] A further classification consists of twenty-eight—outer maras and so forth. If categorized on the basis of their distinct machinations, they are inconceivably numerous. There are as many maras as there are conceptual limitations, specific elements of karma, and afflictive emotional patterns. They can all be subsumed under the single heading of "conceptualization." If you free concepts within the scope of awareness and so realize that the ultimate meaning of awareness lies in its being unobstructed, you are known as "a yogin who is completely victorious over the maras."

Concerning these maras, *The Natural Freedom of Awareness* states:

> Concepts by which one invests things with characteristics are
>   maras that bind.
> They are incredibly numerous, indescribable, and inconceivable.

All concepts that characterize things and stir in the mind are
    by nature maras.
A concise presentation of them, moreover, is as follows:
If one is attached to the sense objects of dualistic perception,
    that is an outer mara.
If one indulges in the confusion of concepts, that is an inner mara.
Getting lost in sounds[60] is the seduction of maras.
Adorning the body with finery is the seduction of maras.
The insincere flattery of friends is the seduction of maras.
Emotional reaction to one's enemies is the seduction of maras.
Conceiving of things as having identity is the seduction of maras.
If one becomes attached to the body, that is also a mara.
If one is attached to the sense objects of dualistic perception,[61]
    that is an outer mara.
If one is attached to the "taste" of meditative absorption, that is
    an inner mara.
If one is attached to apparent sense objects, that is the mara of
    apparent objects.
If one indulges in indecision about what is or is not, that is
    the mara of concepts.
If one is carried away by the distractions of plans and actions,
    that is the mara of samsara.
If concepts take hold deep within one, that is the mara of
    ordinary mind. [171a]
If one is attached to the phenomena of dualistic perception, that
    is the mara of conceptual mind.
If one is attached to wealth and retinue, that is the mara
    of distraction.
If one is attached to the phenomena of samsara, that is the mara
    of the mind-body aggregates.
If one is caught in the mire of contention, that is the mara of the
    afflictive emotions.
If one is attached to pleasing and attractive companions, that is
    the mara of the gods.
If one is too wrathful, fierce, or aggressive, that is the mara of
    the lord of death.
If one is attached to the deity one meditates on, that is the mara
    that binds one.
If one is attached to the five states of emotional reaction, that is
    the mara of lower states of rebirth.

If one is attached to the ten kinds of religious activity, that is
    the mara of one's state of rebirth.
If one is attached to the path of samsara, that is the mara of
    the nonrecognition of awareness.
If one is obsessed with sense objects, that is the mara
    of attachment.
If one denigrates spiritual teachings, that is the mara of envy.
If one causes others to become discouraged,[62] that is the mara
    of pride.
If one ignores others, that is the mara of character flaw.
There are inconceivable ways in which one is similarly seduced
    by maras.
They are so numerous as to defy description,
but if one has vanquished the four primary maras,
other maras will find no purchase.
The foregoing are held to be the distinct kinds of maras.

. . . .

Therefore, concepts are the maras of samsara.
Given nonexistence and emptiness, there is nothing to reify.
The maras, moreover, are understood within one's own context.
From the perspective of supreme timeless awareness,
no maras exist, so there is nothing that can act as a deadening
    influence.
Naturally occurring awareness is a state of oneness.
There is nothing else—no maras exist.
See that the maras themselves are self-knowing awareness!
When that is realized, all maras[63] are automatically nonexistent,
    vanquished as a matter of course.
Before I existed, there was not even the term "mara." [171b]
Because maras themselves came from me,
nothing called a "mara" exists otherwise.
Concepts that reify identity are the major source of maras.
If I myself am realized, maras are cleared away.
All maras—all reifying concepts—are pacified within my scope
    through skillful means.
Therefore, since not a single mara—not a single concept—
has ever existed from the beginning, maras are originally pure.
They are the display of timeless awareness.
Coming from me, they stray from me in confusion.

Therefore, they are my magical expression.
My display is inconceivable.
My magical expression is not problematic—
everything is my display.

Now, I advise you to get to the heart of the matter within the expanse of awakened mind, the true nature of phenomena:

> Regardless of what arises to the six avenues of consciousness—
>   appearances seen, sounds heard—
> everything is naturally clear, an expanse with no division or
>   exclusion.
> Come to this decisive experience within the timelessly free
>   expanse of equalness.

Outer sensory appearances are the five kinds of sense objects—visual forms and so forth. Inner consciousness denies or affirms these. No matter what arises, none of it falls outside the dynamic energy and display of naturally occurring timeless awareness. Within the scope of awareness, you thus come to the decisive experience of these appearances being expressions of emptiness, clearly manifest without truly existing. Awareness—naturally occurring timeless awareness—is the decisive experience of the unobstructed state that is beyond labels and in which phenomena resolve. It is not an object of conceptual or verbal elaboration. *The Perfect Dynamic Energy of the Lion* states:

> I am free of any talk of emptiness.
> Since there is no obscurity in me,
> I am my own supremely illuminating manifestation.
> Since there is no condition to make me manifest,
> I am evident in the five kayas, which manifest as signs.
> Since nothing that is produced applies to me,
> I am timelessly free of origination. [172a]
> Since there are no maras that can take hold of me,[64]
> I am free of conditions in all their variety.
> Since no conceptual limits apply to me,
> I am free of any sense of being something or not.
> Since there are no words to characterize me,
> I am free of the extreme of nihilistic denial.
> Since I entail no substantial sense objects,

I am free of the extreme of naive affirmation.
Since no reifying concepts apply to me,
I am beyond the extreme of nihilistic denial.[65]
Since nothing that involves deliberate recollection applies to me,
I am liberated from the painful phenomena of samsara.
Since no dualistic appearances apply to me,
I am free of the duality of virtue and harm.
Since I am not subject to extremes,
I am free of ordinary confused states of mind.
Since nothing that is produced applies to me,
I occur naturally and am spontaneously present.[66]

The significance of the terms "basic space," "ground of being," "expanse of being," and "awakened mind" can be shown in a general way:

> Awareness is "basic space," because whatever manifests occurs within a single state of equalness.
> It is "the ground of being," because it gives rise to all enlightened qualities.
> It is "the expanse of being," because everything occurs naturally, without division or exclusion.[67]
> It is "awakened mind," because it is experienced as the heart essence that is the source of everything.
> You should understand it to be like space, primordially pure.

In that awareness abides as the ground for the arising of all things, which are equal in emptiness, it is called "basic space." In that it reveals the presence of spontaneous enlightened qualities, it is called "the ground of being." In that it is the heart essence of everything, it is called "awakened mind." These aspects, moreover, are ultimately indivisible, like space. Their meaning is found in the statement "I am naturally occurring timeless awareness, the heart essence of all phenomena." The significance of this statement is discussed in *The All-Creating Monarch*:

> "I" means the heart essence—
> it is the heart essence of all phenomena. [172b]
> As for "naturally occurring,"
> that heart essence has no causes or conditions,
> so it is beyond all effort and achievement.
> As for "timeless awareness,"

it is unceasing and unobscured,
so it reveals all phenomena without exception.
"I" refers to awakened mind.
The significance of "timeless"
is that it implies abiding from the very beginning.
The phrase "all phenomena"
signifies that just as the nature of all teachers is the true nature
     of phenomena,
so the nature of all teachings is the true nature of phenomena.
The nature of the retinues, environments, and occasions[68] is also
     the true nature of phenomena.
There is not a single thing whose nature is not the true nature
     of phenomena.
The significance[69] of "heart essence"
is that it implies the heart essence of all that occurs.
Due to the nature of awakened mind,
the three teachers come from awakened mind.
Their three teachings come from it.
Their retinues, environments, and occasions also come from it.
It is explained to be the heart essence from which everything comes.

The "three teachers" are the three kayas. The "three teachings" are the nirmanakaya teachings, the outer spiritual approaches based on causes, consisting of the three categories of ethical codes, sutras, and metaphysical teachings; the sambhogakaya teachings, consisting of the three inner categories of kriya, upa, and yoga; and the dharmakaya teachings, consisting of the three secret categories of development stage, completion stage, and great perfection.

The "three retinues" are the nirmanakaya retinue, consisting of four groups—monks, nuns, laymen, and laywomen; the sambhogakaya retinue, consisting of bodhisattvas who abide on the ten levels of realization; and the dharmakaya retinue, consisting of all objects of the phenomenal world (arising as the display of their true nature), as well as the vast hosts of timeless awareness.

The "three environments" are the dharmakaya environment, the basic space of phenomena—Akanishtha, the pinnacle pure realm, in its ultimate sense— [173a] which is beyond imagination or expression; the sambhogakaya environment, consisting of the respective pure realms of the five buddha families, as well as Akanishtha, in the sense of the "multi-tiered pinnacle pure realm"; and the nirmanakaya environment, varied and unpredictable, consisting of places like Vulture Peak, which manifest subjectively to those who are to be guided.

The "three occasions" are the occasion of dharmakaya, which is ineffable; the occasion of sambhogakaya, the continuous state of lucidity and purity; the occasion of nirmanakaya, the coming together of conditions that support the occurrence of spiritual teachings.

The significance of the term "awakened mind" (*byang chub kyi sems*) can be explained in detail:

> In the spacious expanse of the ground of being, naturally
>   occurring timeless awareness
> is "refined," because it is timelessly immaculate, unsullied
>   by samsara.
> It is "consummate," because enlightened qualities are
>   spontaneously present, beyond cause and effect.
> It is "mind," because self-knowing awareness is the utterly
>   lucid heart essence.
> Everything is subsumed and completely pure within
>   awakened mind.

Within the essence of awareness, timelessly immaculate, samsara has never known existence, and therefore awareness is said to be "refined" (*byang*). Enlightened qualities are spontaneously present within the heart essence itself, which is said to be "consummate" (*chub*) because it allows for the arising of anything at all. It abides as all-pervasive responsiveness—utterly lucid, permeating all samsara and nirvana, and occurring in each individual's self-knowing awareness—and so it is said to be "mind" (*sems*). In this regard, ordinary mind and mental events, which involve thought patterns, arise in an impure way from the dynamic energy that accounts for the display of awareness, and so they do not constitute awakened mind. Rather, they constitute the ordinary mind of samsara. Thus, there is a substantial discrepancy here, for there is a difference between dynamic energy and what arises as a display due to that energy. Furthermore, *The All-Creating Monarch* states:

> The significance of "refined" is as follows:
> The heart essence, awakened mind,
> is naturally occurring, timelessly and completely pure, [173b]

so all that is created by the all-creating monarch
is completely pure within the wholly positive state.
This is the explanation of "refined."

"Consummate" is as follows:
The heart essence, naturally occurring timeless awareness,
abides pervasively.
It is consummate in everything—
sensory appearances and life forms,
all that is subsumed within the inanimate and animate universe,
all buddhas of the three times,
ordinary beings in the three realms and six classes,
and suchness itself.
Thus, this is the explanation of "consummate."

The significance of "mind" is as follows:
The heart essence, naturally occurring timeless awareness,
imbues, controls, and clearly defines
the entire universe of appearances and possibilities.
Thus, this is the explanation of "mind."

The definitive reasons for the preceding can be summarized:

Within the very essence of what arises as a display due to
dynamic energy,
a "reawakening" to buddhahood in the moment comes
with realization.
In the absence of realization, thought patterns based on
the confusion of nonrecognition arise—
the eight avenues of consciousness that develop from the
ground of all ordinary experience, as well as their objects.
Nothing that arises as the display—the entire universe of
appearances and possibilities—
strays from the expanse of awakened mind.
If you abide in a state of equalness,[70] without straying from
the expanse of mind,
you fully embrace samsara and nirvana, free in the spacious
expanse of enlightened intent.

Awakened mind, like a flawless, transparent gem, is imbued as
a matter of course with a naturally lucid dynamic energy. Due to this

energy, nothing—not even what manifests as awakening to buddha-hood, free of the adventitious distortions of thought—strays from the way awareness itself manifests. In the absence of realization, there is the universe of ordinary beings, whose confusion lies in their nonrecognition of awareness, as well as the eight avenues of consciousness, [174a] but none of this strays from the context of awareness either.

In this regard, it is said that none of the perceptions that manifest to each individual stray from the context of that individual's awareness. But it is not the case that everything is "of one taste" within, and does not stray from, a single state of awareness that is shared by everyone, for this is impossible in light of experience.

The ground of all ordinary experience, which functions as the source of ordinary mind, is the karmically neutral state of the nonrecognition of awareness. From it come the conscious aspect of that ground, simply a subtle, nonconceptual state; the five sense consciousnesses, which are naturally lucid but do not involve concepts; consciousness based on conceptual mind, which does involve concepts in reifying sense objects, but may be experienced as a nonconceptual, one-pointed state of mental abiding; and emotionally biased consciousness based on conceptual mind, which abides as the aspect that allows for any of the three emotional poisons to occur. All of these arise as a display due to the dynamic energy of awareness. Within the scope of awareness, they manifest as the phenomena of samsara—an all-consuming state of emotional affliction—though they simply are clearly apparent without truly existing.

Thus, awareness—the ground from which everything comes—is analogous to a gem, a storehouse, a mirror, a crystal globe, silk brocade, a great garuda, a lion, an ocean, space, and a foundation. *The Pearl Garland* states:

> Mind itself, which is thus,
> is similar to a gem, in that it fulfills wants and needs.
> It is similar to a storehouse, in that all that is required is complete
>   within it.
> It is similar to a mirror, in that what I reveal[71] manifests in it.
> It is similar to a crystal globe, in that it is immaculate and lucid.
> It is similar to silk brocade, in that it manifests in all its variety.
> It is similar to a great garuda, in that it does not waver.
> It is similar to a lion, in that the dynamic energy of view
>   is perfected. [174b]

It is similar to an ocean, in that it is profoundly complete
 and pervasive.
It is similar to space, in that its freedom occurs naturally.
It is similar to a foundation, in that it supports everything.
It is especially superior to all sense objects.

Mind you, using metaphors provides only partial illustration—in no
way does it provide a total comparison. People with scant wisdom take
this language at face value, thinking, "These are in every way comparable," or else they interpret the metaphors incorrectly. For example, they
might miss the point that, in being like a gem, awareness has spontaneously present enlightened qualities, and instead take "gem" as a metaphor for something unaware and inanimate.

In such cases, do not entertain the counterproductive doubts of those
who do not comprehend that such comparisons are only partially valid.
That is to say, the metaphor "gem" just illustrates that enlightened qualities are spontaneously present within the essence of awareness, so do
not think of awareness as if it were something inanimate. As for "storehouse," it just illustrates that everything required is complete in that it
occurs naturally, so do not think of awareness as, for example, some
independent place or thing. As for "mirror," it just illustrates that an
open avenue functions as the ground for the arising of things, so do not,
for example, concern yourself with the display of reflections that have
arisen. "Crystal" just illustrates that original purity is unobstructed,
so do not, for example, think that it has to do with some specific example of purity or something that can be identified. "Silk brocade" just
illustrates the mode of continuous manifestation, so do not think that
it has to do with something that can be established as having color or
shape. "Garuda" just illustrates what abides naturally without wavering, so do not think of awareness as something existing within empty
space. "Lion" just illustrates the absence of anxiety and of hope and
fear, [175a] so do not think that it has to do with something overwhelming something else. "Ocean" just illustrates the quality of limpid clarity, so do not think that it has to do with some deep translucent matrix.
"Space" just illustrates being devoid of anything that can be characterized as real, so do not think that it has to do with some inert void that
is nothing whatsoever. "Foundation" just illustrates that basic space—
which serves as the basis for enlightened qualities and so forth—is the
source of whatever arises, so do not think of awareness as a support

368   A TREASURE TROVE OF SCRIPTURAL TRANSMISSION

upon which something else is supported, in such a way that these are established to be interdependent. Do not think in such terms, because, for example, both awareness and the sensory appearances of samsara and nirvana are beyond the extremes of existence and nonexistence, as are the ground of being and the sensory appearances that arise from it.

Now I will explain the genuine essence, which is fundamentally unconditioned and naturally settled:

> The naturally settled state—samsara and nirvana cannot
>   possibly exist within that fundamentally unconditioned
>   state.
> The naturally settled state—positive and negative, acceptance
>   and rejection, cannot possibly exist.
> The naturally settled state—dualistic perceptions involving
>   renunciation or attainment cannot possibly exist.
> The naturally settled state—the five emotional poisons cannot
>   possibly exist.
> The naturally settled state—restrictions and extremes cannot
>   possibly exist.
> The naturally settled state—dynamic energy and the arising of
>   things cannot possibly exist.
> The naturally settled state—there is nothing to prevent it from
>   being labeled, however inadequately.

Although it is referred to by various conventional designations, ultimate reality—the bare essence of awareness—is beyond any statement that proves or refutes that it is this or that. Therefore, it has never known existence as anything that could be termed "samsara" or "nirvana," "positive" or "negative," "acceptance" or "rejection," "renunciation" or "attainment," "afflictive emotions," "restrictions," "extremes," "dynamic energy," "display," "the context in which things arise," even the "arising." [175b] *The Reverberation of Sound* states:

> The true nature of phenomena, basic space, the very essence
>   of being,
> is such that mental stirring is absent and concepts are resolved.
> It is perfect as the ground of being, without path or fruition.

The true nature of phenomena is not created[72] by anyone
    or anything.
Naturally pure, it is free of elaboration,
beyond being an object of any discrete concept.
The flow of confusion generated by language is interrupted.

And *The Six Expanses* states:

It is beyond the numerous attempts to characterize it.
It is not some phenomenon, for it is beyond all labeling.
There are no buddhas, no ordinary beings.

You may wonder, "Given that there is nothing to prevent them from being labeled, how is it that neither dynamic energy nor any basis for what arises exists?" I will explain:

**Within naturally occurring timeless awareness—a state beyond
    labels, in which phenomena resolve—
whatever arises as its dynamic energy and display is in fact
    without basis.
The way of abiding, in which there is neither bondage nor
    freedom, is the naturally settled state.
What is symbolically labeled "freedom" is simply a state
    in which things vanish naturally, leaving no trace,[73]
and since there is no contradiction in labeling it as anything
    or nothing,
we describe it with the words "timelessly free."**

It is by virtue of the fact that nothing has ever existed that labels can be applied, because there is no connection between the label and the actuality. Given that the actuality does not exist in essence, the label cannot be found even if you look everywhere for it. Therefore, since the label and the actuality have never existed, why would you ever think of them as being connected? Even the terms "awareness," "dynamic energy," "display," and "natural freedom" are merely labels applied to facilitate understanding—simply aids to comprehension through symbols, in light of the fact that there is nothing to label. Since awareness itself does not exist in essence, how could anything that derives from it— a place in which things arise, the process of their arising, or their myriad display—actually exist?

Well, when things manifest in their continuous way due to the fact that they do not exist, [176a] applying such labels is similar to labeling appearances in an illusion. An illusionist, the magical incantations, and the display of horses and elephants generated by those spells—if these three factors are not examined or investigated, mere appearances seem to arise continuously, one from another. Similarly, in the case of awareness, its dynamic energy, and the display that arises due to that dynamic energy—that is, the manifestation of the universe of appearances and possibilities, whether of samsara or nirvana—these simply manifest in light of not being examined or investigated.

If the situation is investigated, the horses and elephants are found to be clearly apparent without truly existing. The incantations are the unity of sound and emptiness, leaving no trace. The illusionist's body can be reduced to subatomic particles until there is nothing left to divide. And given that the illusionist's mind is free of being one thing or many, it has never existed. Similarly, the entire universe, whether samsara or nirvana, manifesting as this display is clearly apparent without truly existing. The dynamic energy of awareness is naturally lucid and empty. And awareness is the unobstructed state in which phenomena resolve; given that it is free of the extremes of being one thing and being many, in fact it transcends any context of conceptual or verbal elaboration.

You might think, "When not investigated or examined, sensory appearances are consciousness, given that they occur due to the potential of dynamic energy." But how could we ever hold such a mistaken notion as that? The issue here is similar to the fact that while illusory horses and elephants arise as the illusionist's display, they are not the illusionist. If the illusory horses and elephants were the illusionist, this would mean that the illusionist would no longer be there once the illusory appearances vanished and that the illusionist was not there before those appearances existed. But whether there is an illusionist or not does not depend on whether there is an illusion or not, or whether it has vanished or not, so these two are not identical in essence. Analogously, sensory appearances and one's own mind are not identical. Appearances are not brought about or eliminated as a consequence of me, nor am I [176b] brought about or eliminated as a consequence of appearances, so they and I are not identical in essence.

You might object, "Well, since these appearances are the display of awareness, it makes perfect sense to assume that they are brought about and eliminated as a consequence of me." But there is no problem here, once my reply has clarified the issue: Since our collective perceptions of sensory appearances are not brought about or eliminated as a consequence of anyone's personal perceptions, even when I am no longer here mountains and so forth will remain in my absence. The display that is an individual's personal perception of a mountain subsides when that individual dies, so while your own personal display is brought about or eliminated as a consequence of you, the collective display is brought about or eliminated in association with the collective situation.

"But surely," you might think, "when I myself am no longer here, the mountain that is my personal perception does not vanish, so my display remains behind." Since what is left behind is the collective perception of apparent sense objects, those appearances are perceived by those who remain behind, not by the deceased. This makes perfect sense and presents no problem, because I am not asserting that the collective display ceases and because of the distinction I have made between sensory appearances in general and one's perception of them as sense objects.

For these reasons, there is no connection between the label and the actuality. Because they are sensory appearances, things have no independent nature. So the label and the actuality have never existed, and therefore you should understand that whatever manifests and however it is labeled, these labels are merely conventional designations. *The Exalted Discourse on the Most Majestic State of Meditative Absorption* states:

> Those to whom a child is born
> give the child a conventional name.
> But that name cannot be found, even if one searches for
>   it everywhere.
> One should understand all phenomena to be just like that.

And *The "Mother"* states:

> Subhuti, all phenomena are merely symbols, merely labels, [177a] merely names, and are adventitious. If you look for them everywhere, you will find that they do not exist inside you and so cannot be conceived of as such; they do not exist outside you and so cannot be conceived of as such; they do not even exist in the interval between these two alternatives and so cannot be conceived of as such. This is because they are by nature empty.

Now, I will explain this mode of timeless freedom in more detail. It can be shown that the essence of the ground for all that arises and the nature of its dynamic energy are timelessly free:

> There is no division or exclusion—there is freedom
>   in the expanse of spontaneous presence.
> There is no union or separation—there is freedom
>   in the expanse of the sphere of being.
> Anything at all arises—there is freedom in the expanse
>   in which everything is indeterminate.

Two modes of freedom pertain to the essence of awareness—the freedom of that very essence as a state of original purity and the freedom of phenomena within that context. In its very essence, awareness has never existed as anything whatsoever and so, from the point of view of its being devoid of substance or characteristics, it is conventionally described as "free of the phenomena of samsara and nirvana." As for phenomena being free within that context, with the realization of awareness in its bare state, phenomena are pristine in that state, in which no sense objects exist. Conventionally it is said that awareness has "gone" to its naked state, when it has simply become evident, and that things are "free in its expanse," but this in no way implies that something has "gone" anywhere or "been freed" within the scope of awareness, like something sinking into a lake. Rather, because neither phenomena nor awareness have a finite essence, the situation is similar to the fact that the child of a barren woman could not possibly drown in a mirage of a body of water.

At this point, three steps can be enumerated on the basis of this bare state of self-knowing awareness—being directly introduced to it, maintaining that context, and training in its dynamic energy. [177b]

Once you have been directly introduced to awareness—which is not subject to division or exclusion—as timelessly free within the spontaneously present expanse, ideally you begin to recognize its very essence. With such recognition, you reach the naked state to which you are led— the natural state of original purity, the true nature of phenomena. Even if you try to proceed further, it is said that "there are no tracks left in the sky"—that is, any state to be reached falls away.

With such realization, there is freedom from fixating reification within the expanse of utter lucidity, the unique sphere that is beyond union with or separation from the limpid scope of awareness. You perceive this pristine limpidity in all its nakedness, and so you gain trust in the meditative stability of the spontaneously present nature of being. Any state of enlightened intent to be reached falls away.

Due to the dynamic energy that is the limpid quality of this awareness, the way sensory appearances and ordinary mind arise is perfectly continuous, like the appearance of reflections in a mirror. By training in this energy in its own place—as freedom within the expanse in which everything is without basis and is indeterminate—you become familiar with the key point that natural freedom does not entail renouncing anything. You come to a decisive experience of things vanishing naturally, leaving no trace.

When you place your confidence in this unobstructed state of genuine timeless awareness, these are the three keystones of the great perfection that enable you to "take your stance" within the spacious state of spontaneous presence, in which nothing need be done. *The Reverberation of Sound* states:

> Furthermore, the essence of the true nature of phenomena
> is ensured as the essence by its very nature.
> Since there is no single predictable way in which it manifests,
> there are different paths to approach it.
> By perceiving the essence, maintaining awareness of it,
>   and perceiving its freedom,
> one approaches it, perceives it, and gains familiarity with it,
> so that the very essence of being lies in that recognition.
> This is the state of trust one reaches.
> Having come to a decisive experience, one places one's
>   confidence in it.
> Thus, action that brings certainty comes through these
>   three steps.
> Since the essence is perfect, there cease to be causes.[74] [178a]

Now, it can be shown that the sensory appearances that arise as a display due to dynamic energy are free in their own place within the expanse in which they have no independent nature:

> Forms manifest—sensory appearances are free in their
>   own place.
> Sounds are audible—what is audible is free in its own place.
> Odors are sensed—sensations are free in basic space.

> Flavors are tasted and tactile sensations are felt—they are free
> in the context of their own place.
> Consciousness and mental events are free, without basis,
> foundation, or support.

Appearances that manifest as the six kinds of sense objects are ex-pressions of emptiness, clearly apparent without truly existing. They are timelessly free within the context of having no independent nature. Since the six sense faculties and their attendant consciousnesses are in essence empty, they have never known existence and so are free within the basic space of emptiness. In having no support, sensory appearances and mind are timelessly free within the very essence of space, and so there is nothing that has ever truly existed, even in the slightest, as some essence or some phenomenon that can be identified. Things simply ap-pear to be false, but they have never existed, even as falsehoods. There-fore, even as these expressions of emptiness—clearly apparent without truly existing—manifest, like the moon's reflection in water, within the "womb" of basic space, supreme emptiness free of limitation, they arise without having any independent nature. So there is no need whatsoever to renounce or accept them, to treat them with hope or fear, or to exam-ine or investigate them. As Aryadeva states:

> Because whatever manifests is the essence,
> one does not engage in investigating it.

That is to say, there is emptiness because, however things manifest, they are in essence empty, are beyond being true or false, and are un-predictable in all their variety. Their unpredictability and variety are such that, due to the dynamic energy of awareness, they arise in interde-pendent connection, with the coming together of conditions and causes [178b] as clear appearances that do not truly exist. The underlying cause of these displays of appearances based on confusion is beginningless habitual patterning, which is present within the ground of all ordinary experience, being aroused by conditions of karma and afflictive emo-tions. Their immediate cause is simply the coming together of adventi-tious circumstances. The underlying cause of Devadatta's perception of the Buddha as a foe was his own karma and afflictive emotions, while what served as the immediate cause was his adventitious displeasure, so that he perceived a foe. The sensory appearances of the universe, which are perceived as pleasurable or painful, are like this. Since they arise adventitiously due to causes and conditions, they are expressions of emptiness that lack authenticity. To be authentic, they would have to occur independent of causes and conditions. Therefore, since appearances manifest in all their variety, they are indeed empty. *The Reverberation of Sound* states:

> Furthermore, I shall explain the true nature of phenomena.
> Something like this cannot be ascertained to be any one thing,
> so however one labels it, that is how it seems.
> As for the variety of labels, they manifest as elaborations—
>   a plethora of terms—
> due to the underlying basis they are meant to designate.
> While there is this variety of arbitrary labels,
> in actuality there is emptiness, for they are merely labels.
> Since this emptiness has never existed as anything whatsoever,
> sensory appearances are superficial manifestations of what is
>   pure by nature.

And as the exalted Nagarjuna states:

> There is not a single phenomenon
> that is not included within interdependent connection.
> Therefore, there is not a single phenomenon
> that is not included within emptiness.

Some might raise the point, "If the preceding discussion is applied to the development of spiritual attainments through meditation on a deity or the development of nonconceptual awareness and other such states through meditation, [179a] then aren't these authentic in their respective contexts, since they manifest as though newly existing?" But I am explaining here that they are not authentic, for it is due to the fact that they are adventitious that they seem to come about. They cannot be authentic if they are not present when you do not meditate, although they certainly do arise through a process like meditation.

Depending on what you investigate at any given point, through the reinforcement of concepts it may seem as though things change due to this or that cause or condition, but there is not even a hair's tip of change in ultimate reality, the true nature of phenomena. For children at play, appearances may seem to change in the moment, but there is no change on any ultimate level; and though appearances in an illusion may seem to change at any given moment, ultimately there is no change, since none of these appearances prove to be permanent. Likewise, whenever anything manifests—whether out of confusion or not—it may seem at any given point that awareness changes, but ultimately there is not even a hair's tip of change in its true nature. So, in manifesting, everything arises as the display of emptiness.

Others might raise another point: "Since things are present such that they are seen and heard, it does not follow that they are empty." But to focus on such an interpretation of emptiness—simply that there is nothing to perceive because nothing whatsoever exists—is termed "nihilistic denial." We will not argue with someone who posits that sort of emptiness. Arguing with nihilists only leads to exhaustion. The eight metaphors for illusoriness can be applied here; they are easy to understand through direct experience, for they concern natural expressions of emptiness. On this basis, it can be posited that what is now seen and heard, manifesting as the universe of appearances and possibilities, whether of samsara or nirvana, is empty. But if things did not manifest, there would be nothing to base this supposition on, so on what basis would one then be speaking? You might think, "On the fundamentally unconditioned nature of phenomena." But since this fundamentally unconditioned nature has never existed as anything whatsoever, [179b] it is not even "emptiness." *The Source Verses on Sublime Knowing* states:

> The four alternatives—empty, not empty,[75] and so forth—
> how could they pertain to this state of peace?

Since phenomena have never existed as anything whatsoever, they occur as imputations, for as the same source states:

> Buddhas teach about "identity,"
> as well as "no identity" and "nothing whatsoever."
> Even as they label something "empty,"
> they also speak of it as "not empty."[76]

The preceding statements are very important paradigms in this philosophical system, so you should understand them thoroughly.

Now, it can be shown that the process of labeling is timelessly free, since it is empty in its very essence:

> **There is freedom in oneness—freedom in the expanse that is
> the true nature of phenomena.**

There is no duality—freedom in the equalness of sense objects
and mind.
There is naturally occurring freedom—freedom in the expanse
of timeless awareness.
There is spontaneously present freedom—freedom in the purity
of the ground of being as basic space.

Because all things are unborn, they are free within a single state of
emptiness, and since they do not fall outside the essence of a single state
of awareness, they are free within that essence. Even as sense objects
and the mind that reifies them appear to constitute a duality, they do
not deviate from a single awareness that involves no such duality, and so
are free within that awareness. Moreover, this awareness—naturally occurring timeless awareness—is not restricted or localized in any way, so
it is free as ultimate timeless awareness, unique and free of elaboration.
And the unique, spontaneously present sphere of being is free in unobstructed basic space, beyond characterization or description.

For these reasons, samsara and nirvana cannot be confirmed or refuted within the essence that is the supremely spacious expanse free of
limitation, and so, having no context, obscurations are cleared away.
This is enlightened intent that cannot be obscured by anything whatsoever—ever-present, naturally occurring timeless awareness.

Let me demonstrate the meaning of this a little. [180a] You should
understand it exactly as discussed in the following citation from *The
Perfect Dynamic Energy of the Lion*:

In applying the timeless seal to the three-thousand-fold universe,
I am not obscured by incidental circumstances.
In the timeless spaciousness of the basic space of phenomena,
I am not obscured by confinement in some narrow abyss.
In the timeless lucidity that occurs naturally,
I am not obscured by the darkness of samsara.
In awareness, which is forever deathless,
I am not obscured by birth and death.
In the timeless abiding of the three kayas,
I am not obscured by the five kinds of emotional reaction.
Since skillful means and sublime knowing abide timelessly,
I am not obscured by either "union" or "liberation."
Since the elixir of immortality cures disease timelessly,
I am not obscured by the source of the five emotional poisons.

Since awareness is timelessly unbiased,
I am not obscured by either error or obscuration.
In dharmakaya, which never entails identity,
I am not obscured by the duality of self versus other.
In the timeless, natural clarity of sensory appearances,
I am not obscured by the five elements.
In the timeless, natural perfection of the three kayas,[77]
I am not obscured by the two stages of development
    and completion.
In lucidity, which is timelessly free of substance,
I am not obscured by phenomena with characteristics.
Since self-knowing awareness is timelessly unchanging,
I am not obscured by either virtue or harm.

. . . .

Since sense objects are awareness's own nonconceptual
    manifestations,[78]
I am not obscured by the perceptions of ordinary mind.
Since timeless awareness is beyond phenomena,
I am not obscured by the myriad expressions of ordinary
    consciousness.
Since apparent sense objects are not perceived dualistically,
I am not obscured by the eight avenues of consciousness.
Since buddhas are not differentiated from ordinary beings,
I am not obscured by the duality of good versus bad. [180b]
Since emptiness and lucidity cannot be divided in two,
I am not obscured by either laxity or agitation.
Since plans and actions cannot be divided in[79] two,
I am not obscured by the striving found in spiritual approaches.
Since there is neither realization nor the lack of it,
I am not obscured by the duality of "is" versus "is not."
Since there is neither understanding nor the lack of it,
I am not obscured by the duality of ordinary consciousness
    versus things.
Since there is no holding to biases and distinctions,
I am not obscured by the duality of foe versus friend.
Since there is no division into limit and center,
I am not obscured by either error or obscuration.
Since there is no duality of what is hidden versus what is not,
I am not obscured by the two kinds of suffering.
Since there is no duality of awareness versus nonrecognition,

I am not obscured by the duality of illumination versus
   darkness.[80]
Since there is no duality of the five emotional poisons versus
   timeless awareness,
I am not obscured by either reification or conceptualization.
Since there is no view directed outwardly or inwardly,
I am not obscured by the influence of the elements.
Since things are not differentiated into many distinct entities,[81]
I am not obscured by being one thing or many.
Since there are no concepts of what is transcendent or not,
I am not obscured by the duality of samsara versus nirvana.
Since there is no reification of the duality of clarity versus
   obscuration,
I am not obscured by distraction or dullness.

Furthermore, with the timeless seal of the true nature of phenomena
having been applied, the unobscured and unobstructed state arises in all
its nakedness. *The Pearl Garland* states:

Awareness's own manifestations are the seal of emptiness.
The vast range of emptiness is the seal of the kaya of
   timeless awareness.
The variety of things is mind itself, the seal of awareness.[82]
The spacious, completely pure expanse is the seal of
   timeless awareness.
The purity of characteristics and substance is the seal of
   self-knowing awareness.
The natural perfection of sensory appearances is the seal of
   basic space.
Superb conduct is the seal of sensory appearances.
Superb meditation is the seal of mind. [181a]
Superb view is the seal of space.
Superb fruition is the seal of a uniquely decisive state.
Superb timeless awareness is the seal of emptiness.
The superb nature of phenomena is the seal of the display.
Superb realization is the seal of consciousness.
Superb authenticity is the seal of awareness.

Let me demonstrate the meaning of this passage as a practical instruction by quoting from *The Tantra of Naturally Occurring Perfection: The River of Empowerment*:

> The supreme way of abiding of awareness itself—
> there is the way it is free, the way it is realized, and the way
>   it is attained.
> When one abides in that unborn state,
> there is the method of viewing it, the method of resting in it,
>   and the method of carrying through with it.

This passage refers to the way in which awareness is realized, in that it is realized to be unobstructed; to the way in which it is free, in that it is pristine in original purity; and to the way in which it is attained, in that it is attained in its natural state of rest. Given that these three occur simultaneously, there are three key points for becoming familiar with this context—to view awareness as unobstructed, to rest in a uniquely decisive state, and to carry it through to the point of resolution. I have already dealt with the stages these points entail.

A key point to determine here is that the display is free in its true nature:

> There is freedom in the variety of things—freedom within
>   the unique expanse.
> There is freedom not subject to extremes—freedom within
>   the spontaneously present expanse.
> There is universal freedom—freedom within the expanse
>   of the heart essence.

All phenomena, which arise in all their variety without being subject to extremes, abide such that in essence they have no basis. So they are free in being empty in their own place. When yogins realize this to be so, their minds are free of the bondage caused by reifying things. That freedom is said to "arise naturally as the realization that the unity of appearance and emptiness is the unity of awareness and emptiness."

However, while your fundamentally unconditioned nature is like that, [181b] it is of no benefit if your ordinary consciousness does not realize this. If you do realize it, though, this true nature ensures the accomplishment of all that has ultimate meaning. It is said to be "pure without anything being renounced," "ensured without having to be sought," and "reached without one's having gone to it." *The Pearl Garland* states:

> Ah! Ah! O lord of secrets, vajra holder!
> If you realize the meaning of samsara itself,

what is called "nirvana" does not exist.
If you realize the meaning of the five afflictive emotions,
timeless awareness is not present elsewhere.[83]
If you realize the meaning of suffering itself,
supreme bliss is not something to seek.
If you totally realize the meaning of the two flawed extremes,[84]
supreme enlightened qualities need not be sought.
If you understand[85] the meaning of confusion itself,
unconfused awareness need not be sought.
If you realize the meaning of the five ordinary elements,
the five great elements are innately ensured.
If you thoroughly investigate the nonrecognition of
     awareness itself,
the very kaya of awareness is ensured without having to be achieved.
If you understand the meaning of the state of ordinary beings,
you discover buddhahood without having to seek it.
If you realize the meaning of sensory appearances in all
     their variety,
you discover the luminous vision of self-knowing awareness[86]
     without having to seek it.
If you search out the traces of thoughts themselves,
confusion itself is freed in its own place.
If you realize the meaning of emptiness manifesting as
     sensory appearances,
the kaya of timeless awareness is spontaneously ensured.
If you perceive the ultimate implication of the manifestation
     of things,
emptiness is perfect without having to be achieved.
If you realize the meaning of the pure nature of phenomena,
you reach the furthest extent of that unborn true nature.

Let me relate the meaning of this passage as a practical instruction.
Whatever manifests or arises, let it all go by settling naturally in imperturbable rest, and so apply your spiritual practice without straying from
the context of naturally pristine awareness. [182a] *The Tantra of Blazing
Remains* states:

Without its having to be bestowed, once one has received the
     empowerment that is perfect within the ground of being,
the pith instructions on resting imperturbably in the natural state
     are revealed.

> One applies them without deviation, but without guarding
>   against anything.
> This is enlightened intent itself—abiding in the single state of
>   natural abiding.

That is to say, even as something manifests, you abide, letting it go within a state of resting imperturbably, so that you experience it as naturally free. In the context of its natural freedom, your immediate perception of the essence of awareness in all its pristine nakedness is unshakable. This is the main method of this practical instruction. *Naturally Occurring Perfection* states:

> During the four phases of understanding,
> one is unshakable in the naturally free state
>   of resting imperturbably.

The expression "four phases" refers to the understanding that sensory appearances have no basis, consciousness has no object, awareness has no foundation, and the resolution of phenomena is a state beyond labels.

Now, everything having been shown to be primordially free by nature, it can be demonstrated that everything is pure in the unwavering unity of emptiness and lucidity:

> There is freedom as utter lucidity—freedom within the expanse
>   of the sun and moon.
> There is freedom as the true nature of phenomena—freedom
>   within the expanse of space.
> There is freedom of objects in the phenomenal world—freedom
>   within the expanse of the ocean.
> There is unchanging freedom—freedom within the expanse
>   of the most majestic mountain.

At any given time, the utterly lucid nature of mind is already free within "the expanse of the sun and moon"—that is, awareness, primordially without any finite essence. So the key point here is that freedom is ensured by your initially realizing and then becoming familiar with naturally occurring timeless awareness as utter lucidity.

What is labeled "supreme emptiness, the true nature of phenomena," is already free within "the expanse of space"—that is, primordially unobstructed awareness. [182b] So the key point here is that freedom is ensured by your initially realizing and then becoming familiar with awareness as unborn and beyond imagination or description.

The display that arises continuously from the unceasing ground for the arising of dynamic energy is already free within "the expanse of the ocean"—that is, supremely lucid, pure awareness. So the key point here is that freedom is ensured by your initially realizing and then becoming familiar with awareness as a naturally free state of resting imperturbably.

The supreme view and intent, with nothing to add or remove, no transition or change, are already free within "the expanse of the most majestic mountain"—that is, primordially unwavering awareness. So the key point here is that freedom is ensured by your realizing the ultimate meaning of awareness—that it is beyond effort or achievement, with nothing needing to be done—and becoming familiar with the infinite state of perfect equalness that is the abiding ground of being.

With regard to this, there are two steps. I will cite a scriptural source that validates such pure realization and then reveal the key points that define how to put it into practice. As for the quotation from the scriptural source, having determined that the preceding four key points pertain to the true nature of phenomena, you further determine that this nature is awareness and that awareness is unobstructed. Moreover, since the very essence of awareness is nondual, although the way things arise is to manifest in all their diversity, you realize that essence to be a supreme state without underlying basis, in which phenomena resolve. You thus reach the state in which they resolve in awareness as their natural place of rest. *The Pearl Garland* states:

> Since there is no duality of ultimate versus relative,
> there is supreme bliss in everyone's own context.
> This is an indication that the true nature of phenomena
>   is nondual.
> Since one does not follow after sensory appearances,
> although they manifest in every way there is no duality.
> Since one does not dwell on plans and actions,
> there is no duality within the range of awareness's
>   own manifestations.
> Since there is no differentiation between one and many,
> there is no duality in the context of realization. [183a]
> Since the skillful means of the secret mantra approach
>   are infinite,[87]

there is no duality in the context of understanding.
Although sense objects based on confusion are diverse,
on the ultimate level they constitute neither a unity nor a duality.
Although not a single thing exists among the sense objects that
   manifest as anything at all,
their variety occurs in the context of consciousness.
One is naturally free of fixating on this variety.
If one understands the true nature of phenomena,
one thoroughly investigates apparent sense objects that are based
   on confusion within that nondual context
and there is no duality within the essence of self-knowing
   awareness.
A completely pure realm is spontaneously present.

In delineating the key points of putting the meaning of the foregoing into practice, there are three aspects—ground, path, and fruition. When you maintain an experience of the ground of being in its own mode, due to the mere identification of bare awareness all sensory appearances and states of mind are free in their natural purity, are experienced decisively in an extremely direct and final way, and hold their own place in original purity. When you maintain an experience of the path as a uniquely decisive state, due to the mere identification of the limpid quality of awareness's unceasing essence and dynamic energy you proceed in natural purity, in your own place, and in the abiding ground of being. When you maintain an experience of the fruition as an unobstructed state, you realize that the way the display manifests is the magical expression of awareness. With everything thus being pure in a pristine state without foundation, like a mirage, you experience it as timelessly pure, timelessly perfect, and timelessly discovered.

Concerning these points, *The Tantra of Supreme Naturally Occurring Perfection* states:

In the context of the four ways of maintaining an experience
   of the ground of being,
there is natural purity, an extremely decisive experience,
   and original purity.
In the context of the four ways of following the path,
there is natural purity, view, and the abiding ground.
In the context of the four ways of bringing this all together
   as the fruition,

there is timeless purity, timeless perfection, and timeless
discovery.[88] [183b]

Now, everything can be summarized in terms of awakened mind (*byang
chub kyi sems*)—which is equal to space—as the unique nature of phenomena that is timeless buddhahood (*sangs rgyas*):

> There is primordial freedom—freedom in the unborn expanse.
> There is freedom in the single state of evenness—freedom in
> the expanse of timeless awakening.
> There is total freedom—freedom in the timelessly unfolding
> expanse.

Awareness, or awakened mind, in essence primordially free as the
unborn expanse of unique dharmakaya, is such that it is beyond being
anything that could be reified as this or that and so be confirmed or refuted; thus, it is refinement (*byang*) that constitutes the expanse of timeless awakening (*sangs*). Since it is already spontaneously present as the
ground for all that arises, it abides as consummation (*chub*) in light of
its timeless unfolding (*rgyas*). The phrase "timelessly awakened to buddhahood within vajra basic space" refers to the unique way in which
great perfection is by nature spontaneously present. *Naturally Occurring Perfection* states:

> Dharmakaya, the state of emptiness,
> is the nonconceptual basic space of naturally occurring
> timeless awareness.
> It is endowed with the heart essence of empty yet lucid awareness.
> It is timeless awareness, empty and without identity,
> and the state of great perfection, the spontaneous presence
> of all phenomena.

Such awareness is naturally occurring timeless awareness, empty yet
lucid. Since it is empty in essence, it is not subject to the extreme of naive
affirmation. Since it is lucid by nature, it is not subject to the extreme of
nihilistic denial. And since as responsiveness it is the continuous ground
for what arises, it is not subject to both extremes or to neither.

It has never existed as anything whatsoever, and so is beyond the
scope of ordinary consciousness. It can be characterized in any way at
all, and so serves as the secret avenue of skillful means. Nonetheless,

being unobstructed, it is free of any conceptual framework that could characterize or describe it. Even if you label it as existent, [184a] in essence it has never existed. Even if you describe it as nonexistent, by nature it is continuous. Since it is beyond view or meditation, it occurs in an unobstructed way. The kaya of naturally occurring timeless awareness—the true nature of phenomena—is vast and spacious. Beyond ordinary mind, it is self-knowing awareness. Unimaginable and inexpressible, it is pristinely lucid. Although you have never known separation from it, it has not been revealed directly to your perception. Although it is coemergent with being itself, present within everyone, it is not within the range of everyone's conscious experience. And although it always arises nakedly, it is not perceived by everyone. It is supremely pure, free of limitation, and beyond any extreme or division.

It is realized by a yogin who experiences the dynamic energy of the vast expanse. It is discovered without being sought, ensured without being achieved, seen without being looked at, reached without being approached, pure without being refined, understood without being studied, and free without being cultivated in meditation. You abide in the natural state of rest, the state of equalness, without renouncing, without accepting, without affirming, without denying, without thinking, without describing, and without wavering. Other than this, there is no phenomenon, no mind, no karma, nothing to do, no effort, no view, no meditation, no conduct, no fruition, no basic space, no timeless awareness, no samsara, not even a nirvana that exists. Since this state is naturally pristine, naturally resolved, naturally empty, naturally pure, and naturally decisive, there is not even the perception of some unique, unobstructed state of timeless perfection—just a freedom from restrictions, unobstructed as the naked state in which phenomena resolve.

It is my opinion that, at this point, you have arrived at the enlightened intent of supreme spaciousness that is Samantabhadra. Why? you ask. [184b] *The Six Expanses* states:

> "O teacher, Samantabhadra! When no deeds are performed by buddhas, how do you, the teacher, abide?[89] By what means are beings guided by the teachings?"
>
> The reply was: "When no buddha's deeds are manifest, my enlightened form is the 'gathering of all aggregates into one.' It arises such that it is not manifest, not differentiated, not accepted, not rejected, not conceptual, not reified, not abiding, not chang-

ing, not obvious, not evident, not created, not eliminated, not imagined, not tangible, not painful, and not void.[90]

"Empty, it has none of the elaborations of a specific context.
Lucid, it is beyond the extremes of existence and nonexistence.
Mindful, it is endowed with total recall.
It is the path of direct visionary experience.
It is beyond the numerous attempts to characterize it.
Not created through mantra, it is timeless perfection itself.
It is completely free of causes and conditions
and free of[91] all distortions of view and meditation.
It is without limit and cannot be conceived of as a center.
It has no specific form and no sensory qualities.[92]
There is no deity, or even a mantra.
It is not some phenomenon, for it is beyond all labeling.
There is no enemy, or even an ally.
There is no body, no sense faculties, no sensory appearances.
Phenomena do not manifest through thought.
Nothing exists, for there is nothing to reify.
I do not exist, nor does my retinue.
There is no basic space or any embodiment of awareness.
There is no virtue or any inevitable consequences of
    harmful actions.
There is no life force, so no idea of it being cut off.
There are no accumulations or objects to be amassed.
There are no buddhas, no ordinary beings.
There is no location, or even emptiness.[93] [185a]
There are no skillful means and no retinue to listen.
There are no sense objects.
Not even the three times exist,
nor does a continuum of the three times.
Therefore, in that nothing whatsoever exists,
I manifest as undivided and indivisible.
Since my objects, deeds, and conduct
cannot be differentiated and are beyond any level of realization,
in the equalness of the three times
I am not an object and am free of any concept or
    underlying basis.
This is explained to be[94] the unique and extremely subtle
    heart essence.

Given the timeless radiance of supreme emptiness,
from the perspective that awareness itself, free of distortion,
has no manifestation,
it is not false, but the direct perception of truth.
Whoever perceives this is my spiritual heir.
My manifestations being what they are,
all of them are the natural radiance of awareness.
In this single expanse in which these manifestations unite,
one engages in this supreme, definitive transmission."

Thus, by integrating what this passage discusses into your realization—spacious like the sky—the enlightened intent of natural great perfection is spontaneously accomplished. This is the point at which everything merges as a blissful expanse within the supreme equalness in which phenomena resolve.

This is the commentary on the twelfth section of *The Precious Treasury of the Basic Space of Phenomena,* demonstrating that all phenomena are by nature timelessly free in awakened mind.

13

Awakening to Buddhahood

When you have thus followed the path to its consummation, the fruition is the nature of sublime enlightenment becoming fully evident. It is like a flawless gem that spontaneously grants everything one could wish for. When you have gained total familiarity with the meaning of natural great perfection, the essence of being becomes fully evident as the spontaneously present unity, beyond union or separation, of the kayas and timeless awareness. [185b]

When the manifest aspect of the ground of being initially arises from that ground, the ingrained habit of investing what manifests with identity gives rise to confused perception and all it entails, as well as ordinary mind and the eight avenues of consciousness that derive from it (including the ground of all ordinary experience) and the five mind-body aggregates that perpetuate samsara. All this constitutes obscuration, which can be compared to a cloud cover. When you are purified of this, spontaneously present dharmakaya—naturally occurring timeless awareness—is the sun within you, shining clearly without anything obscuring it. From the three kayas, which are like the orb of the sun, enlightened activity radiates like the sun's rays in all directions, ensuring benefit. Such is the fruition of this approach.

You should be aware that my extensive explanation of this topic is threefold—revealing the essence of the fruition in general, explaining the underlying logic in particular, and describing the actual fruition in detail.

Essence

The essence of sublime enlightenment is consummate dharmakaya, endowed with twofold purity, becoming fully evident:

> If, through the key point of effortlessness, there is familiarity
> with the very essence of enlightenment—the spontaneous
>   presence of phenomena—
> although buddhahood is timeless, there is awakening to
>   buddhahood anew.
> This is the unsurpassable pinnacle[1] of the vajra heart essence—
> the vast expanse of enlightenment, the very essence of the nine
>   progressive approaches.

The enlightened qualities of the kayas and timeless awareness are timelessly and spontaneously present within the essence of awareness. The adventitious obscurations that keep them from being fully evident are removed once you gain consummate familiarity with the key point of resting naturally and effortlessly. "Buddhahood is timeless," then, for awareness, completely pure by nature, [186a] abides as dharmakaya, and there is "awakening to buddhahood anew," which is made fully evident by complete purity in the moment. This is the consummate perfection of the ultimate goal that all other spiritual approaches strive for. You experience being of "one taste" with dharmakaya. That is to say, perceptions and thoughts based on confusion, along with all they entail, subside in basic space. Thus, you become inseparable from the true nature of phenomena, inconceivable basic space, experiencing a state of supreme nondual equalness. You abide always in this state of suchness without deviating from it, as *The Blazing Remains* states:

> The essence itself dissolves into itself,
> and so there is inseparability, without any division.
> Like water dissolving into water,
> or oil dissolving into oil,
> or space blending with space,
> there is nonduality, without anything to be identified.

And *The Drops of Nectar: A Letter of Advice* states:

> Like water dissolving into water
> and oil dissolving into oil,
> timeless awareness blends completely with, and is
>   inseparable from,
> suchness—the experience of freedom from elaboration.
> This is the nature of all buddhas,
> which is called "dharmakaya."

At that point, the enlightened intent of the spontaneously present kayas and the five aspects of timeless awareness abides as extremely subtle timeless awareness, the naturally perfect heart essence, within the originally pure expanse of inner basic space as dharmakaya. *The Perfect Dynamic Energy of the Lion* states:

> Within the expanse of emptiness—timeless awareness—are the
> five buddhas.
> They cannot be characterized,[2] but are clearly evident as one's
> heart essence.
> Enlightened intent,[3] ultimately unchanging,
> is free of obscuring perception, whether spiritual or not. [186b]
> One enters the realm of the ultimate heart essence—buddhahood.
> In cognition itself, there is freedom from the ordinary thinking
> process.
> In expression itself, one dissolves into an inexpressible state.

In this context, the state that is directed inwardly but is not dull abides as subtle timeless awareness. If dharmakaya did not entail timeless awareness, it would be an inert void, like empty space, but in fact it is inner basic space, which is naturally lucid—lucid yet free of elaboration. It is present simply as the aspect that is the ground from which arise knowledge of everything in general and knowledge of everything in detail. It is from this that all the kayas and aspects of timeless awareness arise to become evident outwardly. *The Six Expanses* states:

> It abides as the ground of supreme, profound lucidity.
> It is pervasive, yet even in being pervasive it is empty.
> Though the way it manifests is unpredictable,
> it illuminates and its manifestation is continuous.
> Since it distills the vital force of the entire heart essence,
> it is free of distortion and totally pure.[4]
> It abides by nature as the aspect
> that is the supreme secret of the buddhas.
> . . . .
> Without the two ways that timeless awareness knows what
> it knows,
> how would it be different from inanimate matter?
> Alternatively, how would it be anything more than an empty,
> inert void?

Furthermore, ordinary mind and mental events—that is, all-consuming thought patterns, together with the eight avenues of consciousness that derive from the ground of all ordinary experience—cease, while the ground within which they cease, awareness itself, becomes fully evident due to the kaya of supreme timeless awareness. With this, the aspects of rupakaya—expressions of enlightened being as form—manifest from dharmakaya to become evident outwardly, abiding for as long as there is samsara or space itself. *The Entrance into the Middle Way* states:

> Once the dry tinder of all that is knowable, without exception,
> has burned up, that state of peace is the dharmakaya of the
>   victorious ones. [187a]
> At that point, there is no origination and no cessation.
> The kayas make the cessation of ordinary mind fully evident.
> ·
> The kaya of peace illuminates like a wish-granting tree,
> yet like a wish-fulfilling gem it involves no thought.
> Until beings are liberated, it is ever-present, so as to be involved
>   with the world.
> It is manifest, yet free of conceptual elaboration.

Underlying Logic

My explanation in particular of the logic underlying the fruition has three topics—establishing the underlying logic of naturally occurring timeless awareness itself being obscured by the arising of the display that is due to its own dynamic energy, and of that obscuration being removed; the underlying logic of attaining buddhahood by recognizing dharmakaya, which arises as a natural attribute, when you become free of the confines of the body; and the underlying logic of benefit for beings coming about due to responsiveness once you have awakened to buddhahood.

The Obscuration of Timeless Awareness and the Removal of That Obscuration

The first topic has three parts—showing in general how timeless awareness is obscured by its own dynamic energy and display, and how that obscuration is removed; explaining the state of obscuration itself in more detail; and discussing the process of purification and the logic underlying it.

Given that timeless awareness is obscured by the display that arises due to its own dynamic energy, it can be shown through several key points how that obscuration is removed:

> Although the orbs of the sun and moon are radiantly luminous
>   in the vault of the sky,
> they can be completely obscured by thick clouds, which
>   prevents them from being seen.
> This parallels the way in which enlightenment, though present
>   within you, is not apparent.

At any given time, buddha nature—the fundamental nature of being, sugatagarbha, mind itself that is utterly lucid by nature—is like the orbs of the sun and moon. Your failure to realize it causes a dualistic state to arise due to the dynamic energy of awareness. [187b] Thus, the components of the animate and inanimate universe—which consist of visual forms and the rest of the five kinds of sensory objects—arise as the display of ordinary mind and mental events, like clouds. Although the very essence of being is utterly lucid and unobscured, it appears to be obscured. This is similar to the sun being covered by clouds. It is due to the influence of adventitious distortions that the natural manifestation of dharmakaya is not evident.

It can be shown that when those adventitious distortions are dispelled, dharmakaya—which is present within you—is made fully evident:

> Thick clouds vanish naturally when left alone in the sky.
> Similarly, the clouds of causality vanish without effort
>   or striving,
> and the very essence of enlightenment shines in and of itself
>   in the vault of the sky.
> Given the varying degrees of acumen, there are different
>   spiritual approaches.

There are different ways to refine away distortions, but here we shall consider the one for those superb individuals of ideal acumen. The key point of resting naturally is as follows: Due to the supreme state of settling naturally, in which one's subtle energy involves no effort or striving, all the cloudbanks of phenomena in samsara—that is, the causes of confusion and their effects, as well as the habitual patterns they entail— are eliminated within basic space, so that the natural purity underlying them is experienced without their having to be renounced.

The sun, which cannot be seen when it is covered by layers of clouds, shines forth the instant it is free of those clouds, unobscured and naturally evident in the vault of the sky. Similarly, the instant it is free of adventitious obscurations, dharmakaya—uncompounded and spontaneously present within you—arises naturally in its very essence as the perspective of the kayas and timeless awareness. Since this "sun" shines, naturally evident, without ever setting, [188a] it is called "dharmakaya endowed with twofold purity, spontaneously present in that it occurs naturally." *The Perfect Dynamic Energy of the Lion* states:

> If sensory appearances do not obscure it, timeless awareness is
> evident everywhere.[5]

Spontaneously present dharmakaya is neither better nor worse in any one of three contexts—that is, initially in the circumstances of an ordinary being, later in the circumstances of someone training on the spiritual path, and finally in the circumstances of someone who has awakened to buddhahood. This is comparable to the fact that there is no change from worse to better with respect to the same sun when it is obscured by clouds, somewhat free of them, or completely free of them. *The Ornament of the Sutra Category* states:

> As for suchness itself, at all times, earlier or later,
> there is no difference in it,
> even when one is purified of all obscurations.

And *The Two Chapters* states:

> Ordinary beings are truly buddhas,
> but this fact is obscured by adventitious distortions.
> Once these are removed, truly there is buddhahood.

As for the way awareness becomes obscured by the display that arises due to its own dynamic energy:

> The essence is like the sun, shining clearly in the expanse of
>   the basic space of phenomena.
> Everything arises without bias due to its dynamic energy,
>   which is like the sun's rays.
> They suffuse the earth and bodies of water with warmth,
> so that a display of clouds arises, formed from water vapor.
> This obscures the essence itself and even its dynamic energy.
> Similarly, due to the impure display of natural dynamic energy
>   deriving from the essence itself,
> one's perception of suchness, the heart essence, is obscured.
> The universe of appearances and possibilities consists of an
>   inconceivable range of perceptions based on confusion.

The fact that the sun is obscured by clouds is fundamentally due to the dynamic energy of the sun itself. As the dynamic energy of the sun's rays touches the earth and bodies of water, the warming effect causes water vapor to rise [188b] as mist into the sky, where it forms clouds, and these obscure the sun itself. Similarly, the natural dynamic energy of awareness stirs, so that the ground of being manifests as sensory appearances. When this is not known to be awareness itself, things are misconstrued in terms of self and other, so the display—of ordinary mind and the confused perception of objects manifesting to the mind— arises as the universe of appearances and possibilities.

The three aspects of ordinary body, speech, and mind obscure enlightened form, speech, and mind, which are aspects of awareness abiding timelessly as the awakened state. These enlightened aspects are not perceived by beings of the six classes, who thus err in confusion. This is called "the perception of confused mind." That is to say, awareness itself is obscured by the impure aspect of its natural dynamic energy and the display of that energy. *The Perfect Dynamic Energy of the Lion* states:

> Buddhahood itself is obscured by buddhahood itself.
> Timeless awareness, as clear threefold vision, is limpid in its
>   natural state.

It can be explained that it is the "sun" itself that dispels the obscuration caused by the dynamic energy and display of awareness itself:

> The dynamic energy of the sun's rays stirs the wind that
>   disperses clouds.
> Similarly, with the realization of the very essence of being,
>   its display is experienced as its adornment.
> Confusion, which has always been free, is now[6] free in its
>   own place.
> Confused perception and reification are purified[7] in basic space
>   without having to be renounced.
> You have no idea where they have gone.
> The spontaneously present sun shines as the kayas and timeless
>   awareness in the limpid sky.
> It does not come from somewhere else, but is simply
>   awareness's own pure manifestation.

The radiance that is the nature of the sun, shining without obscuration in the vault of the sky, amounts to the sun itself. As the sun's rays shine, the wind that reaches everywhere stirs from its natural state of abiding [189a] and gathers force, scattering clouds in the sky, so that the sun shines radiantly. Similarly, awareness, the heart essence of dharmakaya, ensures the open avenue by which its natural dynamic energy arises. So as realization of the very essence of being dawns, you know that the display of sensory appearances and ordinary states of mind is the natural expression of emptiness, without basis or foundation. Perceiving that any attempt to renounce or accept anything is meaningless, you let go in a state of resting imperturbably. These sensory appearances and ordinary states of mind are naturally free in and of themselves, arising as adornments of timeless awareness. Since they are pure in their own place without having to be renounced, at the same time that they are pristine—without any basis for something going somewhere—they arise spontaneously as the natural attributes of being in its very essence.

Furthermore, those with the highest degree of diligence can, in this very lifetime, be purified of the experience of the physical body and the material world, and instead experience the three kayas as awareness's own manifestations. Once they have gained the totality of the fruition within the originally pure ground, basic space, they experience its very essence as dharmakaya, while its own manifestations arise as sambhogakaya and nirmanakaya, so that the two kinds of benefit for beings occur spontaneously.

That is to say, dharmakaya as basic space does not deviate from the context of the true nature of phenomena; it has have never been divided from it and never will be. This means that there is no basis for labeling as "buddhahood" anything that has ever existed as some distinct, substantial entity. Even the fact that there is a ground from which all aspects of rupakaya arise is due to the quality of spontaneous presence, so that these aspects manifest in any given moment in the perception of those to be guided, without existing in the past or future. The manifestations of buddhahood appear to ordinary beings as a guiding influence, and ordinary beings manifest as the basis for the guiding principle of buddhahood. This is the pure interdependence that ensures a connection between responsiveness and the context in which it functions. [189b] *The Reverberation of Sound* states:

> The true nature of buddhas
> is a state of equalness that is undivided and indivisible,
> so how could there possibly be terms or labels for it?
> It is naturally purified of any basis these could rely on, and it is
> purified of confusion.
> The terms "samsara" and "nirvana" are not heard of.
> Not occurring, unborn, and unceasing,
> timeless awareness, from which everything comes, is nothing
> at all.
> It is not something to accept or something that goes.[8]
> In the moment that is free of causes and conditions,
> it manifests as the ground of buddhas and ordinary beings,
> free of all fragmentation.

Awakening to Buddhahood on Being Freed from the Confines of the Body

It can be shown that there is a logic underlying the fact that yogins who realize their very essence attain buddhahood once freed from the confines of the physical body:

> **The wings of a garuda unfold within the egg.**
> **As long as it is enveloped by the shell, this is not evident,**

> but when the shell breaks, the garuda soars into the vault
>   of the sky.
> Similarly, although the contamination of confused dualistic
>   thinking has already resolved,
> when the "shell"—the result of this contamination—breaks,
> spontaneously present awareness immediately arises in and of
>   itself, naturally lucid.
> The vast perspective of the kayas and timeless awareness fills
>   the "sky" of basic space.
> With recognition of the very essence of being comes freedom
>   within the expanse of Samantabhadra.

A garuda chick is capable of soaring into the sky as soon as it is freed from the confines of the egg, for its wings and feathers have grown completely within the egg. Similarly, yogins of natural great perfection have completely grown the "wings and feathers" of realization while still within the confines of the physical body. Although contamination—investing with identity things perceived in dualistic confusion—has resolved in this lifetime, such yogins are not yet free of the body, which remains something to be discarded, a factor born of karmic consequences, the corporeal result of this contamination. [190a] So the enlightened qualities of the kayas and timeless awareness cannot actually manifest to any great extent. However, once they are freed from corporeality, during the pure experience of the true nature of phenomena in the interval after death, their perceptions are suffused with the manifestations of the kayas and timeless awareness, which they recognize to be their very essence. Thus, they are free in the expanse of Samantabhadra. *The Perfect Dynamic Energy of the Lion* states:

> If there is no reification of "I," or self-identity, one meets the
>   "mother," the true nature of phenomena.
> Once the knot of the elements is loosened, the stake of reification
>   comes out.
> If one is free of the cocoon of habitual patterns, one experiences
>   the true nature of phenomena as being encompassed within
>   basic space.
> If one perceives sensory appearances to be timeless awareness's
>   own manifestations, the continuity of corporeality is
>   cut through.

If sensory appearances do not obscure it, timeless awareness is
    evident everywhere.[9]

. . . .

In the very bodies of all ordinary beings
abides the perspective of pure timeless awareness.
For example, what is confined within a womb or an egg
is not evident, but hidden.
Once its natural energy is perfected, however, it emerges.
Similarly, as soon as this body born of concepts has been
    cast aside,
one encounters the realm of awareness's own manifestations.
Self-knowing awareness, abiding timelessly,
perceives its essence nonconceptually.
The pure perspective of timeless awareness
and the truth of buddhahood are perceived.

Even though such yogins may appear in human form, their enlightened intent is pure as the awakened state, and so they are called "nirmanakayas who have completed all that is to be done." While in their
present lifetime they can ensure benefit for only a limited retinue, later
on they will ensure benefit for all beings, who are equal to space in
extent. *The All-Creating Monarch* states:

Although they . . . may look like ordinary individuals, such as
    gods and humans,
their enlightened intent is in accord with the true nature of
    phenomena—they are buddhas. [190b]
While they ensure benefit for beings,
they make no effort or attempt to achieve anything,
    but abide blissfully.[10]

And *Naturally Arising Awareness* states:

Nirmanakayas who have completed all that is to be done
awaken to actual buddhahood with the freeing of their mindstreams,
and then emanations issue forth.
Outwardly and inwardly, all that is to be done has been completed,
so this is held to be the case of nirmanakayas who have
    completed all that is to be done.

The way in which benefit is ensured in the future is as follows:

> Since the display of responsiveness is immeasurable throughout
>   the ten directions,
> emanations issue forth to ensure total benefit for beings.
> Enlightened actions are revealed for as long as samsara lasts.
> This is impartial responsiveness, dynamic energy arising
> from the naturally settled essence of being
> so that[11] through its display there is abundant benefit
>   for others.

Once awareness's own manifestations are evident as the blissful state of enlightenment, your perception of the true nature of phenomena in the interval after death dissolves into originally pure dharmakaya and you abide uniquely in indivisible dharmakaya. *The Blazing Remains* states:

> Then, given the originally pure essence of being,
> just as though the sun's rays were reabsorbed into the sun,
> the essence itself dissolves into itself,
> along with its emanations,
> and so there is inseparability, without any division.

Spontaneously present responsiveness and the pure karmic tendencies of beings who are to be guided allow for countless emanations to appear under any circumstances to guide in any way necessary without straying from the context of dharmakaya. These emanations manifest in worlds in which beings have given rise to the fundamentally positive traits that permit them to behold buddhas. This is the display of responsiveness. Arising in all realms throughout the boundless reaches of the ten directions, it ensures uninterrupted benefit for others for as long as samsara is not emptied. [191a] Furthermore, it occurs spontaneously, without effort or striving. *The Six Expanses* states:

> Responsiveness, which is a natural power,
> timelessly carrying out actions without effort,
> manifests as timelessly undivided
> in ways that make it apparent without anything
>   being done.
> Like light from the sun, it is not created by itself.
> By its very nature, it manifests in just this way.

Ensuring Benefit for Beings Once One Has Awakened to Buddhahood

The underlying logic of responsiveness ensuring benefit for beings once one has awakened to buddhahood is as follows:

> Although the impure display, along with all it entails,[12]
>   thoroughly subsides,
> emanations manifest for beings in impure states.
> They arise out of the responsiveness of teachers—a power
>   that is simply so—
> and the pure karma and aspirations of beings with
>   positive minds.

When one abides entirely at peace within dharmakaya, in its very essence it is beyond being manifest or not, beyond any plan or action. So any sense of something manifesting is eliminated and confused perception is let go, along with all it entails, and so no longer manifests. Thus, the universe of confused perception is absent in this very essence. When one is cured of a disorder of the phlegm humor, the symptom of blurry or distorted vision, or of perceiving a white conch shell to be yellow, no longer manifests in one's experience. Similarly, perceptions based on confusion, which constitute samsara, along with all they entail, do not, from the enlightened perspective, exist as sense objects in their own right.

Although they do not exist as such, the enlightened perspective of responsiveness is one of engaging with ordinary beings. On this note, some people claim that, although the rupakaya manifests in the perceptions of other beings due to their aspirations and the blessings of buddhahood, the rupakaya is absolutely imperceptible to buddhas themselves, and so buddhas cannot perceive ordinary beings. To support this claim, such people use the metaphor of a stupa suspended in space, a wish-fulfilling gem, or a wish-granting tree. [191b] Now, on the one hand, it makes perfect sense that confusion does not manifest in a buddha's own perceptions, but there is absolutely no rationale for saying that a buddha has no knowledge of those to be guided. This contradicts the omniscience of buddhahood and entails the erroneous conclusion that a buddha does not have the timeless awareness that knows things in all their multiplicity.

Some believe that a buddha perceives sensory appearances based on confusion and so can ensure benefit. This seems reasonable from the point of view of a buddha being aware of those to be guided, but it is completely unreasonable to claim that confusion manifests in its own right in a buddha's perception. It would follow that a buddha's development of a pure field of experience had not been completed, because impure, confused perception would still be manifesting. It would also follow that, because of the impure confusion underlying the perception of objects manifesting to the five senses, along with the reification it entails, the buddha had not undergone a profound transformation. Acceptance of this would lead to an erroneous conclusion, for the consequence would be the possibility of a state of buddhahood that was not purified of obscurations. Instead, it is explained that, with the transformation of confused perception, one comes to a pure field of experience on the three pure levels of realization, to say nothing of the level of buddhahood! And as *The Ornament of the Sutra Category* clearly states:

> Because conceptual mind, reifying perceptions, and thought
> have been transformed, one abides, due to a fourfold power,
> in nonconceptual awareness, pure fields of experience,
> timeless awareness, and pure activity.

Therefore, with the unique state of buddhahood being of "one taste" with dharmakaya, the two aspects of rupakaya manifest, and so benefit is ensured for beings by the spontaneously present qualities of timeless awareness and responsiveness. But from the perspective of buddhahood itself, there is no confusion—so perceptions based on confusion do not manifest; rather, a buddha perceives the rupakayas to be merely manifestations that are clearly apparent without truly existing, arising in response to other beings, to whom spiritual teachings are revealed. This is analogous to the case of a clairvoyant with pure insight, whose perception of forms is not confused from his or her own perspective [192a] but who can see that someone else has blurry or distorted vision, perceives a conch shell to be yellow, or is having a dream while asleep, and who can advise that person, "These manifestations are clearly apparent without truly existing; they have never actually existed."

An ordinary being's perceptions based on confusion, which are merely apparent without ever having existed, are eventually cleared away due to a familiarity with the realization that they have never existed with any independent nature. So just as dreams vanish when one awakens from sleep, and just as one's distorted vision and the perception of a conch shell as yellow are eliminated when a phlegm disorder clears up, so one actually comes to abide solely in the pure perception of buddhahood. This, furthermore, brings us back to the key point that buddhahood is timeless.

In this way, while there is no confused perception from the perspective of buddhahood itself, a buddha perceives what arises for others and so can ensure benefit for them. Ensuring benefit involves the arising of emanations due to responsiveness, a natural power present in buddhahood. The ability of ordinary beings to perceive these emanations depends on the purity of their individual karma. If there were no responsiveness, it would make sense that samsara and buddhahood were cut off from one another, one below and the other above, with no benefit coming about for anyone. But this is not the case, and so benefit is ensured for as long as there is samsara. *The Reverberation of Sound* states:

> Due to the empty nature of dharmakaya,
> the quality of perfect knowing—timeless awareness—
> arises automatically for beings.
> This knowing quality is aware and lucid,
> for without it, samsara and nirvana would be cut off
>   from one another.

And *The Six Expanses* states:

> Therefore, omniscient timeless awareness [192b]
> manifests as[13] the quality of responsiveness.
> While there is awareness of everything, this is not perception
>   that reifies objects.
> Given that it abides in its very nature,
> it does not abide as coarse dualistic perception.
> It manifests as a subtle quality of profound lucidity.
> It is the path for ordinary beings.
> Like a seed, it grows upward.
> Without blocking sensory appearances,
> like the curative power of a medicine suited
>   to everyone
> it manifests appropriately to the six classes of beings.
> Therefore, it is responsiveness.

The way in which benefit is ensured without this display straying from basic space is as follows:

> At that point, although there are innumerable emanations
>   in all realms,
> leading countless beings to enlightenment,
> they do not stray from basic space—the dharmakaya
>   of the teachers.
> Naturally occurring timeless awareness is not subject to
>   restrictions[14] or extremes.
> Arising naturally within basic space, in the realm of
>   Ghanavyuha,
> an inconceivable array of the sambhogakaya manifests
> to masters of awareness, dakas and dakinis, and bodhisattvas
>   on the tenth level of realization.
> Moreover, it manifests within basic space as the very essence
>   of spontaneous presence,
> due to the responsiveness of teachers and the inspiration and
>   virtue of those to be guided.

When at any point you are purified of distortions affecting your body, speech, and mind and so perceive the mandala of the three kayas, that is described by the phrase "The mind 'attains' dharmakaya, speech 'attains' sambhogakaya, and the body 'attains' nirmanakaya." This is analogous to the expression "The attainment of the five aspects of time-less awareness is 'caused' by the transformation of the five emotional poisons." There is a substantial contradiction between the five poisons and the five aspects of timeless awareness, so this is not true causality, in which something is created by something else. Nevertheless, since the transformation arises on the strength of purification, it is explained in terms of what is to be purified and what results from the purifica-tion. [193a] Similarly, the intent here is to explain the three avenues of body, speech, and mind and the three kayas as, respectively, what is to be purified and what results from that purification. *The Reverberation of Sound* states:

> Furthermore, as for the stages of fruition,
> dharmakaya is completely attained through the activity of mind,
> sambhogakaya through that of speech,
> and nirmanakaya through that of body.

You might wonder in what environment the kayas are attained. It is the unsurpassable realm of Akanishtha, as *The Tantra of the Sphere of the Secret Moon* states:

> . . . there is the pleasing environment of Akanishtha.
> Those who become perfect buddhas awaken to
>   buddhahood there.

And a commentary on *The Entrance into the Middle Way* states:

> At whatever point one awakens to buddhahood as the unsurpassable state of enlightenment, that first moment takes place solely in the environment of Akanishtha.

You might ask where this is exactly. In general, the "level" on which all buddhas discover their original awakened state is the environment called Akanishtha [Pinnacle Realm; lit. "under nothing"], for it is the "highest" of all and nothing can surpass it. One cannot say, "It is solely here," narrowing it down to some isolated locale, because the environment is a state free of the perception of anything having identity. *The Compendium of the Supreme Spiritual Approach* states:

> Because there is no perception of anything having identity,
> the environment is not some distinct place.

When you ask where humans are born, I reply, "They are born solely in the human realm." But my assertion that they are only in that realm does not narrow their location down to a single isolated place. Given that the environments of the six classes of beings are present throughout the reaches of space, there are countless human realms. Similarly, it is said that those who become buddhas awaken to buddhahood in Akanishtha, but this does not imply some single location to fix your mind on. You should understand Akanishtha [193b] to be the environment in which basic space and timeless awareness are of one taste.

The Akanishtha realm in which our teacher, Samantabhadra Vajradhara, demonstrated how one awakens to full enlightenment and spoke the many classes of tantra—the realm referred to as "supreme Akanishtha"—is the foremost of all realms. It is the pure realm of Ghanvyuha [Dense Array], experienced by innumerable bodhisattvas on the tenth level of realization, dakas and dakinis, and mahasiddhas. This is why, for example, the introductory sections of most tantras contain passages such as "In the environment of Akanishtha, without limit or cen-

ter, an immeasurable ground, the ongoing lucid state of timeless awareness. . . ." *The Discourse of Ghanavyuha* states:

> Beyond the realms of formlessness, desire, and form,
> as well as the state of "no perception"—
> it is beyond these environments.
> Powerful buddhas abide there.
> In the mandala of Ghanavyuha
>
> . . . .
>
> the teachings are a dense, uncompounded array.
> Those who become perfect buddhas awaken to
>   buddhahood there;
> one emanation awakened to buddhahood in our world.

Thus, emanations issue forth from the pure realm of Akanishtha
throughout the ten directions, in the innumerable and boundless realms
of the six classes of beings. They emanate in accord with the specific
perceptions of those beings and ensure benefit for them. For example,
Shakyamuni appeared in our human world of Jambudvipa when the av-
erage life span was one hundred years. As the preceding source states:

> Once even the purest worldly realms have been left behind,
> there is the pleasing environment of Akanishtha.
> Those who become perfect buddhas awaken to
>   buddhahood there; [194a]
> one emanation awakened to buddhahood in our world.

In this regard, in the context of dharmakaya, the fundamentally
unconditioned state of naturally occurring timeless awareness, which
abides in its three aspects of essence, nature, and responsiveness, is the
ground for all that arises. It is due to this quality of timeless awareness
that the two aspects of rupakaya emanate to become evident outwardly.
This is called "the arising of rupakaya from dharmakaya."

In the context of dharmakaya, the teacher is Samantabhadra, the
teacher of perfect mastery. The teaching is natural great perfection,
truly uncompounded. The environment is the inconceivable basic space
of phenomena. The retinue consists of the vast hosts of naturally occurring timeless awareness. The occasion is the time of fourfold perfection,
without transition or change. This is similar to what *The Web of Magic*
calls "indeterminate time."

The circumstances of sambhogakaya are such that the teachers are the five "regent teachers"—the five families of Gangchentso [Lake of Vast Glaciers]. The environment is Ghanavyuha—the pure, naturally apparent realm of Akanishtha. The teaching is solely that of the mahayana approach. The retinue consists of buddhas and bodhisattvas who are the teacher's own manifestations—not other than the teacher—as well as dakas and dakinis, masters of awareness, and others whose good fortune is equivalent to that of bodhisattvas on the tenth level of realization. The occasion is the eternal present. As *The Ocean of Magic* states:

> Naturally manifest victorious ones, bodhisattvas,
> great bodhisattvas, great arhats, [194b]
> primordial victorious ones, those who are victorious on the levels
>   of realization . . .

And *The Entrance into the Middle Way* states:

> The kaya of peace illuminates like a wish-granting tree,
> yet like a wish-fulfilling gem it involves no thought.
> Until beings are liberated, it is ever-present, so as to be involved
>   with the world.
> It is manifest, yet free of conceptual elaboration.

And *The Highest Continuum* states:

> The powerful spiritual lord vanquished the mara of death.
> In essence nonexistent, the guide of the universe is
>   ever-present.

And *The Ornament of Manifest Realization* states:

> This embodiment of the thirty-two major marks
> and eighty minor marks of perfection
> thoroughly enjoys the wealth of the mahayana approach,
> and so is held to be the sambhogakaya of the sages.

And a commentary on the preceding source states:

> Because there is thorough appreciation of the extremely abundant joy and bliss of the mahayana teachings, this embodiment, which in its very essence has the thirty-two major and eighty minor marks of perfection, is the sambhogakaya of the sages who are buddhas, transcendent and accomplished conquerors.

As for the nirmanakaya, the teacher is called "the teacher as a sacred leader," from the point of view that he or she guides impure mortal beings. The environment is as varied as it is unpredictable, due to the variety of the universes of those to be guided. The retinue comprises countless beings to be guided—gods, humans, and so forth. The teaching consists of a variety of spiritual approaches, corresponding to the acumen of these beings. The occasion is any one of the three phases of past, present, or future. [195a] In particular, it is the present moment when spiritual teachings occur due to the coming together of the preceding four aspects of excellence. The nirmanakaya ensures benefit for as long as samsara continues. *The Ornament of Manifest Realization* states:

> An enlightened embodiment who ensures
> a range of benefit for beings impartially
> for as long as conditioned existence continues—
> such a one is the uninterrupted nirmanakaya of the sages.

The three kayas, being of one taste in dharmakaya, are beyond being manifest or not. But within that context, the two aspects of rupakaya arise as a display due to the dynamic energy of responsiveness and are labeled "sambhogakaya" and "nirmanakaya." This is a case of applying the name of a cause to an effect—like saying the sun is shining inside when the rays of the sun enter a house. The actual sambhogakaya is the quality of spontaneously present lucidity—the nature of awareness within the context of dharmakaya—and abides as a ground for what arises. The actual nirmanakaya is the quality of responsiveness inherent in timeless awareness. This being the case, the three kayas constitute an inseparable unity. *Naturally Arising Awareness* states:

> Though by nature a unity, the three kayas
> magically appear to be manifold.[15]
> Dharmakaya is free of being an object of the imagination.
> Sambhogakaya is free of the mara of concepts.
> Nirmanakaya is free of being a phenomenon that can
>   be characterized.

That is to say, dharmakaya is the empty essence of being—unobstructed awareness. Its display is the vast reach of completely nonconceptual timeless awareness. Sambhogakaya is the nature of being—the spontaneous presence of lucidity. Its display consists of the buddhas of the five families, resplendent with the major and minor marks of perfection. Nirmanakaya is timeless awareness as all-pervasive responsiveness [195b] in its aspect as a ground for what arises. Its display consists of teachers who manifest in whatever way is necessary to guide under any circumstances.

It is crucial to distinguish between the three kayas and their display. If you do not, the conclusions you reach will be erroneous. Since the three kayas are identical in essence, it would seem to follow that dharmakaya is manifest, just as nirmanakaya and sambhogakaya manifest for those to be guided. Or it would seem to follow that just as dharmakaya is not manifest, it would be impossible for the two aspects of rupakaya to manifest for those to be guided, because the kayas are identical in essence. This is reminiscent, for example, of the reasoning that there cannot be two aspects, one obscured and one unobscured, to which *The Thorough Determination of Valid Cognition* refers: "This does not follow when things are of an identical nature." But there is a key point here, which lies in the interpretation of such lines of reasoning. Seen in this light, given that the three kayas are present in dharmakaya, it follows that the twofold display of the rupakaya does manifest so that it becomes evident outwardly for those to be guided, just as it follows that, given the potential to refract light of five colors that is present in a crystal, when the crystal is brought into contact with sunlight as a condition, five-colored light shines forth to become evident outwardly. *The Six Expanses* states:

> Therefore, one's fundamentally unconditioned nature is present
> in such a way that
> there is its very essence, as well as the manifestations
> of its nature and its responsiveness,
> appearing to those with ordinary consciousness.
> While the essence has never existed as anything,
> the nature manifests as the clearly apparent aspect of things.
> Due to the quality of responsiveness, two aspects of
> timeless awareness
> arise without plan or action.
> Because of the two aspects of consciousness—arising and
> manifestation—
> there are the corresponding actions[16] of timeless awareness.
> They manifest free of effort or achievement.

The "two aspects of consciousness" referred to are as follows: In the perceptions of those whose minds are purified and who are to be guided by the sambhogakaya, benefit is ensured by the sambhogakaya as the display "arising" due to spontaneous presence, the nature of timeless awareness. [196a] In the perceptions of those whose minds are impure and who are to be guided by the nirmanakaya, benefit is ensured by the "manifestation" of the nirmanakaya as the display that arises due to the all-pervasive responsiveness of timeless awareness.

Fruition

In the preceding discussions, which establish the logic underlying the kayas and timeless awareness, as well as what this implies, I have proved their interrelationship. Now I will explain in detail the classification of the kayas and timeless awareness that are thus interrelated. This involves three topics.

Dharmakaya and Timeless Awareness

First, dharmakaya and the aspects of timeless awareness it entails can be discussed in detail:

> The essence of dharmakaya is naturally occurring timeless
>   awareness.
> Its display is the reservoir of omniscient timeless awareness,
>   abiding as the single sphere of being within primordial
>   basic space.

The timelessly pure essence of awareness, which abides as the heart essence of dharmakaya, has become fully evident at this point. It is referred to as "the precious secret matrix that is originally pure dharmakaya." Since it abides as the unique sphere of being free of elaboration, in which the kayas and timeless awareness are a unity beyond union or separation, it is the province of buddhahood alone, for it is beyond being an object that can be imagined or described. Timeless awareness, as the ground for what arises, has a subtle quality of profound lucidity, but other than this the kayas and timeless awareness have never existed in the slightest as distinct entities separate from one another.

Of the three—essence, nature, and responsiveness—the essence abides as the fundamental kaya, so that it is the ground from which the three distinguishable kayas arise, but it is not a distinct entity that can be characterized. The nature is an utterly lucid ground for what arises, but it is not an entity with distinct colors. And responsiveness is the aspect that is a ground for what arises within timeless awareness, but it is not a distinct form that becomes a sense object. So there are simply the distinguishable qualities of the kayas and timeless awareness, [196b] and the distinguishable qualities of the three kayas are actually present as essence, nature, and responsiveness. *The Reverberation of Sound* states:

> Furthermore, since the essence abides as the fundamental kaya,
> the aspects of dharmakaya, sambhogakaya, and nirmanakaya
> are such that they are undivided and indivisible.
> This is ensured by their natural condition,
> so they are not mental objects, such as forms with colors.
> The way in which the nature accounts for lights arising
> as white, red, yellow, green, and dark blue
> is such that they are not distinct entities[17] that can
>   be characterized,
> for they are ensured by the natural condition of all that can
>   be known—that it is not subject to division.
> Responsiveness is a multifaceted ground for what arises;
> even though it cannot be determined to be any one thing,
> it is called "ground," for sensory appearances manifest in all
>   their variety.

From the standpoint of the essence as the unique state of dharmakaya, it has never existed as anything whatsoever and so reaches consummation at the point of resolution. The same source states:

> Although one cannot describe the fruition,
> one has reached the level on which phenomena resolve.
> One's philosophical system collapses.
> Within this context, the guru's pith instructions are eclipsed.
> Since the limitations imposed by view, meditation, and conduct
>   are absent,
> nothing exists that manifests as a phenomenon.
> Since the continuity of the kayas and timeless awareness
>   is undermined,
> no buddhas exist, no ordinary beings exist.
> In brief, nothing whatsoever abides,
> and since nothing has gone, nothing comes.

And *The Six Expanses* states:

> You should hold well in your mind[18] what I have revealed about the fruition that occurs[19] throughout the three times. Whoever is familiar with the pervasive radiance of dharmakaya, empty yet lucid, is free in his or her very body.

In this context, since dharmakaya abides uniquely, [197a] it is ensured as Samantabhadra, the "original guide." Since benefit for others arises within that context, it is called "vajra holder." The same tantra states:

> This is the fruition of all buddhas of the three times, naturally
>> present as the essence of Samantabhadra.
> Whoever is familiar with this fruition of the buddhas will also
>> become a glorious vajra holder.
> Since the original guide, flawless and pure, arises spontaneously
>> within the matrix[20] of light,
> the kaya of the supreme, sublime secret is attained as the
>> embodiment of the deeds of all buddhas.
> Fortunate ones with powerful, dynamic minds—yogins who
>> know they will not regress—
> have reached the full expression of the entire fruition, their
>> fortune equal to that of Samantabhadra.

To clearly demonstrate dharmakaya, as described, I will discuss the actual dharmakaya as a support and present a detailed categorization of timeless awareness as what is supported.

DHARMAKAYA AS A SUPPORT

My explanation of dharmakaya as a support has three topics—its essence, the meaning of the term, and its classification. The essence of dharmakaya is basic space endowed with twofold purity and free of all limitations imposed by elaboration. Without transition or change, this is the essence of naturally occurring awareness—profoundly lucid timeless awareness. *Naturally Arising Awareness* states:

> The essence of dharmakaya has three qualities—
> it is unchanging, unceasing, and pervasive.

As for the meaning of the term, it is "dharmakaya" [embodiment of truth] (*chos sku*) because it is the "truth" (*chos*) of original purity, empty

yet lucid—the consummate goal one aspires to—and is the "embodiment" (*sku*), or basic space, that is the ground from which the totality of
the kayas and timeless awareness arises. The same tantra states:

> Imperishable, empty, and lucid— [197b]
> these three qualities define "dharmakaya."[21]

As for the classification of dharmakaya, since in its very essence it is
beyond limitations imposed by elaboration, it is indivisible, but there is
no harm in analyzing it from the point of view of certain aspects or facets of its qualities. Thus, if dharmakaya is analyzed according to such
secondary factors, there are two classifications—a general one, of its nature as the five aspects of excellence, and a specific one, of its nature as
the five facets of enlightened form, speech, mind, qualities, and activity.

In the first case, these five aspects of excellence can be considered
from the standpoint of dharmakaya's distinct expressions. In the context of "the dharmakaya aspect of dharmakaya," the pure realm is inconceivable and the environment is the true nature of phenomena, beyond imagination. Meditative absorption is the supreme, unwavering
state. The retinue in all its variety is by nature none other than dharmakaya. The teaching is the inexpressible nature of phenomena. The occasion is that of the true nature of phenomena, in which there is no change
whatsoever.

In the context of "the sambhogakaya aspect of dharmakaya," the
pure realm is the impeccable, immaculate realm and the environment is
the state in which the ordinary mind's concepts have been cut through.
Meditative absorption is the state in which there is none of the purposeful intent of ordinary mind and mental events. The retinue is emptiness,
which allows for the appearance of awareness's own manifestations.
The teaching is the total purity underlying any frame of reference. The
occasion is that of the true nature of phenomena, which is not some permanent "thing."

In the context of "the nirmanakaya aspect of dharmakaya," the pure
realm is emptiness, which is not restricted in any way whatsoever, and
the environment abides as the aspect that is the ground for all that arises.
Meditative absorption is the continuous state of natural lucidity. The
retinue consists of the three indivisible kayas, which are ensured in and
of themselves. The teaching is the uncontrived nature. The occasion is
the overt manifestation of the heart essence. [198a]

Naturally Arising Awareness discusses the preceding extensively, in passages such as the following:

> The realm of dharmakaya has three qualities—
> it is lucid, radiant,[22] and unadulterated.
> The environment of dharmakaya has three qualities—
> it is immeasurable, has no frame of reference, and entails
>   no reification.
> The conduct of dharmakaya has three qualities—
> it is unceasing, without fixation, and without
>   attachment.
> The meditation of dharmakaya has three qualities—
> it is vivid, steadfast, and undistracted.

In classifying dharmakaya as the five facets of enlightened form, speech, mind, qualities, and activity, *The Reverberation of Sound,* for example, states:

> As for dharmakaya, it is enlightened form, speech,
> mind, qualities, and activity.
> Enlightened form is by nature empty, clearly evident,
> and beyond characterization.
> Enlightened speech is free of terms, words, and labels
> and is inexpressible, beyond discussion.
> Enlightened mind entails no thought or mental stirring
> and is beyond proliferating thoughts and analysis.[23]
> Enlightened qualities neither increase nor deteriorate.[24]
> They pervade basic space and timeless awareness
> and are by nature uncontrived.
> Enlightened activity does not "occur," but is unborn,[25]
> automatic, and continuous;
> it is not made to happen and does not cause anything
>   to happen.

And *Naturally Arising Awareness* states:

> One occurs, two occur, everything occurs—
> these are the enlightened qualities of dharmakaya.
> Not to be achieved, already achieved, perfectly achieved—
> this is the enlightened activity of dharmakaya.
> Existing neither outwardly nor inwardly nor in basic space[26]—
> this is the natural body of dharmakaya.

TIMELESS AWARENESS AS WHAT IS SUPPORTED

This discussion of timeless awareness as what is supported has two topics—a general presentation and a specific explanation of timeless awareness as dharmakaya.

In general, when you are free within the unique state of dharmakaya—the consummate state of original purity—"threefold timeless awareness abiding as the ground of being" [198b] functions as the ground from which the kayas and timeless awareness arise to become evident outwardly. "Timeless awareness that exhibits attributes" reveals its manifestations to pure individuals who are to be guided, while "timeless awareness of the knowable" fulfills the hopes of impure individuals who are to be guided. *The Reverberation of Sound* states:

> Mind itself, thus free,
> does not lack responsiveness.
> Timeless awareness abiding as the ground of being
> functions as the ground for what arises naturally,
> of its own accord.
> The influence of timeless awareness that exhibits attributes
> ripens[27] those who are pure.
> Timeless awareness that understands the knowable
> grants spiritual attainments to those with devotion.

Of the three aspects, the first is timeless awareness as dharmakaya. The explanation of this has two parts—a brief presentation and an extensive explanation. As for the brief presentation, the same tantra states:

> Furthermore, when one's experience of mind itself has matured,
> the ground of being is found in dharmakaya.
> Since it is originally pure, distortions fall away;
> its essence is timelessly unconfused.
> It is unceasing spontaneous presence that accounts for all
> that arises;
> such a nature is not finite.
> Since it permeates everything, it is responsiveness;
> samsara is not cut off from nirvana.

The extensive explanation has three parts—timeless awareness as the originally pure essence of being, the empty quality of awareness that is free of elaboration and so is the unique sphere of being as basic space; timeless awareness as the spontaneously present nature of being, its lucid quality, functioning as the ground of enlightened qualities; and timeless awareness as all-pervasive responsiveness, abiding as the open avenue for the process of arising, and so evoking, in all their limpidity, the rupakayas and the aspects of timeless awareness they entail. *The Reverberation of Sound* states:

> Within "timeless awareness as the originally pure essence
>   of being," [199a]
> not even the word "nonrecognition" is possible.
> The limiting enumerations of unity and duality do not apply to it.
> Being only imputations, things have never existed or not existed.
> The true nature of phenomena, which is in no way divisible,
> is such that nothing has ever existed, even as timeless awareness.
> There are no words for it and it has never existed as
>   something describable.
> Pure self-knowing awareness does not abide in extremes—
> the limitations imposed by descriptive words and labels[28]
>   have fallen away.
> It has no cause, no multitude of conditions,
> no dualistic manifestation of sense objects and a subjective perceiver.
> It has no characteristics whatsoever to be analyzed.
> Circumstances on the gross level resolve naturally.
> It is pure, pure in that it has never existed.
> Since there cease to be thoughts based on confusion, it does not
>   act in any way.
> Since it is unborn, it is devoid of cessation.
>
> "Timeless awareness as the spontaneously present nature of being"
> is unborn, unceasing, and does not deliberately intend
>   anything at all,
> because its pure scope is not finite.
> Given that its dynamic energy and enlightened qualities are
>   continuous,
> what manifests is simply a display,
> for it is the ground in which things in all their variety are perfect.
> Because it is nonexistent it can manifest, but because it manifests
>   it is empty.
> This is the embodiment of the primordial unity of appearance
>   and emptiness.
> Buddhas and ordinary beings are its pure objects.

The "ground" truly abides in this way.
Its nature is pure and impeccable,
while from the standpoint of its essence it is devoid of imputation.
Since it gives rise to elaboration, its knowledge is perfect.
Since it abides naturally and is spontaneously present,
it involves neither rejection nor acceptance.

Due to "timeless awareness as all-pervasive responsiveness,"
there is an avenue for the arising of things, uncreated,
    in all their variety,
so that enlightened actions that seem to manifest are perfect
    in its essence.
Due to the empty nature of dharmakaya,
the quality of perfect knowing—timeless awareness— [199b]
arises automatically for beings.
This knowing quality is aware and lucid,
for without it, samsara and nirvana would be cut off from one another.
Due to the very nature of lucid self-knowing awareness,
responsiveness itself as a natural power
is uninterrupted and continuous.
Due to their purity, the elements
are the unobscured natural attributes
of a single state of perfection, without any activity taking place,
like light from the sun.

Sambhogakaya and Timeless Awareness

Now, sambhogakaya and the aspects of timeless awareness it entails can
be discussed:

> The essence of sambhogakaya is the spontaneously present
>   nature of being.
> Its display is the five buddha families and the five aspects
>   of timeless awareness,
> manifesting to fill all realms of space.

The spontaneously present quality that is the nature of awareness
is the actual sambhogakaya, which embodies the perfection of enlightened qualities. While it is in essence inseparable from dharmakaya, it
is due to this quality that the specific forms of the buddhas of the five
families manifest to become evident outwardly and thus fill all realms

of space. These, together with the five corresponding aspects of time-less awareness that exhibits attributes, constitute sambhogakaya as a display, which is referred to as "Gangchentso, occurring naturally as the central principle of all mandalas."

There are two parts—an explanation of the nature of this kaya as a support and a detailed presentation of the nature of timeless awareness as what is supported.

SAMBHOGAKAYA AS A SUPPORT

Sambhogakaya as a support has three topics—its essence, the meaning of the term, and its classification. In essence, it is the embodiment of spontaneously present timeless awareness, endowed with the major and minor marks of perfection, clearly apparent yet without independent nature. *Naturally Arising Awareness* states:

> Having specific colors and distinct names,
> bearing the noble major and minor marks of perfection,
>   radiating rays of light, [200a]
> appearing as masculine and feminine deities,
> and exhibiting the features of enlightened form—
> these are the attributes of sambhogakaya.

As for the meaning of the term "sambhogakaya" [embodiment of the perfection of expressed enjoyment] (*longs spyod rdzogs pa'i sku*), the same tantra states:

> Since its clarity and distinctness are all-pervasive, it is "expressed" (*longs*).
> Since its five manifestations cannot be characterized, it is "enjoyment" (*spyod*).
> Since these manifest simultaneously while in actuality they have no frame of reference, it is "perfect-" (*rdzogs*);
> "-ion" (*pa*) refers to unimpeded emptiness, clearly manifest in various ways.
> Since these manifestations[29] retain their specific attributes, it is an "embodiment" (*sku*).

As for the classification of sambhogakaya, there are three groupings of five elements each.

If it is first classified according to the five aspects of excellence, combining these with its distinct expressions as the three kayas gives a total of fifteen topics. In the context of "the dharmakaya aspect of sambhogakaya," the teacher is the form of Vairochana known as Gangchentso, whose presence manifests as transparent inwardly if viewed from without and transparent outwardly if viewed from within, who has no front or back, and whose face gazes panoramically in all ten directions. The pure realm is that of mastery over the twenty-one universes held in the palms of Vairochana's hands, and the environment is the totally pure realm of Ghanavyuha. The retinue is none other than Vairochana. The teaching is the inherent manifestation of naturally occurring awareness. The occasion is that of realization becoming fully evident.

In the context of "the sambhogakaya aspect of sambhogakaya," the teachers are the principal buddhas of the specific families, whose attributes are such that they are essentially distinct yet identical in nature. The pure realms are the innumerable mandalas of the specific buddha families, and the environment is Akanishtha Ghanavyuha. The retinue consists of the five families of the respective buddhas. The teaching is the five aspects of timeless awareness as a quality of knowing. [200b] The occasion is that of sensory appearances forming and evolving.

In the context of "the nirmanakaya aspect of sambhogakaya," the teachers are the five principal buddhas of the specific families, whose attributes are such that they are apparent yet have no independent nature—clearly evident yet entailing no concepts. The pure realm of this aspect is enjoyed by countless hundreds of thousands of gods and goddesses who abide naturally therein, and the environment is that of pure timeless awareness, the supremely blissful realm of Alakavati [Willowbanks], which is completely uncompounded. The retinue consists of the specific buddhas and mandalas that are these principal buddhas' own manifestations. The occasion is that of awareness's own manifestations becoming apparent.

Regarding the classification into the five families, *Naturally Arising Awareness* states:

> Furthermore, the buddha families manifest as fivefold—
> the tathagata family, the vajra family, the ratna family,
> the padma family, and the karma family.

. . . .

Vairochana, Vajrasattva,
likewise Ratnasambhava, Amitabha, and Amoghasiddhi.

Regarding the classification into the five facets of enlightened form, speech, mind, qualities, and activity, *The Reverberation of Sound* states:

For the sambhogakaya as well, there are the five facets
of form, speech, mind, qualities, and activity.
Enlightened form is clearly apparent yet has no
    independent nature,
and awareness permeates both what is illuminated
    and what illuminates.
Enlightened speech is naturally occurring, naturally manifest,
an ongoing process of proliferation and resolution.
Enlightened mind is uninterrupted vision,
the dynamic energy of knowing, and enlightened intent.
Enlightened qualities consist of the perfection of the major
    and minor marks,
as well as the perfection of lucid enlightened intent and sublime
    states of perception.
Enlightened activity develops on outer, inner, and secret levels
of the wheel of spiritual teachings. [201a]
For the buddhas of the specific families,
as well as for bodhisattvas,
these teachings proliferate from the principal buddhas' "naturally
    occurring tongues."
They reveal themselves to the retinue through their own essence.

TIMELESS AWARENESS AS WHAT IS SUPPORTED

There are two topics concerning the nature of timeless awareness as what is supported. A concise presentation is given in the same tantra:

Timeless awareness in the context of sambhogakaya exhibits
    attributes.
Since things of the sensory world are pure, there is mirrorlike
    awareness—
clearly reflecting samsara and nirvana.
Since there are no extremes or biases, there is awareness as equalness.
Discerning awareness reveals[30] the objects of the senses.

There is awareness as spontaneous fulfillment, since no effort
   is involved.
Since these aspects are not separate and distinct, there is
   awareness as the basic space of phenomena.

The detailed explanation of this has five parts. "Timeless awareness
as the basic space of phenomena" (*chos dbyings ye shes*) is the source of
empty yet lucid awareness. *Naturally Arising Awareness* states:

Timeless awareness as the basic space of phenomena entails
   three factors—
supreme emptiness as its very domain,
lucidity as its luminous manifestation,
and timeless awareness as the sphere of awareness's activity.
With the coming together of these three factors, there is "basic space."

The Reverberation of Sound discusses the essence of this timeless
awareness, as well as the meaning of the term:

The basic space of phenomena, being spacious,
cannot be conceived of in terms of limit or center,
and so it is the pure nature of phenomena, the ground of freedom.
As for how "phenomena" (*chos*) are dealt with,
there is nothing to be done in the world or beyond it[31]—
their nature is clearly evident and pure.
With the open dimension of "basic space" (*dbyings*),
there is the supreme, naturally occurring environment.
"Timeless" (*ye*) refers to the epitome of perfection,[32]
uncontrived from the very beginning.
"Awareness" (*shes*) frees one from the duality of samsara and
   nirvana— [201b]
it is enlightened intent as awareness's own perfect manifestation.

Naturally Arising Awareness discusses "mirrorlike timeless awareness" (*me long lta bu'i ye shes*), as well as the metaphor this term entails:

As for mirrorlike timeless awareness, take this example:
just as anything placed before a mirror
is reflected on its surface,
so also the manifestations of pure timeless awareness
are clearly apparent within immaculate awareness.

And *The Reverberation of Sound* states:

> Within mirrorlike timeless awareness, due to the process
>   of reflection[33]
> the manifest aspect—shapes and colors—is complete.
> Because it is transparent and purified of any distortion, there is light.[34]
> It manifests as a natural attribute, linking samsara and nirvana.
> Since it illuminates[35] the forms of all phenomena,
> it is termed "self-knowing timeless awareness."
> It is lucid yet empty and, being empty, is free.
> Concepts about the extremes of freedom and bondage are
>   resolved.
> It is naturally free without being brought to rest—perfect within
>   the ground of being.[36]

Naturally Arising Awareness discusses "timeless awareness as equalness" (*mnyam nyid ye shes*):

> In the essential equalness of phenomena
> there is no falling to any extreme.

And *The Reverberation of Sound* states:

> What is called "equalness"
> entails two causal factors and three conditions of equalness,
> as well as the occasion and full expression of equalness.
> It is nondual and free of bias,
> undivided, indivisible, and a naturally abiding state.
> The term "equal-" (*mnyam*) means that the true nature
>   of phenomena
> is free of deleterious elaboration;
> "-ness" (*nyid*) means that it is uncontrived and involves no effort
>   or achievement.
> It abides naturally and is empty in essence.
> It is mind itself—all thoughts have resolved.
> Though "timeless awareness" (*ye shes*) abides,
> realization of its attributes shows
> that it does not abide as either samsara or nirvana. [202a]

The "two causal factors of equalness" are samsara and nirvana; the "three conditions of equalness" are sensory appearances, emptiness, and the realization of their nonduality. The "occasion of equalness" becomes fully evident in the context of the consummate fruition, while to be brought to the state of resolution is the "full expression of equalness."

As for "discerning timeless awareness" (*so sor rtog pa'i ye shes*) [lit. "timeless awareness that cognizes things individually"], *Naturally Arising Awareness* states:

> As for discerning timeless awareness,
> it is realized to be awareness free of plans or actions.

And *The Reverberation of Sound* states:

> Discernment involves the various sensory faculties.
> Whatever phenomena manifest, and however they do so,
> they are clearly apparent in their individual contexts.
> When one's perception of awareness's own manifestations
>   is purified,
> they themselves become the scope of awareness.
> Due to their "individual" quality (*so so*), which is to say,
>   their distinctness,
> they occur such that they are antidotes.
> The "cognizing" aspect (*rtog pa*) perceives their
>   characteristics.
> Awareness's own manifestations entail a quality of increase.
> "Timeless awareness" (*ye shes*), since it occurs primordially,
> is awareness that purifies the flaws of the afflictive emotions.

As for "timeless awareness as spontaneous fulfillment" (*bya ba grub pa'i ye shes*), *Naturally Arising Awareness* states:

> As for timeless awareness as spontaneous fulfillment,
> whatever manifests is perfect within the scope of awareness.

And *The Reverberation of Sound* states:

> As for what is called "spontaneous fulfillment" (*bya ba grub pa*),
> effort and striving have naturally ceased,
> and all phenomena are naturally free in a natural state of rest.
> Due to the perfect state of natural freedom—the ground of being
>   manifesting as sensory appearances—

an extremely subtle, immaculate, and undistorted state
is attained.
It is beyond the scope of conceptual analysis—
it is the true nature of phenomena, not divisible in any way.
Since there is natural perfection, the limitations of ordinary
perception have resolved.
Due to instantaneous realization, there is "what is to be fulfilled"
(*bya ba*).
Due to its being spontaneously "accomplished" (*grub pa*),
in a state free of desire there is no need to repeat that accomplishment
and no backsliding from it.
"Timeless" (*ye*) has the meaning of "abiding."
With "awareness" (*shes*), this becomes fully evident,
so that one has reached the state in which phenomena resolve.

Nirmanakaya and Timeless Awareness

Nirmanakaya and the timeless awareness it entails [202b] can be discussed as follows:

> The essence of nirmanakaya is the ground for the arising
> of responsiveness.
> Its display manifests in whatever way is necessary to guide
> under any circumstances,
> while its supreme enlightened activity brings mastery.

In this regard, responsiveness itself is identical in essence to dharmakaya, and nirmanakaya—the display of this responsiveness—manifests as distinct teachers for spiritually undeveloped people, shravakas,
pratyekabuddhas, and other impure individuals who are to be guided.
This detailed definitive treatment of nirmanakaya has two topics—the
nature of this kaya as a support and the nature of timeless awareness as
what is supported.

NIRMANAKAYA AS A SUPPORT

Nirmanakaya has three topics—its essence, the meaning of the term,
and its classification. As for its essence, it is the nirmanakaya because it
manifests in accord with circumstances, is unpredictable, and is transitory. *Naturally Arising Awareness* states:

> Nirmanakayas . . . reveal themselves in whatever way is necessary
>   to guide;
> in manifesting in accord with others' perceptions,
> they are not deluded about what is in the interest of others
> and can appear as anything at all.

The same tantra discusses the meaning of the term "nirmanakaya" [embodiment of emanation] (*sprul pa'i sku*):

> O Lord of Secrets, you should understand that the following statements concern the meaning of "nirmanakaya": It is the embodiment of emanation because it manifests in accord with the perceptions of all ordinary beings in the universe. It is the embodiment of emanation because it is capable of ensuring benefit. It is the embodiment of emanation because it does all that is to be done. It is the embodiment of emanation because it liberates countless beings.[37] It is the embodiment of emanation because it is transitory in any given realm. It is the embodiment of emanation because responsiveness arises without bias.

There are three ways of classifying it. [203a] If it is classified according to its enlightened actions, there are two kinds. Nirmanakayas "who have completed all that is to be done" refers to those who are not yet released from the physical body, but whose minds have matured into dharmakaya, so that benefit is ensured. Nirmanakayas "who do what is to be done" refers to the distinct display that arises from basic space. Or the classification can be threefold—emanations who benefit through artistic expression, those who emanate through conscious rebirth, and sublime emanations. *Naturally Arising Awareness* states:

> There are held to be two kinds of nirmanakayas—
> those who have completed all that is to be done
> and those who do what is to be done.
> Nirmanakayas who have completed all that is to be done
> awaken to actual buddhahood with the freeing of their
>   mindstreams,
> and then emanations issue forth.
> Nirmanakayas who do what is to be done
> reveal themselves in whatever way is necessary to guide;
> in manifesting in accord with others' perceptions,
> they are similar to the preceding kind.

And *The Ornament of the Sutra Category* states:

> The emanations of sublime enlightenment
> are those of artistic expression, conscious rebirth,
>   and supreme enlightenment.
> The nirmanakaya of buddhahood
> is the supreme skillful means of total freedom.

If nirmanakaya is classified according to the five aspects of excellence, these can be considered from the standpoint of nirmanakaya's distinct expressions. In the context of "the dharmakaya aspect of nirmanakaya," the teacher is supreme Vajradhara, whose attributes constitute the commitment to manifest in physical form through any of the four modes of rebirth and to complete the thirty-six deeds of an enlightened being. The pure realm is a state of mastery over countless billions of three-thousand-fold universes, and the environment is the realm called Endowed with a Thousand Lotuses. The retinue consists of beings born through any of the four modes of rebirth. The teaching is *The Reverberation of Sound*, the source of all categories of the teachings. The occasion [203b] is the time when people live for countless years.

In the context of "the sambhogakaya aspect of nirmanakaya," the teacher is the glorious Vajrasattva. The pure realm is that of a billion three-thousand-fold universes, and the environment is in harmony with the perceptions of those to be guided. The retinue consists of bodhisattvas on the eighth level of realization or higher. The teaching is the spiritual approach that concerns the definitive meaning. The occasion is unpredictable.

In the context of "the nirmanakaya aspect of nirmanakaya," the teacher is Shakyamuni, whose nature was such that he was able to ordain himself a monk by virtue of his naturally occurring splendor. The pure realm is a universe such as this—our universe of sorrow, which consists of a billion world systems—and the environment includes places like Vulture Peak. The retinue is varied, made up of gods, humans, and other beings. The teaching consists of a variety of spiritual approaches, oriented toward both causes and results. The occasion is any opportunity to cut through doubt with total certainty.

In classifying nirmanakaya according to the five facets of enlightened form, speech, mind, qualities, and activity, *The Reverberation of Sound* states:

Nirmanakaya, moreover, has five facets—
enlightened form, speech, mind, qualities, and activity.
Enlightened form, with the major and minor marks
    of perfection,
emanates in a body in whatever way is necessary to guide[38] those
    to be guided.
The words of enlightened speech are elegant,
with sixty melodious qualities.
Enlightened mind abides as the enlightened intent to benefit both
    oneself and others
and is timeless awareness of the knowable.
Enlightened qualities are the perfection of wisdom.
Enlightened activity is the perfection
of all actions without exception—outer, inner, and secret—
and abides as the five aspects of excellence.

TIMELESS AWARENESS AS WHAT IS SUPPORTED

There are two topics concerning timeless awareness as what is supported. [204a] A concise presentation is given in the same tantra:

> For the nirmanakaya, through knowledge of things just as they are,
> the benefit for oneself lies in understanding the way of abiding
>   of all things.
> Through knowledge of things in all their multiplicity,
> one understands what is in the minds of those to be guided.

As for the extensive explanation, due to "knowledge of things just as they are" (*ji lta ba mkhyen pa*) there is unerring knowledge of the way of abiding, and due to "knowledge of things in all their multiplicity" (*ji snyed pa mkhyen pa*) there is knowledge of the unlimited causes and effects involved in the way sensory appearances manifest. *The Reverberation of Sound* discusses the essence of these two aspects, as well as the meanings of the terms:

> Timeless awareness that encompasses the knowable
> is understood to have two aspects.
> Of these, I will explain knowledge of things in all
>   their multiplicity.
> This is knowing the minds of those to be guided.
> Due to a thorough mastery of what benefits others,

there is understanding of the true nature of phenomena.
"In all their" (*ji*) refers to the way of abiding,
while "multiplicity" (*snyed pa*) refers to perfect "knowledge"
    (*mkhyen pa*) of everything without exception.
"Timeless" refers to benefit for all beings,
while "awareness" lifts them from the pit of the three realms.
The nirmanakaya's knowing quality
is perfect in light of awareness's own manifestations.

I will explain timeless awareness as knowledge of things just
    as they are.
While there is no basis for describing things, given their
    manifest quality
the pure reflections of awareness's own manifestations are
    clearly apparent.
With knowledge of the way things abide,
one ensures one's own benefit, so the flow of confusion
    is exhausted.
"Just" (*ji*) refers to the way of abiding,
while "as they are" (*lta ba*) means reaching the undistracted state
    of resolution.[39]
Because it is continuous, "knowledge" (*mkhyen pa*) is perfect.
"Timeless" refers to what serves as the path,
while "awareness" is the full expression of that.

Such is the fruition of the kayas and timeless awareness that becomes
fully evident. [204b] If you wonder where these come from, I will explain:

The kayas are not achieved by effort involving cause and effect.
They are timelessly and spontaneously present, manifesting
    within a state of resting imperturbably.
The most sublime secret manifests in this lifetime.
You are not lured away from it in the interval after death,
and so the pinnacle approach of the vajra heart essence
    is exalted above all other approaches, based as they are on
    causes or results.

The sacred fruition of the kayas and timeless awareness is timelessly
and spontaneously present, is uncompounded, and abides within you.
It is made fully evident through the key point of resting imperturbably,

beyond causality, and so this spiritual approach is more exalted than all lower ones. *The Six Expanses* states:

> Born of nonconceptual timeless awareness,
> original buddhahood, timelessly present, is discovered
> through the pith instruction on resting without trying to do so.

Furthermore, *The Highest Continuum* discusses this as being uncompounded and spontaneously present:

> Uncompounded and spontaneously present,
> it is not realized as a result of any circumstances,
> yet is endowed with wisdom, love, and energy.
> This is buddhahood itself, which ensures the two kinds of benefit.

This is the commentary on the thirteenth section of *The Precious Treasury of the Basic Space of Phenomena,* demonstrating that, since all phenomena already constitute the timelessly awakened state of buddhahood, awakening to buddhahood anew happens without effort or achievement.

Conclusion

Thus, the main body of this treatise—the extensive project I have undertaken—is finished. Now the entire work is concluded under seven headings.

The environment in which this work was composed in such an excellent way can be described as follows:

> Such is the song of the vajra heart essence—the true nature
>   of phenomena. [205a]
> This primordially pure nature, equal to space,
> arises naturally in the unchanging environment free of
>   underlying basis or foundation,
> becoming apparent as a display that is without transition
>   or change.

This supreme secret song of the vajra heart essence—the infinite state of spontaneously present genuine being—was composed on the summit of a mountain that is a site of spiritual attainment, a source of all that is precious, a place blessed by the self-arising ruler Padmakara. On this mountaintop, where a hundred visions appeared to me in a single instant and so brought me ease within mind itself, I wrote down this secret song from the dakas and dakinis.

The subject matter, the meaning to be realized, can be identified:

> This is the meaning of the spacious, supreme expanse of being,
>   an infinite state of timeless equalness.

> Without having gone anywhere, you reach your primordial
>   nature.
> This true nature, unwavering and spontaneously present,
> is not subject to restrictions and is free of bias.

I have experienced the universe of appearances and possibilities in its true nature, so I have realized that whatever manifests is naturally occurring timeless awareness. Since I have gained realization of the true nature of phenomena, which involves no coming or going, all effort and striving have been naturally eliminated and I can guarantee my realization, saying, "I have become free of any restrictions or bias." Thus, the auspicious circumstances have been established for me to bless those who study this treatise so that they too may gain realization of the true nature of phenomena. In his song of genuine being, the Glorious Brahmin sings:

> Whatever you perceive, that is suchness.
> Today, like me, your guide, you have cut through confusion.
> Now you do not have to ask anyone about it.

Even in these times in which we live, this became evident to me and so brought me freedom effortlessly. [205b] As the master Haribhadra states:

> Alas! I wearied of various scriptural traditions
> and after a long time, at a place in which I took my ease,
> I beheld the way of the perfection of sublime knowing.

Since I have arrived at the supremely spacious expanse of spontaneous presence, my nature can be shown to be that of one who has mastered the words of this treatise and their meanings:

> The meanings concern the spacious realm equal to space,
>   just as it is.
> There, the monarch of the naturally occurring vast expanse
> never wavers, free in the natural state of things in all their variety.
> I have reached the ultimate womb of basic space, which cannot
>   be characterized as some "thing."

The true measure of those who compose treatises is that they have unerringly fathomed the words and their meanings and thoroughly understand how to compose written commentaries for the sake of others. In my own case, I have unerringly fathomed the vajra themes of natural great perfection. Thus, I am skilled at communicating my bountiful fortune—these words and their meanings—in order to benefit others. I have adorned this text with garlands of scriptural authority, citing commentaries by those who have fathomed the vajra themes—the secrets of the enlightened minds of our teachers, transcendent and accomplished conquerors. While completing this text, I abandoned all external distractions, writing in a one-pointed state of meditative absorption, reflecting on the teachings. Thus, I composed the text on the strength of the ultimate sublime knowing that awakened in me when I arrived at the majestic expanse that is the true nature of phenomena. [206a] To those of you fortunate enough to have a devoted interest in this sublime spiritual approach, my earnest advice is: this text will serve as your eyes, so treat it with the highest respect. As *The Highest Continuum* states:

> Whatever is explained by someone with an undistracted mind—
> solely on the basis of the Victorious One's teachings
> and in accord with the path to the attainment of liberation—
> is treated with as much respect as the words of the Seer himself.

The way in which the text was composed can be described:

> **When my realization was certain, I, a yogin who is like the sky,**
> **wrote this summation of my own experience, together with**
> **appropriate scriptural citations,**
> **setting it down in accord with the twenty-one transmissions**
> **of the Category of Mind,**
> **the three sections of the Category of Expanse, and the four**
> **sections of the Category of Direct Transmission.**

Having accepted the lord of dharma, Kumararaja, as my sacred guru and glorious guide, placing his feet on my head with the utmost respect, I was taken under the care of this spiritually accomplished guide and received his blessings. On the strength of this, I gained mastery over the meaning of natural great perfection and unerring realization of the meaning of mind itself, utterly lucid by nature. Thus, I am not confused about these meanings. With the light rays of my guru's speech shining on the lotus of my mind, I experienced the immensity of his words.

Thus, there unfolded in me an unhindered vision of the vast range of both what was to be discussed and the ways to discuss it.

At that point, once I had become a yogin of the vajra heart essence of utter lucidity, I was certain that the time was right for me to benefit others with my activities. The implication of this is that the opportunities for doing so are as vast as space. Because I have written so well about the meaning of what I have realized, just as it is, [206b] I have ensured benefit for future generations. I have ensured that the philosophical system of my sublime and incomparable vajra master, the second Samantabhadra, will not be impaired and that his teachings have been codified. Though the topics discussed in this text are so profound that ordinary people will find it difficult to fathom their meaning, I have presented them without adulterating them with more common themes, and so have ensured that these teachings concerning the vajra heart essence, the most majestic spiritual approach, will last for a long time in this world. As well, since the themes dealt with in the tantras and pith instructions are so numerous, there are those who cannot synthesize or assemble them. Thus, I have composed this treatise so that by studying it they may easily fathom all these topics.

In answer to potential accusations that I made all this up or am indulging in some personal caprice, I have ensured that masters of the teachings and scriptures will have confidence in it. I have written this work in accord with the three categories—of Mind, Expanse, and Direct Transmission—drawing on citations from scriptures related to them. How could those who are not learned in such scriptural sources gain mastery over these vajra topics? They would be like the congenitally blind, who have no chance or ability to distinguish visual forms. As *The Ornament of the Sutra Category* states:

> A mentor who is disciplined and calm—exceedingly calm—
> who has enlightened qualities, who is diligent, and whose
>   scriptural knowledge is especially rich,
> a person like this is skilled in speaking about consummate realization.
> Cast aside all faintheartedness and rely on such an epitome
>   of kindness.

Apropos of this, there are twenty-one texts in the Category of Mind. Five are the so-called earlier translations—*The Harbinger of Awareness, The Stirring of Supreme Dynamic Energy, The Soaring of the Great*

Garuda, The Smelting of Gold from Ore, and *The Victory Banner That Never Falls.*

Thirteen are the so-called later translations—*The Pinnacle State of Victory Over All Occurrences, The Ruler of Space, The Blissful Array of Inlaid Gems, The General Paradigm of Perfection,* [207a] *The Sphere of Awakened Mind, The Vast Array of Bliss, The Wheel of Life Force, The Six Spheres, The General Definition of Perfection, The Wish-Fulfilling Gem, Awareness in Which Everything Unites, Foremost and Venerable Sanctity,* and *Attaining the Goal of Meditation.*

Together, these two groups are called the "eighteen texts of the Category of Mind." To them are added the following: *The All-Creating Monarch, The Superb Monarch,* and *The Ten Discourses.* In total, then, there are twenty-one texts.

The Category of Expanse has many aspects, but there are three main divisions—the White Expanse, the Black Expanse, and the Multicolored Expanse. The White Expanse has three subdivisions—the Expanse of Space, the Expanse of the Ocean, and the Expanse of Precious Jewels. The Black Expanse has three subdivisions—the Black Expanse of Responsiveness, the Black Expanse of Enlightened Actions, and the Black Expanse of Emanations. And the Multicolored Expanse has three subdivisions—the Multicolored Expanse Conforming to the Category of Mind in Positing Existence, the Multicolored Expanse Conforming to Its Own Key Point in Positing Nonexistence, and the Multicolored Expanse Conforming to the Category of Direct Transmission in Transcending Existence and Nonexistence. The teachings of this category are subsumed within these nine expanses. As for the Vast Array of the Expanse, it is not considered to be in a separate division, for it falls within the larger scope of all the preceding.

The Category of Direct Transmission has four cycles—the outer cycle, inner cycle, secret cycle, and unsurpassable secret cycle. Although this category includes an incredible number of topics that are found in the classes of tantras, these topics are said to be subsumed within the seventeen definitive tantras of the supreme secrets. *The Reverberation of Sound* states:

> *Naturally Arising Awareness, The Natural Freedom of*
> *Awareness,*
> *Naturally Occurring Perfection, The Perfect Dynamic*
> *Energy of the Lion,*

Auspicious Beauty, The Array of Inlaid Gems,
The Pearl Garland, The Tantra Without Letters,
Vajrasattva: Mirror of the Heart, The Mirror of
    Enlightened Mind,
The Conjunction of Sun and Moon, Adornment
    Through Direct Introduction,
The Blazing Remains, The Heaped Jewels,
The Blazing Lamp, and *The Six Expanses*—
In this way, these sixteen distinct texts [207b]
definitely derive from *The Reverberation of Sound*
and manifest to beings who are to be guided.

Thus, considering the Categories of Mind, Expanse, and Direct Transmission in general, among the infinite variety of teachings communicated by the teacher Samantabhadra, manifesting in the form of Vajradhara, they constitute the supreme secret mantra approach. Of the two internal divisions of that approach—the stages of development and completion—these categories constitute the stage of completion, and of the two aspects of that stage—the greater and the lesser—they constitute the greater. These teachings include some six million four hundred thousand verses, thirty-five thousand chapters, twenty-one thousand volumes, one hundred and eighty "keystone" teachings, fifteen hundred overviews, three thousand summaries of key points, and four hundred thousand topics for coming to the decisive experience beyond error and obscuration. These teachings are found in some twenty thousand tantras bearing separate titles. All this is stated in the source text of all the categories in these cycles, *The Reverberation of Sound:*

From natural great perfection
came detailed written analyses.
From the three categories came the nine expanses.
When these were set down in words,
there were six million four hundred thousand verses,
from which came thirty-five thousand chapters
and twenty-one thousand volumes.
What is discussed is equal to space in extent.
It cuts through the concepts of beings who are to be guided.
From this, the subject matter was further condensed
into one hundred and eighty "keystone" teachings,
with fifteen hundred overviews,

three thousand pithy summaries of key points,
and four hundred thousand topics concerning how one errs
    or is obscured.
There are twenty thousand tantras bearing separate titles,
which clearly record the words spoken.

I dedicate my work to the enlightenment of all:

> **By this virtue, may all beings without exception
> effortlessly reach the primordial ground. [208a]
> May they become spiritual rulers who spontaneously
>   accomplish the two kinds of benefit,
> dwelling on the level of Samantabhadra without transition
>   or change!**

An enormous amount of virtue has accrued from the completion of this superb text on spiritual practice. It is my aspiration that all of this virtue serve as a cause for the complete enlightenment of all beings without their having to exert themselves or strive in the least. May they attain the state of buddhas—transcendent and accomplished conquerors, spiritual rulers who are victorious ones, of equal taste within the oneness of dharmakaya on the indivisible level of Samantabhadra—and so spontaneously ensure the two kinds of benefit.

To ensure that everything is completely auspicious, I dedicate this virtue so that well-being and excellence increase on a vast scale:

> **In all directions, may there be well-being, splendor, and wealth,
> so that everything that is wished for is spontaneously
>   accomplished, as though in a pure realm.
> May the drum of spiritual teachings resound and the victory
>   banner of liberation be raised.
> May the sacred teachings never wane, but spread and flourish!**[1]

The manifold merit of finishing this composition is light that radiates throughout our world and the gods' realms. Due to this noble and splendid radiance, may beings in all worlds be happy and may they never suffer, even in dreams; may they always, day and night, enjoy all that is auspicious—the superb joy of the teachings that lead to liberation. Finding themselves in pure realms—such buddha fields as Sukhavati [Realm of Bliss], Abhirati [Manifest Joy], and Padmavati [Lotus-Filled]— [208b] may all beings enjoy the spontaneous accomplishment of everything they wish for in abundance. May the acclaim of the Three Jewels resound without interruption in all times and all places. With the upholding of these unsurpassable teachings—like the planting of the gods' wish-granting tree or the raising of a victory banner topped by a wish-fulfilling gem—may the sacred teachings spread and flourish in the boundless realms of the ten directions, throughout the endless reaches of space!

With such auspicious wishes, I have brought this work to a fitting conclusion.

The colophon found in the source text can now be discussed, beginning with the title:

> **This text, entitled *The Precious Treasury of the Basic Space of Phenomena*, . . .**

Mind itself, utterly lucid by nature and free of all the limitations of conceptual elaboration, is the "basic space of phenomena." Spontaneously present by nature, it is described as a "precious" gem. And since it serves as the source of all phenomena of samsara or nirvana, it is described as a "treasury." So the title epitomizes the meaning of the subject matter of this commentary in its entirety—ground, path, and fruition. The thirteen chapters in which these topics are elucidated are by nature a collection of extensive and profound scriptural sources.

Being the "basic space" from which come words and their meanings in all their variety, it is comparable to a "precious" jewel, for it ensures the spontaneous accomplishment of the bountiful fortune of both the words and their meanings. Because it serves as the basis for the accomplishment of our goals—the two kinds of benefit—and is a repository of terms, words, and idioms, [209a] it is accurately described as a "treasury."

In addition, because the source text is a "treasury" from which comes the "precious" and excellent array of the "basic space of phenomena"—the nature of ground, path, and fruition—it is entitled *The Precious Treasury of the Basic Space of Phenomena*. This title is also based on the superb nature of this treatise, both the excellent text that discusses the subject matter and the excellent meaning of what is discussed.

... by a yogin of the most sublime spiritual approach ...

The vajrayana, the spiritual approach based on the fruition, is the pinnacle of all approaches, and its innermost heart essence, or very pinnacle, is natural great perfection. Because the theme of this text—the vajra heart essence of utter lucidity—is even more sublime, it is called the "most sublime spiritual approach." To thoroughly fathom and become familiar with its meaning is to make that ultimate meaning one's yoga. Having thoroughly fathomed the topics expressed by the words and their meanings, to make the writing of such a text one's spiritual practice is to make the words one's yoga. Such a person is described as "a yogin of the ongoing flow of spiritual teachings."

... Longchen Rabjam ...

This is my personal name as the author. Within the "vast expanse" (*klong chen*) of my realization, as spacious as the sky, awareness—the ongoing experience of the true nature of phenomena, free of laxity or agitation, hope or fear—is "infinitely extensive" (*'byams klas*), day and night, [209b] and so I am called Longchen Rabjam (*kLong chen Rab 'byams*). This name further reveals the subject matter of this commentary.

In fact, I have signed treatises that I have authored in the past by several names. These names also further reveal the subject matter of those works. In works that deal primarily with provisional truth, in connection with such mundane fields of study as poetics, metrics, the etymology of technical terms, and so forth, I have signed the name Samyépa Ngak-gi Tsultrim Lodrö [Disciplined Intellect, the Lord of Speech from Samyé]. In works that discuss topics related to the themes of the outer and inner levels of the secret mantra approach, I have signed the name Dorjé Ziji [Vajra Brilliance]. In works that set forth any profound topics related to developmental spiritual approaches or that primarily discuss meditative absorption (both the letter and the spirit of these topics), I have signed the name Drimé Özer [Stainless Rays of Light]. In works that reveal the way of abiding as an inconceivable, spacious expanse, I have signed the name Longchen Rabjam [Infinitely Extensive Vast Expanse]. And in works dealing with extensive treatments of spiritual approaches, philosophical systems, suchness, and so forth, I have signed the name Kunkhyen Ngak-gi Wangpo [Omniscient Lord of Speech].

These are examples of "the subject matter of a treatise being further re-vealed by a distinctive name."

. . . is now completely finished. [210a]

In Sanskrit this would be *samayathā* . It signifies that "I have com-pletely finished my presentation of the words and their meanings," or "my composition is finished," or "the work has been finished in an excel-lent way."

Such is the ultimate meaning of the utterly secret vajra heart
   essence.
From the vast secret teachings that define the heart drop,
the profound key points have been summarized here in one work,
which sets forth the unlimited ways in which one can follow the
   path to peace and liberation.

This sublime teaching, the commentary on *The Treasury of the
   Basic Space of Phenomena,*
is a vision of realization, the consummate meaning to be realized.
It is the most majestic spiritual approach, the pinnacle of all
   sublime approaches.
Embellished with explanations found in scriptural sources, it is
   entitled *A Treasure Trove of Scriptural Transmission.*

This is not mere verbiage, for I have seen the meaning of
   the heart essence,
meditated on it well, just as it is, and brought together
in a single work the consummate and most profound key points
   from my definitive experience.
Therefore, this commentary on *The Treasury of the Basic Space
   of Phenomena* is a vision of realization.

The meaning of the vajra heart essence—enlightenment
   in this lifetime—
is the pinnacle of everything, utter lucidity that is sublimely
   unchanging,
like the majestic mountain rising in the midst of the four
   continents.

This commentary on *The Treasury of the Basic Space of
Phenomena* concerns the most majestic spiritual approach.

I have sung my vajra song of profound key points.
I have adorned it with garlands of scriptural citations, especially
the authoritative words of buddhas.
It is in accord with all the sutras and tantras that concern
the heart essence of definitive meaning.
This commentary on *The Treasury of the Basic Space of
Phenomena* is entitled *A Treasure Trove of Scriptural
Transmission.* [210b]

Having trained in the past, lifetime after lifetime,
I have been cared for in this lifetime by the holiest of holy beings,
have come to a realization of the meaning of the heart essence,
the most profound of the profound,
and so have reached the far shore of the ocean
of the most sublime of sublime spiritual approaches.

Therefore, in the sky of my spacious intellect
there have gathered great clouds of study and contemplation,
sending forth lightning bolts of benefit and well-being, with the
thunder of realization.
This unfolding play of my meditative absorption
has caused a torrential rain of excellent explanations to fall.

Since I have analyzed, studied, and contemplated on a vast scale,
I have mastered all the meanings of every spiritual approach
without exception.
Since I am learned in this noble path of the vajra heart essence,
I have composed this profound and extensive commentary
concerning the basic space of phenomena.

Any who have abundant devotion and virtue,
who are yogins of the most majestic of sublime spiritual
approaches—
take this wealth that provides the noble riches of peace and
enlightenment,
seize this commentary on *The Treasury of the Basic Space
of Phenomena.*

Thoroughly summarizing the key points concerning
effortless freedom

found in countless texts—the tantras that define the
 supreme secrets
and the pith instructions based on them—
I composed this work in an excellent way on the slopes
 of Gangri Tökar.

By the virtue of this, may the teachings of the buddhas—
the source of benefit and well-being—spread and flourish.
May the holy ones who are the allies of the teachings
enjoy longevity, as well as unlimited activity and opportunity.
May there be happiness and well-being in all universes,
and may lower destinies be blocked, so that beings attain higher
 states of rebirth.
Engaging in spirituality day and night, as though in a pure realm,
may all attain unsurpassable enlightenment.
On the great ship that is the merit of this excellent explanation
 of what simply is,
may all beings cross the ocean of conditioned existence. [211a]
Reaching the Isle of Jewels—the noble state of liberation—
may they become spiritual monarchs of the three spontaneously
 present kayas.
By the merit of this thorough, unerring explanation—
this transmission of awakened mind, the unborn heart essence—
may all beings without exception enjoy an abundance of the two
 kinds of benefit
and may virtue increase effortlessly.

As for me, for as long as conditioned existence continues,
may I carry out the activities of my guru, my glorious guide.
Through my abundant activity, which brings enormous benefit
 to others,
may those who see, hear, think of, or touch me be released
 from samsara.
Any beings who are connected to me—
whether they hate me or have faith in me, try to injure me
or praise me, follow me or not—
may I swiftly guide them all.
However extensive are the basic space of phenomena,
the reach of ordinary space, and the reach of ordinary beings—

may these be my sphere of influence and be permeated
    by my activities,
so that I may guide all beings.

May this spiritual method also remain here in the world,
adorning the earth for as long as conditioned existence continues.
May the branches and foliage of the tree of the teachings grow,
and the flowers and fruit that benefit others be unlimited.
May this method be like the sun and moon, a gem, a great
    wish-granting tree,
the earth, the ocean, a great ship, and a victorious monarch.
May its thousand light rays of benefit and well-being shine,
    satisfying the hopes of all beings,
and may boundless enlightened activity spontaneously
    accomplish benefit for others!

This commentary on the work entitled *The Precious Treasury of the Basic Space of Phenomena,* this vision of realization concerning the most majestic spiritual approach, is called *A Treasure Trove of Scriptural Transmission.* So concludes this composition, written by a yogin of the sublime spiritual approach, the omniscient lord of speech Longchen Rabjam, who has reached the far shore of the ocean of his own and others' philosophical systems [211b] and whose intelligence has thoroughly unfolded to embrace the superb themes found in the sublime speech of the sugatas. Good fortune! Good fortune! Good fortune!

An Exhortation to Read
The Seven Treasuries,
the Excellent Writings of
Omniscient Longchen Rabjam

Paltrul Rinpoche

Nama sarva jnanaya—Homage to the Omniscient One!

The infinite realm, genuine and tranquil from the beginning,
is dharmakaya's expanse of timeless awareness that never wavers.
Its mode is perfect manifestation, the supreme energy of
    enlightened intent.
I pay homage to this omniscient lama.

Listen! It is in the nature of sublime qualities
that if you don't rely on sacred texts, you won't create them.
Rare jewels come from the great ocean.
How would they be obtained from a lesser domain?

Timeless awareness, born of realization bright as the sun,
    will definitely come
from the pith instructions of a lama whose lineage blessings
    are undiminished.
But those who meditate on voidness are casting stones in
    the dark;
few will reach the genuine state on the excellent path.

If you don't study, it is a great defect in your life.
But to study erroneous ideas can cause greater harm.
Now, when you can read the writings of a learned master,
wouldn't it make sense to open your eyes and study them?

In conditioned existence, the precious scriptural tradition
of the omniscient lama is the sole wish-fulfilling gem.
If buddhahood is not found anywhere other than here,
who wouldn't take great delight in it?

The precious *treasury of* meaning intended by the myriad tantras
is *the sublime* vajra heart essence, the highest *spiritual approach.**
The treatment is extensive; the meaning discussed is profound.
To see this is to behold the face of the real Samantabhadra.

You will comprehend the meaning of six million tantras.
You will understand the way of abiding of conditioned existence
     and the state of peace—samsara and nirvana in their entirety.
You will realize extraordinary qualities intended by the profound
     path of the pinnacle approach.
Therefore, study this scripture assiduously.

The *treasury of* Samantabhadra's enlightened intent beyond cause
     and effect
is *the* dharmakaya's *way of abiding,* in which there is nothing
     to protect.
If elaboration is not cut off with such an excellent text,
who could destroy the perverse fixations of intellectual
     approaches?

Summarized in groups of six, the perfect *treasury of* sacred
     dharma
distills the heart essence of all *pith instructions.*
Even if you were to meet the actual Victorious One,
wouldn't it be hard to hear teachings on such an excellent path all
     at once?

The entire Buddhist teachings are completely explained in just
     one treatise—the *precious treasury of philosophical systems.*
An excellent text like this never appeared before
in either India or Tibet and will never come again.

* Italicized words indicate the titles of the treasuries.

The *treasury* concerning study, reflection, and meditation on all
    methods of dharma—
what to accept and reject in every situation—beautifully shows
    how *to fulfill one's wishes.*
Reading this, you will understand the principles of all
    instructions;
you will be trained in hundreds of texts all at once.

The meaning intended by the highest spiritual approach is
    excellently summarized
in a single *treasury of* practical key points of pith instructions
that spins their import into eleven chapters of *words and their
    meanings.*
It is singularly powerful in cutting through the root of
    conditioned existence.

Especially, the precious *treasury of the basic space of
    phenomena*—
the most profound of all—is the depth of mind of the
    omniscient lama
that beautifully reveals the meaning of dharmakaya, genuine
    mind itself,
to be naked awareness, with nothing to be added or dispelled.

It is authentic dharmakaya appearing in the form of a text.
An excellent text like this is an actual buddha—
it directly reveals the enlightened intent of victorious ones,
accomplishing their deeds in this world.
Even if you met a buddha, you would not find more than this.

An excellent text like this is a treasury of all sacred dharma.
The consummate content of all teachings
is nakedly revealed as timeless awareness of dharmakaya.
Even if all teachings were compared, there would be nothing
    more than this.

Such an excellent text is the enlightened mind of all the exalted
    sangha.
The timeless awareness realized by buddhas, bodhisattvas,
    and arhats
throughout the three times does not go beyond this.
The timeless awareness of exalted ones is not other than this.

It is the complete perfection of the three jewels in a shrine of
    dharmakaya—
the unsurpassable path blazed by all victorious ones,
the representation of the omniscient lama's realization.
Those who encounter this will have their last lifetime in
    samsara.

Even hearing a single word of an excellent text like this
has the power to shred the manifestation of conditioned existence
    to tatters.
If you gain the good fortune to read it completely
and you waste it, what could you be thinking?

Listen, the doctrines of the tripitaka and the nine stages
are primarily intended for the industrious and diligent.
They say, "Freedom comes through meditation, so practice
    with effort."
But they do not see timeless awareness, with nothing to be
    dispelled or added.

This vajra pinnacle is effortless, beyond ordinary mind.
Buddhahood is not cultivated; it is the expanse of naked
    emptiness and awareness.
Even the indolent can be introduced to dharmakaya these days,
for it is without the fixations of the intellect—effort and sadhana
    and meditation.

In revealing this path in the transitory world that includes
    the gods,
the omniscient lama is the unique dharmakaya.
Since it contains a wealth of instructions about dharmakaya,
this *Treasury of the Basic Space of Phenomena* is the quintessence
    of dharma.

Therefore, to see such an excellent text in this world
liberates you—it liberates you to hear and to remember it.
Whoever makes a connection with it will become a buddha
    in the future.
If you discover its enlightened intent, you are a buddha
    right now.

Since the acute power of the lineage of blessings has not
    diminished,
by focusing enlightened intent, this text transmits the timeless
    awareness of the absolute lineage.
It is sealed with a seal of entrustment to future generations,
and so it is equal to the presence of the omniscient lama.

Even if you can't unravel the enlightened intent of the words
    and their meanings, just as it is,
if you have devotion, the timeless awareness of the lineage
    of blessings will be transmitted to you.
There is nothing more to the precious word empowerment
    than encountering this text—
it is the complete empowerment of the dynamic energy
    of awareness.

When depression, anxiety, or irritation overwhelms,
if you read this text, supremely joyful timeless awareness
    will arise.
You will be cheerful and in good spirits, your awareness sharp
    and clear.
The confusion you encounter in perceiving sense objects will
    be destroyed.

When joyful experiences flourish and great bliss blazes,
if you read this text, attachment to savoring joy will be
    destroyed.
The infinite and genuine expanse, without the distinctions
    of acceptance and rejection,
is the profound teaching of the omniscient lama's enlightened
    intent.

In this life, when you are distressed by yearning and exertion,
if you read this text, attachment to the solidity of your experience
    will be destroyed.
Regardless of what manifests, you are expansive; whatever you
    do is all right.
Without the usual reactions of hope and fear, you are relaxed,
    resting in equipoise.

This is the middle way and the perfection of wisdom,
the practice of cutting through as well as the pacification
   of suffering,
the real mahamudra and great perfection.
All teachings are subsumed in this, the most exalted of them all.

If you are a follower and heir of the omniscient lama,
never be apart from this excellent text.
It is enough to trust in this, awareness's constant companion.
There will never be anything like this ultimate reliance.

You will gain happiness immediately; in the end, you will attain
   buddhahood.
You will break the fetters of the intellect and not suffer from
   exertion.
If you are exuberant, it will make you level; it is a consoling friend
   if you suffer from depression.
Such an excellent text is unique in that it will never deceive you.

Therefore, sing and chant it as a melodious song.
Utter the words as poetry and read the prose aloud.
If you are never separate from it,
your confused perceptions of samsara will shatter.

Eventually, when the lineage blessings, the key to realization,
   have passed to you,
inexpressible timeless awareness will be born from within.
You will meet the true face of the omniscient dharmakaya lama.
On the basis of your fundamental state of bliss, your happiness
   will be uninterrupted.

Besides studying these texts, there is no other practice.
This itself is the heart essence of meditation and sadhana
   practice.
However long you study these excellent texts,
for that long the enlightened intent of dharmakaya will
   spontaneously arise.

For that reason, do not magnify the stormy mind of intellectual
   exertion.
Consider these noble texts in a carefree state.

The profound meaning expressed is not far away.
With a decisive mind, rest in the naturally settled state.

You don't need to scrutinize the meaning of words with precision,
as is the case with pedantic treatises that are difficult to
    understand.
In the naturally settled state, mingle your mind with these texts
and it will instantly become expansive and nakedly unobstructed.

That is direct introduction.
That is genuine timeless awareness.
That itself is the spiritual advice of the omniscient lama.
That is the main teaching as well as the real bestowal of
    empowerment.
That practice of the heart essence is sufficient in itself.

Whether or not you elucidate the definitions of the literal
    meaning,
whether or not you understand the profound meaning of
    the content,
whether or not you discover the innermost sanctuary of
    enlightened intent—
read these texts in an undistracted state, cutting through doubts
    and expectations.

Read them again and again; read by bringing them into your
    experience.
Mingling your mind with these texts, seal their marrow in
    your mind.
From the state of inseparability, chant melodiously, joyful in your
    experience.
In the blazing dynamic energy of devotion, timeless awareness
    born of realization will arise.

Listen, these are the very heart of the heart essence.
There is nothing more profound than these.
They are a treasury of blessings.
They are the revelation of the heart essence.
They are the presence of the teacher.
They are holding the buddha in the palm of your hand.

If I were to expound for an eon on the qualities of such texts,
even my small mind's intellect—
let alone the eloquence of others with greater minds—would
    never be exhausted.
There is nothing like this excellent path to delight the exalted.

Take care—these are like precious gems.
Whoever has the liberty and good fortune to meet with them,
although remaining here in samsara, won't have too much
    sorrow.
Appreciating them deeply, why wouldn't you become carefree?

Oh, dear friend, cast your mind into these texts
and, with a carefree attitude, find confidence therein.
Your erratic mind, with its contrived plans and actions, will
    collapse therein.
The elaborate advice of many texts will be resolved therein.

What's the point of numerous philosophical systems with
    melodious texts?
What's the point of so many profound pith instructions?
What's the point of so many elaborations of practices?
What's the point of so many explanations of how things are?

Easygoing, yet stable concentration—this is it.
Natural freedom in an expansive carefree mind—this is it.
The excellent way of knowing one thing and liberating
    everything—this is it.
A hundred rivers of pith instructions flowing under one bridge—
    this is it.

Since it rests in you, don't seek it elsewhere.
Don't collect the bark and throw away the heartwood.
Don't practice with exertion, forsaking what is effortless.
Don't have a lot of plans and activities, having cast away the
    effortless state.

Once you have taken birth in the lineage of the omniscient lama,
an excellent tradition like this is your inheritance;
such an excellent path was preserved by your forebears.
If you want to relax completely, you can relax in this.

Ah! Ah! I am so grateful to the three lineages.
What great fortune I have to encounter this noble tradition!
How lucky I am to have this excellent path to practice!
It is definitely true—buddhahood is within you.

Therefore, on this excellent path that pleases the victorious ones,
mingle dharma and your mind, my dear friend.
Try to hold this heartfelt advice deeply in your mind.
If you keep this in your heart, you can become the heart essence.

Lost in a valley without a care, I'm just old Uncle Tatters.
How can I presume to preach to others when I don't have
    anything of my own?
However, I have gained deep confidence in the texts transmitted
by the omniscient Longchenpa—that is my unique experience.

When I met and studied excellent texts such as these—
even for a bad person like me, in whom the five poisons burn,
whose mind is enslaved by distraction,
and for whom it is difficult to dislodge confused perceptions—
the appearances of conditioned existence became evanescent.

Therefore, people like you who have pure samaya and good
    fortune,
stable minds with few thoughts driven by the five poisons,
in encountering these texts, generate again and again your conviction
to definitely attain sublime timeless awareness of the blessing
    lineage.

Whoever is touched by the illumination of blessings
of the omniscient lama—that perfect buddha—
will directly experience simultaneous realization and freedom.
The omniscient lama is the forefather of one hundred siddhas.

The great Lhatsun, a powerful lord among those who are realized,
Rigdzin Jigmé Lingpa, who revealed the expanse of enlightened
    intent,
and Terchen Lama, master of the Buddha's teachings, as well as
    others,
obtained the blessings of the lineage from the texts of omniscient
    Longchenpa.

Dear friend, please think on these things.
From perceiving the meaning of the sublime and beautiful
  writings
of the omniscient lama in this way, you will realize the timeless
  awareness of the lineage.
May you be liberated in the expanse of enlightened intent, the
  basic space of suchness.

Spoken by Paltrul.
Sarva mangalam—May everything be auspicious.

Translated by Susanne Fairclough

Notes

These notes serve four purposes. First, wherever we found what we felt were misspellings or ambiguous readings, we brought them to the attention of one or more of the scholars consulted on this translation. We then rendered these words in the way we thought best reflected the intended meaning and identified our decision in the notes.

Second, Longchen Rabjam quotes from traditional sources to support his arguments. In particular, he cites extensively many of the seventeen tantras that constitute the scriptural basis for the Category of Direct Transmission in the great perfection approach. Occasionally, the version of a passage that he cites differs from the text of the source currently available to us; we indicated such variations in the notes.

Our reference was the edition of these tantras printed at Adzom Chögar in eastern Tibet. We wish to acknowledge the enormous benefit we derived from the work of Mr. James Valby of the Dzogchen Community's Vairochana Translation Project, who had previously transcribed in the Wylie system of transliteration the Tibetan texts of these tantras, as well as a number of other great perfection scriptural sources, making our search for such variant passages much easier.

Third, there are a number of places where Longchen Rabjam's source verses (our translation of which has been published as *The Precious Treasury of the Basic Space of Phenomena*) differ from his citation of those verses in this commentary. We chose the version we thought best reflected the intended meaning and identified our choice in the notes. In some instances, we changed the commentary citation so that it was consistent with the source verse version; in others, we changed the source verse to match the commentary citation. In the latter case, we also changed the Tibetan text facing the source verse to match the English, and so in these places it differs from the source verse text that appears in the Adzom Chögar edition.

Fourth, where we found significant variations among the various editions of the source verses and commentary—the original Adzom Chögar edition (orig. Adzom), the revised Adzom Chögar edition (rev. Adzom), and the Dergé edition (Dergé)—we chose the version we found most relevant and gave the alternative readings in the notes.

The first version listed in a note is the one we chose for the main text; the succeeding version or versions are variants. Unless otherwise indicated in parentheses, "commentary" and "source verse" refer to all three editions. Folio numbers refer to both Adzom Chögar editions.

Introduction

1. Commentary (rev. Adzom): *rgya mtsho'i tshogs thams cad* (all the vast hosts); commentary (orig. Adzom): *rgya mtsho'i tshogs* (the vast hosts).
2. Commentary (rev. Adzom): *thos* (hearing); commentary (orig. Adzom): *mthong* (seeing).
3. Commentary: *gcig kyang med* (There is not a single thing); tantra: *gang yang med* (There is nothing at all).
4. Commentary: *nga la btab* (they are buried in me); tantra: *nga la yod* (there is in me).
5. Commentary: *nga las* (from me); tantra: *nga la* (in me).
6. Commentary: *nga las* (from me); tantra: *nga la* (in me).
7. Commentary: *gsal bya* (what is to be illuminated); tantra: *gsal cha* (an aspect of lucidity).
8. Commentary: *yangs pas* (Since it is spacious); tantra: *yangs pa* (Spacious).

Chapter 1

1. Commentary: *ma 'gags pa* (continuous); source verse: *ma 'gags pas* (being continuous).
2. The tantra adds *zhen med* (which is without fixation).
3. Commentary: *rol* (display); tantra: *thim* (dissolution).
4. Commentary: *'char* (arises); source verse: *snang* (manifests).
5. Commentary: *rig pa ni* (Awareness); tantra: *rig pa 'di* (This awareness).
6. Commentary: *'gag med ngang du 'khor 'das rol par shar* (It arises as the display of samsara and nirvana within a continuous context); tantra: *'gag med rnam dag klong du de bzhin rnam par rol* (It displays itself thus within the totally pure, continuous expanse).

7. Commentary: *sangs rgyas sems can snod bcud kun kyang gnas* (is such that buddhas, ordinary beings, and the entire universe are present therein). The tantra links this with the next two lines, not cited here: *sangs rgyas sems can snang srid snod bcud kun / thams cad rnam par dag pa'i chos nyid la / gnyis su med de sgro skur kun dang bral* (is such that buddhas, ordinary beings, and the entire universe of appearances and possibilites / are all nondual in their true nature, which is total purity, / and are free of all exaggeration and underestimation).

8. Commentary: *'khor lor* (as the ongoing principle); source verse: *ngo bor* (as the essence).

9. Commentary: *tshig gis gsung* (through words as enlightened speech); tantra: *tshig gi gsung* (as words that are enlightened speech).

10. Commentary: *ji ltar dran rig rtog pa thams cad kun* (All consciousness, all thoughts, whatever their content); tantra: *de ltar dran rig rtog pa thams cad kun* (Thus, regarding all consciousness and all thoughts).

11. Commentary: *dpyod* (investigate); tantra: *gcod* (delineate).

12. Commentary: *mtha' yas don spyod rang rig bde chen sa* (The meaning of boundlessness is experienced as that state of self-knowing and supremely blissful awareness); tantra: *mtha' yas don skyod bde chen rang gi sa* (The meaning of boundlessness emerges as the level of supreme bliss itself).

13. Commentary: *spros* (elaboration); tantra: *rtog* (concepts).

14. Commentary: *yul las 'das* (beyond being an object); tantra: *kun las 'das* (beyond everything).

15. Commentary: *rang bzhin gcig gi* (of the single nature); tantra: *rang bzhin gyi ni* (of the nature).

16. Commentary: *zhing khams chos nyid yongs su rdzogs* (I am the pure realm—the completely perfect nature of phenomena); tantra: *zhing khams thams cad yongs su rdzogs* (I am the complete perfection of all pure realms).

17. Commentary: *'byung ba rkyen gyis ma gos bdag* (The elements are the embodiment of what is unsullied by conditions); tantra: *'byung ba rdo rje'i rkyen gyi bdag* (The elements are the very embodiments of vajra conditions), which is also found on fol. 50a.4 of the commentary.

18. Commentary: *snang ba'i ye shes* (Illuminating timeless awareness); tantra: *snang ba'i rdo rje* (The vajra of illumination).

19. Commentary: *grags par ston* (revealed in what is audible); tantra: *grags pas stong* (empty by virtue of being audible).

20. Commentary: *rtogs par sangs* (pristine in light of realization); tantra: *rtog pa sangs* (unsullied by concepts).

21. Commentary: *kun tu bzang po rang rig pa'o* (Samantabhadra is self-knowing awareness); tantra: *kun tu bzang pos kun tu rig pa'o* (Samantabhadra is aware of everything).

22. This line is not found in the version of the tantra available to us.

23. Commentary: *rgyal chen kun tu bzang* (Samantabhadra, the supreme ruler); tantra: *rgya chen kun tu bzang* (Samantabhadra, vast in extent).

24. Commentary: (rev. Adzom and Dergé): *rtogs pa* (realization); commentary (orig. Adzom): *rtog pa* (concepts).

25. Commentary: *gang du* (in any finite way); tantra: *kun rdzob yul du* (as some relative object).

26. Commentary: *don dang* (with what is meaningful); tantra: *don dam* (with ultimate reality).

27. Commentary: *klong* (expanse); tantra: *sku* (kaya).

28. Commentary: *'gro ba yongs la khyab* (completely permeates all beings); tantra: *ma bris yongs la gsal* (though it cannot be drawn, is still totally evident).

29. While the commentary version of this citation refers, almost alternately, to Samantabhadra and Samantabhadrā, the masculine and feminine principles, the tantra refers exclusively to Samantabhadrā, the feminine principle.

30. Commentary: *rnam par dag* (complete purity); tantra: *snang ba dag* (pure manifestation).

31. Commentary: *rig pa* (awareness); tantra: *sems dpa'* (courageous mind).

32. The tantra adds *cir yang* (in anything whatsoever).

33. The phrase *sems la* (to your mind) is found only in the Dergé commentary.

34. Source verse and commentary (Dergé): *med pas* (Since there is no); commentary (orig. Adzom): *med pa* (There is no).

35. Source verse: *chos su med* (nothing exists as some); commentary: *chos med de* (there is no thing that is an).

36. This line is not found in the version of the tantra available to us.

Chapter 2

1. Commentary: *klong nyid do* (is this very expanse); source verse: *klong nyid du,* which appears to be in error.

2. Commentary: *med* (not); tantra: *'das* (beyond).

3. Source verse: *dngos po mtshan ma med* (have no substance or characteristics); commentary: *dngos po'i mtshan ma med* (have no substantial characteristics).

4. Commentary: *rdzogs chen nga yi byang chub sems* (Great perfection

is my awakened mind): tantra: *yang dag rdzogs pa'i byang chub sems* (Awakened mind is truly perfect).

5. Source verse: *dngos po mtshan ma med* (has no substance or characteristics); commentary: *dngos po mtshan mar med* (nonexistent as substance or characteristics).

6. Commentary: *pas* (Since it is); source verse: *de* (It is).

7. Commentary: *dang bral* (free of); tantra: *las 'das* (beyond).

8. Commentary: *rnam pa med cing yul rnams med* (It has no specific form and no sensory qualities); tantra: *snang ba med cing yul yang med* (It has no manifestation, or any object).

9. Commentary: *stong pa nyid* (emptiness); tantra: *ston pa nyid* (a teacher).

10. Commentary: *nga las 'das pa . . . ma phye bas* (cannot be differentiated from me); tantra: *sa las 'das pa . . . ma phye bas* (cannot be differentiated and are beyond any level of realization), which is also found on fol. 185a.1–2 of the commentary.

11. Commentary (rev. Adzom): *lhun grub* (spontaneous presence); commentary (orig. Adzom): *lhun* (spontaneity).

12. These four lines are not found in the version of the tantra available to us. The last two are found, in slightly different form, in *The Array of Inlaid Gems*.

13. We have translated the commentary version of the second part of this citation. The tantra reads:

> The vajra of self-knowing awareness is timeless awareness blazing everywhere.
> The naturally manifest vajra without characteristics is supreme in every way.
> The radiantly fearless vajra is emptiness, supreme in every way.
> The vajra of the immaculate nature of what is subtle and coarse blazes intensely.
> The vajra crown is all-pervasive emptiness, supreme in every way.
> The vajra of the complete conferral of natural empowerment is perfect without being conferred.

14. This passage is actually found in the tantra *Samantabhadra: Mirror of Enlightened Mind*.

15. Commentary: *'khyil* (This encompassing); source verse: *dkyil* (The very center of the).

16. Commentary: *bshad* (are explained to be); tantra: *shar* (are the arising of).

17. The tantra omits *ye shes* (of timeless awareness).

18. Commentary: *brgyud pa'i rtsa ba* (the root of its continuity); tantra: *rgyud kyi skye ba* (the origin of that continuum).

19. Commentary: *bsam pa* (thoughts); tantra: *med pa* (what is ineffable).

20. Commentary: *'gyur med* (without changing); tantra: *rgyu med* (without cause), which is also found on fol. 95b.3 of the commentary.

21. Commentary: *lhun rdzogs sangs rgyas pa* (spontaneous, perfect buddhahood); tantra: *sangs rgyas nyid kyi sa* (the level of buddhahood itself).

22. Commentary: *grags pa* (is audible); tantra: *byung ba* (occurs).

23. Commentary: *na* (In); source verse: *ni* (As for).

24. This line is not found in the version of the tantra available to us.

25. Commentary: *gzhi nas 'dod mi srid pa'i* (about which it is fundamentally impossible to posit anything); scriptural source: *gzhi gnas 'dod mi srid pa'i* (which abides as the ground of being and about which it is impossible to posit anything).

26. Commentary: *rten bral* (having no support); scriptural source: *rten 'brel* (connected to a support).

27. Commentary: *thim shes na* (If one understands that . . . dissolve); tantra: *thim pa na* (Given that . . . dissolve).

28. Commentary: *dri ma nyid* (simply distortions); tantra: *dri ma med* (without distortion).

29. Commentary: *rang byung rang zhi* (occur naturally and subside naturally); tantra: *rang byung rang bzhin* (are inherently natural occurrences).

30. Commentary: *lhun gyis grub* (is spontaneously present); tantra: *de la gnas* (abides).

Chapter 3

1. Commentary and source verse (rev. Adzom): *kyi* (that of); source verse (orig. Adzom): *kyis* (due to).

2. Commentary: *la* (within); tantra: *yis* (by).

3. Commentary: *chos sku mkha' ltar dag* (is dharmakaya, pure like space); tantra: *chos sku'i mkha' la rol* (displays itself in the sky of dharmakaya).

4. Commentary: *bsam med* (unimaginable); tantra: *bsal med* (not to be eliminated).

5. Commentary: *chos nyid* (the true nature of phenomena); tantra: *lus nyid* (the body itself).

6. Commentary: *gsal dag stong pa* (lucid, pure, and empty); tantra: *gsal dang stong pa* (lucid and empty).

7. Commentary: *bsngo dang bral* (free of the need to dedicate anything); tantra: *dngos dang bral* (free of substantiality).

8. Commentary: *blang dor* (acceptance or rejection); tantra: *rtsol sgrub* (effort or achievement).

9. Commentary: *blang dor* (acceptance and rejection); tantra: *rstol sgrub* (effort and achievement).

10. Commentary: *blang zhing dor ba* (Acceptance and rejection): tantra: *blang dor bnyis byung* (The onset of a duality of acceptance and rejection).

11. Commentary: *rang gsal bde ba'i klong* (is the expanse of naturally lucid bliss); tantra: *rang gdangs gsal ba'i shugs* (is imbued with the force of the lucid, natural radiance of being).

12. Commentary: *kun brtags* (which labels everything); tantra: *kun rtags* (which is evident in everything).

13. We have translated the commentary version of this citation. The tantra reads:

> In the sky that is the true nature of phenomena, free of labels,
> soars the golden garuda of awareness's own manifestations,
>> with none of what characterizes sense objects.
> This is uncontrived—occurring as natural bliss.

> In the ocean that is the true nature of phenomena, occurring
>> naturally and free of elaboration,
> swim the golden fish of what cannot be characterized as anything.
> They are sealed as one in naturally manifest dharmakaya.

> In the sky of freedom from fixating on things in all their variety
> soars the golden garuda of dharmakaya, free of elaboration.
> The undistracted mind of effort is fully encompassed within the
>> realm of the "lamps."

> In the completely pure ocean that is the boundless nature of
>> phenomena
> swim the golden fish of the naturally occurring state, free of
>> concepts.
> They are sealed within the empty yet lucid realm free of samsara
>> or nirvana.

> In the sky that is free of thoughts that involve reifying attachment
> soars the golden garuda of naturally abiding enlightened intent.
> It is fully embraced within the scope of the true nature of
>> phenomena, spacious and all-pervasive.
> In the sky in which dharmakaya, free of elaboration, is naturally
>> dispersed in its own place

> soars the golden garuda of awareness's own manifestations,
>   free of plans and actions.
> It is fully encompassed within the scope of the basic space of
>   phenomena, free of effort and achievement.
>
> In the ocean of timeless awareness, uncorrupted and
>   spontaneously perfect,
> swim golden fish—the manifestation of lucidity and purity.
> They are sealed within the naturally occurring realm free of any
>   conditional basis.

14. Commentary: *bzang ngan* (no better or worse); source verse: *bar gsum* (or in between).
15. Commentary: *mthong* (see); tantra: *thob* (attain).
16. Commentary: *kun byed mngon du phyung bar 'dus* (is that of the all-creating one making evident); tantra: *kun byed mngon du byung bar nus* (is that of the all-creating one being able to make evident).
17. Commentary: *spros pa'i chos* (elaboration); source verse: *spros pa'i tshogs* (patterns of elaboration).
18. We have translated the commentary version of this citation. The tantra reads:

> Supreme dharmakaya, free of the four extremes:
> look at the crystal kaya, purified of flaws!
> Dharmakaya, purified of extremes, is the kaya that dispels
>   darkness.
> Flawless and dispelling darkness, it is similar to the halo of
>   a lamp.
> The four fires of awareness dispel the darkness of the four
>   extremes.

19. Commentary: *sku gsum rang bzhin kyang* (By nature, the three kayas); tantra: *sku gsum ston pa yang* (The teachers of the three kayas, moreover).
20. Commentary: *rtogs dang mi rtogs* (whether there is realization or not); source verse: *rtog dang mi rtog* (whether there are concepts or not).
21. Commentary: *gsang* (secret); tantra: *gnas* (abode).
22. Commentary: *rang bzhin 'ga' med de* (none of them has any independent nature whatsoever); source verse: *rang bzhin 'gag med de* (their nature is continuous).
23. Source verse: *bar skabs re 'ga'i chos su rtogs par bya* (You should realize that all these manifestations are temporary, adventitious phenomena);

commentary: *bar skabs re 'ga'i chos sku rtogs par bya* (You should realize these to be temporary, adventitious expressions of dharmakaya).

24. Commentary: *'gag pa'i chos ni* (phenomena subject to cessation are); tantra: *'gags pa'i chos nyid* (the true nature of what is subject to cessation is).

25. Commentary: *rig pa'i chos ni* (expressions of awareness); tantra: *rig pa'i chos lnga* (the five aspects of awareness).

26. Commentary (rev. Adzom): *rang shar bas* (arise naturally, and so); commentary (orig. Adzom): *rang shar ba* (arise naturally—).

27. Commentary: *bsam gtan nyid du rdzogs* (unwavering meditative stability itself); tantra: *bsam gtan chen por rdzogs* (unwavering, supreme meditative stability).

28. Commentary: *re ba nyid ni rang dag pas* (hope itself is pure in its own place); tantra: *re ba nyid dag rang snang bas* (hope itself manifests naturally as pure).

29. Commentary: *gzugs su rnam pa gnyis su rdzogs* (they are perfect in the dualistic way they manifest as forms); tantra: *gzugs sku rnam pa gnyis su rdzogs* (they are perfect as the two rupakayas).

30. Commentary: *bden shar te* (are experienced as true); tantra: *rang shar te* (arise naturally).

31. Commentary: *shar* (arise); tantra: *snang* (manifest).

32. Commentary: *rang snang dag pa'i tshad rnams rdzogs* (the full measure of awareness's own pure manifestations is perfect); tantra: *rang snang dag pa'i tshad rnams ni* (there is the full measure of awareness's own pure manifestations).

33. Commentary: *mtshon med na* (Though . . . cannot be quantified or illustrated); tantra: *mtson du med* (cannot be . . . illustrated).

34. Commentary: *ni* (as); tantra: *tu* (within).

35. Commentary: *rang byung ye shes bdud rtsi* (nectar, naturally occurring timeless awareness); tantra: *rang byung bdud rtsi* (naturally occurring nectar).

36. Commentary: *brtsal bya rtsol byed med par rang byung rang las shar* (arises naturally and occurs naturally, without there being anything to strive for or any effort to make); tantra: *btsal bya btsal byed med par rang las shar* (arises naturally without anything to seek or anyone to seek it).

37. Commentary: *gnas dang 'ong ba med pa'i* (no duration or onset); tantra: *gnas dang 'gro 'org med pa'i* (no duration, coming, or going).

38. Commentary: *rang grol chen po ni* (Supreme natural freedom); tantra: *rang grol chen po 'di* (This supreme natural freedom).

39. Commentary: *rig pa'i ngang* (scope of awareness); tantra: *skye med ngang* (the unborn state).

40. Commentary: *rtsa ba med* (without foundation); tantra: *rtsa ba su la srid* (and there is no possibility that any of them has a foundation), which is also found on fol. 75b.3 of the commentary.

Chapter 4

1. Commentary: *byas pas* (by being made); tantra: *byas pa* (as something made).
2. Commentary: *'dzin pa'i tha snyad* (conventional designations that reify); tantra: *'dzin pa'i tha dad* (separateness of reification).
3. Commentary: *gnas* (abides); tantra: *snang* (manifests).
4. Commentary: *rang byung shes rab mig gsal ba* (what is clearly perceived by the eye of naturally occurring sublime knowing); tantra: *shes rab mig gis gsal ba ni* (what is clearly perceived by the eye of sublime knowing).
5. Commentary (orig. and rev. Adzom): *dpe zla med pa'i don* (which has ultimate meaning in that nothing compares to it); commentary (Dergé) and source verse: *ye zla med pa'i don* (which has ultimate meaning in being timelessly beyond compare).
6. Commentary: *don mi 'grub* (has never existed in actuality); tantra: *don mi 'gyur* (is ultimately unchanging).
7. Commentary: *rang gsal che* (supreme natural lucidity); tantra: *rang sar che* (supreme in its own place).
8. Commentary: *dbyig* (wealth); tantra: *dbyibs* (shape).
9. Commentary: *mtshon ldan* (colored); tantra: *mtshan ldan* (authentic).
10. Commentary: *bsam 'das* (beyond imagination); tantra: *bsam gtan* (meditative stability).
11. Commentary: *rang byung sku nyid* (This naturally occurring kaya itself is); tantra: *rang byung sku gnyis* (The two naturally occurring kayas are).
12. Commentary: *rig pa* (awareness); tantra: *rim pa* (developmental stages).
13. These lines are not found in the version of the tantra available to us.
14. Commentary (Dergé): *dpyod* (known through analytical investigation) and *rnam dpyod* (known when discerned thoroughly); commentary (orig. Adzom): *gcod* (delineated) and *rnam gcod* (thoroughly delineated).
15. Commentary: *zhig pa* (has put an end to); tantra: *med pa* (is without).
16. Commentary: *ngang ring shugs dal ba* (they are patient and relaxed); tantra: *rang nyid shugs dal ba* (they themselves are relaxed).
17. Commentary: *gdal ba'i chos nyid klong* (expanse that is the true nature of phenomena, the infinite extent); tantra: *bdal ba chen po'i klong* (expanse that is the supreme and infinite extent).

18. Commentary: *ma btsal ji bzhin pa ru gnas pa de* (To abide in what simply
is, without its being sought); tantra: *ma rtsol ji bzhin sa ru gnas pa des*
(To abide on the level of what simply is, without effort).
19. Tantra: *bstan* (revealed), which is also found on fol. 87a.4 of the commentary; commentary: *bsten* (relied on).
20. Commentary: *byar med rtsol sgrub kun las 'das pa yin* (The state in
which nothing need be done transcends all effort and achievement); tantra: *rtsol sgrub kun gyi gnyen po 'joms byed te* (The antidotes that entail
all effort and achievement are vanquished).
21. The tantra omits *dngos* (actually).
22. Commentary: *snang bar* (sensory appearances); tantra: *rnam par* (specific forms).
23. Commentary: *'bad med ye nas rdzogs sangs rgyas* (are effortlessly and
timelessly perfect buddhas); tantra: *'bad pa med par ye nas grol* (are
effortlessly and timelessly free).
24. Commentary: *bdag dang 'dzin pa'i zhen yul* (self-identity and the objects
of its reifying perceptions); tantra: *chags dang 'dzin pa'i zhen yul* (the
objects of one's fixated attachment and reification).
25. The tantra has the plural marker *rnams* instead of *kyang* (Moreover).
26. Commentary: *kun* (all that); source verse: *kyang* (that which, moreover).
27. Source verse: *su gsal* (evident within); commentary: *gsal bas* (being
clear as).
28. Commentary: *rdzogs chen nga yi byang chub sems* (Great perfection
is my awakened mind); tantra: *yang dag rdzogs pa'i byang chub sems*
(Awakened mind is truly perfect).
29. The tantra omits *yul les* (the scope of).
30. Commentary: *rang rig byang chub klong* (self-knowing awareness as
the expanse of enlightenment); source verse: *byang chub rang rig klong*
(enlightenment as the expanse of self-knowing awareness).
31. Commentary: *rig pa sku gsum ngo bor gsungs* (Awareness—the three
kayas—is said to be the essence of being); tantra: *rig pa'i sku ni gsum du
gsungs* (The kaya of awareness is said to be threefold).
32. Commentary: *rang snang* (own manifestations); tantra: *snang ba* (manifestations).
33. Commentary: *chos sku dngos bral ye shes gsang ba nyid* (Dharmakaya,
free of substance, is the very secret of timeless awareness); tantra: *chos
sku spros bral ye shes thabs kyi rgya* (Dharmakaya, free of elaboration,
is the seal of skillful means—timeless awareness).

34. Commentary: *'gag med rol pa'i rig pa* (Awareness as a continuous display); tantra: *'gag med sku yi rol pa* (The continuous display of the kayas).

35. Commentary: *mnyam pa nyid* (is a state of equalness); tantra: *gar yang gnas* (abides anywhere and everywhere).

Chapter 5

1. Commentary: *skye med byang chub sems* (unborn awakened mind); tantra: *skye med rang gsal rnyed* (the discovery of unborn natural lucidity).

2. Commentary: *dang bral* (free of); tantra: *las 'das* (beyond).

3. Commentary: *chos las 'das* (beyond any factor); tantra: *phyogs dang bral* (free of any extreme).

4. Commentary: *bya byed 'das* (transcends the plans and actions of); tantra: *byas pa med* (has not created).

5. Commentary: *rig pa'i sku dang dam tshig med* (There is neither samaya nor kaya of awareness); tantra: *rig pa'i sku la dam tshig med* (There is no samaya in the kaya of awareness).

6. Commentary: *lhun grub ster* (spontaneous presence bestowed); tantra: *lhun grub gter* (the treasure of spontaneous presence).

7. Commentary: *dgag dang sgrub pa'i med pa nyid* (The state that entails no repression or indulgence); tantra: *dgag sgrub med pa'i spyod pa ni* (Conduct without repression or indulgence).

8. This last line is not found in the version of the tantra available to us.

9. Commentary: *rang bzhin* (nature); tantra: *yul ni* (scope).

10. Commentary (rev. Adzom and Dergé): *btsal du med* (nothing need ever be sought); commentary (orig. Adzom): *brtsal du med* (no effort need ever be made).

11. Commentary: *chos nyid mi mthong yangs pa yin* (one becomes lost, having failed to perceive that nature); tantra: *chos nyid mi mthong spangs pa yin* (one rejects that nature, having failed to perceive it).

12. Commentary: *sbyong ba* (training); tantra: *spyod pa* (conduct).

13. Commentary: *rang sems spang pa sems* (that is ordinary mind—the abandonment of natural mind); tantra: *rang sems spang pa yin* (this is the abandonment of natural mind).

14. Commentary: *chos chen po* (The supreme teaching); tantra: *ches che'o* (So very supreme).

15. Commentary: *dag kyang rtogs par dka'* (is difficult to realize, even though it is pure); tantra: *kun gyis rtogs par dka'* (is difficult for anyone to realize).

16. Commentary (Dergé) and tantra: *lta* (view); commentary (orig. and rev. Adzom): *lha* (deity).

17. This line actually appears in *The Array of Inlaid Gems*.

18. Commentary: *rang rig* (self-knowing awareness); tantra: *rang sems* (natural mind).

19. Commentary (rev. Adzom): *don rnal ma ma rtogs par* (fail to realize what has genuine meaning); commentary (orig. Adzom): *don rnal ma rtogs par bstan pa* (realize what has genuine meaning).

20. Commentary: *rang byung* (naturally occurring); tantra: *rang snang* (naturally manifest).

21. Commentary: *ye nas rtogs pa* (timeless realization); tantra: *ye shes rtogs pa* (realization of timeless awareness).

22. Commentary: *spros* (elaboration); tantra: *grogs* (ally).

23. Commentary: *mnyam pa chen po'i* (a state of supreme equalness); tantra: *mnyam par gnas pa'i* (which abides in evenness).

24. Commentary: *sprul snang* (emanations . . . manifest); tantra: *yul snang* (the scope . . . manifests).

25. Commentary: *snang bas* (since what manifests); tantra: *shar ba* (what arises).

26. Commentary: *yul ngo* (the essence of sense objects as); tantra: *rang ngo* (the very essence of).

27. Commentary (Dergé) and tantra: *sgra bzhi* (the four sounds); commentary (orig. and rev. Adzom): *sgra gzhi* (the basis of sound).

28. Commentary: *la* (Within); tantra: *'di* (This).

29. Commentary: *dag pa'i snang ba* (pure perceptions manifest); tantra: *rig pa snang ba* (awareness manifests).

30. Commentary: *zug rngu med pa'i* (which is without affliction); tantra: *gzung du med pa* (which cannot be reified as an object).

31. Commentary: *bral ba* (free of); tantra: *med pa* (without).

32. Commentary: *rig pa* (awareness); tantra: *bsgom pa* (meditation).

33. Commentary: *rig pa ma bsgoms lhun grub la* (Given that awareness is spontaneously present and not cultivated in meditation); tantra: *chos dbyings ye nas bsgom med la* (Given that the basic space of phenomena is timelessly such that it is not cultivated in meditation).

34. Commentary: *mthong* (perceive); tantra: *rnyed* (find).

35. Commentary: *mtha' bral* (free of limitation); tantra: *blta bral* (free of being viewed).

36. Commentary: *legs par bstan gyi yid la zung* (I have revealed this thor-

oughly, so keep it in mind); tantra: *'on kyang legs par yid la zung* (However, hold this thoroughly in mind).

37. The tantra adds *dper na* (for example).

38. Commentary: *sems kyi dri ma ci* (how could there be the distortions of ordinary mind?); tantra: *sems kyi dri mas bcings* (there is bondage due to the distortions of ordinary mind).

39. Commentary: *ye shes dam bca'* (what is posited to be timeless awareness); tantra: *ye nas dam bca'* (what has always been posited).

40. Commentary: *dri med dag pa'i* (undistorted and pure); tantra: *dri ma dag pa'i* (purified of distortion).

41. Commentary: *byas med* (is not created); tantra: *byar med* (is such that nothing need be done).

42. Commentary: *rtog med sa la de bzhin gshegs* (One arrives at suchness in the nonconceptual state); tantra: *rtog med pa la de bzhin nyid* (Suchness itself is found in the nonconceptual state).

43. Commentary: *gdangs* (radiance); tantra: *mdangs* (inner glow).

44. Commentary: *ye nas rang gsal* (is timelessly and naturally lucid); tantra: *ye nas rang gnas* (abides timelessly and naturally).

45. Commentary: *mchod bstod lha mi dgyes* (Deities are not delighted with offerings and praises); tantra: *mchod 'bul lha tshogs dgyes* (The hosts of deities are delighted with offerings).

46. Commentary (orig. and rev. Adzom): *brtsal* (involving effort); commentary (Dergé): *bstal* (to seek).

47. Commentary (orig. and rev. Adzom): *dpyad* (to determine); commentary (Dergé): *spyad* (to engage in); tantra: *sbyang* (on which to train).

48. Commentary: *spyod du med pa* (involves no specific conduct); tantra: *bskyod du med pa* (cannot be caused to waver).

49. Commentary (Dergé) has *ltar* (like), missing in the two Adzom editions.

50. Commentary: *'phrin las brtsal med* (no activity involving effort); tantra: *'phrin las btsal med* (no activity that involves seeking anything).

51. Commentary: *bsrung du med* (nothing be upheld); tantra: *bsrung dang bral* (free of being upheld).

52. Commentary: *bskur thob med* (neither bestowed nor received); tantra: *'gyur ba med* (without change).

Chapter 6

1. Commentary: *chos rnams* (phenomena); tantra: *sangs rgyas* (buddhas).

2. We have translated the commentary version of these lines. The closest match in the tantra reads: *dmigs pa'i yul dang bral na sgron ma yul la*

snang / snang 'byed btsal sems med par ye shes dbyings su 'dus (If there is freedom from any objective frame of reference, the lamp manifests in sense objects; / that which causes manifestation [reading *byed* for *'byed*] is subsumed within the basic space of timeless awareness, which is not the ordinary seeking mind).

3. Commentary (orig. and rev. Adzom): *snod bcud thams cad* (The entire universe); commentary (Dergé) and tantra: *snod bcud bsdus pa* (What is subsumed in the universe).

4. Commentary: *ye nas med* (there was never anything that could be called); tantra: *ming yang med* (there was not even the name).

5. Commentary (Dergé) and tantra: *rje btsun* (foremost and most venerable); commentary (orig. and rev. Adzom): *rje btsan* (majestic ruler).

6. Commentary: *nga yi ngang 'dir* (within my realm); tantra: *nga yi sku la* (in my enlightened form), which is also found on fol. 57b.6 of the commentary.

7. Commentary: *chos kun* (all phenomena); tantra: *chos rnams* (phenomena).

8. Source verse and commentary (Dergé): *bsgrub med btsal du med* (nothing to achieve or to seek); commentary (orig. and rev. Adzom): *bsgrub med brtsal du med* (nothing to achieve or effort to be made).

9. Commentary (rev. Adzom): *zla ba rgyal mtshan gyi blo brgya* (the scope of Dawa Gyaltsen's mind); commentary (orig. Adzom): *zla ba rgyal mtshan gyi blo brgya* (the hundredfold mind of Dawa Gyaltsen). We have not been able to determine the source of this reference to Dawa Gyaltsen.

10. Commentary: *btags* (labeled); tantra: *brtag* (examined).

11. Commentary: *rang byung* (occurs naturally); tantra: *rang bzhin* (is so by nature).

12. Commentary (Dergé) and tantra: *btsal* (sought); commentary (orig. and rev. Adzom): *brtsal* (gained by effort).

13. Commentary (Dergé) and tantra: *la* (In); commentary (orig. and rev. Adzom): *las* (From).

14. Commentary (orig. and rev. Adzom): *brtsal* (effort); commentary (Dergé): *btsal* (seeking).

15. Commentary: *nam mkha' kun kyang rtsol sgrub kun las 'das* (space is entirely beyond all effort and achievement); tantra: *nam mkhas kun byas rtsol sgrub kun las 'das* (space, which has created everything, is beyond all effort and achievement).

16. Commentary: *lhun gyis grub* (are spontaneously present as); tantra: *gnas pa yin* (abide within).

17. Commentary: *klong yangs pas* (the spacious expanse of); source verse: *klong du grol* (free within the expanse of).

Chapter 7

1. Source verse: *rtse* (the pinnacle), which parallels the line cited from *The Gathering of Secrets* a few lines later; commentary: *tshe* (longevity).

2. Commentary: *ni* (As for); tantra: *nas* (Within).

3. Commentary: *chos sku rtog med zang thal nyid* (dharmakaya is nonconceptual and unobstructed); tantra: *rtog med rang shar zang thal nyid* (the nonconceptual state arises naturally and is unobstructed).

4. Source verse and commentary (rev. Adzom and Dergé): *bya btsal* (conscious striving); commentary (orig. Adzom): *bya brtsal* (concerted effort).

5. Commentary: *rgya che* (on a vast scale); tantra: *rgyan la* (in its adornment).

6. The tantra omits *rang gsal* (Naturally lucid).

7. Commentary (orig. and rev. Adzom): *gsal* (becomes clear); commentary (Dergé): *'char* (arises).

8. Commentary: *rtsol med chos skur ye nas yid ches pas* (in trusting that this effortless state has always been dharmakaya); tantra: *btsal du med par ye nas yid ches pas* (in trusting that this has always been effortless).

9. Commentary: *ngo bor bshad* (is explained to be the essence); tantra: *ngang la thim* (dissolves within its scope).

10. Commentary: *ting 'dzin mchog* (there is sublime meditative absorption); tantra: *ting 'dzin thob* (meditative absorption is attained).

11. This line is not found in the version of the tantra available to us.

12. This line is not found in the version of the tantra available to us.

13. This line actually appears in *The Array of Inlaid Gems*.

14. This line is not found in the version of the tantra available to us, although the tantra contains a similar line: *sems dang bral ba'i rig pa sangs rgyas dngos* (Awareness free of ordinary mind is true buddhahood).

15. This line is missing in the Dergé commentary.

16. Commentary: *ye nas* (timelessly); source verse: *ye grol* (timelessly free).

17. Source verse: *bya rtsol* (concerted effort); commentary: *bya btsal* (conscious striving).

18. Commentary: *ye shes rang snang* (naturally manifest timeless awareness); tantra: *ye shes yul snang* (timeless awareness manifest in sense objects).

19. The tantra adds *ngo bo* (the essence of being).

20. This line is not found in the version of the tantra available to us.

21. Commentary: *de* (It); tantra: *don* (Its ultimate significance).

22. Commentary: *'gro ba* (movement); tantra: *grol ba* (freedom).

23. Commentary: *mdor na ji ltar snang ba yi chos kun de las byung ba'o* (In brief, all phenomena that manifest as they do come from it); tantra:

mdor na ji ltar snang ba yi / sa chu me rlung nam mkha' dang / 'byung ba che rnams de las byung (In brief, earth, water, fire, and air, / which manifest as they do, moreover— / these great elements have come from it).

Chapter 8

1. Commentary: *rtogs* (realized); scriptural source: *mthong* (perceived).
2. Commentary: *srog* (has life force); tantra: *gsog* (is hollow).
3. The tantra adds *nyon mongs* (and afflictive emotions).
4. Commentary: *kun byed nga yi* (of me, the all-creating one); tantra: *kun byed rgyal po'i* (of the all-creating monarch).
5. Commentary: *chos kun* (all phenomena); tantra: *chos skur* (dharmakaya).
6. We have translated this as "all phenomena" (*chos kun*), assuming that *chos sku* (dharmakaya) is a typographical error, although it is found in all three editions of the commentary.
7. Commentary: *brid* (seduced); source verse: *khrid* (led).
8. Commentary: *rnam rtog* (concepts); tantra: *sems can* (ordinary beings).
9. Commentary: *blo la* (as ordinary consciousness); tantra: *glo bur* (adventitiously).
10. Commentary: *btags* (labeled); tantra: *brtags* (determined to be).
11. Commentary: *btags* (labeled); tantra: *grags* (proclaimed).
12. Commentary: *gzung 'dzin* (dualistic perception); tantra: *yul 'dzin* (the reification of sense objects).
13. Commentary (orig. and rev. Adzom) and tantra: *'dzin rtog bral nas* (With freedom from reifying concepts); commentary (Dergé): *mi 'dzad rtog bral* (With freedom from inexhaustible concepts).
14. Commentary: *'gro 'ong med pa* (nothing comes or goes); tantra: *'gro ba med pa* (nothing comes).
15. Commentary: *'khor dang 'das* (of samsara and nirvana); tantra: *'khor dang 'dres* (blended with samsara).
16. Commentary (Adzom) and tantra: *gsog* (hollow); commentary (Dergé): *srog* (life force).
17. This line is missing in the Dergé commentary.
18. Commentary: *khungs* (underpinnings); tantra: *khong* (inner workings).
19. Commentary: *dngos po mtshan ma med* (has no substance or characteristics); tantra: *dngos po bsam pa med* (has no substance and entails no deliberation).
20. The tantra omits *shin tu* (a great).
21. Commentary: *gsang ba'i nges don rang bzhin gcig* (this single nature—

the definitive meaning of all that is secret; tantra: *gsang ba'i nges don gcig* (this single definitive meaning of all that is secret).

22. Commentary: *chos nyid dkyil yangs mtshan ma med pa'o* (The spacious mandala of the true nature of phenomena is without characteristics); tantra: *chos nyid dkyil 'khor yangs pa na* (Within the spacious mandala of the true nature of phenomena).

23. Commentary: *rmi lam nang zhes* (Am I in a dream?); source verse: *rmi lam nang bzhin* (Is this like a dream?).

24. Commentary (Dergé): *rang sangs* (naturally pristine); commentary (orig. and rev. Adzom): *rang srungs* (naturally protected).

25. Commentary: *grub mtha' rnams* (philosophical systems); tantra: *grub mtha' gnyis* (two philosophical systems).

26. Commentary: *chos su* (as phenomena); tantra: *chos sku* (as dharmakaya).

27. Commentary (rev. Adzom): *kyis* (through); commentary (orig. Adzom): *kyi* (of).

28. Commentary: *rtogs su* (within one's realization); tantra: *rtags su* (as indications).

29. Commentary: *de yang med par* (Otherwise); tantra: *de rnams min par* (Without these being the case).

30. Commentary (orig. and rev. Adzom): *gnyis su med par spyad* (experienced as nonduality); commentary (Dergé): *gnyis su med par byang* (refined in nonduality).

31. Commentary (Dergé) and tantra: *grol ba la* (there is freedom, and); commentary (orig. and rev. Adzom): *grol ba med* (there is no freedom).

32. The preceding two lines are missing in the Dergé commentary.

33. Commentary: *sna tshogs snang bas gdangs zhes bya* (Since it manifests in myriad ways, it is "radiance"); tantra: *sna tshogs gdangs bas sangs zhes bya* (Since it is limpid in various ways, it is "pristine").

34. Commentary: *rang la* (in and of itself); tantra: *ye nas* (timelessly).

35. Commentary: *log pas* (defies); tantra: *'das pas* (is beyond).

36. Commentary: *dmigs byed* (whatever establishes these frameworks); tantra: *dmigs med* (whatever is nonreferential).

37. Commentary: *dpyod* (examination); tantra: *spyod* (conduct).

38. The preceding six lines are missing in the Dergé commentary.

39. We have translated the commentary version of the preceding three lines. The tantra reads:

> How could there be any frame of reference concerning nirvana?
> Since it is nonexistent as cause or condition,
> it is beyond the duality of being empty or not.

40. Commentary: *grol ba na* (are free); tantra: *rang grol bas* (are naturally free).

41. This line is missing in the Dergé commentary.

42. Commentary: *khams gsum ldog pa'i rten med par* (Without any grounds for falling back into the three realms); tantra: *khams gsum 'khor ba'i rten med par* (Without any support for the three realms of samsara).

Chapter 9

1. This sentence is missing in the Dergé commentary.

2. Commentary: *zang thal yin par* (unobstructed); tantra: *zang thal yangs par* (spacious and unobstructed).

3. Commentary: *ngo bo* (essence); tantra: *snang ba* (perspective), which is also found on fol. 190a.4–5 of the commentary.

4. Commentary: *yang dag nga* (the truth that I am); tantra: *yang dag pa* (the truth).

5. Commentary: *dgos* (needing); tantra: *dgongs* (intending).

6. Uttaratantra, I.5.

7. Commentary: *ma rtogs pa* (Without realizing); tantra: *ma brtags par* (Without remarking).

8. Commentary: *rgyu rkyen med pa'i skye* (occurs without causes or conditions); tantra: *rgyu rkyen med mi skye* (is unborn, with no causes or conditions).

9. Commentary: *ma btsal ji bzhin pa ru gnas pa de* (To abide in what simply is, without its being sought); tantra: *ma rtsol ji bzhin sa ru gnas pa des* (To abide on the level of what simply is, without effort).

10. Commentary (orig. and rev. Adzom): *ngang bzhengs* (is experienced intuitively); source verse and commentary (Dergé): *rang bzhengs* (arises naturally).

11. Commentary: *don 'di'i* (these meanings); tantra: *'di yi* (these).

12. Commentary: *mi snang nam mkha' gud lta dang* (Trying to fragment space, which is nonmanifest . . .). The closest line in the version of the tantra available to us reads: *mi snang nam mkha' khu rlangs dang* (. . . and misty vapor [dissipating in] space, which is nonmanifest).

13. Commentary: *rlung bzhi rim gyis zhon nas kyang / rlung chen gcig gis bskyod pa'i tshe* (Having been borne on the four subtle energies in succession, / one is stirred by a single great energy); tantra: *rlung bzhi rim gyis zhi nas kyang / rlung chen dag gis bskyod pa'i tshe* (Once the four subtle energies are pacified in succession, / one is stirred by the major energies).

14. Commentary: *yul gnas* (object and environment); tantra: *lus gnad* (physical posture).

15. Commentary: *nam mkha' dag la kun kyang rtsol mi byed / nam mkha'i rang bzhin rtsol sgrub kun las 'das* (While everyone seeks something in pure space, / the nature of space is beyond all effort and achievement); tantra: *nam mkha' dag la kun kyang btsal bya ru / nam mkhas kun byas rtsol sgrub kun las 'das* (While everything could be sought in pure space, / space—within which all is created—is beyond all effort and achievement).

16. Commentary (orig. and rev. Adzom): *'khrul pa'i blo* (ordinary confused mind); commentary (Dergé) and source verse: *'khrul pa'i klong* (expanse of confusion).

17. These two lines are not found in the version of the tantra available to us.

18. Commentary (orig. and rev. Adzom): *mnyam pa* (equalness); commentary (Dergé) and source verse: *nyams pa* (impairment).

19. Commentary: *brtags dang brtag dpyad* (labels and speculates about); scriptural source: *brgya dang brtag dpyad* (speculates about the hundred implications of).

20. Commentary: *don dang dbyer med* (inseparability from the ultimate); source verse: *don dam dbyer med* (the inseparability of the ultimate).

21. Commentary: *spros* (speculation); scriptural source: *sgro* (exaggeration).

22. Commentary: *rig pa 'ching* (awareness is bound); tantra: *rig pa nyid* (there is awareness itself).

23. Commentary (orig. and rev. Adzom): *blun po'i blo* (a fool's attitude); commentary (Dergé) and source verse: *blun po'i klong* (expanse of foolishness).

24. Commentary: *rig pa'i ngang* (scope of . . . awareness); tantra: *bde ba'i sku* (kaya of bliss).

25. Commentary: *chos nyid ngang* (the . . . true nature of phenomena); tantra: *gtong phod can* (endowed with . . . liberty).

26. Commentary: *'gyur med nam mkha'i klong* (the expanse of unchanging (space); tantra: *'gyur med brtson 'grus che* (great and unchanging exertion).

27. The tantra adds *de yi phyir na* (For this reason) at the beginning of this line.

28. Commentary: *ming* (label); tantra: *yul* (object).

29. Commentary: *rnam rtog yul kyang med* (there are no concepts or objects); tantra: *sna tshogs yul kyang med* (there is no variety of objects).

30. Commentary: *thig le gcig rtogs yangs pa'i* (the spacious realization of the

single sphere of being): tantra: *de ltar bya ba gsum btang* (thus letting go of the three kinds of action).

31. Commentary: *mi ldog sa la 'gyur med nges par gnas* (is one of abiding definitively and without change on a level from which there is no regression); tantra: *phyir mi ldog pa'i sa la nges par gnas* (is one of abiding definitively on a level from which there is no falling back).

32. Commentary: *su la* (for anyone); tantra: *sems can su la* (for any ordinary being).

33. Commentary: *'khor ba 'khrul pa ga la yod* (Where, then, is samsara? Where is confusion?); tantra: *'khor 'das 'du 'bral ga la yod* (How, then, could samsara and nirvana come together and then separate?).

34. Commentary: *rig pa de nyid* (awareness itself); tantra: *de nyid* (itself).

35. This line is not found in the version of the tantra available to us.

36. Commentary: *dag* (pure); tantra: *gsal* (clear).

37. Commentary: *btsal du* (to seek); tantra: *bya ru* (to enact).

38. Commentary: *bsam pa* (thoughts); tantra: *med pa* (what is ineffable).

39. Commentary: *bya dang byed pa'i* (that entails plans or actions); tantra: *bya ba byed pa'i* (of carrying out some plan).

40. Commentary: *ltos* (dependent); tantra: *stong* (void).

41. Commentary: *'dzim pa med* (does not perceive); tantra: *'dzin pa spang* (avoids perceiving).

42. Commentary: *byas dang byung ba med pa* (nothing is created and nothing happens); tantra: *byas pa byung pa med pa* (no creation occurs).

43. Commentary and source verse (rev. Adzom): *dpyad* (engage in examination); source verse (orig. Adzom): *spyad* (engage in conduct).

44. This line is not found in the version of the tantra available to us.

45. Commentary: *rang sangs rgyas kyi sa* (the level of natural buddhahood); tantra: *sangs rgyas nyid kyi sa* (the level of buddhahood itself).

46. Commentary: *de la rang byung stong yul bas* (Since these are naturally occurring, empty objects); tantra: *shes pa 'gyu ba stong yul bas* (Since the stirring of consciousness involves empty objects).

47. Commentary: *kun grol phyir* (Because everything is free); tantra: *kun grol byed* (Everything is made free).

48. Commentary: *yan pa* (unstructured); source verse: *lhun grub* (spontaneously present).

49. Commentary: *dpyad* (avail themselves of); tantra: *spyod* (engage in).

50. Commentary: *gzud* (enmeshed in); tantra: *gzung* (attached to).

51. Commentary: *bsgrub bya'i* (to accomplish); source verse: *bsgrub 'dod* (that one desires to accomplish).

52. Source verse (orig. Adzom): *phyam gdal* (is infinitely uniform); commentary (orig. and rev. Adzom) and source verse (rev. Adzom): *phyam 'das* (is beyond uniformity).

53. Source verse: *bya rtsol* (concerted effort); commentary: *bya btsal* (conscious striving).

54. Commentary: *ma byung byas pa med pa ste* (It does not come about and is not created); tantra: *ma byung byas pa med pa'i chos* (It is something that does not come about and is not created).

55. Commentary: *stong gsal gnas* (abides as the unity of emptiness and lucidity); tantra: *stong par gnas* (abides as emptiness).

56. Commentary: *brtson 'grus* (exertion); tantra: *rtsol sgrub* (effort and achievement).

57. Commentary: *bskyar* (reestablished); tantra: *bskyal* (led).

58. Commentary: *sems la nges 'byung gtan la 'bebs pa med* (In mind there is no definitive conclusion to reach regarding the certainty of one's release); tantra: *sems las nges lung gtan la 'bebs pa med* (From mind comes no definitive transmission of certainty).

59. Commentary: *mi snang yul med* (this does not manifest or exist as an object); tantra: *mi snang yul kun* (all objects are not manifest).

60. Commentary: *rig sngags* (mantras of awareness); tantra: *rigs rnams* (families).

61. Commentary: *bdag bzhin* (my example); source verse: *bdag gzhan* (myself and others).

62. Commentary: *da lta nyid nas rgyal ba'i sa la gnas* (abide henceforth on the level of victorious ones); tantra: *da lta nyid na sangs rgyas sa la gnas* (abide in this very moment on the level of buddhahood).

63. Commentary: *bzung nas* (Appreciating); tantra: *la zhugs* (Entering into).

Chapter 10

1. Commentary: *shes rab ma yin dbang pos mthong* (this experience is not just a sublime form of knowing, but direct perception with one's faculties); tantra: *shes rab mig gi dbang pos mthong* (this is perceived with the faculty of the eye of sublime knowing).

2. Commentary (rev. Adzom): *gzhi lam 'bras bu ltos min pa'o* (there is reliance on ground, path, and fruition); tantra: *gzhi dang 'bras bu ltos min pa'o* (there is no reliance on ground or fruition); commentary (orig. Adzom and Dergé): *ltos yin pa'o* (there is reliance).

3. Commentary: *lhun mnyam* (spontaneous equalness); source verse: *lhun grub* (spontaneous presence).

4. Source verse: *mi g.yo mnyam pa bzhin* (like the unwavering evenness); commentary: *mi g.yo mnyam pa nyid* (—the unwavering evenness).

5. Commentary: *ma bskyod mi bskyod bskyod pa kun las 'das* (It has never varied, does not vary, and is beyond all variation); tantra: *ma spyod mi spyod spyod pa kun las 'das* (It has never been involved, does not become involved, and is beyond all involvement).

6. Commentary: *ye nas ma byung ma bcos cog gzhag nyid* (The uncontrived state of resting imperturbably has never come into being); tantra: *ye shes ma bcos rang byung cog bzhag nyid* (Uncontrived timeless awareness is a naturally occurring state of resting imperturbably).

7. Commentary: *phyi ma shor ba med pa nyid* (is truly ineffable and is not lost to externals); tantra: *phyi la shor ba med pa nyid* (is truly not lost to externals).

8. Commentary: *rig pa nyid kyi gzhag thabs gsal* (is to seek a means of resting in awareness itself); tantra: *rig pa nyid ni bzhag sa btsal* (is awareness itself seeking a place of rest).

9. This couplet (*thig le nyag gcig spros med de blos yi bye brag brjod las 'das*) is not found in any of the seventeen source tantras of the Category of Direct Transmission in the edition available to us. Several lines in *The Tantra Without Letters* are suggestive, however: *thig le nyag gcig kun chub pas / spros pa'i ye ge'i ming yang med* (The unique sphere of being is the consummation of everything, / and so even the term "elaboration" is absent); and *blo yi bye brag brjod 'das shing* (It transcends verbal expression and analysis by ordinary consciousness).

10. The tantra omits *rig pa'i* (of awareness).

11. Commentary: *'byung ba lnga yi sang rgyas lam ltar snang / chen po lnga nyid ma yi snang bar gsal* (The five minor elements are buddhas manifesting on the path. / The five great elements are clearly evident manifestations of the mothers); tantra: *'byung ba lnga yi sang rgyas pha ltar snang / chen po lnga nyid ma yin snang bar gsal* (The five elements are buddhas manifesting as fathers. / The five great elements are the mothers; they are evident in sensory appearances).

12. Commentary: *cer gzhag* (Resting in the immediacy of); tantra: *cog bzhag* (Resting imperturbably in).

13. Commentary: *chos kyi sku yi snang ba thams cad ston* (reveals the entire perspective of dharmakaya); tantra: *chos kyi sku ni snang ba thams cad bstan* (is dharmakaya, which reveals all perspectives).

14. Commentary: *gsang ba'i gzhag thabs* (the secret method of resting); tantra: *gsang ba'i 'gag thabs* (the secret means of bringing about their cessation).

15. Commentary: *nga yi mig la 'di yis mthong* (it looks through my eyes); tantra: *nga yi dmigs pa 'di yis mthong* (it sees my frame of reference).

16. Commentary: *dpyod* (analysis); tantra: *bcos* (contrivance).

17. Commentary: *gzugs* (forms); tantra: *tshig* (labels).

18. Commentary: *nga yi rang snang nyams myong* (meditative experience—my awareness's own manifestation); tantra: *nga yi nyams myong* (my meditative experience).

19. Commentary: *'di tsam* (all this simply ensures); tantra: *ngas brtsams* (I have ensured).

20. The tantra omits "as one" (*gcig tu*).

21. Commentary: *gcig 'dus ngo bo gcig pa* (single unifying essence); tantra: *gcig 'dus ngo bo rtse gcig* (one-pointed unifying essence).

22. Commentary: *rig* (knowing); tantra: *rtogs* (realizing).

23. Commentary: *dran pa nyid* (consideration); tantra: *dran pa rnams* (considerations).

24. The three instances of *sangs rgyas* (buddhahood) found in the passage as cited in the commentary are *nga rgyal* (pride) in the tantra.

25. Commentary: ... *sun ma phyung* ... *zhe ma bcad* ... *yul ma phyung ba* (... does not try to renounce ... is not resigned ... and does not banish); tantra: ... *sun phyung* ... *zhe bcad* ... *yul phyung ba* (... tries to renounce ... is resigned ... and banishes).

26. The tantra adds *chen po* (great).

27. Commentary: *'gyu ba* (mental stirring); tantra: *'gyur ba* (change).

28. Commentary: *gzhir* (support); tantra: *gzir* (focus).

29. Source verse: *bya dang rtsol med* (nothing to do and no effort to make); commentary: *bya dang btsal med* (nothing to do or to seek).

30. This line is not found in the version of the tantra available to us.

31. Commentary: *rtsol* (strives to understand); tantra: *brtsod* (argues about).

32. Commentary: *sngon du* (yet); tantra: *mngon du* (directly).

33. Commentary: *mi 'jog* (Do not focus on); tantra: *mi 'jig* (Do not do away with).

34. Commentary: *ma lus skye med* (that everything without exception is unborn); tantra: *ma skyes skye med* (what is unborn, without origination).

35. Commentary: *las* (from); tantra: *la* (within).

36. Source verse: *chos nyid klong las ngang gis g.yos pa med* (means that, as a matter of course, there is no straying / from the expanse that is the true

nature of phenomena); commentary: *chos nyid klong ste ngang gis g.yos pa med* (is the expansive nature of phenomena: / as a matter of course, there is no straying).

37. The last four lines are not found in any of the seventeen tantras of the Category of Direct Transmission in the edition available to us.

38. Commentary: *rang zhir zhog* (rest in natural peace); source verse: *ngang zhir glod* (relax in innate peace).

39. Commentary: *bzhag na* (If one rests); tantra: *gzhag pas* (Due to one's resting).

40. Commentary: *sna tshogs ye shes rol pa sdud* (so the myriad display of timeless awareness is subsumed); tantra: *sna tshogs ye shes chen por sdud* (the myriad variety of things is subsumed as supreme timeless awareness).

41. Commentary: *ngag ni smra brjod tshig dang bral* (one's speech is free of spoken words); tantra: *ngag gi smra brjod tshig rnams bral* (one is free of the spoken words involved in verbal expression).

42. Source verse: *la* (Given); commentary: *las* (Due to).

43. Commentary: *rang yin gzhan yin* ("This is self, this is other"); scriptural source: *rang min gzhan min* (neither self nor other).

44. Commentary: *yid dang sems kyi cho 'phrul cir snang 'gag / chos bral yid la byed pa'i bar du bdsam* (The implication that whatever manifests is the miraculous expression of ordinary conceptual mind / can be discerned in the "interval" between the state free of phenomena and the mind's conceptual process); scriptural source: *yid dang sems kyi cho 'phrul cir yang 'gag / chos bral yid dang byed pa'i bar du gtams* (The implications of the entire miraculous expression of ordinary conceptual mind / fill the "interval" between the mind free of phenomena and its conceptual process).

45. Commentary: *bsdam* (can be discerned within); scriptural source: *gtams* (fills).

46. Commentary: *gang gnyis* (Any dualism is); scriptural source: *gegs gnyis* (The two hindrances are).

47. Commentary: *bdsam* (can be discerned within); scriptural source: *gtams* (fills).

48. Commentary: *rang yin gzhan yin* ("This is self, this is other"); scriptural source: *rang min gzhan min* (neither self nor other).

49. Commentary: *ma btang* (not relinquished); scriptural source: *ma gtad* (not directed).

50. The scriptural source adds *gnyis* (two).

51. Commentary: *rang sor bskyur te . . . bdsam* (is laid bare in its natural state, discerned within); scriptural source: *rang sor 'gyus te . . . gtams* (stirs in its natural state, filling).

52. This line is not found in the version of the tantra available to us.

53. Commentary: *rmi lam lta bu'i tshig du go* (are understood . . . to be like words heard in); tantra: *rmi lam lta bu'i tshul du'o* (are in a mode . . . like that of).

54. Source verse: *rtog* (conceptualization); commentary: *brtags* (ascription).

55. Commentary: *sangs rgyas kyi thugs ni bdag rtog gi mtha' dang bral bas bsam gyis mi khyab pa'i ye shes nyid do* (The enlightened mind of buddhahood is free of the extreme of conceiving in terms of identity, and so is inconceivable timeless awareness itself); tantra: *sangs rgyas kyi ngo bo ni bdag rtog gi mtha' las 'das te kun khyab kyi ye shes nyid do* (The essence of buddhahood is beyond the limitation of conceiving in terms of identity, and so is all-pervasive timeless awareness itself).

56. Commentary: *di tshe 'khrul pa'i snang ba dag* (At this point, confused perception is pure); tantra: *de tshe nga ni snang ba dag* (At that point, I am pure perception).

57. Commentary: *'gag pa med pa'i rig pa la / 'khrul rgyu med pas ldog pa med* (Within unceasing awareness, / there is nothing to be confused about, so there is no regression); tantra: *'gag pa med pa'i rig pa las / 'khrul pa med pas rtog pa med* (Due to unceasing awareness, / there is no confusion and so no concepts).

58. Commentary: *rten nas 'phags* (exalted above everything); tantra: *gtan nas 'phags* (forever exalted).

59. Commentary: *ma bsgoms bzhag pa'i sa steng rang rig pa* (On the level of resting without meditating, self-knowing awareness); scriptural source: *ma bsgoms bzhag pa'i sa ste de nyid rang rig pa* (The level of resting without meditating—that itself is self-knowing awareness that).

60. Commentary: *rang so nyid de bcos ci dgos* (the natural state itself—what need is there to contrive it?); scriptural source: *rang bzo nyid de bcos mi dgos* (fabricated by itself—there is no need to contrive it).

61. Commentary: *ma bsgoms ye shes lhug pa bcos pa med pa'i gnad* (The key point is that timeless awareness, experienced in a relaxed and uncontrived way, is not cultivated in meditation); scriptural source: *ma bsgoms ye shes lhung pa bcos pa med pa'i gnas* (The uncontrived state is one of falling into timeless awareness, not cultivated in meditation).

62. Commentary: *byas pas* (by being produced); tantra: *bya bas ma zin* (by design).
63. Commentary: *dpyod* (analysis); tantra: *spyod* (conduct).
64. Commentary: *'phro* (proliferate); tantra: *'gro* (go).
65. Commentary: *bya btsal med* (nothing to do or to seek); tantra: *bya brtsal med* (no concerted effort).
66. Commentary: *btsal* (seek); tantra: *brtsal* (strive for).
67. Commentary: *klong* (expanse); tantra: *rlung* (subtle energy).
68. Commentary: *blang dor gnyis su med* (there is no duality of acceptance and rejection); source verse: *blang dor byar med cing* (there is nothing to accept or reject).
69. Commentary: *spyod pa . . . gnyis las 'das* (Conduct is beyond the dualities); tantra: *stong pa . . . yul las 'das* (Emptiness is beyond the scope).
70. Commentary: *spangs thob mtha' gnyis bral* (beyond the dualistic extremes of renunciation and attainment); tantra: *rtog mtha' gnyis dang bral* (beyond the two conceptual extremes).
71. Commentary: *snang ba'i chos rnams* (phenomena that manifest); source verse: *snang ba'i chos nyid* (the true nature of phenomena that manifest).
72. The scriptural source adds *rab tu che* (utterly).
73. Commentary: *rang gsal* (naturally lucid); source verse: *ngang gis* (as a matter of course).
74. Commentary: *shar* (reflection); tantra: *gsal* (clear appearance).
75. Commentary: *gtso* (foremost); tantra: *dngos* (actuality).
76. The tantra adds *yul la* (Within their scope) at the beginning of this line.
77. Commentary: *don gyi gtan tshigs chen po yin* (is the great, ultimate "logical argument"); tantra: *gtan tshigs chen po nga yis bshad* (is what I explain to be the great "logical argument").
78. Commentary: *chos nyid dgongs pa* (the enlightened intent of the true nature of phenomena); source verse: *mnyam pa'i dgongs pa* (the enlightened intent of equalness).
79. Commentary: *gzung ba yul la 'dzin pa sems* (It is the reification of objects and mind); tantra: *gzung ba yin la 'dzin pa yin* (It is what is reified as objects and as mind).
80. Commentary: *'khrul pas bzung* (out of confusion they reify things); tantra: *bzung bas 'khrul* (there is confusion in that things are reified).
81. Commentary: *bcas* (There is its); tantra: *bshad* (It is explained as).
82. Commentary: *lus* (physical embodiment); tantra: *yul* (scope).
83. Commentary: *gzung ba yul la 'dzin pa sems* (It is the reification of objects

and mind); tantra: *gzung ba yin la 'dzin pa yin* (It is what is reified as objects and as mind).

84. Commentary: *sa* (the level of); tantra: *pa* (awakening to), which is also found on fol. 129a.6 of the commentary.

85. Source verse: *bya rtsol med* (no concerted effort); commentary: *bya btsal med* (no conscious striving).

86. Commentary: *chos nyid* (true nature of phenomena); source verse: *chos dbyings* (basic space of phenomena).

Chapter 11

1. Source verse: *dmigs bsam* (conceptual frameworks); commentary: *dmigs pa'i* (frameworks).

2. Commentary: *dag* (pure); source verse: *yangs* (spacious).

3. Commentary: *gcod* (analysis); tantra: *bcos* (contrivance).

4. The tantra adds *med pa'i* (ineffable).

5. Source verse: *gzed* (anticipate); commentary: *gzeg* (crumb, particle), in error.

6. Commentary: *rang grol 'gro ba* (be freed naturally); source verse: *rang sar grol ba* (be free in their own place).

7. Commentary: *sgyur* (change); tantra: *zhi* (pacify).

8. Commentary: *rang sa* (natural state); tantra: *rang sangs* (naturally awakened state).

9. Commentary: *rtogs pa yis* (having realized); tantra: *rtogs pa che* (with the great realization of).

10. Commentary: *thar pa'i lam* (the path to liberation); scriptural source: *thar pa'i gnas* (liberation).

11. Commentary: *stong mun bsal* [read *gsal*] *dang yod dang med pa nyid* [Emptiness (whether darkness or light), existence and nonexistence]; scriptural source: *stong mu gsal dang yod dang med pa gnyis* (Emptiness and lucidity, existence and nonexistence).

12. Commentary: *gsang ba 'chol* (violate secrecy); tantra: *gsang ba 'phel* (broadcast what is secret).

13. Commentary: *gsang chen* (supreme secret); tantra: *gsang don* (secret meaning).

14. Commentary: *gtsub shing me gtsubs* (a stick creating fire by friction); tantra: *gtsub shing mer bcug* (a fire stick thrust into the fire).

15. Commentary: *gzhan yang mtshan mar gyur pa bsreg* (and anything of worth also being incinerated); tantra: *gzhan yang 'tshig par 'gyur ba bzhin* (and so incinerated).

16. The tantra adds *dam pa'i* (sacred).
17. Commentary: *dregs pa* (arrogance); tantra: *grags pa* (fame).
18. Commentary: *dgos pa* (need); tantra: *dgongs pa* (intend).
19. The tantra adds *man ngag* (of pith instructions).
20. Commentary: *gsung 'dzin* (use the words); tantra: *gdung 'dzin* (maintain the lineage).
21. Commentary: *bral* (free of any); tantra: *'brel* (connected to a).
22. Commentary: *su* (anyone); tantra: *sems can su* (any being).
23. Commentary: *bden bsgom* (meditates authentically); tantra: *bden goms* (is acquainted with truth).
24. Commentary (rev. Adzom) and tantra: *de ltar sems la ltad che ba* (A great spectacle thus takes place in the mind); commentary (orig. Adzom): *de ltar soms la ltad che ba* (Think thus: this is a great spectacle).
25. Commentary: *rig sngags kun* (those who hold all mantras of awareness); tantra: *rigs rnams kun* (all families).
26. Commentary: *grol* (free in); tantra: *grogs* (acquainted with).
27. Commentary: *skal che bas* (with the great fortune); tantra: *skal pa can* (with the fortune).
28. Commentary: *snang thabs ma 'gags pas* (manifests in ways that are continuous); tantra: *snang mtha' ma 'gags pas* (manifests such that it is not subject to finite limits).
29. Commentary: *rtogs pa'i nang nas* (among those with realization); tantra: *mi yi nang na* (among human beings).
30. Commentary: *dbang phyug yid kyis* (with a devoted mind to these powerful masters); tantra: *dbang phyug yin gyis* (for these are powerful masters).
31. The tantra adds *ye shes sgron ma* (—the lamp of timeless awareness).
32. Commentary: *dgongs pa* (enlightened intent); tantra: *gsal la ma yengs sgom pa* (meditation, lucid and undistracted).
33. The tantra adds *rang byung ma bcos* (—naturally occurring and uncontrived).
34. The tantra adds *'dzin med rang gsal* (—natural lucidity without reification).
35. Commentary: *rig pa* (awareness); tantra: *rig pa dngos med* (intangible awareness).
36. The tantra adds *kun gyi snying po yin pas* (is the heart essence of everything and).
37. Commentary: *sangs rgyas* (buddhahood); tantra: *sang rgyas kun gyi* (of all buddhas).

38. Commentary: *lta ba'i snying po rang rig ye shes sgron ma ni* (self-knowing awareness, which lies at the very heart of the view, is found to be the lamp of timeless awareness); tantra: *lta ba'i snying po sgron ma rin po che ni* (the very heart of the view is the precious lamp).
39. Commentary: *zhing* (realm); tantra: *gzhi* (ground).
40. Commentary: *ye shes gsang bcud* (The secret distillation of timeless awareness); tantra: *lus kyi gnad gcud* (The key point of physical posture).
41. Commentary: *lus* (the body); tantra: *las* (action).
42. Commentary: *theg pa'i* (of spiritual approaches); tantra: *thog mtha'i* (of beginning and end).
43. Commentary: *nyon mongs dngos rnams 'dul bar byed* (tames the patterns of afflictive emotions); tantra: *dngos rnams zad par byed* (ensures the resolution of things).
44. Commentary: *dmag dpung zlog par byed* (turns back the forces); tantra: *smag rum bzlog par byed* (banishes the gloom).
45. Commentary: *gsang ba'i* (secret); tantra: *yang gsal* (most lucid).
46. Commentary: *bcos bslad med pas* (uncontrived and unadulterated); tantra: *bcos pa med pas* (uncontrived).

Chapter 12

1. Commentary: *ming tsam btags pas stong* (are empty, mere labels that are applied); scriptural source: *ming tsam yang dag btags pas stong* (are mere labels that are applied but devoid of truth).
2. Commentary: *ngang* (state); tantra: *mkha'* (sky).
3. The tantra adds *e ma ho* (How marvelous!) at the beginning of this line.
4. Commentary: *btsal* (sought); tantra: *bcos* (contrived).
5. Commentary: *sems* (mind); tantra: *lus* (body).
6. Commentary: *btsal med* (nothing to seek); tantra: *rtsol med* (no effort).
7. Commentary: *rang rig pa la* (within self-knowing awareness); tantra: *rang gi sa la* (in one's natural place).
8. Commentary: *chos nyid zhi ba'i ngang* (the true nature of phenomena is a state of peace); tantra: *zhi ba'i ngang* (there is a state of peace).
9. Commentary: *snang ba rang la rnyed pa'i rang rig zang thal nyid* (Unobstructed self-knowing awareness itself, the illumination found within one); tantra: *snang ba rang la yas pa'i rang snang dngos med nyid* (Awareness's nonsubstantial appearances, the illumination that resolves within one).
10. Commentary: *rang gi gdangs* (its own radiance); tantra: *rang rig gdangs* (its own self-knowing radiance).

11. Commentary: *spro bsdu ma byed rig pa'i ngang la blta bar bya* (Do not complicate or oversimplify it, but look within the scope of awareness); tantra: *spro bsdu ma byas rang gi yul la blta bar bya* (Look within your own scope, which involves no complication or oversimplification).

12. Commentary: *yod min med pa'i mtha' gnyis rnam par bsal* (The two extremes of "is" and "is not" are completely eliminated, for it is neither); tantra: *yod dang min pa'i mtha' gnyis rnam par gsal* (The two extremes of "is" and "is not" are completely illuminated).

13. Commentary: *ye shes 'od gsal* (utterly lucid timeless awareness); tantra: *ye shes 'od lnga* (the five lights of timeless awareness).

14. Commentary: *gsal* (lucid); tantra: *sangs* (awakened).

15. Commentary: *dkyil 'khor rnam dag* (totally pure mandala); tantra: *rnam dag chen po'i dkyil 'khor* (mandala of supreme total purity).

16. Commentary: *stong par 'gyur* (are devoid of); tantra: *ltos par 'gyur* (are dependent on).

17. Commentary: *mtshan med ye shes rgyan nyid mthong* (Though it cannot be characterized, timeless awareness is perceived through its adornment); tantra: *mtshan ma ye shes rgyan nyid mthong* (What can be characterized is perceived to be the adornment of timeless awareness).

18. Commentary: *dpe med rang byung ye shes nyid* (Incomparable, naturally occurring timeless awareness itself); tantra: *dpe med ye shes rang nyid snang* (The manifestation of incomparable timeless awareness itself).

19. Commentary: *gyis* (by); tantra: *la* (on).

20. Commentary: *'das dang ma 'das tshig las 'das* (beyond the words "transcended" and "not transcended"); tantra: *'das dang ma 'das dus gsum bzhugs* (and transcendence and the lack thereof abide throughout the three times).

21. Commentary: *nyon mongs las* (afflictive emotions and karma); tantra: *nyon mongs tshogs* (accumulations of afflictive emotions).

22. Commentary: *lcags kyi khang pa* (iron house); tantra: *lcags kyi khang yangs* (spacious iron house).

23. Commentary: *byed mun pas gtibs* (opens, there is enveloping darkness); tantra: *byed gtibs* (opens, it is enveloped).

24. Commentary: *bdag dang 'dzin pa'i zhen yul* (self-identity and the objects of its reifying perceptions); tantra: *chags dang 'dzin pa'i zhen yul* (the objects of one's fixated attachment and reification).

25. Commentary: *gzhi nas 'dod mi srid pa'i* (about which it is fundamentally impossible to posit anything); scriptural source: *gzhi gnas 'dod mi srid pa'i* (which abides as the ground of being and about which it is impossible to posit anything).

26. Commentary: *rten bral* (having no support); scriptural source: *rten 'brel* (connected to a support).

27. Commentary: *lus dang sems kyi gnas med* (the body and mind have no location); scriptural source and same passage cited on fol. 25a.1–2 of the commentary: *lus la sems kyi gnas med* (the mind is not localized in the body).

28. Commentary: *gnyis kyi mtha' las 'das* (is beyond the dualistic extremes of); tantra: *gnyis kyi snang bar med* (involves no perspective of).

29. Commentary: *rtog pa'i yul las rnam par 'das* (Completely beyond the realm of thought); tantra: *rtog pa'i rnam pa yul las 'das* (Beyond the realm of discrete thoughts).

30. Commentary: *grol* (free of); tantra: *'das* (beyond).

31. Source verse: *ma dpyad ma dpyad yul sems rjes ma dpyad* (Don't analyze! Don't analyze! Do not analyze sense objects and ordinary mind!); commentary: *ma bcad ma bcad yul sems rjes ma bcad* (Don't cut! Don't cut! Don't cut through sense objects and ordinary mind!).

32. Commentary: *mtshon* (represented); tantra: *chod* (cut through).

33. Commentary: *goms pa ye yod* (familiarity that is timelessly present); tantra: *bsgom pa ye rdzogs* (meditation that is timelessly perfect).

34. Commentary: *gnyis* (twofold); tantra: *nyid* (actual).

35. Commentary: *rnam pa* (distinct forms); tantra: *snang ba* (sensory appearances).

36. Commentary: *dbyings kyang so na med* (not even basic space exists innately); source verse: *dbyings kyi so na med* (they do not exist within the innate state of basic space).

37. The tantra omits *snying po* (heart essence of).

38. Commentary: *'dug tshul* (way in which things are present); tantra: *gnas tshul* (way things abide).

39. The tantra omits the vocative particle *kye* (O).

40. The tantra omits *snying po* (heart essence of).

41. Commentary: *'du 'dral med pa* (beyond union or separation, they are a unity); tantra: *'du 'dral med pa'i chos nyid* (their true nature is such that they are beyond union or separation, a unity).

42. Commentary: *kun mnyam* (a state of universal equalness); tantra: *kun mnyam kyi ye shes* (timeless awareness as a state of universal equalness).

43. Commentary: *de'i tshe* (At that point); tantra: *de yis kyang* (Then [Samantabhadra said]).

44. Commentary: *sangs rgyas kyi* (a buddha's); tantra: *sangs rgyas thams cad kyi* (all buddhas').

45. Commentary: *stong pa nyid rang byung gi spyod pa* (the naturally occur
ring conduct of emptiness); tantra: *stong pa nyid kyi rang shugs kyi
spyod pa* (the conduct of the natural force of emptiness).

46. The tantra omits *rang sad* (naturally awakened).

47. Commentary: *ye bkod dang ye grol chen por rang grol* (timelessly arrayed,
and supremely and timelessly free); tantra: *ye bkod chen por rang grol*
(timelessly and supremely arrayed, and timelessly free).

48. The tantra omits *rig pa'i ngo bo mthong ba la* (in perceiving the essence of
awareness).

49. Commentary: *ngas* (I); tantra: *nga nyid kyis* (I myself).

50. Commentary: *dngos po* (reality); tantra: *ngo bo* (the essence of being).

51. The tantra omits *ngo bo rtogs pa la* (regarding realization of the essence
of being).

52. Commentary: *yid chos kyi spros pa* (conceptual elaborations); tantra: *yid
ches kyi spros pa* (elaborate belief systems).

53. Commentary: *rang gi rnam rtog 'du 'dzis g.yengs* (are distracted by the
busyness of their concepts); tantra: *rang rig rnam rtog 'du 'dzis g.yengs*
(find themselves distracted from recognizing awareness by the busyness
of concepts).

54. Commentary: *chags pas* (attachments to); tantra: *chags sdang* (attachment and aversion in).

55. Source verse (orig. and rev. Adzom): *don la 'ching grol gnyis med* (In actuality, there is neither bondage nor freedom); source verse (Dergé): *'ching
grol gnyis dang bral bas* (Since there is freedom from both bondage and
freedom).

56. Commentary: *med la yod par* (in the existence of what does not exist);
source verse: *ming la yod par* (that labels refer to what exists).

57. Commentary: *dngangs* (terrified); tantra: *sdangs* (angered).

58. Commentary: *gnas* (abides); tantra: *shar* (arises).

59. Source verse (orig. and rev. Adzom): *'dzin* (perceiving); source verse
(Dergé): *'dod* (positing).

60. Commentary: *grags pa* (sounds); tantra: *rtog pa* (concepts).

61. Commentary: *gzung 'dzin* (of dualistic perception); tantra: *'dzin pa* (that
one reifies).

62. Commentary: *gzhan la sun 'byin byed* (causes others to become discouraged); tantra: *gzhan la skyon 'dzin byas* (seizes on the faults of others).

63. Commentary: *de nyid rtogs pas bdud rnams kun* (When that is realized,
all maras); tantra: *de ma gtogs pa'i bdud rnams kun* (Any other maras,
as well).

64. Commentary: *'jug pa'i bdud* (maras that can take hold of me); tantra: *'byung ba'i skyon* (faults that originate from me).

65. Commentary: *chad pa* (nihilistic denial); tantra: *chad rtag* (nihilistic denial and naive affirmation).

66. Commentary: *nga ni rang byung lhun gyis grub* (I occur naturally and am spontaneously present); tantra: *nga ni 'byung bar lhun gyis grub* (In occurring, I am spontaneously present).

67. Commentary: *thams cad rang byung dbye bsal med pas* (because everything occurs naturally, without division or exclusion); source verse: *thams cad bya byed med par grol bas* (because everything is free, without plan or action).

68. Commentary: *'khor gnas dus* (the retinues, environments, and occasions); tantra: *'khor gnas kun* (all retinues and environments).

69. Commentary: *don 'di* (significance); tantra: *chos nyid* (true nature).

70. Source verse: *mnyam pa'i ngang gnas na* (If you abide in a state of equalness); commentary: *mnyam pa'i ngang nyid du* (In that very state of equalness).

71. Commentary: *nga bstan* (what I reveal); tantra: *gang bstan* (whatever is revealed).

72. Commentary: *byas pa med* (is not created); tantra: *bcos su med* (cannot be contrived).

73. Source verse: *rang yal rjes med tsam* (is simply a state in which things vanish naturally, leaving no trace); commentary: *rang yal rjes med cing* (vanishes naturally, leaving no trace).

74. Commentary: *rgyu 'gags so* (there cease to be causes); tantra: *rgyud 'gags so* (there ceases to be continuity).

75. Commentary: *stong dang mi stong* (empty, not empty); scriptural source: *rtag dang mi rtag* (permanent, impermanent).

76. Commentary: *stong ngo zhes kyang brtags gyur la / mi stong zhes kyang brjod pa yin* (Even as they label something "empty," / they also speak of it as "not empty"); scriptural source: *stong ngo zhes kyang brtags gyur la / mi stong zhes kyang brjod pa yin* (They do not speak of something as "empty," / nor do they call it "not empty").

77. Commentary: *sku gsum* (three kayas); tantra: *longs sku* (sambhogakaya).

78. Commentary: *yul la rtog med rang snang bas* (Since sense objects are awareness's own nonconceptual manifestations); tantra: *yul la rtog byed mi snang bas* (Since concepts about sense objects do not manifest).

79. Commentary: *'byed* (divided in); tantra: *'dzin* (held to be).

80. Commentary: *mun snang gnyis kyis* (by the duality of illumination versus darkness); tantra: *mun ngang snang bas* (by the manifestation of darkness).

81. Commentary: *tha dad du mar mi 'byed pas* (Since things are not differentiated into many distinct entities); tantra: *tha dad gcig tu mi 'byed pas* (Since nothing can be differentiated into some distinct entity).

82. Commentary: *shes pa* (awareness); tantra: *shes rab* (sublime knowing).

83. Commentary: *ye shes gzhan du yod ma yin* (timeless awareness is not present elsewhere); tantra: *ye shes ming du yod ma yin* (there is nothing that can be called timeless awareness).

84. Commentary: *skyon gyi mtha' gnyis* (the two flawed extremes); tantra: *skyon gyi mtha' nyid* (flawed extremes).

85. Commentary: *shes* (understand); tantra: *rtogs* (realize).

86. Tantra: *rang rig* (self-knowing awareness); commentary: *ma rig* (nonrecognition of awareness), in error.

87. Commentary: *tshad med* (infinite); tantra: *tshegs med* (not insignificant).

88. Commentary: *ye rnyed* (timeless discovery); tantra: *ye nyid* (timelessness itself).

89. Commentary: *ston pa ji ltar bzhugs pa lags* (how do you, the teacher, abide?); tantra: *ston pa ci skad bya bar bzhugs* (what explanation do you, the teacher, give?).

90. Commentary: *mi sdug mi stong* (not painful, and not void); tantra: *mi 'dug mi gtod* (not present, and not fixed).

91. Commentary: *dang bral* (free of); tantra: *las 'das* (beyond).

92. Commentary: *rnam pa med cing rul rnams med* (It has no specific form and no sensory qualities); tantra: *snang ba med cing yul yang med* (It has no manifestation and no object).

93. Commentary: *stong pa nyid* (emptiness); tantra: *ston pa nyid* (a teacher).

94. Commentary: *bshad* (This is explained to be); tantra: *gnas* (This abides as).

Chapter 13

1. Commentary: *rtse* (pinnacle); source verse: *don* (meaning).

2. Commentary: *mtshan mar* (characterized); tantra: *bskyed pa* (developed).

3. Commentary: *dgongs pa* (enlightened intent); tantra: *dgongs pa ma yin* (Without being intended, it is).

4. Commentary: *rnam par dag* (totally pure); tantra: *rang sar dag* (free in its own place).

5. Commentary: *mtha' la* (everywhere); tantra: *mkha' la* (in space).

6. Source verse: *da* (now); commentary: *de* (that which is).

7. Commentary: *dag* (are purified); source verse: *zhi* (subside).

8. Commentary: *'gro ba* (that goes); tantra: *grol ba* (to be freed).

9. Commentary: *mtha' la* (everywhere); tantra: *mkha' la* (in space).

10. Commentary: *bde bar gnas* (abide blissfully); tantra: *bde bar 'gyur* (become blissful).

11. Commentary: *las* (so that); source verse: *ste* (—).

12. Source verse: *cha bcas* (along with all it entails); commentary: *cha shas* (in part).

13. Commentary: *la* (as); tantra: *las* (from).

14. Commentary: *rgya chad* (restrictions); source verse: *rtag chad* (affirmation and denial).

15. Commentary: *du mar snang bar 'phrul pa yin* (magically appear to be manifold); tantra: *du mar snang ba 'khrul pa yin* (appear to be manifold, but this is confusion).

16. Commentary: *mdzad pa 'di lta bu* (the corresponding actions); tantra: *mdzad pa gnyis lta bu* (two seeming aspects to the actions).

17. Tantra: *ris can* (distinct entities); commentary: *rig can* (sentient), apparently in error.

18. The tantra omits *yid la* (in your mind).

19. Commentary: *'byung* (occurs); tantra: *bzhugs* (abides).

20. Commentary: *sbubs* (matrix); tantra: *dbus* (center).

21. Commentary: *mi 'jig stong dang gsal ba gsum / chos kyi sku yi nges tshig go* (Imperishable, empty, and lucid— / these three qualities define "dharmakaya"); tantra: *mi 'jig stong dang gsal ba dang bya ba thams cad rdzogs pa ni / chos kyi sku yi nges tshig go* (Imperishable, empty, lucid, the perfection of all that is to be done— / these qualities define "dharmakaya").

22. Commentary: *gdangs* (radiant); tantra: *dvangs* (limpid).

23. Commentary: *dpyod pa* (analysis); tantra: *spyod pa* (conduct).

24. Commentary: *phyir 'ong ldog pa med* (neither increase nor deteriorate); tantra: *phyi mi 'ong dang ldog pa med* (are irreversible and are not lost).

25. The tantra adds *byas pa med* (not undertaken deliberately).

26. Commentary: *dbyings* (in basic space); tantra: *dbus* (in the middle).

27. Tantra: *smin* (ripens); commentary: *min* (not), in error.

28. Commentary: *brjod tshig ming* (descriptive words and labels); tantra: *gzung 'dzin ming* (the labels of dualistic perception).

29. The tantra adds *kha dog* (of colors).

30. Commentary: *bstan* (reveals); tantra: *brten* (is dependent on).

31. Commentary: *'das dang 'jig rten bya ba med* (there is nothing to be done in the world or beyond it); tantra: *'das dang 'jig rten bya ba byed* (all that is to be done in the world or beyond it is done).

32. Commentary: *rdzogs* (perfection); tantra: *gnas* (abiding).

33. Commentary: *gzugs brnyan las* (due to the process of reflection); tantra: *gzugs can gsal* (forms are clearly reflected—).

34. Commentary: *dkar po dri ma med phyir 'od* (Because it is transparent and purified of any distortion, there is light); tantra: *dkar po dri ma med phyir ro* (It is transparent because it is purified of any distortion).

35. Commentary: *snang* (illuminates); tantra: *mthong* (perceives).

36. Commentary: *gzhag med rang grol gzhir rdzogs pa'o* (It is naturally free without being brought to rest—perfect within the ground of being); tantra: *gzhan med grol gzhi rdzogs pa'o* (There is nothing but this—the perfect ground of freedom).

37. Commentary: *sems can grangs las 'das pa rnams sgrol ba'i phyir na yang sprul pa'i sku'o* (It is the embodiment of emanation because it liberates countless beings); tantra: *sems can las sad pa rnams skye med dbyings su sgrol nus pa'i phyir na yang sprul pa'i sku* (It is the embodiment of ema-nation because it is capable of liberating into unborn basic space those beings whose karmic tendencies have awakened).

38. Commentary: *'dul* (is necessary to guide); tantra: *byung* (occurs for).

39. Commentary: *yeng med zad sar phyin* (reaching the undistracted state of resolution); tantra: *yengs pa med par spyod* (experiencing this without distraction).

Conclusion

1. Commentary: *dar rgyas shog* (May . . . spread and flourish!); source verse: *rgyas par shog* (*May . . . flourish!*).

Sources Cited

Tibetan authors seldom cite sources by their full titles; rather, they use contractions, and often different versions thereof. In the following list of sources, the entries are alphabetized according to the most commonly used short title. In many cases, we have provided the Tibetan for both the short and full titles, separated by semicolons. Where we have been able to determine that the source is a Tibetan translation of a Sanskrit original, we have also listed the Sanskrit title. If known to us, we have noted the author's name.

In the commentary itself, we replaced any contraction that seemed ambiguous or ungrammatical in English—for example, *The All-Creating (Kun byed)*—with a longer version of the title—for example, *The All-Creating Monarch (Kun byed rgyal po)*.

Adornment Through Direct Introduction
  Ngo sprod spras pa; Ngo sprod rin po che spras pa'i zhing khams
  bstan pa'i rgyud

All-Creating Monarch
  Kun byed; Kun byed rgyal po; Chos thams cad rdzogs pa chen po
  byang chub kyi sems kun byed rgyal po (Skt. *Sarva dharma mahāśānti
  bodhicitta kulaya rāja*)

Amassing of the Rare and Sublime
  dKon brtsegs; 'Phags pa dkon mchog brtsegs pa; 'Phags pa dkon
  mchog brtsegs pa chen po'i chos kyi rnam grangs stong phrag brgya pa
  las sdom pa gsum bstam pa'i le'u zhes bya ba theg pa chen po'i mdo
  (Skt. *Ārya mahāratnakūṭa dharma paryāya śatasāhasrika granthe
  trisaṃvara nirdeśa parivarta nāma mahāyāna sūtra*)

Array of Inlaid Gems

Nor bu phra bkod; Nor bu phra bkod chen po'i rgyud; Nor bu phra bkod rang gi don thams cad gsal bar byed pa'i rgyud

Avatamsaka

Phal po che; Sangs rgyas phal po che zhes bya ba shin tu rgyas pa chen po'i mdo (Skt. Buddha avataṃsaka nāma mahāvaipūlya sūtra)

Blazing Remains

sKu gdung 'bar ba; sKu gdung 'bar bu rin po che'i rgyud; dPal nam mkha' med pa'i sku gdung 'bar ba chen po'i rgyud

Chapter on the Sacred Collections of Meditative Absorption

Ting nge 'dzin tshogs dam pa'i le'u (Skt. Samādhi sambhāra parivarta nāma), by Kṛṣṇapa

Clear Words

Tshig gsal; dBu ma rtsa ba'i 'grel pa tshig gsal ba zhes bya ba (Skt. Mūla madhyamaka vṛtti prasannapadā nāma), by Chandrakīrti

Commentary on the Awakening Mind

Byang chub sems 'grel; Byang chub sems kyi 'grel pa zhes bya ba (Skt. Bodhicitta vivaraṇa nāma), by Nāgārjuna

Compendium

sDud pa; 'Phags pa shes rab kyi pha rol tu phyin pa sdud pa tshigs su bcad pa (Skt. Ārya prajñā pāramitā sañcaya gāthā)

Compendium of the Supreme Spiritual Approach

Theg bsdus; Theg pa chen po bsdus pa (Skt. Mahāyāna saṃgraha), by Asanga

Conjunction of Sun and Moon

Nyi zla kha sbyor; Nyi ma dang zla ba kha sbyor ba chen po gsang ba'i rgyud

Detailed Analysis of Empowerments

dBang rnam par phye ba

Detailed Commentary on Valid Cognition

rNam 'grel; Tshad ma rnam 'grel gyi tshig le'ur byas pa (Skt. Pramāṇa vārttika kārikā), by Dharmakīrti

Discourse of the Ever-Turning Wheel
Phyir mi ldog pa 'khor lo'i mdo; 'Phags pa phyir mi ldog pa'i 'khor lo zhes bya ba theg pa chen po'i mdo (Skt. Ārya avaivartacakra nāma mahāyāna sūtra)

Discourse of Ghanavyuha
rGyan stug po bkod pa'i mdo; 'Phags pa rgyan stug po bkod pa zhes bya ba theg pa chen po'i mdo (Skt. Ārya ghanāvyūha nāma mahāyana sūtra)

Discourse on the Most Majestic State of Meditative Absorption
Ting nge 'dzin gyi rgyal po; 'Phags pa chos thams cad kyi rang bzhin mnyam pa nyid rnam par spros pa ting nge 'dzin gyi rgyal po zhes bya ba theg pa chen po'i mdo (Skt. Ārya sarva dharma svabhāva samatā vipañcita samādhi rāja nāma mahāyāna sūtra)

Discourse Unifying the Enlightened Intent of All Buddhas
Sangs rgyas thams cad kyi dgongs pa 'dus pa'i mdo lung; De bzhin gshegs pa thams cad kyi thugs gsang ba'i ye shes don gyi snying po rdo rje bkod pa'i rgyud rnal 'byor grub pa'i lung kun 'dus rig pa'i mdo theg pa chen po mngon par rtogs pa chos kyi rnam grangs rnam par bkod pa zhes bya ba'i mdo (Skt. Sarva tathāgata citta jñāna guhyārtha garbha vyūha vajra tantra siddhi yogāgama samāja sarva vidyā sūtra mahāyānābhisamaya dharma paryāya vyūha nāma sūtra)

Drops of Nectar: A Letter of Advice
sPring yig bdud rtsi'i thigs pa

Engaging in the Conduct of a Bodhisattva
sPyod 'jug; Byang chub sems dpa'i spyod pa la 'jug pa (Skt. Bodhisat-tvacaryāvatāra), by Śāntideva

Entrance into the Middle Way
'Jug pa; dBu ma la 'jug pa zhes bya ba (Skt. Madhyamakāvatāra nāma), by Chandrakīrti

Exalted Discourse of the Rare and Sublime Meteor
'Phags pa dkon mchog ta la la'i mdo; 'Phags pa dkon mchog ta la la'i gzungs shes bya ba theg pa chen po'i mdo (Skt. Ārya ratnolkā nāma dhāraṇī mahāyāna sūtra)

*Exalted Discourse That Completely Consolidates Precious
Enlightened Qualities*

> 'Phags pa yon tan rin po che yongs su sdud pa'i mdo

Exalted Discourse on Transcendent Timeless Awareness

> 'Phags pa 'da' ka ye shes; 'Phags pa 'da' ka ye shes shes bya ba theg
> pa chen po'i mdo (Skt. *Āryā ātyaya jñāna nāma mahāyāna sūtra*)

Garland of Jewels

> Rin chen phreng ba; rGyal po la gtam bya ba rin po che'i phreng ba
> (Skt. *Rājaparikathā ratnamālā*), by Nāgārjuna

Gathering of Secrets

> gSang 'dus; De bzhin gshegs pa thams cad kyi sku gsung thugs kyi
> gsang chen gsang ba 'dus pa zhes bya ba brtag pa'i rgyal po chen po
> (Skt. *Sarva tathāgata kāya vāk citta rahasya guhyasamāja nāma mahā
> kalpa rāja*)

Great Garuda

> Khyung chen; Khyung chen mkha' lding, by Śrī Siṃha

Heaped Jewels

> Rin po che spungs pa; Rin chen spungs pa yon tan chen po ston pa
> rgyud kyi rgyal po

Heart Essence of Secrets

> gSang snying sgyu 'phrul drva ba; sGyu 'phrul gsang ba; aPal gsang
> ba snying po de kho na nyid rnam par nges pa (Skt. *Śrī guhyagarbha
> tattva viniścaya*)

Highest Continuum

> rGyud bla ma; Theg pa chen po rgyud bla ma'i bstan bcos (Skt.
> *Mahāyānottaratantra śāstra*), by Maitreya

Intermediate-Length "Mother"

> Yum bar ma; Shes rab kyi pha rol tu phyin pa stong phrag nyi shu lnga
> pa (Skt. *Pañcaviṃśati sāhasrika prajñā pāramitā*)

Natural Freedom of Awareness

> Rig pa rang grol; Rig pa rang grol chen po thams cad 'grol ba'i rgyud

Naturally Arising Awareness

Rang shar; Rig pa rang shar; Rig pa rang shar chen po'i rgyud; De bzhin gshegs pa thams cad kyi ting nge 'dzin yongs su bshad pa ye shes 'dus pa'i mdo theg pa chen po gsang ba bla na med pa'i rgyud chos thams cad kyi 'byung gnas sangs rgyas thams cad kyi dgongs pa gsang sngags gcig pa'i ye shes rdzogs pa chen po'i don gsal bar byed pa'i rgyud rig pa rang shar chen po'i rgyud

Naturally Occurring Perfection: The River of Empowerment

rDzogs pa rang byung dbang gi chu bo'i rgyud; sKu thams cad kyi snang ba ston pa dbang rdzogs pa rang byung chen po'i rgyud

Ocean of Magic

sGyu 'phrul rgya mtsho

Ornament of Manifest Realization

mNgon rtogs rgyan; Shes rab kyi pha rol tu phyin pa'i man ngag gi bstan bcos mngon par rtogs pa'i rgyan zhes bya ba'i tshig le'ur byas pa (Skt. Abhisamayālaṃkāra nāma prajñā pāramitopadeśa śāstra kārikā), by Maitreya

Ornament of the Sutra Category

mDo sde rgyan; Theg pa chen po mdo sde'i rgyan zhes bya ba'i tshig le'ur byas pa (Skt. Mahāyāna sūtrālaṃkāra nāma kārikā), by Maitreya

Pearl Garland

Mu tig phreng ba; Mu tig rin po che phreng ba'i rgyud

Perfect Dynamic Energy of the Lion

Seng ge rtsal rdzogs; Seng ge rtsal rdzogs chen po'i rgyud

Precious Detailed Instructions Concerning Perception

sNang ba rin po che'i pra khrid

Precious Treasury of Philosophical Systems

Grub pa'i mtha' rin po che'i mdzod; Theg pa mtha' dag gi don gsal bar byed pa grub pa'i mtha' rin po che'i mdzod, by kLong chen pa

Precious Treasury of the Sublime Spiritual Approach

Theg mchog rin po che'i mdzod, by kLong chen pa

Precious Treasury of Utter Lucidity
  'Od gsal rin po che'i mdzod

Precious Unborn Treasury
  sKye med rin po che'i mdzod

Reverberation of Sound
  Thal 'gyur; sGra thal 'gyur rsta ba'i rgyud chen po; Rin po che 'byung
  bar byed pa sgra thal 'gyur chen po'i rgyud

Samantabhadra: Mirror of Enlightened Mind
  Kun tu bzang po thugs kyi me long; Kun tu bzang po thugs kyi me
  long gi rgyud ces bya ba thams cad ston pa'i rgyud

*Scriptural Transmission of Supreme Dynamic Energy: The Perfection of
Enlightened Qualities*
  rTsal chen yon tan rdzogs pa'i lung

Secret Conduct: Tantra of the Potential
  gSang ba spyod pa sa bon gyi rgyud

Single Time
  Dus gcig pa

Six Expanses
  kLong drug pa; Kun tu bzang po klong drug pa'i rgyud

Source of Precious Riches
  sDeb sbyor Rin chen 'byung gnas zhes bya ba (Skt. *Chandoratnākara
nama*), by Ratnakaraśanti

Source Verses on Sublime Knowing
  rTsa ba shes rab; dBu ma rtsa ba'i tshig le'ur byas pa shes rab ces bya
  ba (Skt. *Prajñā nāma mūla madhyamaka kārikā*), by Nāgārjuna

Superb Ruler
  rMad byung rgyal po; Byang chub kyi sems rmad du byung ba (Skt.
  Bodhicitta sopaśika)

Supreme "Mother"
> *Yum chen mo; 'Bum; Shes rab kyi pha rol tu phyin pa stong phrag brgya pa* (Skt. *Śatasāhasrikā prajñā pāramitā*)

Supreme System of Ati
> *A ti bkod pa chen po*

Tantra of the Sphere of the Secret Moon
> *Zla gsang thig le'i rgyud*

Tantra Without Letters
> *Yi ge med pa; Yi ge med pa'i rgyud; Yi ge med pa'i rgyud chen po zhes bya ba rin po che rgyal mtshan gyi rgyud rgyal po'i gdud rgyud lta ba nam mkha' dang mnyam pa'i rgyud chen po*

Testament
> *'Das rjes*

Thorough Determination of Valid Cognition
> *rNam nges; Tshad ma rnam par nges pa* (Skt. *Pramāṇa viniścaya*), by Dharmakīrti

Treasury of Higher Teachings
> *mDzod; Chos mngon pa'i mdzod kyi tshig le'ur byas pa* (Skt. *Abhi dharma koṣa kārikā*), by Vasubandhu

Two Chapters
> *brTags gnyis; Kye'i rdo rje zhes bya ba rgyud kyi rgyal po* (Skt. *Hevajra tantra rāja nāma*)

Two Truths
> *bDen gnyis; bDen pa gnyis rnam par 'byed pa'i tshig le'ur byas pa* (Skt. *Satya dvaya vibhaṅga kārikā*), by Jñānagarbha

Universal Theme of Perfection
> *rDzogs pa spyi chings*

Vajra Cutter
> *rDo rje gcod pa; 'Phags pa shes rab kyi pha rol tu phyin pa rdo rje gcod pa zhes bya ba theg pa chen po'i mdo* (Skt. *Ārya vajracchedikā nāma prajñā pāramitā mahāyāna sūtra*)

Vajra Pavilion

> *rDo rje gur; 'Phags pa mkha' 'gro ma rdo rje gur zhes bya ba'i rgyud kyi rgyal po chen po'i brtag pa* (Skt. *Ārya ḍākinī vajra pañjara mahā tantra rāja kalpa nāma*)

Vajrasattva: Mirror of the Heart

> *rDo rje sems dpa' snying gi me long; rDo rje sems dpa' snying gi me long gi rgyud*

Word List

We have compiled this word list because the translation of Tibetan terms has yet to be standardized and readers may encounter alternative translations of key terms in other texts and teachings. To aid readers unfamiliar with the Wylie system of transliteration, we have included phoneticized equivalents of the terms according to the Kham dialects of eastern Tibet.

When more than one English translation is given for a single Tibetan term, the entry listed first is the most common version. If several versions are equally common, they are listed separately. Some terms are not listed individually but can be found in an idiomatic expression (for example, "description" is listed under the idiom "beyond description, imagination, or expression"). Some of the translations occur only in negative constructions (for example, "independent nature" is found under "without independent nature").

English	Wylie Transliteration	Pronunciation
abandon	spong ba	pōng wa
abide, remain, dwell	gnas pa	nay pa
acceptance and rejection, value judgments	blang dor	lang dor
accomplished	grub pa	drūp pa
achieve, achievement	sgrub pa	drūp pa
adornment	rgyan	jen
adventitious distortions	glo bur gyi dri ma	lo būr ji dri ma

English	Wylie Transliteration	Pronunciation
affirmation and denial	rtag chad	tak chay
afflictive emotions	nyon mongs pa	nyön mōng pa
all-consuming concepts/thought patterns	kun rtog	kūn tōk
all-creating	kun byed	kūn jay
all-embracing seal	rgyas 'debs	jay dep
apparent/manifest (sense) objects	yul snang	yūl nang
apparent yet empty	snang stong	nang tōng
arise	'char ba	char wa
attributes	mtshan nyid	tsen nyi
authentic	bden pa, yang dag pa	den pa, yang dak pa
awakened mind	byang chub kyi sems	jang chūp chi sem
awareness	rig pa	rik pa
awareness's own manifestations	rang snang	rang nang
bare, pure and simple	zang ka	zang ka
basic space of phenomena (Skt. dharmadhatu)	chos dbyings	chö ying
become fully evident	mgnon du gyur pa	ngön du jūr pa
beyond characterization or expression	msthon brjod las 'das pa	tsön jö lay day pa
beyond description, imagination, or expression	smra bsam brjod las 'das pa	ma sam jö lay day pa
bias, distinction	ris	ree
body, speech, and mind	sgo gsum	go sum
boundless, unlimited	mtha' yas, mtha' med	ta yay, ta may
calm abiding	zhi gnas	zhi nay
cannot be characterized	mtshan ma med pa	tsen ma may pa

English	Wylie Transliteration	Pronunciation
Category of Direct Transmission	man ngag sde	men ngak day
Category of Expanse	klong sde	lōng day
Category of Mind	sems sde	sem day
cause and effect/ result, causality	rgyu 'bras	ju dray
cessation	'gog pa	gōk pa
characteristics	mtshan nyid, mtshan ma	tsen nyi, tsen ma
clarity	gsal ba	sal wa
clear distinction	shan 'byed	shen jay
cleared away	sangs	sang
clearly apparent without truly existing	med pa gsal snang	may pa sal nang
complete evenness	phyam phyam	cham cham
composite, compounded	'dus byas	dü jay
conceptual mind	yid	yi
concerted effort	bya rtsol	ja tsol
conditioned existence and the state of peace	srid zhi	si zhi
conduct	spyod pa	chö pa
confirmed or refuted	grub bsal	drūp sal
confusion	'khrul pa	trūl pa
consciousness	rnam shes, shes pa	nam shay, shay pa
consciousness as the ground of all ordinary experience	kun gzhi'i rnam shes	kūn zhee nam shay
consummate	thar thug pa	tar tūk pa
consummation	thar phyin pa	tar chin pa
continuous	'gag med, ma 'gags pa	gak may, mon gak pa
continuum	lu gu gyud	lu gu jü
continuum of being	gyud	jü
conventional designation	tha snyad	ta nyay
cutting through solidity	khregs chod	trek chö

English	Wylie Transliteration	Pronunciation
decisive experience (come to a)	la bzla ba	la da wa
definitive conclusion (reach a)	gtan la 'bebs pa	ten la bep pa
definitive meaning	nges don	ngay dön
direct experience	car phog tu	char pōk tu
direct introduction	ngo sprod	ngo trö
direct perception/ experience	mngon sum	ngön sūm
discern the implication	'gag bsdams pa	gak dam pa
discerning timeless awareness	so sor rtog pa'i ye shes	so sor tōk pay ye shay
dispel constraints	'phrang bsal	trang sal
display	rol pa	rōl pa
distillation, vital essence	bcud	chü
distinction, classification	dbye ba	ye wa
do not come together or separate	du dral med pa	du dral may pa
domain, range, environment	yul, spyod yul	yūl, chö yūl
dualistic perception(s)	gzung 'dzin, gnyis 'dzin, gnyis snang	zung dzin, nyee dzin, nyee nang
dynamic energy	rtsal	tsal
effort and achievement	rtsol sgrub	tsōl drūp
effort and striving	'bad rtsol	bay tsōl
eight avenues of consciousness	tshogs brgyad	tsōk gyay
elaboration	spros pa	trö pa
elicited in all its nakedness	rjen la bud pa	jen la bü pa
embrace the larger scope	chings su bcing ba	ching su ching wa
embraced	bcings pa, 'dus pa	ching pa, dü pa
emptiness	stong pa nyid	tōng pa nyi

English	Wylie Transliteration	Pronunciation
empty yet lucid	stong gsal	tōng sal
encompassed	'khyil ba	chil wa
enlightened activity/ action/deed	phrin las	trin lay
enlightened dimension	sku	ku
enlightened intent	dgongs pa	gōng pa
enlightened mind	thugs	tūk
enlightened perspective	snang ba	nang wa
enlightened speech	gsung	sūng
enlightenment	byang chub	jang chūp
ensured	grub pa	drūp pa
environment, place	gnas	nay
equalness (state of)	mnyam pa nyid	nyam pa nyi
essence (of being)	ngo bo	ngo wo
evanescent	yal ba	yal wa
evidence	rtags	tak
evident	gsal ba	sal wa
exaggeration and underestimation, misinterpretation	sgro skur	drō kur
existence	yod pa	yö pa
expand into evenness	phyam gdal	cham dal
expanse	klong	lōng
expressions of emptiness	stong gzugs	tōng zūk
extreme	mtha', phyogs, ris	ta, chōk, ree
fade away	yal ba	yal wa
final resolution	phu thag bcad pa	pu tak chay pa
fixation	zhen 'dzin	zhen dzin
fixed construct	gtad 'dzin	tay dzin
four methods of resting	gzhag thabs bzhi	zhak tap zhi
framework, frame of reference	dmigs pa	mik pa
free, freedom	'grol ba	drōl wa
free of anything needing to be done	bya bral	ja dral

English	Wylie Transliteration	Pronunciation
free of restrictions	rgya grol	ja drōl
free in their own place	rang sar grol ba	rang sar drōl wa
freedom in immediate perception	cer grol	cher drōl
freedom in oneness	gcig drol	chik drōl
fruition	'bras bu	dray bu
fully embraced/ encompassed	'ub chub	ūp chūp
fundamental nature (of being)	khams	kham
fundamentally unconditioned	gshis	shee
genuine, what has genuine meaning	rnal ma	nal ma
great perfection (approach)	rdzogs chen	dzōk chen
ground of all ordinary experience	kun gzhi	kūn zhi
ground for all that arises	'char gzhi	char zhee
ground (of being), matrix	gzhi	zhi
ground of being as basic space	gzhi dbyings	zhi ying
ground of being manifesting as sensory appearances	gzhi snang	zhi nang
habitual pattern	bag chags	bak chak
has never existed	ma grub pa	ma drūp pa
heart drop	snying thig	nying tik
heart essence	snying po	nying po
identifiable essence	ngo bo ngos gzung	ngo wo ngö zung
identify	ngo bzung ba	ngo zung wa
identity	bdag	dak
illumination	'od, snang, gsal	ö, nang, sal

English	Wylie Transliteration	Pronunciation
immediate perception	cer mthong	cher tōng
imputation	btags pa	tak pa
in direct response to	thog tu	tōk tu
in the immediacy of	thog tu	tōk tu
in its/their own right	rang mtshan du	rang tsen du
in light of	ngor	ngor
inconceivable	bsam med	sam may
indescribable	brjod med	jö may
indeterminate	ma nges pa, nges med	ma ngay pa, ngay may
indivisible, not subject to extremes	ris med	ree may
ineffable, ineffability	med pa	may pa
inexpressible	brjod med	jö may
infinite	byams klas pa	jam lay pa
infinite evenness	phyam gdal/brdal	cham dal
infinitely pervasive	khyab gdal/brdal	chap dal
inherently pristine	rang sangs	rang sang
innate clarity/ limpidity	ngang dvangs	ngang dang
innate (state of) immediacy	thog babs	tōk bap
inner glow	mdangs	dang
intangible	mthong med	tōng may
interdependent connection	rten 'brel	ten drel
investigate	dpyod pa	chö pa
knowing quality, knowledge	shes pa	shay pa
knowing quality of timeless awareness	mkhyen pa'i ye shes	khyen pay ye shay
label, name	ming	ming
laxity and agitation	bying rgod	jing gö
level (of realization), state	sa	sa
level of truth	yang dag sa	yang dak sa
limitation, limit	mtha', phyogs	ta, chōk

English	Wylie Transliteration	Pronunciation
limpid, limpid clarity	dvangs	dang
lucidity	gsal ba	sal wa
luminous, illuminating	'od	ö
magical/miraculous display, magical expression	cho 'phrul	chom trūl
manifest yet nonexistent	med snang	may nang
master of awareness	rig 'dzin	rik dzin
meaning (ultimate)	don	dön
meditation (cultivate in)	sgom pa	gōm pa
meditative absorption	ting nge 'dzin	ting ngay dzin
meditative experience	nyams	nyam
meditative stability	bsam gtan	sam ten
mind (ordinary)	sems	sem
mind itself	sems nyid	sem nyi
mindstream	rgyud	jü
mirrorlike timeless awareness	me long lta bu'i ye shes	me lōng ta bui ye shay
mode of freedom	grol lugs	drōl lūk
natural attribute	rang chas	rang chay
natural condition	babs	bap
natural freedom	rang grol	rang drōl
natural great perfection	rang bzhin rdzogs pa chen po	rang zhin dzōk pa chen po
natural mind	rang sems	rang sem
natural place/state	rang sa, rang so	rang sa, rang so
natural place/ state of rest	rang mal	rang mal
naturally clear/evident manifestation of what is nonexistent	rang gsal med snang	rang sal may nang

English	Wylie Transliteration	Pronunciation
naturally occurring	rang byung	rang jūng
naturally settled, settled in its own place	rang babs	rang bop
nature (of being)	rang bzhin	rang zhin
nature of mind	sems kyi rang bzhin	sem chi rang zhin
nondual	gnyis med	nyee may
nonexistence	med pa	may pa
nonrecognition (of awareness)	ma rig pa	ma rik pa
nonreferential	dmigs med	mik may
not made or unmade	'du 'bral med pa	du dral may pa
not subject to bias or division	phyogs ris med pa	chōk ree may pa
objects of the phenomenal world	chos can	chö chen
omnipresent	spyi blugs	chi lūk
one taste	ro gcig	ro chik
oneness	gcig pu	chik pu
one's perception of sense objects	snang yul	nang yul
open avenue	sgo ma 'gags pa	go mon gak pa
open dimension	go skabs	go kap
openness	phyal ba	chal wa
ordinary consciousness	blo	lo
ordinary mental processes	byung tshor	jūng tsor
original purity	ka dag	ka dak
origination	skye ba	chay wa
own mode	rang lugs	rang lūk
own place	rang sa/so	rang sa/so
perceive	'dzin pa, mthong ba	dzin pa, tōng wa
perceiver	yul can	yūl chen
perception	snang ba	nang wa
perspective	snang ba	nang wa
phenomenon	chos	chö

English	Wylie Transliteration	Pronunciation
pith instructions	man ngag	men ngak
pivotal (point)	gnam gzer	nam zer
plans and actions	bya byed	ja jay
positive	bzang po	zang po
positive and negative	dkar nag, dge sdig	kar nak, gay dik
primordial	gdod ma'i, thog ma'i	dö may, tōk may
pristine	sangs pa, sangs se ba	sang pa, sang se wa
produced, created	byas pa	jay pa
profound insight	lhag mthong	lhak tōng
pure, innately pure	dag pa	dak pa
pure perception/ vision	dag snang	dak nang
qualities (positive/ enlightened)	yon tan	yön ten
radiance	gdangs	dang
rationale	'thad pa	tay pa
reach full expression	rtsal rdzogs pa	tsal dzōk pa
reactions	spang blang	pang lang
real	dngos	ngö
realization	rtogs pa	tōk pa
recognition, recognize	ngo shes	ngo shay
reference point	gtad so	tay so
reflection	gzugs brnyan	zūk nyen
reification	'dzin pa	zin pa
reifying fixation	gtad 'dzin	tay dzin
reject, renounce	pong ba	pōng wa
relative reality/level	kun rdzob	kūn dzōp
relax(ed)	lhug pa	lhūk pa
renunciation and acceptance	spang blang	pang lang
resolution of phenomena	chos zad	chö zay
resolution of phenomena in their true nature	chos nyid zad pa	chö nyi zay pa

English	Wylie Transliteration	Pronunciation
resolve, fall away	zad pa	zay pa
responsiveness, innate responsiveness	thugs rje	tūk jay
rest	'jog pa	jōk pa
resting in equipoise	mnyam bzhag	nyam zhak
resting in the immediacy of	cer gzhag	cher zhak
resting imperturbably, imperturbable rest	cog bzhag	chōk zhak
resting imperturbably in awareness	rig pa cog gzhag	rik pa chōk zhak
resting imperturbably like a mountain	ri bo cog gzhag	ri wo chōk zhak
resting imperturbably like an ocean	rgya mtsho cog gzhag	ja tso chōk zhak
Samantabhadra (Skt.)	kun tu bzang po	kūn tu zang po
scope, state, context, realm	ngang	ngang
seamless	bar med, bar mtshams med pa	bar may, bar tsam may pa
self-identity	gang zag gi bdag	gang zak gi dak
self-knowing awareness	rang rig	rang rik
self-knowing timeless awareness	rang rig ye shes	rang rik ye shay
sense faculties	dbang po	wang po
sensory appearances	snang ba	nang wa
significance	don	dön
six avenues of consciousness	tshogs drug	tsōk drūk
skillful means	thabs	tap
spacious	yangs pa	yang pa
sphere	thig le	tig lay
spontaneous fulfillment	bya ba grub pa	ja wa drūp pa
spontaneous presence	lhun grub	lhun drūp
stray, deviate	g.yo ba	yo wa

English	Wylie Transliteration	Pronunciation
subject to restrictions	rgya chad	ja chay
sublime knowing, knowledge	shes rab	shey rap
substance, (substantial) thing	dngos po	ngö po
subsumed	'dus pa	dü pa
suchness	de bzhin nyid	de zhin nyi
sugata (Skt.)	bde gshegs	de shek
sugatagarbha (Skt.), buddha nature	bde gshegs nying po	de shek nying po
suppression or indulgence	dgag sgrub	gak drūp
surpass	zil gyis gnon pa	zil jee nön pa
ten attributes	rang bzhin bcu	rang zhin chu
tension or laxity	sgrim glod	drim lö
thinking (recollection and)	dran bsam	dren sam
thing	chos	chö
thorough discernment	rnam dpyod	nam chö
thoughts, thought patterns, concepts	rtog pa, rnam rtog	tōk pa, nam tōk
timeless awareness	ye shes	ye shay
timeless awareness of all that there is	ji snyed mkhyen pa'i ye shes	ji nyay chen pay ye shay
timeless awareness as the basic space of phenomena	chos dbyings ye shes	chö ying ye shay
timeless awareness as equalness	mnyam nyid ye shes	nyam nyi ye shay
timeless awareness functioning as cognition	rig byed ye shes	rik jay ye shay
timeless awareness as spontaneous fulfillment	bya ba grub pa'i ye shes	ja wa drūp pay ye shay

English	Wylie Transliteration	Pronunciation
timeless awareness of what simply is	ji lta ba mkhyen pa'i ye shes	ji ta wa chen pay ye shay
timelessly	ye nas	ye nay
timelessly and innately present	ye babs	ye bap
total freedom	yongs grol	yōng drol
total purity	yongs dag	yōng dak
transmission (scriptural)	lung	lūng
true existence, truth	bden pa	den pa
true nature (of phenomena)	chos nyid	chö nyi
ultimate level/reality	don dam	dön dam
unbiased	phyogs med	chōk may
unborn	skye med	chay may
unceasing, ceaseless	'gag med, ma 'gags pa	gak may, mon gak pa
uncompounded, noncomposite	'dus ma byas	dü ma jay
uncontrived	ma bcos pa	ma chö pa
underlying logic	'thad pa	tay pa
understand	rtogs pa	tōk pa
undistorted, flawless	dri med	dri may
unfettered	rgya yan	ja yen
unhindered	thogs med	tōk may
uninterrupted	rgyun chad med pa, bar med	jūn chay may pa, bar may
unique	nyag gcig	nyak cheek
uniquely decisive	gcig chod	cheek chö
unity of appearance and emptiness	snang stong	nang tōng
unity of awareness and emptiness	rig stong	rik tōng
unity beyond union or separation	'du 'bral med pa	du dral may pa
universe (of appearances and possibilities)	(snang srid) snod bcud	(nang si) nö chü

English	Wylie Transliteration	Pronunciation
unobscured	sgrib med	drip may
unobstructed	zang thal	zang tal
unpredictable	ma nges pa, nges med	ma ngay pa, ngay may
unrestricted, without restrictions	rgya yan	ja yen
utter lucidity, utterly lucid	'od gsal	ö sal
vanish	'grol ba, yal ba	drōl wa, yal wa
vast expanse	klong chen	lōng chen
very essence	rang ngo, ngo bo nyid, snying po	rang ngo, ngo wo nyi, nying po
vision, perspective	snang ba	nang wa
waver, vacillate	g.yo ba	yo wa
way of abiding	gnas lugs	nay lūk
wholly positive	kun tu bzang po	kūn tu zang po
without anything needing to be done	byar med	jar may
without differentiation/ division or exclusion	dbye bsal med pa	ye sal may pa
without finite essence	ngo bo med pa	ngo wo may pa
without independent nature	rang bzhin med pa	rang zhin may pa
without transition or change	pho 'gyur med pa	pon jūr may pa
without (underlying) basis	gzhi med	zhi may
yoga	rnal 'byor	nal jor
yogin	rnal 'byor pa	nal jor pa